T0332132

66 This book is brilliantly written—concisely sophisticated, substantive in content, and comprehensive. But it is a sad story that reveals how prejudice and dishonesty were given priority over the dignity and credibility of the United States as the pillar of freedom, patriotism, and democracy. South Vietnam was taken for a ride by Henry Kissinger."

—Kasit Piromya, former Thai foreign minister

66 The period of the Vietnam War was arguably as divisive for the American polity as is the polarization of today. Time heals, but history reveals. Steve Young has contributed to the history of that divisive epoch by revealing the true cost of peace in this superb volume. There is now evidence that peace might have come earlier to Vietnam but for active interference by Richard Nixon at the end of the Lyndon Johnson administration. Nixon won the 1968 election suggesting that he had a "secret plan" to end the war. "Peace with honor" was his mantra. But the war went on and on. Now, as Young reveals, the peace that came eventually was neither honorable nor fair to those Vietnamese who were America's allies. Young presents compelling evidence that Henry Kissinger sanctioned the continuing presence of regular North Vietnamese troops in South Vietnam. In achieving a peace agreement, Kissinger signed the death warrant for the South Vietnamese government. For that he received a Nobel Peace Prize, but it was a peace that was far from honorable."

—J. Brian Atwood, former undersecretary of state, administrator of USAID, and Dean of the Humphrey School at the University of Minnesota

66 Stephen Young has produced an account of Vietnam's tragedy that is as moving as it is erudite. He takes readers inside the mind of a nation that struggled for its distinct national identity against three empires—Chinese, French, and Soviet—and was betrayed by its American ally. He offers a plethora of evidence to show that Vietnamization of the war was succeeding until it was sandbagged. Young combines the inside knowledge of a participant with the precision of a scholar in a persuasive indictment of Henry Kissinger as the author of South Vietnam's fall to Communism. It is a unique combination of testimony and analysis that stands out in the voluminous literature on the Vietnam War. It is indispensable reading for anyone who wants to understand the troubled history of Southeast Asia as well as the damage that arrogant elitists have inflicted on America's world standing."

—David P. Goldman, deputy editor, *Asia Times*

66 From a Japanese point of view, this book is a major contribution to our understanding of Asian history. From the first years of the twentieth century, Japan was compassionately supportive of the Vietnamese Nationalists in their struggle against French colonialism and then Communism as a continuing expression of European cultural imperialism. In the 1970s, first as Japanese ambassador to Saigon and later as Japan's deputy foreign minister, my father felt helpless to do anything but expressed deep sympathy to the government in Saigon. Later, as ambassador to the United States, he maintained the highest respect for, and his friendships with, those Vietnamese whom he had met in Saigon but who were now refugees in America."

—Kazuhiko Togo, former Japanese ambassador to the Netherlands and visiting professor, Shizuoka University

66 All the days of my husband's youth were dedicated to being a teammate in the ranks of fighters protecting the territory of South Vietnam, especially to protect the soul of our nation and our spirit of nationalism in resisting the aggression of a foreign ideology—Communism.

In April 1975 luck turned against the struggle; Communist soldiers conquered the South. Since then many books and articles have shined a light on this truth: the South lost the fight but not the rightful cause. The spirit of nationalism was not defeated. For my husband, he preserved the silent dignity of the defeated warrior because he always believed that he had fought for a just cause, upholding the sacred soul of rivers and mountains.

While reading the book *Kissinger's Betrayal* by Stephen Young, I was taken aback and moved by the thoughtful understanding on the part of an American of the national feelings of Vietnamese.

I (along with the spirit of my late husband and also, I believe, in accord with millions of other Vietnamese) thank Stephen Young for his efforts. With high regard, I recommend this book to every Vietnamese—whether inside Vietnam or overseas; Communist and non-Communist—in order to seek out the origins, put aside ideologies, and understand the national spirit of the Vietnamese that we have sustained for thousands of years."

—Nguyen Tuong Nhung, wife of Lieutenant General Ngo Quang Truong of the Army of the Republic of Vietnam; daughter of Nguyen Tuong Vinh (pen name Thach Lam); niece of Nguyen Tuong Tam (pen name Nhat Linh)

66 In 1973, the Nobel Peace Prize Committee voted to give the award jointly to Henry Kissinger and Le Duc Tho (North Vietnam's chief negotiator) for the cease-fire agreement that enabled the US to withdraw its forces from South Vietnam.

While Kissinger accepted, Le Duc Tho declined. Both were consistent with their public positions. In 1975, the South fell. Had the Peace Prize been awarded in 1975, Kissinger would probably have refused, while Le Duc Tho might have accepted. Stephen Young has told me his account of the Vietnam War and its peace negotiations from years ago. I am glad that he has finally published it with supporting evidence, some only recently available. It is a provocative but important perspective that should be neither ignored nor forgotten by future generations."

—George Yeo, former Singapore foreign minister

66 I first met Steve Young more than half a century ago when I was an Army captain on detail to the American embassy in Saigon as an expert on Vietnamese Communism. Steve was an extraordinary figure even then, held in the highest esteem by Ambassador Ellsworth Bunker and Deputy CORDS Director Bill Colby. The reason was clear—few if any Americans in Vietnam at the time rivaled his in-country experience and extraordinary command of Vietnam and its language and culture. After the war, he distinguished himself as a legal scholar and dean at Harvard and other law schools and in the private sector.

Kissinger's Betrayal is arguably the most important single source published in decades for understanding why America went to war in Vietnam, why doing so was important, and what went wrong and ultimately led to a Communist victory.

Honorable people can disagree about the relative American contributions to that outcome—and Robert McNamara, the news media, Congress, and John Kerry certainly played notorious roles—but it is difficult to read the once highly classified documents disclosed in this landmark study without concluding Henry Kissinger betrayed his public trust and contributed to the deaths of millions of South Vietnamese and Cambodians and the loss of freedom for countless more.

This book is highly recommended for scholars, students, policymakers, and the public alike seeking to understand this important if painful part of our history. Failing to understand the lessons of history would add to the tragedy."

—Prof. Robert F. Turner, SJD, former president of the U.S. Institute of Peace, author of *Vietnamese Communism: Its Origins and Development*, and co-founder of the Center for National Security Law at the University of Virginia

www.realclearpublishing.com

Kissinger's Betrayal: How America Lost the Vietnam War

Author photo by Matthew Clark Henseler.

For more information, please contact:
RealClear Publishing, an imprint of Amplify Publishing Group
620 Herndon Parkway #320
Herndon, VA 20170
info@amplifypublishing.com

Library of Congress Control Number: 2021924933

CPSIA Code: PRV1222A
ISBN-13: 978-1-63755-359-6

Printed in the United States

In grateful memory of:

My father, Kenneth Todd Young, whose life showed me how to respect Asian wisdom and cultures;

Ellsworth Bunker, whose trust in me opened access to an inside story of the Vietnam War;

William Egan Colby, whose confidence in me inspired resolve;

Nguyen Ngoc Huy, a teacher of Vietnamese courage and idealism;

and Mr. and Mrs. Pham Do Binh, for welcoming me into their family.

And I only am escaped alone to tell thee.

Book of Job

One who walks by night and bears
A light behind him, not to help himself
But to give light to those who follow after.

Dante Alighieri, *The Divine Comedy*
(*Purgatorio*, canto 22)

KISSINGER'S BETRAYAL

How America Lost the Vietnam War

STEPHEN B. YOUNG

CONTENTS

ACKNOWLEDGMENTS

The writing of this book has taken forty years of lonely effort. Those who helped along the way are too numerous to thank individually.

They include: my family—my wife, Pham Thi Hoa, and my children; my colleagues—American and Vietnamese—in South Vietnam during the war; Vietnamese colleagues and friends in exile after 1975 in Europe, Canada, Australia, and the United States; scholars and archivists; and advisors and friends who gave encouragement and helped to bring forth a better book. May this book be sufficient repayment for all those supportive contributions.

PREFACE

WHY THIS BOOK?

To finally share the story of why the Vietnam War ended so badly for both the South Vietnamese and the United States.

The ending of the Vietnam War in April 1975 has shaped our history ever since, both domestically in our culture and politics as they have become more and more divisive, and in international affairs, where we could neither prevail as expected in our limited but "forever wars" in Iraq and Afghanistan nor deter Vladimir Putin from invading Ukraine.

Reality is a hard taskmaster; it does not yield to our desires, and it does not adopt our ideals. Much about our world has not changed and will not. Ancient wisdom still provides sound insights. Human nature is pretty much the same now as it was ten thousand years ago, affixed in each of us by the social/psychological matrix building out our identities.

Events have consequences; tragic events traumatize especially. Losing the Vietnam War was traumatic for Americans. The effects of that experience are with us still, with the old who have personal memories of those years and with the young who have heard only hand-me-down narratives about the war.

From the pages of this book, you may draw your conclusions as to what was historically true and what meanings should be ascribed to those realities.

One lesson we all need to learn is to take history seriously. History is more than narrative; it is more than opinion. What happened yesterday and what happens today transcend our opinions and our narratives. Taking history seriously is a moral act taking us outside ourselves into the realms of others and of facts.

But knowing the truth and changing our beliefs accordingly are not the only benefits provided by uncovering this sad story of our country's failure to responsibly defend an ally. The lessons to be learned from Henry Kissinger's diplomacy of fifty years ago apply with special force to today's challenge from a new alliance between Russia and China.

The balance of power in the world changed for the worse on February 4, 2022, when Vladimir Putin for Russia and Xi Jinping for China signed a pact declaring that

> as every nation has its own unique national features, history, culture, social system and level of social and economic development, [the] universal nature of human rights should be seen through the prism of the real situation in every particular country, and human rights should be protected in accordance with the specific situation in each country and the needs of its population . . .
>
> [Russia and China] believe that the advocacy of democracy and human rights must not be used to put pressure on other countries. They oppose the abuse of democratic values and interference in the internal affairs of sovereign states under the pretext of protecting democracy and human rights, and any attempts to incite divisions and confrontation in the world. The sides call on the international community to respect cultural and civilizational diversity and the rights of peoples of different countries to self-determination. . . .
>
> Certain States' attempts to impose their own "democratic standards" on other countries, to monopolize the right to assess the level of compliance with democratic criteria, to draw dividing lines based on the

grounds of ideology, including by establishing exclusive blocs and alliances of convenience, prove to be nothing but flouting of democracy and go against the spirit and true values of democracy. Such attempts at hegemony pose serious threats to global and regional peace and stability and undermine the stability of the world order.

[Russia and China] reaffirm their strong mutual support for the protection of their core interests, state sovereignty and territorial integrity, and oppose interference by external forces in their internal affairs.

Consistent with the terms of this agreement, Russia invaded Ukraine on February 24, 2022. The United Nations General Assembly voted to condemn this aggression.

However, in 1935, the League of Nations had voted to condemn Mussolini's invasion of Ethiopia after hearing Emperor Haile Selassie movingly appeal to the conscience of humanity. What happened as a result? Only that the international community slid closer to World War II.

Invoking its pact with Russia, will China now invade Taiwan?

Who will step up to defend an international community of open societies, human rights, and constitutional democracies?

How should we think of America's role in this unhappy world so prone to misunderstandings, differences of opinion, and abuses of power?

Should not we Americans now consider what is to become of our country? What our individual responsibilities are in that respect? What lessons might we learn from how, two score and ten years ago, the Vietnam War was lost—lessons that would help bring forth the "better angels of our natures"?

Stephen B. Young
October 2022

CHAPTER 1

PRELUDE
TO BETRAYAL

PART 1: WHO ARE THE VIETNAMESE?

When a vast image out of Spiritus Mundi
Troubles my sight: somewhere in sands of the desert
A shape with lion body and the head of a man,
A gaze blank and pitiless as the sun,
Is moving its slow thighs, . . .
And what rough beast, its hour come round at last,
Slouches towards Bethlehem to be born?

—William Butler Yeats, "The Second Coming"

This book tells the story of how the Vietnamese Communists ruling from Hanoi in North Vietnam were able to invade and conquer South Vietnam in April 1975, defeating both the South Vietnamese and the United States of America in their joint defense of Vietnamese Nationalism. The story turns on Henry Kissinger, the national security advisor to American president Richard Nixon. On May 31, 1971, in his secret negotiations with the Vietnamese Communist leadership, Kissinger made a crucial military concession, putting in place the conditions that later enabled Hanoi to conquer South Vietnam. Kissinger, however, had previously and informally made that fatal concession on January 9, 1971, in a private meeting with Anatoly Dobrynin, the ambassador of the Soviet Union to the United States.

But to fully understand the tragedy of the American and South Vietnamese defeat, we must go back in history and learn about who the Vietnamese are and how their Nationalist ideals were crushed by French colonialism after World War II. We can begin the story as French colonial rule over Vietnam came to an end.

In July 1954, an international conference of the great powers convened in Geneva, Switzerland, to end two wars, one in Korea and one in Southeast Asia. The Korean War saw the Communist government of North Korea invade South Korea to unite the Korean people under Communism. The North Korean government had support from the Soviet Union and the People's Republic of China. The United States came to the aid of South Koreans who refused to live under Communism. The United States sought and obtained support from the United Nations in fighting to defeat an aggression that was in violation of the charter of the United Nations.

The second war, largely fought in Vietnam, was one of the last European colonial enterprises. It saw the French attempting to extend their cultural and economic hegemony over Vietnam, Laos, and Cambodia under a revised protocol of subordinated political rights for the peoples of Indochina.

In Vietnam, the war was also one of Communist Vietnamese against Nationalist Vietnamese, with the Communists seeking to keep the Nationalists out of power. But it was a more complicated struggle than North Korea's war to invade and conquer South Korea because a third belligerent party, France, fought to keep all of Vietnam in some form of colonial subordination to France. Before World War II, Vietnam had been a French colony in part, with the other two-thirds of the country under French dominance as a protectorate. After World War II, seeking to sustain their colonial privileges, the French allied with some Vietnamese to fight other Vietnamese. The leader of the resistance to France had taken the nom de guerre of Ho Chi Minh. He was chairman of a united front called the Viet Minh. Ho presented himself not as a Communist but more as a patriot, seeking the independence of Vietnam from French colonialism. After the Chinese Communists conquered China and expelled the Chinese Nationalists to Taiwan, they came to the assistance of Ho Chi Minh and turned the military struggle in Vietnam in his favor. In May 1954, a major French position in the valley of Dien Bien Phu was captured by Ho's forces. A new French government in Paris decided to sue for peace and give up the war.

The Geneva Conference first ratified an armistice between North Korea and South Korea, and the fighting between the two Koreas stopped. Then the conference sought terms acceptable to the French and the Vietnamese Communists that would end the fighting in Vietnam. Granting independence to the former French colonies in Laos and Cambodia was not difficult to arrange. With respect to Vietnam, it was decided to divide the country into two zones, as Germany and Korea had been divided after World War II, one for the Communists and the other for the Nationalists. The armistice agreement between France and the Viet Minh provided that neither zone would be used to attack the other. Non-Communists in the North were free to move to the southern zone, while Communists in the South were given the right to move to the North. Then a nonbinding, unsigned statement was issued by the conference that in 1956 the two zones would collaborate on an election for a single government and unification.

In July 1954, without French approval, Ngo Dinh Diem was appointed prime minister of the southern zone, the one reserved for the Nationalists, called the Republic of Vietnam. He set in immediately to build a strong non-Communist state in his zone, much to the dismay of the French government. On October 23, 1954, American president Dwight D. Eisenhower committed the United States to the defense of South Vietnam with economic and military assistance. Eisenhower's letter of commitment made express reference to Vietnamese Nationalism as a legitimate political aspiration of the Vietnamese, providing a profound moral justification for the independence of South Vietnam.

Eisenhower's letter said,

We have been exploring ways and means to permit our aid to Viet-Nam to be more effective and to make a greater contribution to the welfare and stability of the Government of Viet-Nam. I am, accordingly, instructing the American Ambassador to Viet-Nam to examine with you in your capacity as Chief of Government, how an intelligent program of American aid given directly to your Government can serve to assist Viet-Nam in its present hour of trial, provided that your Government is prepared to give assurances as to the standards of performance it would be able to maintain in the event such aid were supplied.

The purpose of this offer is to assist the Government of Viet-Nam in developing and maintaining a strong, viable state, capable of resisting attempted subversion or aggression through military means. The Government of the United States expects that this aid will be met by performance on the part of the Government of Viet-Nam in undertaking needed reforms. It hopes that such aid, combined with your own continuing efforts, will contribute effectively toward an independent Viet-Nam endowed with a strong government. Such a government would, I hope, be so responsive to the Nationalist aspirations of its people, so enlightened in purpose and effective in performance, that it will be respected both at home and abroad and discourage any who might wish to impose a foreign ideology on your free people.[1]

Within six months of the American commitment of support for Diem's Nationalist government, the smoldering antipathy of senior French officials for his intransigent lack of cooperation with Vietnam's former colonial overlords led to violence. The French schemed to have Diem removed as prime minister, even winning the most senior American representative to their point of view. Diem then sent the army against the Binh Xuyen mafia, a French client quasi-criminal organization with a zone of control in the Chinese section of Saigon. Diem's determination not to succumb to French wishes forced the Americans to choose between their European ally France and Nationalism in Vietnam. The Americans chose Vietnamese Nationalism as the more honorable cause and the better alternative for preventing Communist conquest of South Vietnam.

THE ESSENCE OF VIETNAMESE NATIONALISM

The Southern Emperor lives in the mountains
and rivers of the Southern nation
This destiny is enshrined in Heaven's Book.
—Ly Thuong Kiet

Phuc duc tai mau.
(Good fortune and happiness come from mothers.)
—Nguyen Trai, statesman and poet

Neu khong thanh cong, thi thanh nhan.
(Even if we don't succeed, at least we will become worthy men.)
—Nguyen Thai Hoc, Viet Nam Quoc Dan Dang (VNQDD) martyr

We can rather easily learn about the basic dynamics of the Vietnamese through their language, in descriptive concepts that are unique to them. What are the uniquely Vietnamese beliefs and understandings that separate them from other ethnic nationalities?

First, for example, we find that Vietnamese look for leadership to individuals who possess the personal trait of *uy tin*. We can easily learn the general meaning of *uy tin* by examining the character of those Vietnamese who are accepted as leaders within their social contexts. People with *uy tin* have a moral efficacy; they are trustworthy and reliable and will not abuse power. They have a personal reserve and are firmly comfortable giving directions and making decisions.

While it has a cognate in Chinese, *uy tin* is more predictive of Vietnamese politics than the similar Chinese word is for Chinese politics. To succeed among Vietnamese, you need to work with individuals believed to possess *uy tin*.

Second, Vietnamese deeply value private property as the dividend paid out by their individual karmic investment account. The dividends—wealth and other incidents of good fortune—are called *phuc duc*; the process of investing in karmic wealth accumulation is called *lam phuoc* and consists primarily of virtuous behavior. Someone who lives virtuously and may therefore expect material good fortune in the future is said to be a person possessing *duc,* or a virtue that changes circumstances.

One's educational achievement, the quality of one's marriage, the ability of one's children, the ownership of land and houses, and the social position one arrives at all come from *phuc duc.* To have a good education; a capable and loving wife or husband; attractive and talented children; ownership of fields, houses, factories, and bank accounts; and high social position is to be blessed because of past virtue, especially from your mother and other maternal forebears. Individuals therefore have a right to personal wealth and property.

To suffer from bad fortune, poverty, a nagging or lazy wife, a wastrel husband, no employment, or other low and oppressive circumstances is similarly one's karmic entitlement to a life of poor outcomes. This sad result may be blamed largely on one's mother and other maternal forebears for not having been sufficiently virtuous in their times on earth.

The value placed on *duc* and the possessive appreciation of whatever comes as the blessings of *phuc duc* orient Vietnamese away from Communism. Communism, in fact, is very much contrary to core Vietnamese values and culture. Vietnamese are very protective of their personal property and individual autonomy.

Thus, the evolution of Vietnamese society under Communist control after 1975 was consistently toward a regime of crony capitalism and systemic corruption where everyone, with Communist Party members at the fore, sought money, land, and the power to get more.

Given a level playing field, one would expect that the vast majority of Vietnamese would never support a Communist agenda of expropriation and socialist ownership of the means of production. And in fact the Vietnamese Communist Party never made Communism the centerpiece of its politics when popular support had to be mobilized. In late 1945, the party publicly disbanded, leaving only a private network of Marxist/Leninist study groups. Its political leadership was offered through the Viet Minh Front seeking an end to French colonialism.

Later, when the party sought control over South Vietnam, Communism as a cause was never put front and center before the South Vietnamese people. A new front, one for the liberation of South Vietnamese from American intervention and "lackeys" associated with the Americans (*My Nguy*), was created to recruit and deploy South Vietnamese on Hanoi's behalf. There was no proposal put on the table to unite South Vietnam with the Communist North.[2]

A third core cultural dynamic animating *tinh than dan toc*, or ethnic Vietnamese-ness, drove the Nationalist struggle against Communism as a Western ideology. Vietnamese are great believers in the powers of fate—*so mang*. There are skilled disciplines of fortune-telling that are dear to the hearts of many Vietnamese, such as casting horoscopes, reading patterns of geomancy in the earth, or observing facial features, all of which neatly reveal all our destinies and confirm the relevance of egocentricity for our lives. This orientation to fate has converted nearly every Vietnamese into a determined individualist. Each Vietnamese firmly believes in his or her own private, individual destiny and struggles for self-assertion against the world. The regimentation imposed by the Communist Party, the obsequious submission of individual needs and wishes demanded by fidelity to proletarian solidarity, and the necessity of obedience enforced by the Communist secret police alienate Vietnamese from the cause of Communism. Vietnamese want to be free to enjoy the blessings of their promised *phuc duc* and to give scope and energy to their private destinies. They don't like organizational hierarchies, and they suffer authoritarian "bosses" only when they have no practical alternative to such obedience.

Freedom and liberty have a deep appeal to Vietnamese. The modern Vietnamese translation of the word "freedom" is *tu do*, which uses the signifier for self *tu*. *Tu* is an ancient word with deep associations with Taoism, where "selfness" is taken for granted as a building block of the natural order. That which is natural is legitimate to Vietnamese; therefore, the desires and needs of the self—one's personal identity—can make legitimate claims on society. Thus, political ideals of liberty come naturally to Vietnamese. Buddhism and Confucianism are seen as guiding the self on the moral level to a fit accommodation with others and with the cosmos. Both religions offer strong ethical teachings promoting self-control and self-reliance, habits of mind and heart that are rooted in individualism.

Vietnamese have not been so thoroughly repressed by the conformist social constraints of filial piety as have the Chinese.[3] Chinese culture is more patriarchal than Vietnamese culture is. While they have superficially adopted a patina of Chinese family paternalism, women as mothers and wives are the centers of power in all Vietnamese families. The Le Dynasty Law Code correspondingly provided that daughters could inherit land reserved to support the costs of ancestor worship.[4]

A great distinction between Vietnamese and Chinese cultures can be found in the dominant role of women among the Vietnamese. Accumulated *phuc duc* results from the virtues of one's maternal ancestors, a famous poem has it. A wife is known as the *noi tuong*—the general of the within. After a marriage, mothers and daughters-in-law are expected to struggle for control of the son/husband. Many husbands escape the power struggle between their mother and their wife by flight and avoidance of responsibility, which only confirms the power of women in the family.

In the shifting, coalition-based structures of their politics and in their fluid social interactions, Vietnamese are more Southeast Asian than Chinese in their mores. This makes sense, for in their origins several thousand years ago, the Vietnamese were part of the non-Chinese world of peoples who lived south of the Yangtze River. Chinese cultural forms are little more than ill-fitting robes put on Vietnamese shoulders by various ruling elites to impose forms of submission on a people once undisciplined, tribal, and almost matriarchal in their ancient ways.

What prevents Vietnamese from becoming extremely individualistic to the point of anarchy are the demands of virtue—*duc*—and their belief in fate. It is fate that they are Vietnamese, part of a group that has its own destiny. In Buddhist terms, this arises from a *dong ngiep*, or a common karma shaped by the actions—good and bad—of generations of ancestors. Vietnamese trace their *dan toc,* or peoplehood, through descent back to common ancestry under mythical kings, the Hung Dynasty, who arose separately from the mythical origin figures of the Chinese—Yao and Shun. The emotional tie of individuals to others through descent is tightly braided by domineering mothers when Vietnamese are very young.

The sense of ethnicity is also brought forward by non-Buddhist beliefs in geomancy—the presence of heavenly forces in the rivers and mountains around the community. These heavenly forces provide distinctive opportunities and limitations. They make living under their influences, being enveloped day in and day out by their influences, and being buried within their influences a process of shaping character and destiny.

Vietnamese individualism rests on cosmic realities, not so different in concept from the natural law doctrines providing for individual rights in the American Declaration of Independence. Vietnamese, however, believe in individual destiny, which they call *so.* Vietnamese have expectations that they should be free to realize whatever their talents can bring them within the bounds set by heavenly forces. No emperor, family, or Communist Party has the moral right, they believe, to interfere with heaven's separate plan for each individual. Accordingly, each person has the right and the power to communicate directly with heaven regarding that plan. No intermediary—whether commissar or bureaucrat—is necessary. Individuals stand at the center of things directly under heaven. It is an Asian version of Martin Luther's "priesthood of all believers."

For Vietnamese, the intentions of heaven are known through specialized sciences known in the West as "fortune-telling." First, there is the art of reading horoscopes, known as *tu vi* or *la so.* Then there is interpreting the sizes and shapes of facial features, a discipline known as *coi tuong.* And third, there is geomancy (*dia ly*), now popular in the West in its decorative Chinese form known as feng shui. Finally, an all-around guide to destiny can be found in the sixty-four hexagrams of the *I Ching*.

Now for Vietnamese, a determinant of destiny is what they call *phuc duc*. This is something of a Buddhist concept whereby good deeds bring about good fortune and bad deeds the reverse. The good deeds of a mother are believed by Vietnamese to be especially powerful in determining the fates and fortunes of her children. This may explain why Vietnamese refer to their country as a "motherland" rather than a "fatherland."

This special Vietnamese moral vision can be easily encountered in the poem *Kim Van Kieu*, written about 1820. The poet reflects on individualism and fate and how the two can be adjusted for a worthy life. *Kim Van Kieu* tells the story of a beautiful and very talented young woman who must pay for the hubris of her passions with repeated sufferings, until the effects of her selfless deeds overbalance the detrimental consequences of her selfishness and win her release from the slings and arrows of this world. Finding a moral to his story, the poet tells us that "within us each there lies the root of good." Fate turns on the ability of each person to overcome his or her passions; individuals, not governments or parties or even priesthoods, work out their own fates in direct communion with universal laws.

With its evocative language, the *Kim Van Kieu* poem also ratifies Vietnamese subordination to fate:

> All things are fixed by Heaven, first and last.
> Heaven appoints each creature to a place.
> If we are marked for grief, we'll come to grief.
> We'll sit on high if destined for high seats.[5]

The passion of the Vietnamese to be free and independent of other countries, a conviction that sustained them through one thousand years of Chinese rule and many subsequent wars with China, derives from this fatalism. Heaven gave them a birthright of freedom. The geomancy of

Vietnam, known as *nui/song*, or "mountains and rivers," provides for independent communion with heaven through an emperor, or *de*, of the south who was the equal of the emperor, or *de*, of China in the north.

Some Vietnamese are convinced that their country was lost to the French in the nineteenth century because an emperor built his tomb in the wrong place. The site by a pond was lovely. The emperor had read poetry and drunk tea there while alive. But from the rules of geomancy, the location was deficient in its concentration of yin and yang forces. A burial there would not confer good fortune on the descendants of the deceased.

Other Vietnamese very sincerely believe that the suffering brought on by the Communists was recompense for wrongs done by ancient Vietnamese kings to the Cham people during the fifteenth century in cruel wars of conquest and spoilation.

South Vietnam's constitution of 1967 had 117 articles because one plus one plus seven equaled nine, an auspicious yang number.

Surprisingly, there is to date no accurate and illuminating study in either French or English of Vietnamese Nationalism. American policy in Vietnam has received numerous reviews, histories, and analyses; Vietnamese Communism and Ho Chi Minh have similarly been extensively written up. Several scholarly studies of non-Communist political parties and leaders avoided examination of Nationalism as a cultural force in Vietnamese life.

The Dai Viet political platform was first set forth in 1939 by Truong Tu Anh, a young intellectual from Central Vietnam.[6] His proclamation to the Vietnamese people that year contained these provocative and evocative passages:

> *Episodes of glory and shame came after one another on this land of Dai Viet, forged our people into a race experienced, dogged, strong enough to oppose every unusual twist of fate. At times courage was high and perfect, at times weak, always holding pure the special identity waiting to rise up in arms more courageous than ever before . . .*

Under 50 years of rule by French colonialists, our nation was reduced to a warehouse of raw materials, a market for consumption, and a cook stove for cheap labor. They plundered clean all sources of profit, and pushed our people down into backwardness in culture and industry. To the point that agriculture, the economic basis of the nation came to an end of growth and development. The level of progress of our people thus every day got lower and lower. They poisoned our hearts and spoiled our customs, dividing south from north to rule more easily. They used profits and wealth to buy those with base values, greedy, to night and day to waylay curry favor with, creating in the country a very vile atmosphere of spying on and mistrusting each other. Those with talent, haughty brave because they would not humble themselves were killed or exiled and pushed into misery. While our group of traitors, selling the nation seeking status not knowing honesty at all, wormed and toadied as their way to preferment, turning around to kill the people, whispering or boasting, showing off power, shaky in the highest positions in society.

French imperialists took over the authority for education and pulled into their hands all leading organizations of opinion to retard the learning of the people and convert them into a foundation for colonial rule as a class of slavish intellectuals easy to order about. A self-reliant mind was cleansed away, a flattering feeling for the foreigners, turning us into self-denigration, considering that being a servant was natural, not even knowing what shame was any more. Bowing the head is the role of slaves, only waiting to struggle to grab the position of a mincing disciple.

The result of decades under French rule is exploited resources, degraded economy, degraded culture, and more and more slavish dispositions . . .

Our country of Dai Viet wants to become strong, taking a brilliant place under the sun and honorable before the heavenly spirit which the Creator has endowed our people, so it must solve these two important problems:

Liberate the country

Reform society

Our people must understand: rebuilding the foundation of self-determination for the rivers and mountains of Dai Viet is the sacred duty of Vietnamese. Only we sincerely dedicated because of our survival, because of our happiness. To rely on others, to trust others, is to lead ourselves into the way of destroying our aspirations . . .

If we want to implement thoroughly the general liberation of the country and reform society, we must realize that we must have a purely Nationalist party to unite all the genuinely patriotic forces and with enough power to lead the people in every struggle . . .

The goal of the Dai Viet Quoc Dan Dang is to gather all the outstanding ones from every part of the country, to establish a very powerful strength. That strength is ready to overthrow the force of any powerful nation intending to invade the land of Dai Viet, to attain the foundation for complete independence and because of the common happiness of all the people (hanh phuc) to build a rich and strong nation.[7]

In the comprehensive political program put forth by Truong Tu Anh were several goals that put the party on a path of confrontation with the Communists. First, the Dai Viets set as the first objective of any Vietnamese government the "good fortune of all the people." As Nationalists, the Dai Viets expressly rejected in 1939 class struggle and divisive class warfare among the Vietnamese themselves. Thus, the Dai Viet political program pledged that "the high or low status of each person in the social order will depend on the individual's worth (talent, virtue, sincerity with duties and obligations)."[8] This provision was completely in line with the Vietnamese cultural foundation of individualism and personal fate.

As for the Communists, the Dai Viets held that their ideology of Marxist-Leninism was a puppet or lackey theory coming from the West through the process of French colonialism. The 1939 Dai Viet program affirmed as a goal the elimination of "all lackey theories about class struggle to preserve the spirit of unity of the people from being wounded."

Unfortunately, the naturalism of fate so profoundly part of Vietnamese culture and personality orientations has a dark side. Fatalism includes bad outcomes as well as good ones. Nature, even heaven itself, may not favor us with blessings at all times. There are powers in the world and all around us that are beyond our control and to which we must accommodate ourselves in order to get through life as best we can. Those powers are called *the*—pronounced as "tay." Vietnamese will seek to gain possession of *the* if their *phuc duc* is deficient or their desires outrun what their karma has provided for them.

The facility with which many Vietnamese could subordinate *duc* to *the* both facilitated support for the Communists as the holders of *the* and also undermined the quality of government on the Nationalist side. Nationalist military officers and civil officials could easily look upon their offices as sources of personal advantage and not as stewardship of a higher cause of national honor and collective prosperity. They would not perform with diligence or out of concern for the public good. They would not put personal energy into their official undertakings. They would not live by virtue but rather by self-seeking power and so would not gain *uy tin*.

Further, the intense individualism inherent in the Vietnamese national ethic leads to easy fragmentation of political participation. Vietnamese would, in many cases, rather lead a small group than follow someone else. Non-Communist Vietnamese political associations therefore tend to be small networks that often split when leaders have a falling out with each other over often rather small issues or choices of words. Formation of coalitions among Vietnamese demands intricate and arduous interpersonal maneuvering and positioning of egos. And the resulting alliances rarely last for long. Vietnamese like *phong trao,* or sudden movements that pop up like wind and rain only to fade away just as quickly.

Only remarkable Vietnamese, those personally credited with having *uy tin*, can provide social islands of organizational stability. Such Vietnamese are few and far between. Whenever the Communists would kill Nationalists with *uy tin*, they degraded the political effectiveness of their rivals. Such murderous eliminations began in late 1945 and continued for decades. As the pacification program took hold in South Vietnam in 1969 and 1970 and the Viet Cong were defeated in the rural villages, Le Duan in Hanoi issued orders for the assassination of Nguyen Ngoc Huy, the Tan Dai Viet leader whose ideas inspired the program on the Vietnamese side. He had acquired too much *uy tin*. Killing him would cause the Tan Dai Viet fellowship to lose spirit and splinter into factions. Huy was well protected by his followers, and the assassination team sent south to take him out was apprehended. However, they did kill Huy's close associate Professor Nguyen Van Bong.[9]

HANOI'S WAR OF CONQUEST

No elections were held in 1956 to unify the Communist and Nationalist Vietnams into one country under one government. A formula for free and fair elections was not found. In addition, the Soviet Union was loath to have elections held in a divided Vietnam, as it would be an alarming precedent for them in the cases of the divided Koreas and Germanys.[10] During 1957, the Communist Party's armed units in the South were kept on duty but withdrew from contact with South Vietnamese government forces. Nevertheless, a type of violence that the Communists called *Tru Gian*—extermination of traitors—was encouraged in local areas. Those with *uy tin* who stood in the way of party control in villages were killed.

A Viet Cong cadre confirmed that

> *the principal purpose of 'the extermination of traitors' movement
> was to protect the very existence of the Party. Without exterminating
> the [government's] hard-core elements, the Party apparatus could
> not have survived. A second purpose was to aid in the development
> of the Party by creating fear in the enemy ranks and by creating
> faith among the masses in the skilled leadership of the Revolution.
> Extermination activities had an enormous psychological impact,
> because the masses saw that the government hard-core elements
> were being eliminated.*

He said that honest hamlet chiefs who had done much for the people and
who clearly understood the party's intentions and teachers who were pure
Nationalists and who could assume anti-Communist leadership in their
area were classified by the party as "Traitors of Major Importance."[11]

In early 1958, Hanoi politburo member Le Duan met with leaders of
the party from Interzone 5 in South Vietnam. He advised them that "when
the situation permits," they must launch an insurgency in the South, mobilizing guerilla units and using hit-and-run attacks on fixed military targets.
Thus, secure bases needed to be prepared to support that low-intensity
war against the new Nationalist government in Saigon. Violence would
be supplemented by political agitation in populated areas of South Vietnam. That summer, the Interzone 5 Party Committee expanded base areas
in the Central Highlands and organized armed platoons and community
self-defense units. By the end of 1958, base areas had been established in
Quang Nam, Quang Ngai, Binh Dinh, Phu Yen, Kontum, Darlac, and Ninh
Thuan provinces.[12] By 1959, Hanoi had under its control 173 platoons of
armed soldiers and hundreds more of secret part-time guerilla units in the
villages and hamlets of South Vietnam.

In January 1959, the Central Committee of the Communist Party
met in Hanoi for the Fifteenth Plenum Session since the party congress
of 1951. Representatives of the party's committees for the Mekong Delta

region (the Cochin China Party Committee) and for the central provinces of South Vietnam (the Interzone 5 Committee) joined the plenum. In the plenum, war against South Vietnam was commenced. The Central Committee decided to "liberate South Vietnam" and "build a peaceful, unified, independent, democratic and prosperous Vietnamese nation."[13] The Central Committee further decided to "make vigorous preparations aimed at launching a popular uprising to overthrow the US-Diem regime."[14] The party's goal was to impose its dictatorship over South Vietnam through aggression and violence. That year, 542 soldiers were sent into South Vietnam, and Group 559 was formed to create a supply line from North Vietnam through Laos into South Vietnam to support the coming war. In South Vietnam, uprisings were planned and successfully undertaken in many rural areas. Assassination of village leaders happened in community after community.

Though it is only legal formalism, it is quite relevant to an understanding of the ambitious dedication of the Vietnamese Communists to the seizure of total power over all Vietnamese to note that this decision of the party was a violation of the peace agreement signed with the French on July 20, 1954. Article 19 of that agreement committed the Vietnamese Communists to never using the territory of North Vietnam for a resumption of hostilities against the Nationalists or to further "an aggressive policy."[15]

Thus, when the US government later accused Hanoi of aggression against South Vietnam in violation of international law and the rights of the South Vietnamese people, it told the truth. The US government never lied about the cause of the war in South Vietnam.

The opportune time for Hanoi to launch its planned movement to overthrow the Diem government in Saigon came at the end of 1960. Anxiety over the ability of Diem and his small circle of advisors and lieutenants to successfully resist Hanoi began to spread among South Vietnamese Nationalists after Hanoi had decided on war. In 1959, Diem permitted his sister-in-law Mme Nhu to pressure the National Assembly into passing a law forbidding divorce. This offended many. It was seen by many as the Diem family forcing other Vietnamese to live by Catholic teachings on family solidarity and gave the Communists an opportunity to decry the Saigon government not as a Nationalist one but as only *gia dinh tri*—a one-family government. Diem relied most on his three brothers. His sister-in-law was stridently prominent in politics as well.

In December 1959, the Region 8 Party Committee, under the Cochin China Party Committee, began planning uprisings in the eastern Mekong Delta province of Ben Tre (Dinh Tuong for the Nationalists). From January 17 to 24, 1960, forty-seven villages in the province rose up in protest. Twenty-two village leaders were executed. In twenty-five other villages, followers of the party killed local leaders and attacked police posts and small military outposts.[16]

On January 26, 1960, armed soldiers of the Cochin China Party Committee attacked and captured a South Vietnamese regimental base near Tay Ninh during the New Year's holiday celebration, when the base was on stand down. Nationalist elders in Saigon met in the Caravelle Hotel in Saigon and issued a manifesto calling on Diem to reform his government. Diem refused.

In September 1960 in Hanoi, the Vietnamese Communist Party held its third congress. The congress set forth two goals for the party: 1) to push ahead vigorously the socialist revolution in North Vietnam and 2) to complete the popular democratic nationalist revolution in South Vietnam. The congress proposed that building socialism in North Vietnam would drive forward the goal of reunifying the nation and that party members in South Vietnam would participate directly in the "fight to break the yoke of oppression of the American imperialists and their puppets in order to liberate South Vietnam."[17]

On November 11, 1960, young Nationalist officers in the Dai Viet Party launched a coup calling on Diem to remove his brother Ngo Dinh Nhu from power. Diem stalled in negotiations with the coup leaders while loyal forces were mobilized to move on Saigon in support of the government. The failed coup presented Hanoi with the right time to organize an insurgent organization across South Vietnam.[18]

The insurgency, however, would be led secretly by the Communist

Party. Publicly, it was to be an organization of southern Vietnamese independent of Hanoi, not seeking union with the North or the imposition of Communism on the South. The resulting organization was to be a front for the Communists in Hanoi, a puppet structure of fellow travelers casting their lot with Hanoi.

The Communist Party of Vietnam has published once-secret party documents that confirm that the creation of the National Liberation Front (NLF, or Viet Cong) and of the insurgency to overthrow the Nationalist government in Saigon took place only upon the orders of the party leadership. The ten-point program of the NLF was written by party leaders in Hanoi.[19]

Accordingly, the premise of the American antiwar movement was wrong. The position of the American government that North Vietnam was the cause of the war in South Vietnam was correct.

The antiwar movement therefore destabilized American culture and politics and set in motion a culture war that would continue for fifty years by acting on a lie or on what, years later, would be called "disinformation."

A set of veritable "smoking guns" incriminating the Vietnamese Communists in starting an insurgency in South Vietnam was published by the Communists in a collection of official party documents. The documents that follow are official documents that instruct Communist cadres in South Vietnam to launch the NLF. One document dictates the demands to be made by the NLF, acting as an agent of the Communist Party in Hanoi.

POLITBURO CABLE NO. 17-NB, 11 NOVEMBER 1960

Sent to the Cochin China Region Party Committee and the Interzone 5 Region Party Committee

1. According to reports we have received from the enemy and through news broadcasts by Saigon, British, American, and French radio stations, a coup began at 3:00 in the morning on 11 November 1960. The

coup is being conducted by a number of officers in Diem's army, using airborne units in coordination with police forces and a number of infantry and armored units, all under the command of Colonel Nguyen Chanh Thi and other individuals opposed to Diem.

The coup forces have surrounded Independence Palace and the National Assembly building and have occupied important locations in Saigon. There has been fighting in the area around Independence Palace (where Diem and Nhu are located, protected by a security battalion) and around the National Assembly.

At 2:00 this afternoon, the coup group, calling itself the National Revolutionary Council to have broad appeal, broadcast a statement making clear its opposition to the Diem's oligarchy and dictatorial regime and its anti-communist policies. At the same time it promised to implement freedom and democracy, to stimulate the economy, and form a Constitutional Assembly. As for its foreign policy, it said that it would still stand alongside the Western nations. As of 8:00 tonight, Diem was still dragging his feet, had still not agreed to negotiate, and was moving additional forces from Military Region 5 and elements from Military Regions 1 and 4 up to counter the main coup forces in Saigon.

The situation is still unclear. We need to continue to monitor it closely.

2. Based on the situation as we understand it at this time, the Politburo has reached the following preliminary conclusions:

Because of this new situation, we must shift to new forms of struggle using new and appropriate slogans and demands to gain further support and isolate and topple our enemies.

In order to accomplish these goals, we must publicly issue the program of the National Liberation Front for South Vietnam, which we may call the national liberation movement of South Vietnam if we feel that is appropriate, with the following primary slogans:

—Completely topple the Ngo Dinh Diem ruling clique.

—Form a broad-based national democratic coalition government.

—Implement national independence, freedom, and democracy, and improve living conditions for the people.

—Peace, neutrality.

—Release all political prisoners.

—Establish relations with all nations of the world.

—Work toward achieving unification of our nation.

Depending on the situation in specific areas, at specific time, and among specific classes and levels of society, raise additional slogans [demands] that are specific and suited to the situation and the interests of each class and strata of society.

POLITBURO CABLE NO. 20-NB, 12 NOVEMBER 1960

Sent to the Cochin China Region Party Committee and the Interzone 5 Region Party Committee

1. According to information we have received, as of 4:00 on the afternoon of 12 November 1960, Diem had mobilized many forces from the provinces and the various military regions to come to the relief of Saigon. Diem's troops have recaptured the radio station and a number of important locations in Saigon. It appears that the siege of Independence Palace has been lifted. Diem's information agencies are reporting that the situation in Saigon has returned to normal. By the time you receive this cable, the coup forces may have already collapsed.

2. The Politburo has sent a directive to the Cochin China and Inter-Zone 5 Region Party committees and has received the cable from the Cochin China Party Committee. In general, the Politburo agrees with Cochin China's assessment and policy plans.

The Politburo would like to add the following points: . . .

b) At present Diem is in control of the situation. It is certain that Diem will take direct action to purge opposition in the army and in the government. It is also possible that, because of American pressure, the hatred of the masses of the population, and the damaging blow struck against his regime by the coup, Diem may be forced to reorganize and broaden his government. No matter what happens, however, the contradictions and disruption within the enemy camp will continue, and the prestige and power of the Diem faction will suffer a significant decline.

    The above situation has occurred under conditions in which we have powerful mass forces in the rural countryside and the urban masses hate and despise the Diem regime. This means that our forces will continue to play an active role and will have an important impact on how the situation develops.

c) Our basic policy remains as outlined in the cable we sent to you. We must seize this opportunity to create further political crisis and disruption among the enemy's ranks, to further weaken the enemy's power. At the same time, we will use this opportunity to rapidly strengthen our own forces through the appeal of the National Liberation Front to unite public opinion and lead the masses in a struggle to transform the situation in a manner favorable to our side. . . .

e) We must present the Liberation Front to the public immediately, without waiting to determine the personalities who will make it up. In the current situation, we do not need to announce the entire Front program. We need only put forward the primary points in the Front's program in order to have our voice heard at this opportune moment. In order to quickly lead the masses and unite public opinion under the Front's banner, we must issue a short appeal regarding the rotten US-Diem regime, the seriousness of the current situation, the historic mission of the Front, and a number of major slogans [demands], such as:

1. Topple the Ngo Dinh Diem government and dissolve the South Vietnamese National Assembly.

2. Elect a democratic National Assembly and form a broad-based national democratic coalition government.

3. Implement freedom and democracy, including freedom of expression, freedom of the press, freedom of assembly, freedom to travel and conduct business, freedom of religion, etc.

4. Improve living conditions, provide work for the unemployed, increase wages for workers and soldiers, reduce taxes and fees, lower the cost of living, end forced military conscription and forced coolie labor, etc.

5. End military sweep operations that murder and arrest the people, and eliminate Law 10/59 and other anti-democratic laws.

6. Release all political prisoners and disband the agrovilles, plantations, and concentration camps.

7. Implement progressive national education, oppose the imperialist education designed to keep the people ignorant, guarantee education and reform the testing system for high school students.

8. Guarantee equal rights for all ethnic groups and implement a program granting autonomy to ethnic minority groups.

9. Implement a diplomatic policy of peace and neutrality and establish diplomatic relations with all nations of the world.

10. Advance toward reunifying our nation.

11. Oppose war and protect peace.

PARTY SECRETARIAT CABLE NO. 34/ NB, 16 NOVEMBER 1960

Sent to the Cochin China Region Party Committee

1. The Secretariat believes we should present the National Liberation Front for South Vietnam to the public in the following manner: . . .

f. Issue a Proclamation with major slogans [demands] (The nine slogans laid out in the previous cable with two additional slogans: "Guarantee equal rights to all ethnic groups and grant autonomy to ethnic minority groups" and "Oppose war and protect peace."). If the Party Committee believes it necessary to add any other major slogans, you may draw them from the Front's program. Make sure that the Proclamation does not try to cover too much. It should contain major items only, so that everyone can understand and remember them.

g. The Proclamation should be signed by the National Liberation Front for South Vietnam or under another more appropriate name. Let us know so that we can provide our opinion.

Do not sign it as the Organizing Committee or as representatives of the Organizing Committee, Doctor [Phung Van] Cung and Huynh Tan Phat, because to have it signed by only a few people will not provide the effect of a national appeal or demonstrate the broad base of the Front.

h. When the Proclamation has been issued and attached to the Program of the Front, local areas (provinces and zones, or districts and villages) that are able should establish Front organizations in accordance with the Front program and appoint people to the Front committees at each location.

i. Later we will convene a meeting of representatives of the Front from all areas and a number of people from the different upper strata of society to further discuss the content of the Front's program (we might add or subtract a little) and to form the Front Central Committee.

j. In each locality, you must make sure to select people who are widely representative, reflect the different strata of society, and who have influence among the population. For example, in areas where the Cao Dai, Hoa Hao, or Catholic religions are strong, you must have someone representing them, elders, intellectuals, etc.

2. We must derive lessons learned in leadership and guidance of all types from our experience during the recent coup, because it is possible that similar situations will occur in the future. Pay attention to this matter so that you can contribute your experiences to the Central Committee.

3. For the immediate future, you must make sure that you have a good grasp of the situation and that you have a clear picture of the enemy's plans and schemes so that we can take the initiative in dealing with them in a timely fashion and that you continue to ensure that the movement grows wider and more powerful.

CABLE OF THE PARTY SECRETARIAT, NO. 40/NB, 24 NOVEMBER 1960

Sent to the Cochin China Region Party Committee

3. We are sending you the Proclamation of the National Liberation Front for South Vietnam that the Politburo has approved.

    You can edit the writing style however you feel necessary to make it suitable for use in South Vietnam. With regards to the content and major ideas, however, if you feel that there are any problems, send us a cable so we can discuss the problem.

    Send a cable to inform us what words or phrases need to be changed in terms of writing style so that the copy we send to Inter-Zone 5 will be identical to your copy.

4. You must have a careful, detailed plan ready for use when you present the Proclamation within the Party, to the civilian population outside the Party, etc., so that when the Proclamation is announced everyone is enthusiastic and confident so that we strengthen solidarity and our struggle. For that reason you must expand your infrastructure and expand your political activities among all classes and strata of the population to ensure that our movement continues to advance.

Following these instructions from the Communist Party Central Committee in Hanoi, on December 20, 1961, in a jungle location northwest of Saigon, the NLF was founded. The 1987 summary by the Military History Institute in Hanoi of its report entitled (translated from Vietnamese) "Draft Summary of the Resistance War Fighting the Americans Saving the Country by the Vietnamese People" said flatly: "Following the roadmap of the Congress, on December 20, 1960, the Front for the Liberation of the South was established."[20]

The NLF was positioned as a political movement supervising a territorial administration to take over South Vietnam. NLF committees were established in provinces and districts to provide local leaders across the country. Military commands were established at regional, provincial, district, and village levels to command soldiers attacking government forces and installations. The politburo of the party Central Committee authorized these forces to be named the Liberation Army of South Vietnam. In January 1961, the party's General Military Committee stated, "The Liberation Army of South Vietnam is part of the People's Army of Vietnam, having been organized, developed, educated and led by the Party."[21]

On February 15, 1961, the Central Committee of the NLF followed in lockstep, announcing the unification of all its armed forces under the name of the Liberation Armed Forces of South Vietnam.[22]

In February 1961, the Politburo of the Vietnamese Communist Party, meeting in Hanoi, "gave the Central Military Party Committee the responsibility for directing military activities in South Vietnam." Between 1954 and 1960, the party office directing the "revolution" in South Vietnam had been the Central Unification Committee.[23]

John F. Kennedy assumed the presidency of the United States on January 20, 1961. One of his first policy challenges was how to respond to Hanoi's launch of a war to conquer South Vietnam. Kennedy decided upon a program of expanded US military assistance to the South Vietnamese army, including advisors to accompany Nationalist units into combat and flying helicopters in support of South Vietnamese operations. Economic assistance was also increased.

In his inaugural address, President Kennedy affirmed that his administration would engage in the long twilight struggle against insurgencies and political subversion by the Communists and the ability of Communist Parties to impose their dictatorships on non-Communist peoples. President Kennedy pledged that the United States would "pay any price, bear any burden to insure the cause of liberty."

To counter Hanoi's tactic of organizing villagers under local leaders reporting ultimately to the party Central Committee, the South Vietnamese, with American support, adopted a tactic from the successful British counterinsurgency effort in Malaya. Rural people were moved into fortified communities called strategic hamlets and provided with Nationalist leaders and self-defense capabilities.

In Saigon, Diem refused to open his government to other Nationalists. For political support and to staff his administration, he relied mostly on Catholics and members of a political party established and managed by his younger brother Ngo Dinh Nhu. Nhu's party was called the Can Lao and used a French Catholic ethic of personalism to legitimate its mission and vision. Diem made no attempt to compromise with anti-Communist leaders of the Cao Dai, Hoa Hao, and Buddhist faiths. He also did not invite any leaders from the Dai Viet and Viet Nam Quoc Dan Dang (VNQDD) networks to join his government.

Resistance grew to Diem's overconcentration of power among a few trusted colleagues and family. In setting up a front organization in South Vietnam to oppose Diem, the Communist Party leaders in Hanoi adroitly capitalized on Diem's lack of *uy tin* in the eyes of many South Vietnamese.

In 1963, a shooting incident against Buddhists in Hue escalated into mass protests challenging Diem's legitimacy as a paramount Vietnamese leader. As support for Diem evaporated both in South Vietnam and in Washington, DC, a group of younger officers, principally Dai Viet in loyalty, began to plan for a coup d'état to remove Diem from power. A different group of more senior generals also formed with the same plan in mind. The generals made contact with the Americans and were encouraged to proceed. On November 1, 1963, the Diem government was overthrown, with the younger officers leading the coup units and the generals taking credit and forming a new government. At the order of several generals, Diem and his brother Nhu were murdered.[24]

At the Ninth Plenum of the Central Committee elected in the Third Party Congress, the Communist leadership resolved to send regular North Vietnamese units to the battlefronts in South Vietnam and escalate massed combat in the South.[25] Three regiments of the 325th Division were sent south.

French president Charles de Gaulle called for the neutralization of South Vietnam and an end to American support of Saigon. Two Vietnamese, formerly military officers close to the French during its war against the Viet Minh, returned to Saigon to further French efforts to hand South Vietnam over to the Communists. Younger Dai Viet officers then arrested the four leading generals presiding over the Saigon government for flirting with neutralism and cooperation with the French to betray the Nationalist cause. The military government was reorganized to include leaders from all Nationalist orientations: Buddhist, Catholic, Cao Dai, Hoa Hao, Dai Viet, and VNQDD. In a tense compromise between the coup leaders and senior general Duong Van "Big" Minh, General Nguyen Khanh was installed as prime minister. This proved to be a terrible mistake.[26]

Out of touch with the Dai Viets and so unnerved by this unexpected change of leadership, the Americans, especially Secretary of Defense Robert McNamara, publicly rallied behind General Khanh as their "boy."[27] Khanh took American support as a license to install personal supporters in key positions of power. He put responsibility for village cadres in the hands of a small Nationalist faction, the Duy Dan Party, refugees from North Vietnam but connected to him by marriage. He encouraged the Buddhists to make demands of the Catholics and the Catholics to resist and deepen their mistrust of the Buddhists. He fomented a split in the Dai Viets and refused to promote the best-qualified officers to senior commands. In late 1964 Khanh went so far as to reach out to Huynh Tan Phat, secretary general of the Central Committee of the NLF. Phat responded with a letter on January 28, 1965, praising Khanh and offering to join with him in friendly cooperation.[28] As a result, in 1964 and 1965, the Dai Viets organized several coup attempts to drive Khanh from power. When they finally succeeded in the spring of 1965, the military situation for the Nationalists was dire.

Taking advantage of poor leadership in Saigon, the evaporation of village governments and police across South Vietnam, and incompetence and low morale in the South Vietnamese army, Hanoi had increased its fighting strength and political control of rural areas. Hanoi sent 17,475 soldiers south to stiffen NLF units. To discourage Hanoi from such escalation, the United States started bombing North Vietnam and infiltration routes through Laos. Several American combat units were dispatched to South

Vietnam to set up defense perimeters around important bases.

In late 1964, the Vietnamese Communist Party decided to escalate its efforts to win a decisive victory within a few years. A special offensive campaign was set in motion to unfold in late 1964 and spring 1965. Politburo member and senior general Nguyen Chi Thanh was sent south. More regiments were sent south. In 1965, Hanoi sent at least 46,796 soldiers to the battlefields of South Vietnam.[29]

In June of 1965, the senior American military advisor General William Westmoreland requested the deployment of forty-four maneuver battalions to South Vietnam to seek out and destroy large Communist units. President Johnson granted the request, and the Vietnam War became very serious for Americans. Justifying his decision to commit Americans to the defense of South Vietnam, the president very correctly pointed to Hanoi's aggression as the cause of the war. He said, "We did not choose to be guardians at the gate, but there is no one else."

With the guidance of his superiors in the Department of Defense, General Westmoreland used his American units jointly with South Vietnamese regular forces in search-and-destroy missions to deplete Communist fighting strength and to push Communist forces as far as possible away from populated cities, towns, and villages. General Westmoreland applied these tactics in the tradition of Ulysses S. Grant, who had used them to wear down the Confederacy during the American Civil War. Grant once said, "The art of war is simple enough. Find out where your enemy is. Get at him as soon as you can. Strike him as hard as you can, and keep moving on."[30]

By the end of 1967, Westmoreland had achieved considerable tactical success with this use of force. But in the United States, an emotionally powerful antiwar movement had emerged, convinced either that the United States could not defeat the insurgency or that the insurgency was more legitimate than the Saigon government, which therefore did not deserve American support. And during 1966 and 1967, Hanoi continued its infiltration of regular forces from North Vietnam while the Saigon government failed to successfully contest Viet Cong guerillas in the villages.

In January 1968, during a truce observing the family-focused Lunar

New Year holiday, Hanoi launched offensives at South Vietnamese cities, bypassing American forces. It was the infamous Tet Offensive. Communist forces took massive casualties and were defeated. They never recovered their military momentum in South Vietnam. The fight to evict Communist forces from the city of Hue was arduous.[31]

But the effect of the Tet Offensive in the United States was dramatic. It came as a great surprise to Americans and was presented as evidence that their government either had not told the truth about progress in the war or did not know how to win. In any case, public opinion shifted more and more against the war. President Johnson declined to run for reelection and defend his war strategy. He initiated peace negotiations with Hanoi and the Viet Cong. Robert Kennedy declared himself as a candidate running against the war. Upon Kennedy's assassination, Senator Eugene McCarthy carried the antiwar standard to the Democratic Party convention in Chicago. He lost the nomination to Vice President Hubert Humphrey, but Humphrey then lost a close election in November to Richard Nixon. Nixon told the voters that he had a secret plan to end the war.

Nixon assumed the presidency in January 1969. He chose Henry Kissinger for his national security advisor. Nixon's conundrum was figuring out how to achieve peace with honor. How could he end the war for American forces but not abandon South Vietnam to Hanoi?

Nixon's secretary of defense, Melvin Laird, visited Saigon and was briefed by Ambassador Ellsworth Bunker. Bunker, as instructed by President Johnson, had already put American policy on track to turn the war over to the Vietnamese.[32] He described this strategy to Laird, who returned to Washington and proposed it to President Nixon. Nixon accepted it. In March of 1969, Nixon announced that American forces would withdraw from the fighting in a program called "Vietnamization."

At the urging of Henry Kissinger, Nixon also accepted a parallel track to achieve "peace with honor," which was to have Kissinger conduct secret negotiations with Hanoi seeking agreement on terms to end the fighting. Kissinger used a French friend of long standing, Jean Sainteny, to approach Hanoi and facilitate the commencement of secret negotiations in Paris.

CHAPTER 2

PRELUDE
TO BETRAYAL

PART 2: THE FRENCH POISON THE WELL

The Soul selects her own society
Then—shuts the door—
To Her divine Majority—
Present no more—

—Emily Dickinson, "The Soul Selects Her Own Society"

Henry Kissinger had known Jean Sainteny before Kissinger assumed the position of national security advisor to President Richard Nixon after the 1968 American presidential election. Kissinger had sought Sainteny's assistance in opening doors to negotiation with the Vietnamese Communist leadership in Hanoi.

In June 1966, Kissinger had met with Jean Sainteny in Paris. At the request of French President Charles de Gaulle, Sainteny was preparing for a July trip to Hanoi. President de Gaulle was sending him to meet with the North Vietnamese leaders to explore the possibilities of a peace agreement ending the Vietnam War. Kissinger then had advised his French friend that the Americans would withdraw their forces from Vietnam once there was a ceasefire and a promise from the Communists that they would not invade South Vietnam for at least eight more years. Kissinger demanded that Sainteny keep this peace proposal secret and not to let the American embassy in Paris know of Kissinger's proposed terms. Then in late 1968, on behalf of president-elect Nixon, Kissinger arranged for Sainteny twice to pass on to the North Vietnamese word of American readiness for "serious negotiations."[1]

Jean Sainteny, the son-in-law of Albert Sarraut, French governor general of Indochina (1911–1914 and 1916–1919), took at face value a French misunderstanding of the Vietnamese. Kissinger described Sainteny as having given him "my first insights into the Vietnamese mentality." Sainteny had previously "spent much time with me recounting his experiences in Hanoi and giving me his assessment of our Vietnam involvement." Kissinger said, "Like many Frenchmen who had served in Indochina he considered our enterprise hopeless . . . how could America presume to succeed where France had failed?"[2]

Before her marriage to Jean, Sainteny's wife, Claude, had taken a seminar from Kissinger at Harvard in 1953.

Sainteny's influence on Henry Kissinger over many years could only have been malign. Here was the colonial operative who had chosen Ho Chi Minh for his political partner now advising a most influential American government official whose responsibility was to defeat Sainteny's old friend. Sainteny had no personal reason to assist Kissinger in supporting the cause of the Vietnamese Nationalists in South Vietnam.

When Henry Kissinger chose Jean Sainteny to counsel and assist him in negotiating with the Vietnamese Communists, he exposed himself to prejudice, the deep and abiding prejudice of French colonialists marginalizing and demeaning Vietnamese Nationalists while giving Vietnamese Communists every benefit of the doubt. In French minds, the intransigence, even bad faith, of those Vietnamese who rejected the *mission civilisatrice* of colonial France was presumed, and the inevitability of Communist success was assumed instead.

Perhaps the most extensive documentation of Kissinger's views of the Vietnamese can be found in his January 1969 article in the journal *Foreign Affairs*.[3] First, he made little mention of "Communists" and none of the "Nationalists." Kissinger referred to one Vietnamese protagonist only as the "North Vietnamese and the Viet Cong." He wrote that Hanoi was "xenophobically Vietnamese"—in other words, that the Communists were deep down really only Nationalists.

The "other" side he saw only as "non-Communists" or as protagonists without any compelling moral vision of their own. Thus, he was left completely ignorant of the deep reasons for which Vietnamese were fighting to determine the political future of their homeland—the Communists to impose an ideology imported from France and the majority of Vietnamese to resist the imposition of that foreign ideology. The Nationalist Vietnamese fought to live as Vietnamese had lived, on their own terms, since time immemorial.

Second, Kissinger was of the opinion that in 1961 and 1962, the US government had failed to "analyze adequately the geopolitical importance of Viet Nam." In other words, Kissinger implicitly accepted the conclusion that containment of Communism in Southeast Asia was a questionable use of American resources and prestige. This conclusion was precisely that of the French, as expressed by de Gaulle to President Kennedy. It reflected the French understanding that defending the South Vietnamese could not be a worthy undertaking, as they were a kind of "nothing" in human history.

Third, Kissinger did not believe that the Vietnamese "non-Communists" had any capacity for courage or commitment to their ideals. He saw them as opportunistic, amoral, and essentially nihilistic. For the Vietnamese, Kissinger applied the maxim of the Athenians in the Peloponnesian War: "The strong do what they can; the weak suffer what they must."

He was disparaging in his comments on the Vietnamese:

> *This has compounded the already great tendency of the Vietnamese population to await developments and not to commit itself*

irrevocably to the Saigon Government. . . . The Vietnamese people have lived under foreign rule for approximately half of their history. They have maintained a remarkable cultural and social cohesion by being finely attuned to the realities of power. To survive, the Vietnamese have had to learn to calculate—almost instinctively—the real balance of forces. If negotiations give the impression of being a camouflaged surrender, there will be nothing left to negotiate. Support for the side that seems to be losing will collapse. . . . Even the non-communist groups have demonstrated the difficulty Vietnamese have in compromising differences. It is beyond imagination that parties that have been murdering and betraying each other for twenty-five years could work together as a team giving joint instructions to the entire country.

Thus, Kissinger predicted that "as long as Hanoi can preserve some political assets in the South, it retains the prospect of an ultimately favorable political outcome."

In accord with this assessment, in his secret negotiations with Hanoi, Kissinger would ensure that the Vietnamese Communists would enjoy "the prospect of an ultimately favorable political outcome." Kissinger carried into his work as President Nixon's national security advisor seeking an honorable peace in Vietnam a cast of mind that did not provide much respect for the values and aspirations of his Vietnamese allies. He referred to Vietnamese in his memoirs as "difficult, even obnoxious" and described his ally President Nguyen Van Thieu as "hapless."[4] When South Vietnam was spiraling into its death throes in April 1975, Kissinger would put the blame for defeat on Thieu—calling him "the little guy," picked by the Americans and acting like a maniac.[5]

In his memorandums to President Nixon in September 1969, Kissinger discounted the possibility that the South Vietnamese would make a success of Vietnamization.[6] On October 30, he wrote to his president, "The actual ability of the South Vietnamese Government and armed forces to replace American withdrawals—both physically and psychologically. (Conclusive evidence is lacking here: this fact in itself, and past experience, argue against optimism.)."[7] Here, Kissinger evinced no knowledge of or interest in the existential reasons why Vietnamese might fight willingly and with dedication over the long term against Communist domination of their society and culture. He seems to have drunk too much of the French colonial Kool-Aid as far as the Vietnamese were concerned.

Sainteny applied to Vietnam only the intellectual heritage of French thinking about the Vietnamese that began in the early 1600s. Sainteny saw the Vietnamese through the myopia-inducing eyeglasses of colonial prejudice.

The nearly universal contemporary Western perception of the Vietnamese as only replicating a smaller version of Chinese culture and politics, the conceit of Vietnam as the "smaller dragon," was created by the French.[8]

Perhaps the first, and so most important, French misunderstanding of the Vietnamese, one that did not recognize any of their ethnic nationalism, was written by the French Jesuit missionary Alexandre de Rhodes (1591–1660). De Rhodes arrived in Vietnam in 1624. He assiduously studied Vietnamese, compiling a dictionary and a grammar of Vietnamese words in Latin. In 1651, his catechism written in Vietnamese to support the evangelization of Vietnamese was published in Rome.[9]

In making his case that Christianity should be accepted by Vietnamese as their religion, de Rhodes addressed his arguments to refute existing Vietnamese religious and cultural beliefs as he perceived them. Almost exclusively, de Rhodes assumed that Vietnamese followed conventional imperial Chinese Neo-Confucian customs of moral and political submission to an emperor appointed by heaven and of patrilineal ancestor worship.

Contrary to de Rhodes's understanding, outside the Chinese official cults of filial piety and imperial supremacy but within the Chinese folk tradition of the three religions (*tam giao*), Vietnamese could make a comfortable place for themselves in seeking succor from Taoist deities and through Buddhist rituals. Similarly, de Rhodes's catechism makes no showing of deeper Vietnamese soulfulness and cultural themes around the ethnic ideal of *phuc duc,* or merit virtue, which owes no allegiance to any emperor or mandarin. De Rhodes also did not evince any understanding of the profoundly Vietnamese artful yin/yang practices of geomancy (*dia ly*), casting horoscopes (*tu vi*), or reading faces (*coi tuong*).[10]

What evidently escaped de Rhodes was the evolution of Vietnamese politics and culture since the early 1400s. A robust flourishing of Vietnamese-ness, or the cultural authenticity of being Vietnamese, occurred around 1430 under Emperor Le Loi. He had waged a twenty-year war of resistance against Chinese domination attempted by the Ming Dynasty. Upon the withdrawal of the Ming army and administrators, Le Loi promulgated a new law code for Vietnam. This extensive and impressive work of jurisprudence did not copy or imitate the Ming Code, which had been used in Vietnam by the Ming colonial administration. Rather, the Le Code reached back in time to take inspiration from China's Tang Dynasty (618–907 CE) code of laws.[11] Tang Dynasty China had thrived in a very Buddhist cultural environment prior to the development of imperial Neo-Confucianism under the Sung emperors (960–1276 CE). Buddhism is permissive to the individualism treasured by the Vietnamese in ways not permitted by state-managed Neo-Confucianism.

Notable expressions of Vietnamese national identity were authored under Le Loi by the great scholar-official Nguyen Trai. As the Ming forces withdrew, Trai wrote a paean to the eternal justice of being Vietnamese called the *Binh Ngo Dai Cao*. In this proclamation confirming Le Loi's victory, Trai asserted that it had been ordained by heaven itself. Heavenly forces, he claimed, provided for an independent emperor (*de*) in the South autonomous from an emperor (*de*) in the North. For the emperor in the North to subdue the emperor in the South was counter to natural justice. The different realities of North and South were imprinted in the very earth itself by the forces of yin and yang, to be discovered by geomancy. The Chinese therefore had no ethnic claim or any other moral justification for seeking to rule the Vietnamese.

Then, at that juncture in Vietnamese history, another quintessentially authentic statement of Vietnamese-ness was written and has been ascribed to Nguyen Trai. This is the didactic poem *Gia Huan Ca* ("Poem for Family Instruction").[12] In a dramatic clash of cultural norms, this text rejects Chinese patrilineal values and practices to recognize and guide the psychosocial power of women for the Vietnamese. So too did the Le Code provide inheritance and other rights for Vietnamese women, unrecognized in Chinese law and custom.

Crucially, the *Gia Huan Ca* states categorically that *phuc duc tai mau*—merit virtue comes from the mother. Thus, by virtue of cosmic ordering, women among the Vietnamese must be elevated in stature within the family, followed by their husbands in many things, and obeyed without question by their children.

However, the early Le promotion of immemorial Vietnamese-ness was not to last. Under Le Loi's grandson Le Thanh Ton, the legal culture would begin to evolve, followed by changes in the normative outlook of elite families associated with state power. Le Thanh Ton would borrow from Ming Dynasty Neo-Confucianism and apply Chinese practices in Vietnam through state regulation. These practices, bit by bit, were emulated by mandarin families obtaining social and political status through serving as officials of the state.[13]

By the time de Rhodes and his missionary colleagues arrived in Vietnam in the early 1600s, this process of elite evolution was well underway. The Vietnamese were dividing themselves into two classes along cultural lines: a small upper class copying Chinese imperial norms and practices and the rest of society, mostly villagers, who continued to live by traditional norms preserving age-old ambitions, family patterns, and cultural identities. While elite families sought imperial careers for their sons and complementary Neo-Confucian lifestyles for social advancement, ordinary Vietnamese still took stock of their lives by means of Buddhism, spirit worship in village shrines, and consultation with masters of geomancy, horoscopes, and face reading.

After the reign of Le Thanh Ton, Vietnam experienced some two hundred years of state failure, political warfare, and decentralization. These trends enhanced the rise of a Neo-Confucian elite among Vietnamese. First, while the Le family continued to sit in Hanoi as emperors, other families contested their political power. The Mac family, with Chinese assistance, tried to seize the throne for themselves but failed. Then two powerful warlord clans took real power for themselves under the titular and ritualized social preeminence of the Le rulers. The Le emperors were permitted to use the symbolic color yellow and have dragons as personal motifs, to receive ambassadors from China, and to bestow diplomas on graduates from the official examinations. In Hanoi, the Trinh clan ran the government, and to the south, the Nguyen clan ran a fiefdom along the coast. Side by side with ministries reporting to the Le emperor, special supervisory bureaus called *phien* were established by the Trinh so that their family retainers would make decisions for the ministers. The Trinh fought campaigns to conquer the Nguyen, who successfully resisted but never sought to challenge Trinh power in the North.

While the cult of Chinese imperial Neo-Confucianism was favored by the Trinh policy makers and grew more and more attractive to elite families, Vietnamese reality was that the supposed center of this ideological system of hierarchy and subordination was inconsequential. Imported Chinese Neo-Confucianism could not supplant but only supplement a fundamental ethnic of Vietnamese-ness as a varnish.

As secular rulers promoted an alliance with elite families who served the court or adopted the Neo-Confucian ways appropriate to the examination system of recruitment into government or the achievement of high social status, Vietnamese Nationalism was preserved in village communities living underneath a thin layer of gentry families.[14]

By the twentieth century, Nationalism in Vietnam was an ethnic reality, not a political movement. Its social support system was not in the urban middle classes, as had been the case in Europe with the formation of nation-states tied to cities where administrators lived and middle classes were growing in numbers and wealth. The 1789 revolution in France was carried out by the "third estate," largely urban and middle class. Vietnamese Nationalism thrived in the villages and from there sent tentacles into towns and cities.

In 1663, the Trinh administration ordered a change in the official moral code for village life in order to better subordinate villages to elite Neo-Confucianism. Forty-seven articles of good conduct according to Neo-Confucian norms were to be read aloud before gatherings of villagers on a regular basis for their education in proper behaviors. Village chiefs were empowered to enforce these behaviors as laws. In his collection of notable history documents, the eighteenth-century scholar Phan Huy Chu copied a report of 1719 written by the inspectorate. The report protested that

> *ignorant ones with no sophistication are called before the courts by others on the most trivial provocations. Lawyers stir up lawsuits. Not taking any responsibility, they go to court anyway. Examining magistrates don't see through to the trickery involved or else don't clearly set aside malicious slander, so that the wily slip through the net of the law and those who stir up suits continue to open wide their mischievous mouths. Those who seek the straight path have no one to show them the way; those who value propriety must suffer behind closed doors . . . The expense of litigation daily mounts, the scope of injustice daily increases . . . The officials set themselves above the people as if they were Chinese looking down on Vietnamese.*[15]

Ironically, in reading de Rhodes's catechism, we can infer that the appeal of Christianity presented by the Jesuit actually took hold at the level of traditional Vietnamese-ness and not among the emerging Neo-Confucian elite. De Rhodes presented the Christian God in Vietnamese as *chua troi dat,* or "lord of heaven and earth." Through Jesus Christ as part of the trinitarian deity, individual Vietnamese could approach heaven on their own and not via mediation through an emperor and his mandarins. Christian Vietnamese would thus have no need to submit their minds and souls to Neo-Confucian rituals and strictures. Thus, they could become new in their religious expression and yet still remain very Vietnamese. And the Roman Catholic elevation of Mary as the mother of the savior sat very well with reverential Vietnamese attitudes toward mothers.

There was a major challenge to the Neo-Confucian elite in a late eighteenth-century revolt led by the Tay Son brothers, so named for their place of origin. Under the younger brother, Nguyen Hue, ordinary Vietnamese mobilized to defeat both the Nguyen and Trinh clans. The Chinese Qing Dynasty invaded Vietnam once again on the pretext of coming to the aid of the Le family, who feared being overthrown by the Tay Son. Nguyen Hue smashed the Chinese army in a surprise attack on the outskirts of Hanoi, motivated by a prognostication received from the occult master La Son Phu Tu.

Nguyen Hue united all the Vietnamese under his authority and assumed the imperial throne. His court used the Vietnamese version of Chinese characters, known as Nom, rather than Han Chinese writing. He died, leaving a young heir. A scion of the Nguyen clan then rose in rebellion against the Tay Son family, defeated them after many years of fighting, and proclaimed himself Emperor Gia Long in 1802. He and his successors then systematically and comprehensively grounded the legitimacy of their rule on Chinese Neo-Confucianism.

After de Rhodes, French liaisons with Vietnam continued. Another French cleric, Pigneau de Behaine, a French Catholic bishop, assisted the future emperor Gia Long in his long fight to gain the throne. Gia Long eagerly sought French military assistance. Theodore Lebrun built citadels, Jean-Marie Dayot built naval vessels, and Olivier de Puymanel trained soldiers. The Vietnamese these and other Frenchmen encountered during the early decades of expanding Western enterprises in Asia were mostly either Catholic or members of warlord families. Estranged from Vietnamese culture, the French were very limited in their ability to think or feel as Vietnamese did. They had little alternative than to accept the surface realities of Vietnam, only a patina, as a polity seeking to create a smaller version of the Chinese imperial state along Neo-Confucian lines—which indeed was Emperor Gia Long's cultural project to legitimate his family's claim to the throne of Vietnam.

De Rhodes's conviction that the best way to engage with Vietnamese was to take them as a lesser version of the Chinese carried over to the major French intervention into Vietnamese affairs in the 1860s and later after the French had established a thriving colonial presence in Vietnam. A French expeditionary force arrived in Vietnam to defend Catholics from oppression imposed by the son and grandson of Gia Long. By something of an accident, the French ended up as masters of the southernmost provinces of the Nguyen Dynasty along the Mekong River and a little to the north of that river's vast delta. This new colony of France was given the name of Cochin China. Thus did French colonialists append the name "China" to what was very Vietnamese in culture.

One can forgive the first French colonialists for deeply misunderstanding the Vietnamese. They arrived from Europe to live in a land governed by a law code written in Chinese and borrowed nearly character for character from the Qing Dynasty to the north. The Nguyen Dynasty administration copied most every punctilio from Neo-Confucian China for its operations and its moral justification as a legitimate ruler under heaven.

But underneath the structure of dynastic administration, Vietnamese lived to themselves in village communes. A saying arose that "*phep vua thua le lang*" (imperial law bows before village customs). An ethnic cultural reality passed down over the generations for two thousand years held sway among the people. For example, villagers continued to allocate inheritances and empower women, as provided by the former Le Dynasty Law Code but not mentioned in the new code promulgated by Gia Long and taken from Qing China.

Why shouldn't the French assume that Vietnamese looked up to China for moral guidance? Colonial arrivistes could not openly see much evidence of Vietnamese-ness in the laws, buildings, rice fields, or commerce that they saw around them or in the habits of the families they encountered most as their interpreters or elite interlocutors. Few French bothered to learn Vietnamese.

Thus was solidified in French beliefs and colonial practices a serious dissonance between their conceptions of who the Vietnamese might be and who the Vietnamese actually were.

In 1875, Paul-Louis-Félix Philastre translated Gia Long's law code into French. In his personal preface, Emperor Gia Long adopted the Chinese imperial theory of rule as first fully articulated in the Han Dynasty (206 BCE–220 CE)—that sage rulers employed both the regeneration of virtue in subjects and punishments to provide for public felicity. But in his realm of Vietnam, he affirmed that, since the turbulence set off by the Tay Son rebellion, all social cohesion had collapsed. Therefore, he argued, no humane person could tolerate such conditions. He looked to the evolution of jurisprudence under the Han, the Tang, the Song, the Ming, and the great dynasty of the Qing as a process of correcting and improving the fundamentals of law. Gia Long thus dismissed the relevance to his administration of previous Vietnamese laws in favor of the contemporary Chinese alternative.[16]

Philastre began his introduction to the translation as follows: "The Annamite race, the history of which rests sufficiently unknown, appears after its language, to be a branch of the same strain as the Chinese."

There it is in plain words: French confusion and misunderstanding.

Philastre did not even use the proper name of the people his countrymen were ruling, Vietnamese, but rather categorized them with a word of Chinese origin and usage—Annam, the pacified South, a word to which no ethnic identity or pride attaches.

And he clearly subordinated the Vietnamese to Chinese culture in all things. There was no place in French colonial imagination for Vietnamese Nationalism.

After the establishment of direct French administration of Cochin China, the provinces of Central Vietnam and the northern region of Tonkin were left under the legal suzerainty of the Nguyen emperors. The French referred to that state as Annam and the Nguyen did as Dai Nam, or Great South. The Chinese had recognized the Nguyen emperors as the rulers of Viet Nam, or the "Southern Viet," a condescending echo of the time when all the Viet peoples living south of the Yangtze River had lived under Chinese rule.

Through treaties, especially in 1874, the French extracted concessions from the Nguyen court mandarins, providing the colonialists with vast administrative powers, making Annam a protectorate of France.

In 1885 the young and newly enthroned emperor Ham Nghi fled the palace for the hills and proclaimed a rebellion against French colonialism. His resistance movement was called Can Vuong, or Rally to Protect the King. He used not Nationalism to inspire his people to take up arms and fight the French but rather Neo-Confucian norms of loyalty to the emperor. His movement failed. His family's cause was just not important to the majority of Vietnamese. They did not rise to support the Nguyen clan. The few who joined him in the hills were psychosocially linked to him by ties of family or high position. And many high-ranking officials and their families were willing to work out an accommodation with the French to secure their elite social standing and political powers. No notable persons from either Cochin China or the northern provinces around the Red River, the region known as Tonkin, joined the movement. Thus was exposed the superficiality of Chinese-style Neo-Confucianism as a powerful, populist ethic for Vietnamese.

In 1889, J. L. de Lanessan wrote his study of French Indochina.[17] He described the Vietnamese not as an ethnic people but as "les Annamites," an imposed nomenclature. He placed the Annamites as belonging to the "yellow race." He ventured that their civilization had ancient roots that had disappeared over the centuries in China. He noted that the French who took time to socialize with them found the Vietnamese scholar gentry charming in conversation and most engaging. Their general edification was not without value and not off-putting for the cultivated among the French.

In another avoidance of Vietnamese Nationalism, de Lanessan stressed the fragmentation of Vietnamese into families and village communes. He described each family as a small church that did not recognize nonconforming priests, a minuscule civil society directing all of its self-interests. The French colonial administrator could detect no spirit of the whole people that animated Vietnamese in common cause. They had no "La Marseillaise" to sing.

But de Lanessan was to exploit the dynamics of family as a cultural basis for Vietnamese acquiescence in French colonial domination—if the French would only share power and opportunity with those tiny congregations. After the revolt of Ham Nghi, de Lanessan reported that an important faction of mandarins and scholar gentry families accepted the French protectorate over Annam after the French promised to share certain privileges with them. In particular, the French had to respect their political institutions and customs and make them prosperous but subservient clients of a partnership dominated by French policies. "At the heart, they would owe us everything and they would be thankful."

The treaty of June 6, 1884, between the French and the Nguyen court left the acquiescent mandarins with more administrative autonomy over the provinces of Central Vietnam, as well as a royal army supplemented with French cadres and commanded by French officers and given an autonomous budget for the royal administration, with Vietnamese ministers doubled by French officials.

The scholar gentry spokespeople requested that the French also accept and privilege Neo-Confucian values of propriety and moralized self-expression. As part of the bargain providing for a sort of joint rule with elite Vietnamese families, it also became necessary for the French to provide education to the sons of the elite families so that they would gain qualifications to serve a modernizing administration. This process of "uplifting" the scions of elite families bound the French ever closer to those Vietnamese cut off emotionally from the oldest and most compelling traditions of their ancestors. For most practical reasons of state, the French recognized the "Party of Scholars" as a de facto national political party with which to collaborate for mutual benefit.

As de Lanessan wrote, "It was necessary to accept with fidelity and without restrictions of any sort the sole rule for governing a protectorate, which is to say to govern Annam and Tonkin by our pressing all the forces living in the territories: the king, the court, the secret council, the mandarins and the scholars."

Having agreed to rule with and by means of the Neo-Confucian elite, the French were in no position to solicit the good offices of the ethnic traditionalists in the middle and lower classes and, especially, in the villages.

Thus did French colonialism marginalize Vietnamese Nationalism. An alliance was made with the Neo-Confucian elite, preserving the institutions of the Nguyen family's dynasty; with Catholics; and with others who would support France in return for economic opportunity, such as licenses to do business and titles to land.

The failure of the Can Vuong movement caused one young loyalist to think anew about Vietnamese Nationalism as a political alternative to Neo-Confucian elitism, and as a loyalty potentially more powerful in energizing Vietnamese to fight for their independence from colonialism.

Phan Boi Chau began his lifelong struggle to end French dominance over Vietnam with participation in Ham Nghi's Can Vuong movement. But after its disappointing collapse, Chau came to reject the Nguyen Dynasty as a legitimate leader of the Vietnamese and then also the Neo-Confucian elitism that sustained its pretensions. He wrote in Vietnamese the history of the ancient dynasties. He thus laid the moral and intellectual foundation for the Viet Nam Quoc Dan Dang and Dai Viet Nationalist political parties, the Cao Dai religion, and the Hoa Hao sect of Buddhism, which all arose in the 1920s and 1930s to challenge French colonial hegemony.[18]

But the French were obdurate in perpetuating their misperceptions. In 1926, Georges Coulet published an analysis of Vietnamese secret societies.[19] To better understand the causes of various uprisings and plots against French rule, he studied court records of investigations and trials. The documents included the very marginal revolts of 1913 and 1916 in Cochin China and the case of Gilbert Chau, who had disseminated patriotic writings in 1908. Coulet concluded that such instances of clandestine opposition to French rule were not "necessarily and solely anti-French." To buttress his point, Coulet noted that secret societies in China were not anti-French.

Coulet added that most members of these clandestine networks were mostly "simpletons" or "wanderers" who were adrift in society and responded to the mumbo jumbo of priests and sorcerers. He concluded that the fundamental motivation for anti-French protest was a "love of property." The Vietnamese, he said, had three social classes: the mass of poor peasants; a small, struggling middle class; and a tiny elite, enjoying comfort and luxury. Clandestine organizations, he inferred, were vehicles for the middle class and the poor to gain property and rise in status. "It is logical that those who have nothing should tend toward possession."

"Egoism" and the desire for upward mobility therefore sufficiently accounted for sedition and temptations to rebel among Vietnamese. The French colonial enterprise had no need to worry about political opposition arising from a political culture of nationalism.[20]

Coulet's way of thinking about the Vietnamese set in place a cultural colonial framework that would be open to Communists and could never dignify nationalism among Vietnamese.

One noted scholar said in the 1930s that Marxists were the Vietnamese thought leaders most comfortable in French intellectual circles. He wrote,

> On many occasions in Viet Nam, newcomers from France were surprised to realize that they were closer to the Communist Vietnamese than to other local political groups when talking about the nature of society. These Communists spoke the French language of society even though it was in a Marxist dialect, and, despite their differences, their terminology and their logic blended in with that of the West.[21]

Communism therefore could be appreciated and welcomed by French intellectuals as a successful result of France's civilizing mission—its *mission civilisatrice*—whereas Vietnamese Nationalists evidenced its failure. Communism was in a way a credit to French rule, and Nationalism was a rejection of its goodness and legitimacy. Even under the Communists, it could be said by many French that the Vietnamese were progressing from the myths and falsehoods of the past into a modern future.

Communism, of course, came to Vietnam through French educational institutions. It did not evolve—and never could have—out of the Vietnamese belief in *phuc duc*. Communism in Vietnam was a bastard child of colonial cultural miscegenation.

The alliance between the French as patrons and elite Vietnamese families as clients was given a more noble purpose under the cultural assimilation framework of *mission civilisatrice,* under which France would give privileges of equality and opportunity to those who spoke, wrote, and read in French; adopted French clothing; and adopted French manners in food and social intercourse. Education in French schools thus became a new cultural glue attaching younger members of the Vietnamese elite to French ways of thought and politics. It was a program of westernization that confined the French within their oblivion about the existence of Vietnamese Nationalism. There just was no room for talking about Vietnamese Nationalism in any process of thoroughly "civilizing" Vietnamese with French norms, beliefs, and practices.

A two-track educational system evolved. There was the *chuong trinh Phap* in excellent French schools, such as the Couvent des Oiseaux, Lycée Albert Sarraut, Lycée Marie Curie, and others, which taught in French under French instructors. Separately, there was the *chuong trinh Viet* in lower-status schools, which taught in Vietnamese. Obtaining a degree from a French school was necessary for more prestigious and rewarding employment in French companies and institutions.

Implementing the *mission civilisatrice* forged deep psychological and intellectual bonds between many young Vietnamese and French culture and cut them off from popular values and traditions.

In fact, many leading Communists emerged from *mission civilisatrice* educational institutions. They came from Neo-Confucian families serving the Nguyen Dynasty administration and educated themselves in the cultural milieu of French institutions.

Ho Chi Minh, for example, born Nguyen Sinh Cung and also using the name Nguyen Tat Thanh, was born the son of a scholar mandarin, attended the prestigious Nguyen Dynasty academy Quoc Hoc, and was self-educated in Paris. When he first arrived in France in 1911, the future Communist leader asked to be admitted to the school training colonial administrators because, as he wrote, he wanted to be of use to France. Ho learned his Marxism not in Vietnam but in Paris from Jean Longuet, Paul Vaillant-Couturier, Jules Raveau, and Jean Duret, not Neo-Confucians, to be sure, but similar elitists in the tradition of Jean-Jacques Rousseau, who would conform a society and its politics to the normative demands of a general will discovered by their intellect as informed by their education.[22]

In late 1945, Ho said to a French reporter, "France and Vietnam were married a long-time ago. The marriage has not always been a happy one, but we have nothing to gain from breaking it up . . . France is a strange country. It is a breeding ground of admirable ideas, but when it travels, it does not export them." And to another reporter, he said, "If Frenchmen were sent here in a spirit of peace, anyone who tried to molest them would do so over my dead body."[23]

Jean Lacouture described meeting with Ho Chi Minh in November 1961. He found Ho still to be genial and keen to recall his connections with France but unwilling to speak on matters of political importance.[24] The novelist Duong Thu Huong similarly used Ho's "Frenchiness" as an insight into his light character in her novel about his fall from power in 1957.[25]

The famous Communist general Vo Nguyen Giap was born to a minor Nguyen Dynasty official and also attended the Quoc Hoc academy in Hue. From 1933 to 1938, he attended the National University in Hanoi, studying law. Not getting a sufficiently high score on the entrance examination for admission to the bar, he became a high school teacher, and his ideal was Napoleon. He founded the French-language newspaper *Le travail*, at which the future Communist prime minister Pham Van Dong also worked.

Pham Van Dong, the first prime minister of a Communist state, was born to a mandarin family in Quang Ngai province.

Truong Chinh was a senior Communist Party leader, once a party secretary general (1941–1956) and later chief of state of a Vietnam unified under the dictatorship of the Communist Party. His grandfather received the highest score in the imperial examination of 1856. His father was a scholar but had no success in the official examinations. In his youth, Chinh received a traditional Neo-Confucian education from his father. In 1927, Chinh studied at the Hanoi college for commerce. Later, he too wrote for *Le travail*.

Le Duan, who manipulated the Communist Party's policies and leadership from 1958 until his death, was the son of a railway clerk. He received a French education and worked in Hanoi as a clerk for the French railway company.

Le Duc Tho, a senior party official and close associate of Le Duan, spoke excellent French and in his youth worked in the colonial postal service.

The poet To Huu, a leading member of the politburo for many years, was born near the royal capital of Hue to scholarly families. His father and maternal grandfather were Neo-Confucian in education and social outlook. Huu attended the Quoc Hoc school in the royal capital of Hue.

On the death of Stalin, To Huu wrote the following poem:

> *Oh Stalin! Oh Stalin!*
> *The love I bear my father, my mother, my wife, myself*
> *It's nothing beside the love I bear you.*
> *Oh Stalin! Oh Stalin!*
> *What remains of the earth and the sky*
> *Now that you are dead?*[26]

Frantz Fanon bitterly critiqued the psychopolitical results of colonialism, writing that

> *colonialism came to lighten their darkness. Drive into the natives'*
> *heads the idea that if the settlers were to leave, they would at once*
> *fall back into barbarism, degradation, and bestiality.*
>
> *The intellectual, when he comes to the need to take on two national-*
> *ities, chooses the negation of one of those determinations if he wants*
> *to be true to himself.*
>
> *The individual has greedily thrown himself upon Western culture.*
>
> *The native intellectual will try to make European culture his own.*

*The native intellectual who comes back to his people by way of cul-
tural achievement utilizing techniques and language borrowed from
the stranger in his country behaves in fact like a foreigner.*[27]

Paul Mus saw that "the Communists . . . have incorporated Western principles, and they intend to finish what the West started in Viet Nam by
transcending it."[28] He continued, "Revolution had to come and in fact did,
between France and the advanced Vietnamese—those who had forsaken
their own ways of life and tended toward France's."[29] No acknowledgment
here from a thoughtful French cultural anthropologist of any substance at
all in Vietnamese ethnic pride and Nationalist fervor.

As World War II entered its final phase in Asia, the Japanese took
power from the French colonial administration in both the state of Vietnam and the colony of Cochin China on March 7, 1945. They installed
a Nationalist intellectual, Tran Trong Kim, a historian of Vietnamese
history, as prime minister. North and Central Vietnam were now an independent country with its own government, albeit one recognized only by
the Japanese. On March 11, that government abrogated all prior treaties
with France. On March 24, the new French government under Charles
de Gaulle announced its intention that, after the end of World War II, it
would transform its colonies into a French union, a more evenly balanced
collaboration, with the states of Indochina welcomed as a federation. In
July, of all the Vietnamese leaders, only the Communists replied posi-
tively to this French proposal.[30] Some French officials interpreted this as
an attempt by Ho Chi Minh, leader of a front movement supporting the
Allied powers in the war, to dispel any fears the French might have of his
political intentions, wanting to placate the former colonial power as it
sought to resume its control of Vietnamese events.

In August 1945, after the atomic bombing of Japan and Japan's surrender to the Allies, the Vietnamese Communist leadership decided on a coup
d'état in Hanoi, posing as the Vietnamese representatives of the soon-to-be
victorious Allied forces. The Communists were indeed directly linked to
the Soviet Union, one of the powers allied against Japan, and Ho Chi Minh

had bargained for some modest assistance from the regional office of the American Office of Strategic Services (OSS) in Kunming, China. The Communist coup was successful. On September 2, Ho Chi Minh proclaimed a government for the Vietnamese under his leadership. On September 5, his minister of the interior, Vo Nguyen Giap, outlawed several Dai Viet Nationalist parties. Upon demand, Emperor Bao Dai abdicated, and the Nguyen Dynasty passed unmourned into history.

Vietnam was in chaos. The new government under Ho Chi Minh sought to establish its police control over the country. Japanese forces needed to be repatriated home. French administrators and residents agitated to assert their influence, and local factions spoke up and sought positions of power—the Cao Dai and Hoa Hao religions with followers in Cochin China; the VNQDD party leaders coming back from exile in China; the Dai Viet Party throughout the country; and others.

The French government in Paris had declared on March 24 that France would resume control of Vietnam. De Gaulle sent several representatives, including Jean Sainteny, to Vietnam to work for the reestablishment of French colonial hegemony. When Sainteny arrived in Hanoi, he faced a conundrum: With whom among the Vietnamese should the French propose a reestablishment of their patronage in return for collaboration?

An American officer from the Kunming station of the OSS, Archimedes Patti, and his team, along with Sainteny and four French colleagues, flew from Kunming in China into Hanoi on an American C-47, landing on August 22, 1945.[31] Patti's American colleagues had no great trust in his judgment.[32] Upon driving into the city, Sainteny was unprepared emotionally for the banners supporting Ho Chi Minh festooning the streets. Patti told him that Ho's would shortly be the government in power. But posters of the Nationalist VNQDD party were also before the public. Sainteny was kept isolated in a hotel. He warned Patti about letting the "Annamites" have free reign over their country.[33] For his part, Sainteny considered Patti to be "a rabid anti-colonialist."[34]

Ho Chi Minh's stature at that point rested most on his having been recognized by the American OSS branch in Kunming.[35] He was perceived by Vietnamese as sitting on the shoulders of the paramount victor in World War II. Ho had obsequiously ingratiated himself with the OSS office in Kunming to volunteer his tiny political movement as sources of information on the Japanese in Vietnam. Of particular immediate interest to the Americans had been regular weather reports from Vietnam, which were necessary for flight operations over Indochina and the South China Sea.

Ho did not present himself as a Communist.[36] In fact, he said little about his political beliefs or ambitions, just reassuring the Americans that he could serve their needs. Ho was trying to augment his *the*—his ability to determine outcomes—in the minds of Vietnamese by leveraging American power on his behalf. The OSS officers in Kunming and those assigned to Ho's headquarters inside Vietnam had absolutely no knowledge about Vietnamese history or Nationalism. They got from the French a morsel of colonial prejudice against Ho as being anti-French and a Communist, but they ignored it. One American called Ho "an awfully sweet guy."[37]

Of particular importance to Ho while in Kunming was getting a picture of US general Claire Chennault, the founder and commander of the Flying Tigers. Ho respectfully asked Chennault to autograph the photo. The American obliged. On his return to Vietnam, Ho used the picture of Chennault with his autograph as evidence that he, Ho, had been designated especially by the Americans as their agent. This enabled Ho to establish himself as first among equals with his colleagues. The Communist leadership recognized that it needed American support to overcome its Vietnamese Nationalist rivals, and Ho was a channel to get that support.

Thus, in late August and September 1945, the American OSS, on the one hand, was a sponsor of Ho Chi Minh and, at the same time, also a sponsor of Sainteny. The Americans had no idea what they were doing with respect to Vietnamese political dynamics. They had no engagement with any Vietnamese Nationalists.

At first, Ho Chi Minh was reluctant to meet Sainteny. Ho assured Patti that he was not a Communist or an agent of the Comintern and pressed the Americans to resist French overtures for support. Later, Ho did say that his reading of Lenin's analysis of colonialism had given him a *point d'appui*, or point of pressure, the better to push his way to power. Ho had then become a champion of Leninism. But in late 1945, Ho had been assigned the role of chairman of a front movement—the Viet Nam Dong Minh Doc Lap Hoi, or Viet Minh for short. The secretary general of the Indochina Communist Party with operational control of party cadres was Truong Chinh. Truong Chinh was also in charge of the party committee planning the countrywide uprising.

General Vo Nguyen Giap would later say, "Uncle Ho was the soul of the Resistance against the French, but coming up with practical policies, giving real leadership on theory for the certain victory of the Resistance, was Truong Chinh."[38] Thus, Ho Chi Minh was only something of a poseur, an actor engaged to play upon the public stage.

Sainteny, considering Ho to be the "new leader" of the Vietnamese, requested a meeting with him. Ho sent his senior commander Vo Nguyen Giap instead. Giap offered to exchange views—one government to another, thereby cutting off all Vietnamese Nationalists from any claims to power.[39]

Later, when Patti left Vietnam and called on Ho to say goodbye, Ho promised to be open to discussions with "enlightened" Frenchmen on Vietnamese problems based on mutual trust and honest intent. A Nationalist leader enjoying the patronage of Chiang Kai-shek's government in China proposed a coalition government to Ho to better mobilize the Vietnamese for political independence. Ho neither accepted nor refused the proposal.[40] Ho described his French education as "a lake of Western thought pouring out a stream of colonial philosophy to irrigate and raise a crop of obedient Vietnamese servants useful to France." But with a struggle for the power to rule Vietnam, Ho affirmed that he would have to find allies—American or Russian. Ho gave Patti a letter for the Americans asking for their patronage.

The only Vietnamese leader who would meet with Sainteny was Ho Chi Minh. Even the former emperor Bao Dai refused to see him.[41] By the end of September 1945, Sainteny wrote that his encounters with Vietnamese Nationalists were "disappointing."[42] He therefore concluded, "Thus everything brought me back to Ho Chi Minh. He was the one I had to see, the one with whom I must discuss the situation." He acquired a "conviction that Ho Chi Minh was a personality of the first class."

Thus, Sainteny found himself limited in his options. He proposed a revision to the formula for colonial authority. He would switch French patronage from the old social elements of elite Neo-Confucian families associated with the Nguyen Dynasty, Catholics, and those with economic privileges provided by colonial administrators, and transfer it to a new elite—the Communists and their allies in the anti-Japanese Viet Minh united front.

Sainteny's rationale for this innovation was hardly forced. It adopted the consequences of the *mission civilisatrice* for its justification. Vietnam's Neo-Confucian elite had evolved. A new generation following new Western cultural and intellectual orientations had emerged from its womb, thanks to French educational efforts over the preceding fifty years. Sainteny wrote, "The intellectuals of Vietnam possessed the language and culture of France, which would facilitate cooperation."[43] He judged that Ho Chi Minh certainly had more affinities with France than with any other nation. Nguyen Dynasty Neo-Confucianism had been replaced by French sophistication, or even by Western Marxism, as justification for elite rule over the Vietnamese people.

It does not appear that Sainteny ever gave a moment to serious reflection regarding rapprochement with Vietnamese Nationalists. They were beyond the pale and had no interest in collaboration with the French.

But the Communists were not interested in the full return of French colonialism either. In his declaration of September 2, Ho Chi Minh had called for the independence of Vietnam. De Gaulle in Paris was prepared for some compromise with the Vietnamese. In March, the French had proposed a union of former French colonies with local governments, with local governments having much autonomy in the administration of domestic affairs and the French retaining control over national security and foreign affairs. Sainteny began discussions with Ho Chi Minh within this framework of a somewhat independent Vietnam within a French union. These discussions would come to fruition in March 1946 with an agreement that

Ho would permit the return of French military forces to the northern and central provinces of Vietnam. And, in turn, the French would recognize Ho as the leader of Vietnam and its people.

De Gaulle had sent his orders to his commander in Saigon, French general Philippe Leclerc: "Your mission is to re-establish French sovereignty in Hanoi."[44] Working with Leclerc to accomplish this, Sainteny faced great obstacles. Sainteny desperately needed an agreement with an effective Vietnamese ruling administration. French forces in Saigon available to go north and take up positions in the northern provinces of Tonkin were only some eight thousand strong—not enough to fight their way to control of the territory and not enough to put down any substantial uprising of the Vietnamese or contain a guerilla war. But Sainteny later reported that his job was to persuade Ho Chi Minh to agree to the return of French troops to the northern provinces of Vietnam around Hanoi.[45]

According to Lacouture, Sainteny recognized that he needed a strong political movement as a Vietnamese partner in the restoration of French influence in Vietnam.[46] Hence, Lacouture wrote later that Sainteny "chose the path of negotiating with the hard-core Vietminh rather than doggedly trying to disunite the revolutionary movement by encouraging the rivalries existing between the pro-Chinese nationalists, the pro-Japanese nationalists, the 'progressives' and the communists."[47] From this comment, it seems clear that neither Sainteny nor Lacouture saw any political or cultural substance in Vietnamese nationalism, only marginal factions tying their fortunes to foreign powers.

Ho needed the French, and the French needed Ho. Each made the other into a temporary friend. It was a bargain with the devil for each party, necessary but distasteful. For the French, Sainteny put the best face he could on his Faustian deal—he painted Ho as a fine person, a leading personality, quite French, and an admirable patron of his people. Ho's ability to rationalize his opportunism was reflected in his comment that "manure is dirty isn't it? But if it is good for the rice plants, would you refuse to use it?"

Ho was a Leninist. He had no plan to cooperate in any meaningful mutual and collegial relationship with his fellow countrymen who were just "Nationalists." In late 1945 and 1946, he preferred to work with the French against the Nationalists rather than with Nationalists in sincere common cause against the French. In a very short autobiographical reminiscence, Ho would later insist that by his early twenties, he had outgrown faith in the "mountains and rivers" of his homeland to embrace in Paris the "fact" that "only Socialism and Communism can liberate the oppressed nations and working people throughout the world from slavery."[48]

Sainteny justified his dealing with Ho Chi Minh only with reference to Ho's willingness to compromise with the French.

> *While his rivals demanded total and immediate independence as a condition of any negotiation, Ho Chi Minh declared that he understood quite well that he could not attain what he wanted immediately and that he would be content with relative independence, accepting a gentleman's agreement with France that would bring about, after a lapse of time, the total independency of his country.*[49]

Nevertheless, Sainteny, loyal to his country and its still vibrant colonial ambitions, resolved to put Ho Chi Minh and his Viet Minh associates on a pedestal above all other Vietnamese as the proper party for France to recognize and court as Vietnam's most important leadership faction, deserving respect and the status of partner, even if only for the time being. For so many in the West for decades to come, Ho was never to lose the symbolic stature conferred upon him by Sainteny in the early months of 1946.

Of course, what Ho and his fellow Communists wanted in return from Sainteny was French help in repressing the Nationalists. France could give them what the Vietnamese people were not willing to—recognition as the legitimate government of Vietnam. The French acted accordingly and did not then give support to any other Vietnamese political leaders or movements.

Communist leader Le Duan would later substantiate Sainteny's judgment that in late 1945 and early 1946 the Communists were seeking alliances of convenience with foreign powers. Le Duan revealed that

> *under the leadership of President Ho Chi Minh, our party pursued*
> *an extremely clear-sighted political line, rigorous in principle and*
> *flexible in tactics . . . We would reach a temporary compromise*
> *with [the Chinese Nationalists] to be free to cope with the French*
> *Colonialists, only to do the same with the French in order to drive*
> *out [Chinese Nationalist] troops and wipe out the reactionaries and*
> *their agents [the Vietnamese Nationalists]. Thus we gained time to*
> *consolidate our forces and prepare for nationwide resistance to the*
> *inevitable French colonialist aggression.*[50]

Le Duan also hailed this insincere modus operandi as the art of revolutionary leadership—knowing how to win judiciously step by step.[51] Years later, from 1971 through 1975, Le Duan would again deploy this strategy with Henry Kissinger, taking over South Vietnam step by step. One step was just to get the Americans to withdraw their forces from the war. A later step would be to conquer South Vietnam with a regular army after the Americans had given up the fight.

An important Leninist precedent for the 1946 Communist compromise with French colonialists was the Treaty of Brest-Litovsk, which ended Russia's participation in World War I. Signed on March 3, 1918, the treaty abrogated all Russia's obligation to the Allied powers and gave hegemony over the Baltic states to Germany, but it gave Lenin's new Bolshevik government relief. Lenin no longer had to fight a war but could turn his attention to consolidating his infant police state and winning the civil war against non-Communist Russians.

What the March 1946 agreement negotiated by the Vietnamese Communists with the returning French colonialists could not resolve was the status of Cochin China, the southernmost Vietnamese provinces, then a French colony. In the fall of 1945, British troops had been sent there to supervise the surrender of Japanese forces and see to their return to Japan and had permitted the French in those provinces to reestablish direct administration of their former colony.

For Vietnamese, the principal issue after World War II was not independence from France. That was a goal unchallenged by nearly all. The more decisive issue was more complex and intractable. It was, in brief, what kind of society would an independent Vietnam become?

Would it continue a Neo-Confucian elitism? Would it be westernized, and, if so, by how much? Would it be a Communist westernization or a constitutional one? What role would there be for the reassertion of deeply rooted Vietnamese values? What role would the Cao Dai, Hoa Hao, and Buddhist religions play in an independent Vietnam?

The opposition of Nationalist Vietnamese to Communism had already been a political reality in the 1930s. The Communists did not support the February 10, 1930, Yen Bay revolt of the VNQDD Nationalist leadership under Nguyen Thai Hoc, and the Nationalists did not support the later Communist uprisings to establish soviets in several central provinces.

The 1939 proclamation establishing the Dai Viet Party called for the liberation of Vietnam in the name of the Viet people. The party's founder, Truong Tu Anh, published in Vietnamese a political philosophy of Nationalism called *Dan Toc Sinh Ton*. It does not appear to have been studied by any French intellectual or taken seriously by any French official. The party rejected class warfare and promised to rejuvenate the country's "mountains and rivers" for the benefit of all Vietnamese.[52] Truong Tu Anh would be killed by the Communists in 1946.

On September 21, 1946, Huynh Phu So, the charismatic young founder of the Hoa Hao religion in the Mekong Delta, who had attracted more followers by far than had Ho Chi Minh and his Communist colleagues, launched the Vietnam Democratic Socialist Party. The party's objective was to oppose any imperialist ideology in order to bring prosperity and happiness to every class of Vietnamese.[53] The party rejected class struggle. In February 1947, Huynh Phu So and two other prominent Nationalist leaders from Tonkin formed an alliance. On April 16, 1947, Huynh Phu So was murdered by the Communists.[54]

The Communists knew their position: there would be no compromise with the Nationalists. Vietnam would become a Communist Party dictatorship, with party members gathering for themselves all the economic and social privileges that come with having the power to rule—just as the families serving the Nguyen Dynasty had done for themselves and still other families that had served the French directly had done for themselves.

From the fall of 1945, the Communists began to eliminate through violence and murder their rivals, even their fellow Communists the Trotskyites. From the perspective of the Communists, their March 1946 agreement with the French, negotiated with Sainteny, was very valuable because it would permit them to crush their rivals more quickly, more efficiently, and more thoroughly. After they had so consolidated their power among Vietnamese, they could then attend to the French from a position of greater strength.

But the Communists knew they would never receive loyal support for their ideology, as it was contrary to ethnic Vietnamese norms and practices. By definition, all Vietnamese were potential "enemies" of the proposed Communist solution as to who should rule Vietnam. Keenly aware of this, the Communists proceeded to seek power under false pretenses. First, to pose as Nationalists, they officially disbanded the Communist Party. It became a shadowy, nonpublic network of Marxist study groups. Second, they put before the people the Viet Minh alliance as a non-Communist front. This was consistent with Stalin's policy of forming coalitions against the Fascists and by no means a surrender of the party's aim to establish a dictatorship. The extermination of their most prominent Nationalist opponents occurred by stealth in as much secrecy as possible.[55]

As a Communist affirmed to French scholar Paul Mus, "Nothing can prevent us from executing those whom we regard as traitors."[56] Perhaps it was more than coincidence that the Communist Party's program of eliminating "traitors" seemed modeled on the Law of 22 Prairial (June 10, 1794), passed under the Jacobins during the French Revolution to use "terror" to cleanse the new French Republic of "traitors."[57] The Law of 22 Prairial did not provide those accused with any right to a defense. The law stipulated, "The proof necessary to convict enemies of the people

comprises every kind of evidence, whether material or moral, oral or written, which can naturally secure the approval of every just and reasonable
mind; the rule of judgments is the conscience of the jurors, enlightened
by love of the nation; their aim the triumph of the Republic, and the ruin
of its enemies." In short, just as in France under the Jacobins, in Vietnam,
the Communists could try, convict, and kill anyone they wanted to.

In the scholar Paul Mus, Sainteny found a colleague who could set
forth a polished argument that Neo-Confucians had become Marxists and
so were entitled to be the new elite for Vietnam. Mus was an advisor to
General Leclerc, then commander of what French forces could be had in
Vietnam—not enough to subdue Vietnam by military power.

Mus's father had arrived in Vietnam in the first decade of the twentieth
century to establish the system of schools and education, which would
fulfill simultaneously France's *mission civilisatrice* and its commitment
to partner with elite Vietnamese Neo-Confucian families in management
of the country's culture, society, and economy. Even years later, Mus did
not see Vietnamese Nationalism but rather ascribed to the Vietnamese a
universal state of mind—a profound human predicament, one shared by
people all the world over groping toward new values for modern lives.[58]
Mus concluded that after World War II, Vietnam's traditional values
proved inadequate to organize the power to sustain a modern government
unifying all Vietnamese within one nation. His depiction of Vietnamese
ethnic nationalism was as "vestigial remains of a long-decayed communal spirit."[59] A modern state had to be built in Vietnam, an evolution of
the French *mission civilisatrice*, and such a new community required
new values, giving to the Communists as the more astute possessors of
the needed newer values strategic advantage in their struggle with the
Nationalists.

Mus wrote of a single "Sino-Vietnamese civilization," synthesizing in
one turn of phrase the essence of French misperception about the Vietnamese as an autonomous people with a four-thousand-year history of
their own values.[60] "The traditional Vietnamese state was conventionalized
in accordance with Confucian political thought; it was withdrawn behind

a wall of Chinese characters." And "Confucius was universally accepted in Viet Nam as in China and altars to him flourished even in the villages."[61] "For centuries, even in the poorest villages, there were a few local literati who progressively familiarized the national consciousness with the principles of Chinese political thought."[62]

Mus found the source of Vietnam's struggle in the collapse of a Neo-Confucian order, not in an ideological clash between a populist ethnic identity and a Western vision of social justice imported under French license.

French aversion to Vietnamese Nationalism and individual Vietnamese Nationalists became so ingrained in their conventional wisdom as to later prejudice them day in and day out against South Vietnam's efforts at self-defense against Communist aggression.

At the Geneva Conference of 1954, the French agreed with the Communists to divide Vietnam into two administrative zones, with each promising not to invade the other. But in the spring of 1955, when South Vietnamese prime minister Ngo Dinh Diem stubbornly refused to take French counsel and seemed fixated on building an effective regime of Nationalists in South Vietnam, the French moved to have him replaced. The French convinced the American ambassador General J. Lawton Collins that Diem was ineffective. Collins flew back to Washington to persuade President Eisenhower to follow this French advice. He succeeded but only momentarily. After the State Department sent a cable to the American embassy in Saigon with instructions not to oppose the removal of Diem through political intrigue, the CIA received a cable from its chief operative in Saigon, Edward Lansdale, that Diem had ordered the South Vietnamese military into action against the French-affiliated mafia, the Binh Xuyen, and that government soldiers had gone into the operation with enthusiasm. On learning of this and at the direction of Secretary of State John Foster Dulles, State Department officer Kenneth T. Young, in charge of Southeast Asian affairs, consulted with CIA director Allen Dulles. They decided to break with the French and support Diem as a fulcrum for levering Vietnamese Nationalism into a position of power vis-à-vis the Communists in Hanoi.

This decision followed through on the American commitment of October 1954 to Prime Minister Diem that promotion of Nationalism was the foundation for continued American support for South Vietnam. Diem was well known to Americans and Vietnamese as a determined opponent of French colonialism. Intellectually, though a devout Catholic, he had traveled in Nationalist circles since the 1930s.

French bias against Vietnamese Nationalists appeared again in reporting on the emergence of the Viet Cong insurgency in South Vietnam in 1959. This time, the French predilection favoring the Communists showed itself in denial that Hanoi had created the Viet Cong in order to first cripple and then overthrow the Nationalist government in Saigon. Helping Hanoi camouflage its leadership of the guerilla war in South Vietnam would again ingratiate France with its sometime protégés around Ho Chi Minh.

Jean Lacouture reported that a March 1960 declaration of former followers of Ho Chi Minh's Viet Minh movement against the French who had stayed in South Vietnam after the 1954 armistice was a genuinely autonomous effort by some South Vietnamese to oppose the Ngo Dinh Diem administration in Saigon.[63] Lacouture touted the ten-point program of the NLF as evidence for its independence. Philippe Devillers and Georges Chaffard wrote to the same effect.[64]

As documented in chapter 1 in the instructions from the Communist Party politburo in Hanoi to its cadre organizing a guerilla war inside South Vietnam, this French narrative about the new guerilla war in South Vietnam was poppycock.

Further, the South Vietnamese chosen in December 1960 to serve on the leadership committee of the NLF were largely from elite families who had been prominent under French colonialism but who had seen their status deteriorate under the Nationalist administration of Ngo Dinh Diem. This placed them in the orbit of deserving French solicitude as a counterweight to Hanoi's dominance of the insurgency.[65] The head of the NLF was Nguyen Huu Tho, described by Lacouture as "an intellectual of French culture" who had studied law in Aix-en-Province. Lacouture also noted that most members of the NLF Central Committee had been "moving spirits" in the Congress of Peace in the Saigon area in 1954, what he called an "insignificant pro-Viet Minh organization."[66]

After the fall of Ngo Dinh Diem in the coup of November 1, 1963, there was a murky episode when de Gaulle called for the neutralization of South Vietnam, and two Vietnamese, former officers for the French, returned to Saigon. After the fall of Diem's administration, political leadership in South Vietnam was in the hands of a military directorate. Leading generals of that directorate had first gained rank and prominence serving in the French forces fighting Ho Chi Minh. In late January 1964, young Nationalist officers from the Dai Viet Party mobilized and arrested four of these generals. Their objective was to prevent the French from using these generals to push South Vietnam into the hands of Hanoi.

French bias against Vietnamese Nationalists even corrupted the thinking of the American antiwar movement that arose in the 1960s to protest American support for South Vietnam. Americans who stridently but ignorantly argued that the American effort to succor Vietnamese Nationalists was either unjust or impossible expressly followed French cultural stereotypes about the Vietnamese. Starting in 1965 with President Johnson's decision to send American combat forces to the defense of South Vietnam, antiwar leaders rejected the truth as argued by their government and instead took up a lie proffered by French writers.

During the Kennedy administration, American journalists had already begun to shape their reporting to align with French colonial tropes about the Vietnamese.

Framing the morality of defending South Vietnam only from the prejudiced perspective of French colonialism, English novelist Graham Greene wrote a short novel, *The Quiet American*, disparaging the naïveté of Americans who cared about the Vietnamese and believed in their Nationalism and their right to shape a modern society after their core values. The fictional American in question, Pyle, is murdered in the novel for his wrong-footed interference in the struggle between the French and the Communist-led insurgents. Greene condemned Vietnamese Nationalism as only some vague "third force," opposed to both the Communists and the French. The historical Nationalist fighter disparaged by Greene as low and thuggish was Trinh Minh The of the Cao Dai faith, a hero for many Vietnamese but feared by both the Communists and the French for his charisma.

Frenchman Bernard Fall wrote a history of modern Vietnam that influenced many American journalists sent to South Vietnam in the early 1960s to cover the increasingly difficult struggle of the Vietnamese Nationalists. It was used in the academic teach-ins that challenged the cogency and therefore the legitimacy of the US government's decisions to support the Vietnamese Nationalists. Following the French misunderstanding, Fall asserted without question that

> *it becomes fully understandable why such highly respected non-Communist observers as Jean Lacouture and Philippe Devillers argue, that up to a point, the anti-Diem resistance inside South Vietnam . . . in fact began and developed at a politically opportune moment for Hanoi . . . it would be difficult, to say the least, to build anything else but an ex post facto "aggression" case against North Vietnam on the evidence presently available. A far more solid argument could be made for . . . Hanoi entering the game rather late and at a relative slow pace.*[67]

Influential journalist Neil Sheehan told the American people in 1966 that "I can only conclude that the Vietnamese will die more willingly for a regime, which though Communist, is at least genuinely Vietnamese and offers them some hope of improving their lives, than for one which is committed to the galling status quo and is the creation of Washington."[68] He continued: "Most Non-Communist Vietnamese are incapable, because of the values of the society in which they live, of looking beyond individual and family interests. Their overwhelming concern with 'me and my relatives' deprives the society of a social consciousness which Americans take for granted in their own culture and fosters the corruption and nepotism that exist in the administration." So much for Vietnamese Nationalism—and what a surrender to the French narrative that the Vietnamese have no national values and ideals of their own.

Citing Jean Lacouture as a source, the noted scholar of international power relationships Hans Morgenthau was convinced that "the war is first of all a South Vietnamese civil war, aided and abetted by the North Vietnamese government but neither created nor sustained by it."[69] Professor Morgenthau affirmed as truth that "to call it foreign aggression is to misrepresent the facts. The great mass of the South Vietnamese people are today either indifferent or hostile to our policies."[70] Thus also in 1966, he added his voice and prestige to the nascent antiwar movement.

Kennedy family advisor and loyalist Harvard professor Arthur Schlesinger joined the growing movement of academics and intellectuals in fostering the legitimacy of a political movement to stop American support for the Vietnamese Nationalists. In 1966, Schlesinger wrote that Ho Chi Minh had emerged as the hero of Vietnamese Nationalism in the country's war for independence from France. He affirmed for his readers that "the civil insurrection in South Vietnam began to gather force by 1958; it was not until September 1960 that the Communist Party of North Vietnam bestowed its formal blessing and called for the liberation of the south from American imperialism."[71]

Schlesinger described South Vietnam as a "morass," insinuating that no "morass" was worth American solicitude.[72] He passed on the opinion that "yet the best evidence remains that the war began as an insurrection within South Vietnam which, as it has gathered momentum, has attracted support and direction from the north." And that "to reduce this war to the simplification of a wicked regime molesting its neighbors and to suppose that it can be ended by punishing the wicked regime, is surely to misconceive not only the political but even the military character of the problem."[73]

Boston University professor Howard Zinn in 1967 cited Devillers and Lacouture on the asserted truth that the war "appears to be a revolution in the south against an unpopular regime."[74]

He wrote, "The withdrawal of the United States, by leaving the field open to the play of forces which are Vietnamese, will probably leave the National Liberation Front, which is Communist dominated . . . to become the chief force in a new South Vietnamese government."[75]

In 1972, Frances FitzGerald published a well-received study of the Vietnamese and their war under the title *Fire in the Lake*.[76] She dedicated it in part to Paul Mus. Her thesis was, in line with Mus, Graham Greene's novel, and many other Western journalists, that only the Communists could triumph in war and establish an effective government ruling the Vietnamese. The effect of her book was powerful in Washington and in elite circles, which had turned against the war to protect South Vietnam but still needed to assuage their guilt in rejecting their own government. FitzGerald purported to express the values and views of "true" Vietnamese as a cultural anthropologist, thereby affirming that the American antiwar movement was not defeatist or insufficiently empathetic with another "race" but rather was fully in line with the good of those "others." Harvard professor Stanley Hoffmann called it "a compassionate and penetrating account"; linguist Noam Chomsky praised it as "a work of rare insight and lasting importance . . . a sympathetic understanding of the Vietnamese."[77]

Her book had no small influence in creating a critical mass of opposition to the war among Democrats and even some Republicans. The political consequence of their turning completely against the South Vietnamese Nationalists came in 1973 with congressional legislation restricting the president's ability to send American forces into combat and later with cutting American aid to the South Vietnamese after the 1973 Paris Peace Accords were signed.

This shift in American capacity to defend South Vietnam, enhanced by President Nixon's resignation in 1974, emboldened Hanoi to resume its military aggression against South Vietnam in early 1975.

FitzGerald did not believe that the government in Saigon was naturally for and of Vietnamese Nationalists. She believed it to have been created by the United States.[78] Following Mus, FitzGerald associated Vietnam with the "Celestial Empire of China" in form and essence, speaking of "Confucianism" as the "very foundation of the state."[79] FitzGerald interpreted

Vietnamese identity as derived from Chinese overlordship: "Vietnamese history began in Chinese writing, and the Vietnamese nation took shape along the political and cultural lines of force emanating from China," adding that "Vietnamese leaders assumed Chinese political culture."[80]

Not giving the Vietnamese credit for having any real identity of their own, FitzGerald could breezily conclude that "'Nationalism' in Vietnam did not wait like a brass ring to be 'captured' by the most energetic pursuer: it had to be created." Again following Mus, FitzGerald assured her readers that "Vietnam had, after all, disappeared under the French to be replaced by 'Indochina.'"[81]

She did, however, accurately note that educated Vietnamese "modeled themselves on their conquerors."[82] Assimilated thanks to the French *mission civilisatrice*, they looked to Paris as the center of civilization.

Again rooted in the misperceptions of Mus, a young American only passing through Vietnam definitively concluded that Marxism was an extension of Neo-Confucianism in that both repressed individualism to privilege a social cohesion imposed by the state. FitzGerald evidently saw evidence of the individualism and factionalism all around her among Vietnamese not as part of an autonomous ethnic identity but as the breakdown of order.[83]

She ended her rejection of both American policy and Vietnamese Nationalists with perhaps the most fatuous and demeaning dismissal of a people written by an American about the war. Writing of the coming victory of the Communists "when individualism and its attendant corruption gives way to the discipline of the revolutionary community," she inferred that "it will simply mean that the moment has arrived for the narrow flame of revolution to cleanse the lake of Vietnamese society from the corruption and disorder of the American war."[84]

The founding American dean of antiwar scholarship for journalists, academics, and teach-in participants was Cornell professor George McTurnan Kahin. Also relying on Devillers and Lacouture and not trusting his government, Kahin pontificated that *in sum, the insurrection is southern rooted; it arose at Southern initiative in response to Southern demands. Contrary to US policy assumptions, all available evidence shows that the revival of the civil war in the South in 1958 was undertaken by southerners at their own—not Hanoi's—initiative. To reach the unescapable conclusion that the Liberation Front is not "Hanoi's creation"; it has manifested independence and it is Southern.*[85]

In the 1967 book *Vietnam: Crisis of Conscience*, Michael Novak wrote that Americans should help Communism evolve in more constructive directions to deal with humanity's real enemies—hunger, poverty, ignorance, and disease; Rabbi Abraham Heschel believed that "revolutionary change is a moral necessity" and that the NLF was a "recalcitrant heretic community"; and Professor of Religion Robert McAfee Brown was of the fixed opinion that it was wrong to believe that "this is a war of Communist aggression from the North" and that Communist aggression from the North did not begin until after the US military presence in South Vietnam had been overwhelmingly established.[86]

But the greatest impact of French colonial conceit about the Vietnamese on the destiny of Americans was its influence on Robert Kennedy. French misperceptions were used to justify his turning against the war and President Lyndon Johnson. In the presidential campaign of 1968, Robert Kennedy, then a senator from New York, sought the nomination of his party, the Democrats, for the presidency. A major theme of his campaign, before his tragic assassination, was opposition to the war in Vietnam. By early 1968, Kennedy had broken with the Vietnam policies of President Johnson and was calling for withdrawal of American combat forces and negotiations with the Communists.

In his definitive biography of Robert Kennedy, his friend and advisor Arthur Schlesinger Jr. tells of Kennedy's intellectual evolution from supporter to opponent of the war. In mid-1965, his staff sent him books by Frenchman Bernard Fall and other "incendiary" writings that ridiculed the American justification for helping Vietnamese Nationalists.[87] The journalist

Joseph Kraft, also under the influence of French thinking on Vietnam, arranged for Kennedy to intercede with the Algerian government to win the release of a captured American. The effort moved Kennedy closer to an understanding that the Viet Cong was "truly a National Liberation Front with a political structure and legitimacy of its own." On February 19, 1966, Kennedy issued a statement calling for negotiations that would give the Viet Cong a role in the political structure of South Vietnam.[88] At the end of January 1967, Kennedy visited Paris. There, Henry Kissinger introduced him to Jean Sainteny, who opined that Ho Chi Minh should be considered an open-minded Nationalist determined to be independent of Communist leaders in Moscow and Beijing. Kennedy called on French president de Gaulle, the man who had selected Sainteny to reestablish French dominance over the Vietnamese in 1945. De Gaulle affirmed that Hanoi would never take over South Vietnam. The South Vietnamese would never permit it, he told the American, adding, "History is the force at work in Vietnam and the United States will not prevail against it."[89] On February 6, 1967, Kennedy spoke in Chicago. Now he adopted the self-serving French conceit about the Vietnamese: Kennedy said that Vietnamese Communism was "a native growth with its own revolutionary traditions and dynamism."[90]

Then, on March 2, 1967, Kennedy stood in the Senate Chamber and called for a halt in the bombing of North Vietnam to test the sincerity of the Vietnamese Communists and start a process of removing the American people from complicity in a horrid war of brutality and destruction.

In breaking with President Johnson over the Vietnam War, Kennedy did more than position himself as a candidate for the presidency; he split the Democratic Party into a pro–South Vietnam faction loyal to American internationalism and an anti–South Vietnam camp seeking a new role for Americans in the world, one that rejected attributes of hegemony and moral imperialism. During the ensuing presidential campaign, a cultural war among Americans opened that would, within fifty years, polarize the American people and elect Donald Trump as president. Thus did French colonialism indirectly turn Americans against one another and so undermine the self-confidence of the American people and their national ability to be a force for good.

Subsequently, during the Vietnam War to defend South Vietnam against Communist aggression, American journalists and scholars adopted without independent scrutiny this French misperception. Thus, their commentaries, analyses, conclusions, and recommendations for American policy in Vietnam did not reflect Vietnamese realities. Their narratives about the war were only that—personal narratives—not the truth.

Susan Sontag recognized that the Vietnam War was not appropriated by those opposed to traditional American values and institutions in an ideological vacuum:

> *Radical Americans have profited from the war in Vietnam, profited from having a clear-cut moral issue on which to mobilize discontent and expose the camouflaged contradictions in the system. Beyond isolated private disenchantment of despair over America's betrayal of its ideals, Vietnam offered the key to a systemic criticism of America. In this scheme of use, Vietnam becomes an ideal other.*[91]

Here Sontag reveals why many Americans chose to believe a false French narrative about right and wrong in Vietnam rather than accept the truth put forth by their own government. The French colonial disparagement of the Vietnamese as a people was necessary intellectually to support rejection of official American policy in South Vietnam. The disloyalty and lack of patriotism revealed by opposition to the war would trigger intolerable angst and shame—especially for the sons of fathers who had fought in World War II. Thus, many who chose to oppose the Vietnam War developed a festering psychosocial need to find a compelling way to reject the official reasons given for why the United States should help the Vietnamese Nationalists. French colonial misperceptions gave these Americans just what they needed to so reject the policy of their government toward the Vietnamese Nationalists. It was no surprise, then, that so many Americans adopted without a second thought the French fiction about who the Vietnamese were. It was of the utmost importance for those opposed to the war to prove that it was unjust and/or unwinnable. The French conviction that the Vietnamese were not really much of a people in their own right, possessing the dignity of having their own ancient, non-Chinese values, provided more than sufficient justification for intense antiwar protest.

Cultural and psychological needs drove American intellectuals and the many young men who did not want to serve in the war (and their parents) to embrace colonial prejudice and ditch the Vietnamese as fully deserving of servitude under Communist tyranny.[92]

Senator J. William Fulbright, a great force in the creation of the antiwar movement, once told President Lyndon Johnson that the war was unworthy because the Vietnamese "are not our kind."[93]

CHAPTER 3

BETRAYAL

Mere anarchy is loosed upon the world,
The blood-dimmed tide is loosed, and everywhere
The ceremony of innocence is drowned;
The best lack all conviction, while the worst
Are full of passionate intensity.

—William Butler Yeats, "The Second Coming"

On January 9, 1971, Henry Kissinger met with Soviet ambassador Anatoly Dobrynin in Washington.[1] Toward the end of their discussion, which also included considerations of US/Soviet relations and Berlin, Kissinger raised the topic of how the United States might extricate itself from the defense of South Vietnam. He proposed withdrawal of American forces while leaving North Vietnamese forces inside South Vietnam to continue their war of conquest after the disengagement of the Americans. Kissinger presented this alternative as only "hypothetical." Kissinger was then working in the White House as President Richard Nixon's national security advisor.

After the meeting, Dobrynin sent a report of the conversation to his superiors in Moscow.[2] Dobrynin's report is as follows:

Kissinger said President Nixon had taken note of the Soviet Prime Minister's interview with the Japanese newspaper Asahi [Shimbun], *particularly his statement that the Soviet Government was ready "to help the Americans leave Vietnam."*

After specifying that he would now be speaking unofficially, Kissinger said he would like to "articulate" for the Soviet Government's information the President's current "way of thinking" regarding the problem of a Vietnam settlement, to which he and the President continue to devote a great deal of time.

The administration is still determined to retaliate against the DRV [Democratic Republic of Vietnam] with military strikes if Hanoi, now or in the near future, launches large-scale operations against South Vietnam. But right now they would like to focus on another aspect pertaining to a settlement.

The President knows that one of the key issues to which the DRV attaches great importance is the issue of the withdrawal of US troops. He and the President are currently discussing "with each other" this possibility:

- *What if the US were to commit to withdraw all of its troops by some absolutely specific deadline, of which they would inform the Vietnamese?*

- *At the same time, the Americans could refrain from demanding a reciprocal withdrawal of North Vietnamese troops from South Vietnam, since that would be clearly unacceptable to Hanoi, which has never acknowledged the presence of its troops there.*

It is important, however, that the North Vietnamese, for their part, then commit to a cease-fire for the period of the US troop withdrawal plus at least some brief amount of time after the withdrawal.

Kissinger did not mention any specific deadlines. However, as far as one could make out from his deliberately vague and cautious explanations, an important factor in all this is Nixon's campaign considerations, namely that a cease-fire be observed mainly during the decisive period of the election campaign, as well as considerations involving his personal prestige, that a serious, new deterioration of the situation in South Vietnam not occur right after the troop withdrawal.

Kissinger made a rather curious remark that ultimately it will no longer be their, the Americans', concern, but that of the Vietnamese themselves if some time after the U.S. troop withdrawal they start fighting with each other again.

In this connection, Kissinger let drop a general remark to the effect that he himself is ready, with the President's approval, to resume at any time his direct contacts with DRV representatives in Paris.

Ambassador Dobrynin's memorandum about Henry Kissinger floating a proposal that the North Vietnamese could leave their forces inside South Vietnam was confirmed by Vietnamese Communists Luu Van Loi and Nguyen Anh Vu in their book on the secret Paris negotiations.[3] They reported that around the end of January 1971, Soviet Ambassador Serbakov in Hanoi informed North Vietnam's Prime Minister Pham Van Dong that in mid-January Kissinger told the following to Soviet ambassador Dobrynin in Washington:

If the US undertakes to withdraw all its forces by a certain time limit and does not demand a simultaneous withdrawal of DRVN forces

> *from SVN . . . the North Vietnamese should undertake to respect a*
> *cease-fire during the US withdrawal plus a certain period of time,*
> *not too long, after the US withdrawal, that is the important point*
> *. . . If the Vietnamese can agree among themselves on a reasonable*
> *compromise, and, if thereafter, war breaks out again between North*
> *and South Vietnam, that conflict will no longer be an American*
> *affair, it will be an affair of the Vietnamese themselves, because the*
> *Americans will have left Vietnam. It will be beyond the scope of the*
> *Nixon Administration.*

And so the Soviets rather quickly informed Hanoi's Communist leaders of Kissinger's proposed possibility of Hanoi winning the war after accommodating American requests for a peace agreement and at least a temporary cease-fire.

Kissinger related in his memoirs of working in the White House that by May 1970 he had developed a very strong conviction that "for the internal peace of the [United States] the war had to be ended."[4] With this in his mind, as antiwar protests grew stronger and stronger around him, he was not really all that personally concerned for the fate of Vietnamese Nationalists.

According to his January 1969 article in *Foreign Affairs*, Kissinger was then already convinced that there was no reasonable possibility that the Americans and South Vietnamese could ever secure the long-term independence of South Vietnam. He had concluded, for example, that "the Tet offensive marked the watershed of the American effort. Henceforth, no matter how effective our actions, the prevalent strategy could no longer achieve its objectives within a period or with force levels politically acceptable to the American people"; that "we have been unable so far to create a political structure that could survive military opposition from Hanoi after we withdraw"; and that "once North Vietnamese forces and pressures are removed, the United States has no obligation to maintain a government in Saigon by force."[5]

Along with most opponents of the war, Kissinger believed in the political autonomy of the National Liberation Front (NLF) and its independence from Hanoi's control:

> *Both the Hanoi Government and the United States are limited in their freedom of action by the state of mind of the population of South Viet Nam which will ultimately determine the outcome of the conflict.*

> *In order to retain its autonomy, Hanoi must maneuver skillfully between Peking, Moscow and the NLF.*[6]

But even with his pessimism, in late 1968, Kissinger had advocated withdrawal of North Vietnamese forces from South Vietnam:

> *American objectives should therefore be (1) to bring about a staged withdrawal of external forces, North Vietnamese and American, (2) thereby to create a maximum incentive for the contending forces in South Viet Nam to work out a political agreement . . . The United States, then, should concentrate on the subject of the mutual withdrawal of external forces and avoid negotiating about the internal structure of South Viet Nam for as long as possible. The primary responsibility for negotiating the internal structure of South Viet Nam should be left for direct negotiations among the South Vietnamese.*[7]

Kissinger's "hypothetical" alternative of permitting Hanoi to keep its army in South Vietnam, which he presented to Dobrynin on January 9, 1971, was very much his recommendation of two years earlier in his *Foreign Affairs* article—with one exception: now he abandoned the requirement of mutual North Vietnamese and American withdrawals of their respective combat forces.

In his memoir *White House Years*, Kissinger exposed his justification for turning against South Vietnam. "When a concession is made voluntarily it provides the greatest incentive for reciprocity. It also provides the best guarantee for staying power. In the negotiations I conducted I always tried to determine the most reasonable outcome and then get there rapidly in one or two moves." Kissinger dismissed holding firm for principle or for advantage in negotiations: that course is for novices who want the appearance of toughness and usually proves, he wrote, to be self-defeating—"shaving the salami encourages the other side to hold on to see what the next concession is likely to be, never sure that one has really reached the rock-bottom position."[8]

In line with this practice, if Kissinger had concluded by 1970 that South Vietnam could not become a viable state holding off continued aggression from the Communist leadership in Hanoi and that the Vietnamese Nationalists had nothing worth defending in any case, then his preemptively conceding victory to Hanoi was sensible, even if it was a cruel betrayal.

But Kissinger did not share this proclivity of making concessions with his president. Richard Nixon was a positional bargainer of the old school. He thought of himself as "tough-minded" and wanted to be seen as "tough" in deed as well.

In his report to President Nixon of his January 9, 1971, meeting with Ambassador Dobrynin, Kissinger did not disclose his presentation to the Soviet diplomat of a unilateral US withdrawal from South Vietnam. President Nixon, therefore, did not know that Kissinger had, in secret, with the Soviets, followed his own thinking on how the Vietnam War was to end—the South Vietnamese fighting all on their own against the Communists, winner take all.

Thus did Kissinger leave President Nixon and all his senior officials, including Ambassador Ellsworth Bunker and General Creighton Abrams in Saigon, in the dark about Kissinger's personal plans for the future of South Vietnam.

In the memorandum making a record of his January 9, 1971, meeting with Soviet ambassador Dobrynin, Kissinger wrote only:

> We then turned to Vietnam . . . Dobrynin then said he wanted to ask me a hypothetical question. If Hanoi dropped its demands for a

coalition government, would we be prepared to discuss withdrawal separately. I said as long as the matter was hypothetical, it was very hard to form a judgment, but I could imagine that the issue of withdrawals was a lot easier to deal with than the future composition of a government in South Vietnam. Indeed, if he remembered an article I had written in 1968, I had proposed exactly this procedure. Dobrynin asked whether I still believed that this was a possible approach. I said it certainly was a possible approach and, indeed, I had been of the view that it would be the one that would speed up matters. Dobrynin said he would report this to Moscow.[9]

A few months later, as Operation Lam Son 719—South Vietnam's attack on North Vietnamese forces in Laos bringing soldiers and supplies into combat in the South—drew to a close, President Nixon announced large additional withdrawals of American troops from South Vietnam. Pointedly, he refused to set a deadline for the final exit of all American troops from the war. Nixon wanted the United States to leave South Vietnam in a way that offered "a brave people a realistic hope of freedom" and never in a way that would "by our own actions consciously turn the country over to the Communists."

In his speech of April 7, 1971, Nixon said pointedly:

The issue very simply is this: Shall we leave Vietnam in a way that—by our own actions—consciously turns the country over to the Communists? Or shall we leave in a way that gives the South Vietnamese a reasonable chance to survive as a free people? My plan will end American involvement in a way that would provide that chance. And the other plan would end it precipitately and give victory to the Communists.

In a deeper sense, we have the choice of ending our involvement in this war on a note of despair or on a note of hope. I believe, as Thomas Jefferson did, that Americans will always choose hope over despair. We have it in our power to leave Vietnam in a way that offers a brave people a realistic hope of freedom. We have it in our power to prove to our friends in the world that America's sense of responsibility remains the world's greatest single hope of peace. And above all, we have it in our power to close a difficult chapter in American history, not meanly but nobly—so that each one of us can come out of this searing experience with a measure of pride in our Nation, confidence in our own character, and hope for the future of the spirit of America.[10]

In failing to disclose to President Nixon his consequential concession presented in secret to Soviet ambassador Dobrynin, Henry Kissinger violated his duty and abused his power. Kissinger then held a public trust as an employee of the US government. He was an agent of a higher authority empowered to serve with fidelity and due care. He was not a free agent to do anything he pleased or thought best. He was a servant empowered to seek the good of others. His duty was to think of them first and foremost, subordinating his own predilections and ideological peculiarities of whatever sort to their best interests as they saw their best interests.

Every public office is a public trust. Along with all others who work for the United States, Kissinger had no personal dominion over his office. He had no authority to impose at will his personal feelings and beliefs arbitrarily or capriciously. His responsibilities were, first, loyalty to his principal and, second, due care in the execution of his office. Every president of the United States takes a personal oath to "faithfully execute the office of president." In particular, and in special contrast to Henry Kissinger, Ellsworth Bunker had long since internalized this noble ethic of fiduciary responsibility. In Kissinger's case, taking due care required presenting his best ideas to his president and other senior officials, such as the secretaries of state and defense and members of the National Security Council, for review and consultation. His fiduciary duty of loyalty obligated him to disclose all material information regarding a foreign power, such as the Soviet Union, that was a threat to his government and his people.[11]

Operation Lam Son 719 ended on March 25, 1971. Once again, foreigners misjudged Vietnamese realities. Foreign press coverage of Lam Son 719 portrayed the operation largely as a defeat for the South Vietnamese army, the Army of the Republic of Vietnam (ARVN). Helicopters flying back to the Khe Sanh Base where journalists were stationed were photographed with South Vietnamese rangers hanging on to the struts in desperation. This made for upsetting film footage for the nightly news shows in the United States. Correspondents interviewing returning American helicopter crews took down stories of fearful combat and intense antiaircraft fire—a classic view of war from a lieutenant's perspective, where everything about him is going wrong and all seems lost.

In Washington, Henry Kissinger had been particularly nervous during the operation. From Saigon, Ambassador Bunker had kept him supplied with constant messages on developments. Bunker, however, was as unrattled as ever. He was privately even somewhat surprised by how well the South Vietnamese were doing compared with the situation only a few years before.

The operation, initially oversold by the Nixon administration, was perceived in Washington as a defeat. Journalist Stewart Alsop questioned whether the South Vietnamese still had a will to fight. Hugh Scott, leader of the Senate Republicans, concluded that hawks had become ex-hawks. "The Senate," he said, "must tell the President to get out of the war."

While Lam Son 719 had been underway, ARVN forces elsewhere had performed credibly. Firebase 6, in the mountains near Dak To, held off a North Vietnamese siege and ground attacks that had used some six to ten thousand soldiers in the attempt to capture the base. In the far south, ARVN forces entered the last remaining Communist base area in South Vietnam, the U Minh Forest, in the southernmost tip of the country jutting out into the Gulf of Siam and the South China Sea. Some sixty thousand people took that campaign as an opportunity to become refugees and flee Communist control. The Ninth ARVN Division neutralized the Communist base area in the Seven Mountains of the western Mekong River Delta. ARVN executed two drives into Cambodia around the Parrot's Beak, the traditional Communist route of infiltration just west of Saigon. Simultaneously, ARVN units probed in the rugged A Shau Valley along the Laos border south of Lam Son 719.

For their part, the Communists could mount only a handful of desultory shellings and minor ground assaults inside South Vietnam. But in Cambodia, North Vietnamese units drove elements of the Fifth ARVN Division out of Snoul as the South Vietnamese were pulling back for the start of the rainy season. Much important equipment—tanks, trucks, armored personnel carriers, and artillery—was foolishly lost to the enemy. The withdrawal had been botched by an inept division commander, a man whom General Abrams and Bunker had asked Thieu to relieve of his division command. Thieu had promised to take action but just couldn't seem to get around to it.

Bunker now told Thieu calmly but coldly that the South Vietnamese president could ill afford to lose men and equipment through incompetence. Bunker said he would not authorize the giving of sophisticated weapons to people who would not use them properly. Thieu needed quality leadership more than weapons, Bunker told his South Vietnamese counterpart. Thieu's caution in replacing his subordinates was a leadership characteristic Bunker found frustrating and exasperating. It was a deep part of Thieu's personality, one that Bunker could not succeed in changing. While decisive in many executive matters, Thieu was very hesitant in sacking his subordinates for their poor performance.

Henry Kissinger was not in agreement with his president on what was best for the Vietnamese Nationalists. Disparaging South Vietnamese efforts in the Lam Son 719 operation into Laos, Kissinger now sought progress in the secret peace negotiations, where he could pursue his plan for a unilateral US withdrawal from the war. Kissinger was more inclined to follow the thinking of the antiwar movement, which was demanding "Out, now!" as the only way to end American involvement in the Vietnam War.

In a conversation on April 7, Kissinger told his president that they should wait to see what "Dobrynin brings back."[12]

On April 12, Winston Lord, special assistant to Henry Kissinger, submitted a memorandum for Kissinger's personal attention. Though the memorandum was written under Lord's name, Kissinger in his memoirs affirmed that "it had been worked out by me, Lord, and Smyser of my staff," putting his imprimatur on a plan that would leave North Vietnamese forces inside South Vietnam, as he had suggested to Dobrynin the previous January 9.[13] Lord recommended that Kissinger "immediately reopen your channel" to Hanoi, seeking a private meeting with the Vietnamese Communists, but that he do so through "our usual contact in Paris," no longer using the Soviets as intermediaries with the Hanoi government.

As terms to put before the Communists, Lord recommended 1) an irrevocable withdrawal of US forces from South Vietnam; 2) a standstill cease-fire across Laos, Cambodia, and the two Vietnams; 3) release of all US prisoners of war held by Hanoi; 4) rotation of North Vietnamese troops in and out of South Vietnam but no net increase in their unit strength in the South; 5) international supervision; 6) reaffirmation of the Geneva Accords; and 7) the discussion of political matters between the Saigon government and the "other side."

Later, these terms would, in the main, be put to Hanoi in a secret meeting in Paris on May 31 and would become the framework for the 1973 Peace Accords ostensibly ending the Vietnam War.

Holding up the Geneva Accords of July 1954 as a template for peace between Communist North Vietnam and Nationalist South Vietnam was a bit sophomoric. The actual agreement ending the war between France and Ho Chi Minh's Viet Minh organization was the Agreement on the Cessation of Hostilities in Viet-Nam, signed on July 20, 1954, in Geneva. In Article 19 of that agreement, the French for the territory which was to become South Vietnam (the Republic of Vietnam) and the Vietnamese Communists for the territory that would become North Vietnam (the Democratic Republic of Vietnam) agreed that "neither territory would adhere to any military alliance" and would not "be used for the resumption of hostilities or to further an aggressive policy."[14]

The Victnamese Communists never honored that peace agreement. Expecting them to honor a similar agreement in 1971 was most naive.

Importantly, Lord recommended that the United States not obtain the withdrawal of Hanoi's army from South Vietnam as a condition for ending the war. Instead, Lord noted the possibility of just letting the South Vietnamese negotiate on their own with the Communists on the future "disposition" of Communist military units as the Americans withdrew from combat.

Lord also proposed that the United States unilaterally try to make "rapid progress" in the secret negotiations in May and June and then present South Vietnam's President Nguyen Van Thieu with an update on their progress in late June or early July.

In his memo, Lord raised the issue of how much to disclose to President Thieu. He presented arguments for ignoring Thieu and counterarguments for informing him of the US decision to let Hanoi keep its forces in the South. But in either case, Lord proposed going ahead unilaterally to let Hanoi maintain a powerful military capacity inside South Vietnam.

The recommendation suggested by Lord that the United States withdraw its forces from South Vietnam and leave the South Vietnamese on their own to contend with an invading army of North Vietnamese regular soldiers easily and immediately could have been presented to President Nixon for his approval. It was not. Lord's memo making this recommendation was also not shared with Ambassador Bunker and General Abrams in Saigon. Ambassador Bunker was again left in the dark about Henry Kissinger's plans for South Vietnam's future.

But on April 13, the day after receiving Winston Lord's proposal, Kissinger sent a secret cable to Bunker saying, "We plan to approach other side soon to reopen special Paris forum . . . If they agree to resume talks our thinking is to table a concrete package, say that we want to know promptly if genuine negotiations are possible, and indicate that time for negotiated settlement is in fact running out."[15]

Searching for new options to end the war through negotiations and not by force, Kissinger asked for Bunker's "personal views" on what should be "in the package," including "possible new elements," and on "how . . . we handle Thieu, including his likely reaction to the proposals." Kissinger reminded Bunker that Bunker had suggested testing Hanoi's position before informing Thieu, but Kissinger noted that failure to take Thieu into "our" confidence held "pitfalls" for the relationship between Saigon and Washington.

Bunker, born to a Yankee heritage of service and protestant intentionality in living up to high aspirations, had a very different mind and personality from Henry Kissinger. Kissinger was voluble and finessed his words with cleverness and guile. Bunker was reserved, measured, calm, reflective, and spoke in such a way that his listener would have clarity of meaning and not be misled. As a businessman, and then as an amateur diplomat, Bunker had learned the strategic value for getting things done that comes from being trusted by others. Bunker had easily internalized the good sense to choose wisdom over glib salesmanship and duty over intrigue. Bunker's charm was his integrity and his sincerity. He was loyal, up-front, and frank, always thinking of how to bring about the best results for the common good. Accordingly, he had been highly trusted by Presidents Eisenhower, Johnson, and Nixon.

Bunker thought the complicated matter over for three days and then on April 17 sent back to Kissinger a strategy for negotiations with Hanoi.[16] His recommendations were, with one existentially vital exception, consistent with Winston Lord's recommendations and constituted the first comprehensive American plan for ending the Vietnam War.

For his plan, Bunker reached back to his concept of the year before, dividing the negotiations with Hanoi into two phases, a preliminary one focused on general principles and a subsequent one digging into the details of actual implementation. He also tied his thinking about the preliminary phase to Kissinger's point of April 13 that the United States wanted to know promptly whether the politburo was open to serious discussions seeking genuine compromise.

Bunker wrote, "It seems to me that the aim of this first meeting should be exclusively to establish whether Hanoi is interested in negotiations or not. Depending on the outcome we can then determine whether to table a package at the next meeting."

Bunker was concerned about the impact of secret negotiations on Thieu. He advised that Thieu should be informed in advance of the resumption of private talks between Kissinger and Hanoi. Moreover, Bunker did not want to table new proposals with Hanoi so soon after Lam Son 719, in which the South Vietnamese forces had taken "heavy losses" and after which American withdrawals were to be accelerated. Bunker noted in addition that any new proposal at this time would be subject to a misunderstanding of American resolve on the part of Hanoi. He concluded, "As RVNAF [Republic of Vietnam Armed Forces] demonstrates its strength, resilience and recuperative powers, as it is already beginning to do, confidence will increase and Thieu (and the GVN [Government of Viet Nam]) will prove receptive to proposal."

In the first meeting with Hanoi for the first phase of discussions over general principles, Bunker advised Kissinger to make an argument about why Hanoi should negotiate terms of peace. Bunker's proposed argument was little more than a description of situational realities where facts would carry persuasive weight with Communist leaders. Bunker noted that American forces were on their way home. All American forces would be out of ground combat by the end of 1971. South Vietnam had 1.1 million men in its regular military forces and another 1.5 million in the People's Self-Defense Forces. This force could not be defeated in the field even after American troops left. The United States would supply those South Vietnamese forces with all essential military equipment indefinitely. Furthermore, South Vietnam's economy was solidly based, and its growth would continue. With continued American financial support, there would be no economic collapse in South Vietnam.

If Hanoi wanted to negotiate, the United States would agree to withdraw all its forces, but if not, the United States would maintain a minimum force in South Vietnam indefinitely. If there was no negotiated settlement, the people of South Vietnam would continue to fight, and a war that neither side would win would go on and on. The longer such a war continued, the more difficult it would become to arrange any peace settlement. It was in everyone's interest to open negotiations now. South Vietnam would not give up its constitution or its elections in favor of Hanoi's proposals for a provisional government. That was a reality that Hanoi had to face. For its part, South Vietnam had to face the reality that Hanoi would not accept its constitution and elected government. But after a cease-fire was in place, a serious attempt to find a middle way in which the interests of all sides were protected could produce a negotiated settlement.

If the North Vietnamese accepted negotiations within the framework of this understanding, Bunker wrote, then the United States could move to phase two—presentation of terms for ending the fighting. But if Hanoi stuck to its old positions, then Bunker saw no point to continued meetings and discussions with its senior representatives. Faced with North Vietnamese intransigence, the negotiations should be closed as a waste of time. The United States would exit the Vietnam War under the terms of Vietnamization, leaving the burden of future fighting to the South Vietnamese.

Bunker then proposed for Kissinger a "package" of proposals for phase two of negotiations, assuming that Hanoi had agreed in phase one to move forward toward substantive discussions of peace. His recommended "package" had the following components:

- A date for the withdrawal of all US forces.

- Understanding that US forces would not leave entirely until US prisoners of war were released.

- A cease-fire in all of Southeast Asia effective September 1, 1971.

- Infiltration limited to the amount needed to provide for the rotation and supply of troops and to make up losses.

- International supervision of the cease-fire.

- Condition that on completion of the withdrawal of US forces and exchange of prisoners, all foreign troops would begin withdrawal from countries of Indochina (NVA [North Vietnamese Army] from Laos, Cambodia, and SVN [South Viet Nam]; Thais from Laos), such withdrawal to be completed within six months (i.e., by March 1, 1973).

Bunker's framework for an end to Hanoi's aggression took as its starting point President Nixon's speech of May 14, 1969.[17] Nixon had said then, "We have also ruled out either a one-sided withdrawal from Vietnam, or the acceptance in Paris of terms that would amount to a disguised American defeat . . . As soon as agreement can be reached, all non-South Vietnamese forces would begin withdrawals from South Vietnam."

Additional components included in Bunker's negotiating proposal were the following:

- Over a period of twelve months, by agreed-upon stages, the major portions of all US, allied, and other non–South Vietnamese forces would be withdrawn. At the end of this twelve-month period, the remaining US, allied, and other non–South Vietnamese forces would move into designated base areas and would not engage in combat operations.

- The remaining US and allied forces would complete their withdrawals as the remaining North Vietnamese forces were withdrawn and returned to North Vietnam.

With Bunker's proposal in hand, Kissinger approached Hanoi on April 24 to set up a secret meeting. After three weeks, the Communists agreed.

However, on April 22, six Democratic senators had spoken out on television against President Nixon's Vietnam policy. Only one, Henry Jackson, opposed unilateral withdrawal. The five others wanted a deadline to end American involvement supporting South Vietnam. Senator Birch Bayh said that the United States had no commitment to any government in South Vietnam. Senator George McGovern said that Vietnamization would not gain the release of American prisoners held in Hanoi. He was sure that if the United States pledged to bring all its troops home, Hanoi would release the prisoners. Edmund Muskie said that America had done for the South Vietnamese as much as anyone could reasonably expect. He wanted all American troops out by December 31, 1971, to terminate "bloodshed and terrible human suffering, the devastation of the lands of Indochina and the waste of resources desperately needed at home." Harold Hughes affirmed that there was no honor in prolonging the war "another week."

Two days later, several hundred thousand demonstrators began converging on Washington for a May Day protest against the Vietnam War.

The Senate Foreign Relations Committee opened hearings on legislation to end the war.

Nixon authorized Kissinger to reopen secret negotiations with Hanoi. This was the political context for the Nixon administration when Kissinger asked Bunker to formulate a new strategy for negotiations with Hanoi. At this time, Henry Kissinger saw himself as a bridge over the policy chasm separating President Nixon from his domestic opponents.

On April 25, the Gray Lady herself—the *New York Times*—pontificated, "Mr. Nixon can be assured of broad public support if he will abandon the cruel delusion of Vietnamization and declare unequivocally his intention to withdraw all American forces from Vietnam by an early fixed date."

Nixon talked to Kissinger, who was worried that the rising antiwar protests would weaken his negotiating position with Hanoi. Nixon told him not to worry about it and later made the point to his chief of staff, H. R. Haldeman, that he was going to let Kissinger go to Paris only once, or at the very most twice, and then give up on the negotiations.[18]

On April 29, Nixon rejected demands for unilateral withdrawal by a certain date. Without knowing it, Nixon thus rejected the "thinking out loud" proposal presented to Dobrynin by Kissinger on January 9.

The first days in May brought mass demonstrations into downtown Washington. Some eight thousand demonstrators were unconstitutionally arrested just to get them off the streets. Buses were lined up all around the White House enclosure as a temporary defensive perimeter against a potential angry mob bent on storming the president's home and office.

Caught between an unrelenting president and emotionally intense antiwar paranoia among the nation's intelligentsia and in Congress, Henry Kissinger buckled under the pressures exerted by these two policy extremes and secretly gave up the cause of defending South Vietnam against Communist aggression. It is also most likely that Kissinger was worried about his personal reputation among members of the Harvard faculty. He would need their approval to be reappointed to a tenured professorship after he left the government. He told one aide that he did not want to become "another Walt Rostow," who, just two years before, could not return to his professorship at MIT after serving as Lyndon Johnson's national security advisor.

In effect, Kissinger adopted the antiwar position of "Out, now!" But his policy of negotiating an agreement with Hanoi to save the "face" of South Vietnam while putting Hanoi in a position to win all in the last round after full American disengagement is better known as providing the South Vietnamese with a "decent interval" between American withdrawal and North Vietnamese conquest.

Before his May 31 secret Paris meeting with the Vietnamese Communist negotiator, Kissinger had several meetings and phone conversations with his president in which they discussed the secret negotiations.

In none of these conversations did Kissinger ask for Nixon's approval of a concession to Hanoi that would allow it to station its army divisions, tanks, and other supplies in South Vietnam after American combat forces withdrew in order to resume their aggression at a later date. As far as the official record of these conversations reveals, at no time did President Nixon authorize his national security advisor to make such a concession.

On February 18, 1971, Kissinger had spoken with Nixon to review the progress of the very large, full-scale "big battalion" South Vietnamese Operation Lam Son 719 into Laos to degrade Hanoi's capacity to reinforce and resupply its battalions in South Vietnam. Without revealing his concession to Hanoi passed on through Soviet ambassador Dobrynin, Kissinger adroitly slipped into his discussion with his president an indirect mention of that proposal to let Hanoi keep its army in South Vietnam, possibly forever. Nixon did not notice what Kissinger was really telling him through the silence of omission.

Nixon's concern in the conversation was South Vietnam's fighting capacity to take on and defeat North Vietnamese battalions:

Nixon: The main thing I'm interested in is just to be sure the South Vietnamese fight well—

Kissinger: That's right.

Nixon: —because they're going to be battling in there for years to come. I guess if they fight well, North Vietnam can never beat South Vietnam. Never. And it's because our South Vietnam has more people, and more—

In his mind that day, Nixon's objective in the Vietnam War was the following:

Nixon: I am thinking more in terms of Vietnam. For us, the objective of all these things is to get out of there and [unclear] it's not going to be done. We can't lose. We can lose an election, but we're not going to lose this war, Henry. That's my view. Do you agree with it?

Kissinger: I agree, Mr. President—

At the end of their discussion of Vietnam, Kissinger said:

Kissinger: What I think we can do, what I would recommend, Mr. President, in our game plan is if we get through this [unclear] bomb September, close to the election [November 1972], I ask for a meeting with Le Duc Tho. Then have it October 15th, and tell him, "Look, we're willing to give you a fixed deadline of total withdrawal next year for the release of all prisoners and a ceasefire." What we can then tell the South Vietnamese, "You've had a year without war to build up." And, I think, then, we can settle. We may have a fifty-fifty chance to get it.

> *Nixon: We should be able to get it. What the hell is their choice? [unclear]*
>
> *Kissinger: I think they may take it. But it's too early, because it would panic the South Vietnamese. But, after Thieu's election, I think we may able to do that.*
>
> *Nixon: Okay.*

What Kissinger left out of his proposed peace terms was the requirement for North Vietnam to remove its army from South Vietnam. Nixon did not seem to notice that omission.[19]

President Nixon's anxiety was narrowly focused on publicly positioning his Vietnam policy to undermine the antiwar movement and secure approval from the American people as measured by public opinion polls. Nixon instructed Kissinger to make a proposal that would commit the Americans to complete withdrawal of their combat forces from the war but that the Vietnamese Communists would reject. He did not discuss with Kissinger long-term strategic issues of the balance of forces between North and South Vietnam after a peace agreement. He also did not discuss betrayal of President Thieu and his government in Saigon. As Kissinger was preparing to leave for Paris in late May, President Nixon had fixed in his mind that the terms to be offered Hanoi were only 1) a deadline by which all American forces would leave South Vietnam, 2) a cease-fire in place across all battlefields in Indochina, and 3) a return of all prisoners of war. Nixon said nothing that was inconsistent with his public commitment to a North Vietnamese withdrawal of its army from South Vietnam.

Nothing had been said between the two men or included in the terms they discussed regarding the presence of North Vietnamese forces in Laos, Cambodia, and South Vietnam after the cease-fire went into effect.

On April 17, Nixon had a private conversation with his aides H. R. Haldeman and Henry Kissinger where he worried over the fate of the South Vietnamese if the Communists should ever conquer the country.[20]

In response, Kissinger committed in his forthcoming negotiations only to giving a terminal date for Americans in combat linked to a cease-fire and a return of American prisoners of war. Nixon insisted on an announcement of the "end of the American combat role."

On April 21, Nixon and Kissinger held a discouraging conversation on the negative public reaction to the South Vietnamese military operation inside Laos to degrade Hanoi's ability to send more men and supplies into South Vietnam. In the course of an emotional, rambling review of events, Nixon said, "I had no intention of announcing a cave-in as you know." But he also said, "I've got to have good news . . . People have got to know the war is over." Then he asked Kissinger, "Henry, how far could we go short of a bug out?"[21]

On April 23, President Nixon affirmed for his national security advisor that American policy was "to win the war," by which he meant "letting South Vietnam survive, that's all."[22] Kissinger added, "To come out honorably." Nixon affirmed, "That wins the war." Later in the conversation, Nixon stated that "and then we will be supporting the Thieu-Ky government with military assistance."

One can conclude from this that Nixon had no intention of turning South Vietnam over to the Communists after all American combat forces returned home.

Nixon was clear on what Kissinger was to accomplish: "The idea that the purpose is, is not to get them to accept the offer—we hope to Christ they don't."

Kissinger again affirmed that his plan was "I'd say, 'We'll give you a date, if you're willing to do—have a ceasefire and a repatriation of prisoners.'" Nothing about terms and conditions to be followed after the cease-fire went into effect.

On April 26, Nixon told Kissinger that "you've got to show them right after these demonstrations that we're not going to be affected by them."[23] But Nixon alerted Kissinger to the politics of getting something on the record about American prisoners of war: "I don't give a damn about the Congress, demonstrators, or anything else, but I've got to keep the POW wives from taking off. They could really hurt us."

On May 6, in a private conversation with White House Chief of Staff Haldeman and Deputy Assistant for National Security General Alexander Haig, Nixon disparaged Kissinger's fixation on the secret negotiations, referring to "his little Mickey Mouse game of going over to Paris and seeing those fellows."[24] Nixon gave instructions that he wanted to have a meeting with President Thieu in June to make some announcement about ending America's combat role "at a certain time." He reiterated his understanding of the forthcoming American offer to Hanoi: "As of a date certain, if you'll give us a ceasefire and release our prisoners, we'll be out." He wanted Thieu to announce that the South Vietnamese would "assume full combat responsibility at a certain time."

On May 10, Nixon again noted in a conversation with Kissinger that the American proposal to Hanoi would be "for a deadline, ceasefire and prisoners"—with no additional concessions tabled.[25] Pointedly, Nixon did not propose any deal that would threaten South Vietnam with annihilation.

The next step in the betrayal of South Vietnam came on May 25. That day, Kissinger commented in passing during a conversation with his president that the Frenchman Jean Sainteny was in Washington and that the two had met.[26] Sainteny had brought up the package of proposals that Kissinger was about to present to Hanoi, and Sainteny's judgment was that "just to do it for the prisoners is too little." Insidiously, Kissinger did not disclose to his president that Sainteny also brought to Kissinger assurances from Hanoi confirming its willingness to save American face and prestige if the Americans would agree to let Hanoi win the war at the end of the day. Sainteny had closed the loop between Kissinger and Hanoi in Kissinger's unauthorized personal dealmaking with Hanoi inside the secret negotiations he was charged with undertaking as an official of the US government to talk with officials of the Vietnamese Communist government, secret negotiations carried out rather behind the back of the American allies the Vietnamese Nationalists. Kissinger's personal exploration—as a faithless agent of his president—of an unauthorized deal within a deal linked him to the Soviets, the Soviets to the Vietnamese Communists, the Vietnamese

Communists to their old patron Jean Sainteny, and finally Sainteny back to Kissinger in Washington. Left out of this closed communications loop were President Nixon, Ambassador Bunker, and South Vietnamese president Nguyen Van Thieu.

A memorandum of Kissinger's May 25 conversation with Sainteny was made.[27] Sainteny reported to Kissinger and some of his staff over lunch that "Hanoi" did not fully believe that the Americans would leave Vietnam but that "if they were assured of this and of a certain number of seats for the NLF in the Assembly, they would come to terms on POWs, ceasefire, and the separation of the two Vietnamese for a number of years."

The memorandum also noted that Hanoi's point about having its NLF subordinates join South Vietnam's National Assembly might satisfy them only "for the time being," Sainteny having said nothing about Hanoi's willingness to abandon its war of conquest at any time in the near or distant future.

Here Sainteny put on the table for Henry Kissinger Hanoi's assurance that a "decent interval" tactic would let the Americans leave South Vietnam without losing face immediately but would give Hanoi the victory it craved after "a number of years" had passed.

Kissinger would later write of Sainteny's views on war between Communist and Nationalist Vietnamese that "like many Frenchmen who had served in Indochina, he considered our enterprise hopeless; unlike many of his compatriots, he understood the importance of an honorable exit for America and for other free peoples."[28] Years later, on September 30, 2010, in a State Department conference on the history of American involvement in Southeast Asia, Kissinger would parrot Sainteny's dismissal of Vietnamese Nationalism and Vietnamese Nationalists. Kissinger affirmed that the central American objective of "preserving an independent, viable South Vietnamese state was unachievable."[29]

The substance of what Sainteny conveyed about Hanoi's policy was that it would not give up its effort to conquer South Vietnam, though it could delay the timing of its victory. Years later, in 1988, Hanoi leader Le Duc Tho confirmed the accuracy of Sainteny's report to Henry Kissinger about Hanoi's strategy.[30] Tho said then, "For us the most fundamental question was that the US had to pull out its forces but ours would remain where they were . . . The withdrawal of the US from SVN and the keeping of our forces there was an extremely fundamental and important question that would change the relation of force on the battlefield to our advantage."

However much Kissinger's low opinion of the Vietnamese Nationalists had been stimulated by Sainteny's colonialist disdain for them, Kissinger's lack of respect for and confidence in the South Vietnamese cause had been augmented by his trips to Vietnam in 1965 and 1966. In August 1965, American ambassador to Saigon Henry Cabot Lodge had invited Kissinger to visit and advise him.[31] After his visit, Kissinger had concluded, "Since there were no front lines within South Vietnam and since the Johnson Administration refused to pursue the guerillas into the sanctuaries just across the border in Laos and Cambodia, I advocated a negotiated solution."

In 1966, Kissinger visited South Vietnam again. He left doubting the chances for a Nationalist victory over the Communists, and so he encouraged pursuit of negotiations with Hanoi in order to extricate the United States from the conflict.[32]

On the same day that he had lunched with Sainteny and received word of Hanoi's acceptance of his "decent interval" proposal, May 25, 1971, Kissinger informed Bunker that, at his next meeting with Hanoi, the Americans would omit any discussion of Bunker's suggested phase one and would immediately put on the table with the Communists Bunker's substantive proposals for a peace settlement. That meeting with Hanoi's representative, Xuan Thuy, was only six days away, on May 31, in Paris.

This decision by Kissinger to drop the stern recital of hard facts that Bunker had included in his phase one meeting now had the Americans on the defensive, becoming a supplicant to Hanoi, making no commitments to the future security of South Vietnam, and only seeking a way out for US forces. In his phase one, Bunker had been emphatic that the United States would have a long-term commitment to the people of South Vietnam. Now that moral commitment was to be abandoned. In effect, Kissinger was acting on Sainteny's recommendation that in its negotiations with Hanoi, the United States should focus only on leaving South Vietnam and providing space for the NLF inside the Saigon government.

Kissinger therefore made three changes to Bunker's proposal. Two were inconsequential. One was betrayal.

President Nixon's national security advisor deleted mention of any specific dates in connection with the complete withdrawal of US forces and the coming into force of a cease-fire. These dates were dependent on the completion of negotiations and thus had no importance in and of themselves.

Then Kissinger rejected Bunker's requirement that North Vietnamese forces leave Laos, Cambodia, and South Vietnam. He told Bunker that the United States' position on that point would be only that the peoples of Indochina should discuss this question among themselves.[33]

With this decision, Kissinger condemned the Vietnamese Nationalists to almost certain defeat after the coming American withdrawal of combat forces. The correlation of forces would then be very much against them. First, they would have to fight cheek by jowl with not just weakened and demoralized Viet Cong guerilla platoons and companies but also North Vietnamese regiments supported by tanks, artillery, and antiaircraft missiles. Second, with the North Vietnamese army left in Laos along that country's long border with South Vietnam, Hanoi could continue to use the Ho Chi Minh Trail to resupply its forces inside South Vietnam and reinforce them at will with new battalions and regiments, recruited and trained in North Vietnam and then sent south.

Kissinger made this invidious decision to give up a proper defense of South Vietnam in the long run even though, on April 17, President Nixon had told him that if the negotiations did not make progress, "it tells the enemy that in no uncertain terms that, by God, you're going to do—we're going to stay right there, and also, I've thrown out something there, as you noticed: that we're going to bomb 'em, which we damn well will. If we've withdrawn and they haven't returned a thing, we'll bomb the hell out of North Vietnam. Get my point? Just bomb the living bejeezus out of it."[34]

In an earlier conversation on April 7, Nixon had affirmed to Henry

Kissinger that: "Yeah. And if it doesn't work, I don't care. I mean, [Kissinger attempts to interject] right now, if it doesn't work, then let me say, though, I'm going to find out soon. And then I'm going to turn right so goddamn hard it'll make your head spin. We'll bomb those bastards right out of the—off the earth. I really mean it."[35]

Bunker was unaware of Kissinger's fundamental change of heart on how best to end the war—the idea that Kissinger had proposed to the Russian ambassador in January, which Winston Lord had put in writing on April 12, and which had been accepted by Hanoi as confirmed by the Frenchman Sainteny. Kissinger did not inform Bunker of the terms proposed by Hanoi as presented by Sainteny—that the Americans could get a peace agreement if they would just let South Vietnam lose the war after a "decent interval" had passed after the American disengagement. Bunker was unaware that, now, Kissinger was no longer following the policy enunciated by his president.

Bunker responded to Kissinger's rather cursory communication of the three changes he would make to Bunker's recommended negotiating "package" with the comment that the changes seemed "advisable."[36]

On May 27, 1971, Bunker met with President Thieu, informing him that Kissinger would again meet with a representative of Hanoi on May 31 in Paris only to "probe the other side's thinking." Bunker reported to the South Vietnamese president that only political issues—not military ones, like withdrawal of North Vietnamese regiments from South Vietnam, Laos, and Cambodia—would be "discussed among the Vietnamese parties themselves." Bunker reported that "Thieu interposed no objection and thought it a good idea to probe the other side's views once again."[37]

Thieu was left completely in the dark about how Kissinger really intended to approach Hanoi's negotiators—not with a passive probing of their views but with a heartrending concession of his own, a concession threatening the survival of South Vietnam in line with the stipulation passed on by Sainteny. Of course, Bunker too had not been fully informed by Kissinger about his new approach to extrication of the United States from any further obligation to defend South Vietnam. Bunker simply passed on his lack of understanding to Thieu.

Not until 1980, when he and I were going over these old secret messages while working together on his memoirs, did Bunker realize that Kissinger had not kept him fully informed.

General Creighton Abrams, the American commander and senior advisor to the South Vietnamese military, was also not told about the American concession—that after American forces withdrew, the Vietnamese Nationalists, his allies, would have to fight on against Hanoi's divisions based in South Vietnam.[38] Abrams therefore never modified his plans for the equipping of South Vietnam's military with additional tanks, aircraft, logistics capabilities, reserves of ammunition, and everything else needed to fight intense conventional battles with North Vietnamese regular battalions, regiments, and divisions. Failure to plan for such future conflict left South Vietnam very much at a disadvantage whenever any peace agreement would be reached between Hanoi and Washington.

On May 28, 1971, Kissinger sent to President Nixon a memorandum outlining the elements in the new proposal he would present to Hanoi in Paris.[39] He did not disclose to his president 1) that Ambassador Bunker had proposed that Hanoi withdraw all its forces from South Vietnam as a condition for ending the war, 2) that Kissinger himself had overruled Bunker and would tell Hanoi that it could keep its army in South Vietnam after the withdrawal of American combat forces, and 3) that President Thieu was ignorant of this proposed abandonment of South Vietnam's long-term prospects for freedom and independence. President Nixon was not told that if Hanoi would in the future use its forces left inside South Vietnam to conquer that country, the sacrifice of so many Americans in the war would have been in vain.

Kissinger's May 28, 1971, memo to his president said, in relevant part,

As you know, I am scheduled to meet with Xuan Thuy again Monday morning, May 31, in Paris . . .

Second, I will lay out our package proposal which includes our readiness to set a terminal date for the withdrawal of all our forces from South Vietnam as part of an overall settlement; an Indochina ceasefire-in-place; no infiltration of outside forces into the countries of Indochina; international supervision of the ceasefire and its provisions; respect for the 1954 and 1962 Geneva Accords; and the release of all prisoners of war . . .

If we could negotiate something along these lines I think we and the South Vietnamese would be in a good position . . .

Ambassador Bunker has informed Thieu of our meeting. He told Thieu that we will follow up the other side's recent ambiguous public statements in Paris and discuss the relationship between ceasefire, POWs, and the US withdrawals. He reaffirmed that we will not agree to the other side's political demands and stressed again the need for absolute secrecy about this channel.

Thieu made no objections and thought it a good idea to probe the other side's view again.

When he met with the North Vietnamese on May 31, 1971, Kissinger's proposal read in relevant part as follows: "Second, the Vietnamese and the other peoples of Indochina should discuss among themselves the manner in which all other outside forces would withdraw from the countries of Indochina."

With this reference to the "Vietnamese" as a single people, Kissinger conceptually abandoned South Vietnam. His new negotiating proposal made no reference to South and North Vietnam as two independent, equal nation-states owing one another respect and mutual tolerance under international law. Kissinger also did not put on the table for Hanoi to accept an American demand that the North Vietnamese withdraw all their forces from South Vietnam. The people of South Vietnam were thus abandoned to whatever fate Hanoi would and could impose on them in the years to come.

Kissinger's decision to minimize American demands on Hanoi to the detriment of its ally South Vietnam contradicted his personal recommendations of January 1969.[40] He had then advised,

> *American objectives should therefore be (1) to bring about a staged withdrawal of external forces, North Vietnamese and American, (2) thereby to create a maximum incentive for the contending forces in South Viet Nam to work out a political agreement. The United States, then, should concentrate on the subject of the mutual withdrawal of external forces and avoid negotiating about the internal structure of South Viet Nam for as long as possible. The primary responsibility for negotiating the internal structure of South Viet Nam should be left for direct negotiations among the South Vietnamese. Similarly, we cannot be expected to rely on Hanoi's word that the removal of its forces and pressures from South Viet Nam is permanent.*

Kissinger also knew that the terms of any cease-fire that he proposed would very likely become the last word on control of the territory and so shape the balance of power in the final settlement of the conflict. In 1969, he had written, "However, negotiating a ceasefire may well be tantamount to establishing the preconditions of a political settlement . . . If Saigon is prevented from entering certain areas, it means in effect partition which, as in Laos, tends toward permanency." Accordingly, on May 31, 1971, Kissinger can be held to have known with certainty that whatever he gave away to Hanoi would be a permanent concession. His failure to demand withdrawal of North Vietnam forces from South Vietnam was creating a partition of that war-torn country and was giving the Vietnamese Communists very important military assets inside South Vietnam, strategic assets making possible their ultimate victory over the Nationalists.

The transcript of Kissinger's presentation to the North Vietnamese reads as follows:

Here is our final proposal for a settlement. There will be no other in this Administration.

First, we are prepared to set a terminal date for the withdrawal of all our forces from South Vietnam. We would, as I have indicated earlier, arrange for roughly the same timetable for the withdrawal of other Allied forces.

Second, the Vietnamese and the other peoples of Indochina should discuss among themselves the manner in which all other outside forces would withdraw from the countries of Indochina.

Third, there should be a ceasefire in place throughout Indochina, to become effective at the time when US withdrawals based on the final agreed timetable begin.

Fourth, as part of the ceasefire, there should be no further infiltration of outside forces into the countries of Indochina.

Fifth, there should be international supervision of the ceasefire and its provisions.

Sixth, both sides should renew their pledge to respect the 1954 and 1962 Geneva Accords, to respect the neutrality, territorial integrity, and independence of Laos and Cambodia. This could be formalized at an international conference.

Seventh, I want to reiterate our proposal for the immediate release of all prisoners of war and innocent civilians held by both sides throughout Indochina. We believe this issue should be settled immediately on a humanitarian basis. If this is not done, the men must be released as an integral part of the settlement we are proposing in our final offer. We would expect your side would present a complete list of all prisoners held throughout Indochina on the day an agreement is reached. The release of the prisoners would begin on the same day as our withdrawals under the agreed timetable. The release of prisoners would be completed at least two months before the completion of our final withdrawals. We are prepared to talk concretely and to make rapid progress.

Later in the discussion, Kissinger said, "With respect to the second question, we believe that the proposal we have made reflects the reality of the current situation. When US forces are finally withdrawn, the political future of South Vietnam will have to be left to the Vietnamese."[41]

Luu Van Loi and Nguyen Anh Vu, members of Hanoi's delegation in the secret negotiations, noted in their book that Kissinger's proposal was the first time the United States had not demanded a withdrawal of North Vietnamese troops from South Vietnam.[42] They reported that Hanoi's Foreign Ministry concluded that the United States was "making concessions from a weak position."

Seymour Hersh reported that North Vietnamese diplomat and foreign minister Nguyen Co Thach later recalled, "Kissinger touched on the question of the Decent Interval, saying that the withdrawal of American troops would have a big effect on the internal political processes of South Vietnam, and the USA would accept a neutral South Vietnam."[43]

So Kissinger officially put before the Vietnamese Communists the terms that he had suggested to Soviet ambassador Dobrynin on January 9 and that had then been accepted by Hanoi as Sainteny reported to Kissinger: 1) withdrawal of US combat forces and 2) no withdrawal of North Vietnamese combat forces.

In his memoir *White House Years*, Kissinger described the proposal he tabled with Xuan Thuy of Hanoi on May 31, 1971, as "a turning point in our diplomacy in Vietnam." Kissinger went on to say, "Indeed, in its essence it was accepted sixteen months later by Hanoi."[44] But what Hanoi finally accepted was not Bunker's proposal but Kissinger's betrayal of South Vietnam's aspirations for freedom and independence.

Hanoi, of course, liked Kissinger's proposal as soon as he presented it because his few requirements presaged future American abandonment of South Vietnam. In *White House Years*, Kissinger recalled, "Xuan Thuy was too subtle not to recognize immediately that we had made a major change on the military issues."[45] Hanoi was suddenly eager to negotiate and to meet again with Kissinger.

To be fair, Kissinger was candid—to a point—in his memoirs regarding his decision to accept the continued presence of North Vietnamese forces in Laos, Cambodia, and South Vietnam. He wrote that his proposal "recognized that since we were withdrawing most of our forces unilaterally, we could not use them to bargain for total Hanoi withdrawal."[46]

From other points of view, there was sense to Kissinger's decision that American forces would withdraw unilaterally from fighting to defend Vietnam, Laos, and Cambodia. First, unilateral withdrawal was the growing demand of the antiwar movement and the Democratic Party. Second, Kissinger had always wanted to separate the "military" from the "political" issues in order to reach an end to the war through negotiations.[47] With a unilateral withdrawal of American forces, the U.S. military confrontation with Hanoi just disappeared; only political issues between Communists and Nationalists were left. They could be easily turned over to the local parties to negotiate a balance of interests and advantages.

Apparently, what Kissinger did not appreciate enough intellectually is that in a struggle to become the sovereign authority in a state, there can be no compromise. There can be only one ultimate winner. Such a struggle under the norms of international law has to be a win/lose zero-sum game of thrones. A sole sovereign may be magnanimous in victory and permit some decentralization of authority, say, in a federal system, but such an arrangement about how a country shall be ruled occurs or does not occur at the discretion of the sovereign and no one else. Military power cannot be separated out from the struggle as who shall be sovereign and so divorced from political questions such as who will control the army and the police and who will organize elections. Somebody has to set the obligatory national rules for politics, and that somebody is the sovereign. Monopoly control of violence is the basis for sovereign authority in a state. So possession of military and police powers is necessary to gain such a monopoly. By giving Hanoi robust military power in South Vietnam, Kissinger tipped the balance of political competition among the Vietnamese living there very much in favor of the Communists in the long run.

More insidiously, Kissinger, a highly educated man, had made a categorical mistake in his understanding of war. He presumed that the "military" could be isolated and kept separate from the "political." This misapprehension of human reality blinded him to the very real-world consequences of negotiating with Hanoi to compartmentalize "military" issues, like the presence of American, Australian, Thai, South Korean, and North Vietnamese forces in South Vietnam, and put in another compartment the "political" issues of who was to be accepted as having legitimate authority over the South Vietnamese people. Kissinger did not seem to have internalized the fundamentals of war as notoriously explicated by Carl von Clausewitz in his 1832 masterwork, *On War*.[48]

Von Clausewitz understood with perfect rationality that war is a duality, the product of material means and strength of will. He postulated that the war of a community "always starts from a political condition and is called forth by a political motive. . . . Under all circumstances War is to be regarded not as an independent thing, but as a political instrument." In his famous words taught to generations of military officers, "war is a mere continuation of policy by other means."

In particular, the will of the enemy must be subdued.

The moral forces are among the most important subjects in War. They form the spirit which permeates the whole being of War. These forces fasten themselves soonest and with the greatest affinity on to the Will which puts in motion and guides the whole mass of powers, uniting with it as it were in one stream, because this is a moral force itself. . . . We might say the physical are almost no more than the wooden handle, whilst the moral are the noble metal, the real bright-polished weapons.

In war, politics cannot be separated from the military. South Vietnam's President Nguyen Van Thieu understood this very well. So did Le Duan in Hanoi.

Later in 1974 and 1975, Kissinger would learn to his distress that his Vietnamese Communist collaborators in the secret Paris peace negotiations would never forget Mao Zedong's iron law on the origin of political power—guns.

They would then, with great enthusiasm, use "guns" to gain total control over South Vietnam and all South Vietnamese. And so would Le Duan and Le Duc Tho teach Kissinger a hard lesson on the strategic advantages of never separating the "military" from the "political."

Or, perhaps, Henry Kissinger, the Harvard professor of diplomatic history and geopolitical rivalries among states, was only using the words "military" and "politics" as rhetorical devices.

To mask his desire to abandon the Nationalists in South Vietnam, he used the word "military" to mean American interests and the word "politics" to mean South Vietnamese interests. When he spoke of a strategy to separate the "military" from the "political" in his peace negotiations, in reality he was indirectly advocating an uncoupling of American interests from South Vietnamese interests, a divorce without alimony for the more dependent spouse—a legal separation leaving the Vietnamese Nationalists to go it alone against Hanoi.

By following this contrived understanding, in Kissinger's negotiations, the Americans could unilaterally further their own interests when discussing "military" issues with Hanoi and let the South Vietnamese separately worry about their future in their independent discussions with Hanoi about "politics." Such clever word play would be in keeping with a conscience unable to honor the moral obligations of one alliance partner to another in times of great difficulty for both.

This way of thinking could quite easily justify Kissinger's not giving Nguyen Van Thieu any power to shape the outcomes of the secret negotiations and leaving him out in the diplomatic cold—even perhaps letting him freeze to death. Thieu's right to negotiate for his country's survival would arise only when "political" issues could be discussed. By then, however, the Americans would no longer be at the table in his support.

Moreover, using such rhetoric diverted American attention away from responding effectively to the realities of war as so precisely described by von Clausewitz. This distraction from the truth could only point the Americans towards failure.

And during the war to defend South Vietnam, one of the most overused American cliches was the need to "win the hearts and minds." In other words, to base strategy and tactics on a continuum of morality, politics, policing, and the most violent combat. With the Vietnamese, the wellspring of their "morale," the drive of their will, and the political half of the war was Nationalism. To defeat the Communists, Vietnamese Nationalism had to be put front and center in every effort, just as von Clausewitz recommended. This was just as President Eisenhower insisted in his October 1954 letter to South Vietnam's then prime minister, Ngo Dinh Diem.

Tragically, Henry Kissinger was personally and spiritually incapable of doing what was necessary to win the Vietnam War. Relying most of all on the French colonialist Jean Sainteny to help him understand the Vietnamese, Kissinger never felt the real presence of genuine Vietnamese-ness, the mystical prowess of "mountains and rivers," and so never comprehended the psychic and political reality that was a Vietnamese ethic and ethnic identity some two thousand years in the making. He would learn that Vietnamese—both Communist and Nationalist—were stubborn and single-minded, but he would never come to see the big picture of just how "politics" and "war" were integrated in that culture. Therefore, Kissinger never got to the bottom of the Vietnam War—as von Clausewitz insisted should be done—if it were to be won by the United States and the South Vietnamese Nationalists. By separating the "military from politics," what Kissinger accomplished was a dramatic change in "politics."

Accordingly, Kissinger never conducted his negotiations with the Vietnamese Communist leaders in Hanoi in ways that would hammer at their will, undermine their morale even a little, and use the politics of Vietnamese Nationalism to overcome their self-promoting militarism. Ironically, it would be the Vietnamization program begun by President Lyndon Johnson in 1967, carried out by President Richard Nixon from 1968 to 1972 and supervised by Ellsworth Bunker that would do exactly that and, by 1972, would defeat the Viet Cong and impose a stalemate on the North Vietnamese army. Vietnamization brought together the political and the military sides of war, just as von Clausewitz had taught.

To his credit, Bunker was more sophisticated than Kissinger, or—much more likely—he was less eager than Kissinger for a deal in the secret talks. Bunker knew that residual US forces in South Vietnam combined with continued US assistance to South Vietnam could still be traded with Hanoi for substantial concessions on military and political issues. Bunker's understanding of that favorable linkage supported his recommendations for stressing a phase one in the secret negotiations, the phase that Kissinger dropped from his negotiating strategy.

Why had Kissinger really given up on demands for the withdrawal of North Vietnamese troops?

That demand was fixed and absolute on Thieu's part as necessary for the long-term survival of South Vietnam.

On June 3, Ambassador Bunker met with President Thieu to brief him on the results of Kissinger's secret May 31 meeting with North Vietnam's Xuan Thuy.[49] Again, Bunker reassured Thieu about the future withdrawal of North Vietnamese troops from South Vietnam. Bunker told South Vietnam's president that Kissinger was still negotiating within the framework of President Nixon's speech of October 1970: "i.e., cease-fire in all Southeast Asia, international supervision of cease-fire, prisoner exchange, withdrawal of our troops and eventual withdrawal of all foreign troops from Indo-China." Accordingly, Thieu did not know on June 3 that Kissinger personally had crossed a Rubicon to now provide support for Hanoi's aggression in the long run, putting at hazard all American and Vietnamese sacrifices in the war.

In his memoir of his years as President Nixon's national security advisor, Kissinger inexplicably wrote about Thieu that "with his concurrence also, we had formally abandoned the demand for mutual withdrawal in our secret proposal of May 31, 1971."[50]

Bunker then reported to Kissinger his discussions with Thieu, repeating for Nixon's wily national security advisor the representations made to President Thieu on behalf of the government of the United States that the secret negotiations were still taking place within the framework of demanding complete withdrawal of North Vietnamese troops from South Vietnam.

Kissinger said nothing in reply to Bunker's report of his conversation with Thieu.

Kissinger's silence served to lull both Bunker and Thieu into a misunderstanding regarding his real intentions. Kissinger did not correct Bunker about the reassuring falsehood that the elderly ambassador had passed on to Thieu. For his part, Bunker construed Kissinger's silence as evidence that Bunker's interpretation was correct, and that Washington was still on a path in the secret negotiations of unyielding determination to save South Vietnam from aggression.[51]

However, in Hanoi the Politburo had in May decided to once again launch a mighty offensive in South Vietnam to "force the US imperialists to negotiate an end of the war from a position of defeat." Accordingly, in June the Central Party Military Committee approved a combat plan to use in South Vietnam during the coming year, 1972, with the principal objective of trashing Vietnamization. The plan called for the deployment of from nine to twelve North Vietnamese regular divisions, supplemented by armor and heavy artillery, to three attack zones in South Vietnam—northeast of Saigon, the mountainous Central Highlands, and north and west of the city of Hue. One goal of the planned offensive was to "move our main force units back into the various battlefields of South Vietnam and provide them with a firm foothold there."[52] Thus, Hanoi moved adroitly to have in place inside South Vietnam an invasion force to activate in the future after 1) the withdrawal of American forces from South Vietnam and 2) the expiration of a "decent interval" during which the people of South Vietnam would have experienced freedom and independence.

On July 1, Kissinger left Washington for a secret trip to Beijing to advance President Nixon's dramatic and unprecedented diplomatic effort to move toward a détente with the two great Communist powers, the Soviet Union and Mao Zedong's People's Republic of China. On his way, he stopped in Saigon. When meeting there with President Thieu, he reported that "there was nothing new" in the secret Paris talks with Hanoi.[53]

Mao Zedong, the Great Helmsman, as he was reverently called in China, never made Kissinger's mistake of wanting to separate the military from the political. Mao even quoted von Clausewitz's dictum that war is the continuation of politics, adding in his own words, "War is politics and war itself is a political action." Then Mao famously proposed his own dictum: "Every Communist must grasp the truth 'political power grows out of the barrel of a gun.'"

Mao's quote is even more powerful in Vietnamese: "*Sung de ra chinh quyen*" ("Guns give birth to government.")[54]

To prepare for his meetings with Chinese leaders in Beijing, Kissinger had been provided by his staff with a briefing book compiling in one place many important summaries of facts and circumstances, along with accepted official wording on policy issues and options. In the section of the briefing book on Indochina, Kissinger scribbled some words to conform what had been written by his staff with his intentions. After this sentence—"On behalf of President Nixon I want to assure the prime minister [Zhou Enlai] solemnly that the United States is prepared to make a settlement that will truly leave the political evolution of South Vietnam to the Vietnamese alone. We are ready to withdraw all of our forces by a fixed date and let objective realities shape the political future"—Kissinger wrote by hand in the left margin, "We want a decent interval. You have our assurance."[55]

Here Kissinger expressly referred to giving the South Vietnamese only a "decent interval" after the withdrawal of American forces from the defense of their homeland against Hanoi's aggression.

Just a few days previously, when meeting in Saigon with President Thieu and Ambassador Bunker, Kissinger had not used the words "decent interval" to describe the future he envisioned for the South Vietnamese, leaving his allies completely in the dark about his plans for them.[56]

On July 4, 1971, Henry Kissinger and Ambassador Bunker had called on President Thieu. In their meeting, Kissinger did not reveal to his South Vietnamese allies that he had made a unilateral but existential—from the South Vietnamese point of view—decision about the future war-making capacity of North Vietnam: that Hanoi could leave its forces in South Vietnam after signing a "peace" agreement.

The memorandum making a record of their discussion of progress in the Paris negotiations includes these points:

» *Dr. Kissinger told President Thieu about the last Paris meeting with Le Duc Tho and Xuan Thuy. He said that as Ambassador Bunker had explained, the first meeting (May 31) had no real content and was simply an exploration of their willingness to negotiate. In the second meeting (June 26) the North Vietnamese gave us a nine point program which was roughly the same as the seven point program of Madame Binh (a senior NLF spokesperson) in Paris on Thursday. Four days after promising not to make the proposal public, Madame Binh's proposal, which was almost exactly the same, was published. One could see how trustworthy they were.*

» *He told President Thieu that the U.S. had said that under no circumstances would it do anything to interfere with the government in Saigon. He assured President Thieu that under no circumstances would the U.S. agree with any such proposals.*

» *Another interesting aspect of the North Vietnamese proposal [said Kissinger] was that for the first time they said it was negotiable, and they were willing to bargain. Always before they said, "you must" while this time they said, "you should." When Dr. Kissinger would object, they would say, let's bargain, whereas formerly they would say their proposals were the basis of negotiations. This time they said that we should talk about both our proposals and their proposals and bargain.*

» Secondly, President Thieu said, having studied the proposal he thought that the only new thing was on prisoners, which was aimed at the U.S. public rather than the Vietnamese.

» Thursday [a forthcoming meeting] the US and GVN should primarily ask questions, bringing out points like "agree" versus "discuss" and the fact that "national concord" was no real change in position.

» Dr. Kissinger, Ambassador Bunker, and President Thieu agreed that the allied side should concentrate on asking questions this week and avoid a flat answer within a week, there being many points to clarify.

Thus did his private meeting with his agent in the peace negotiations—the American National Security Advisor—leave President Thieu with no knowledge of Kissinger's decision to accept a peace agreement which would leave South Vietnam subject to continued invasion and renewed war.

Nguyen Phu Duc, Thieu's special advisor on foreign relations, commented in his memoirs that, on this occasion, Kissinger "could have taken that opportunity to keep the GVN abreast of the major concessions he had made and discussed them in an exchange of views on general negotiating strategy."[57]

In his meetings with Chinese prime minister Zhou Enlai, Kissinger reviewed the state of his secret Paris negotiations with the North Vietnamese.[58] In his July 10, 1971, meeting with Zhou, Kissinger affirmed for the Chinese leader, a patron of and arms supplier to Hanoi, the enemy of America's ally South Vietnam, that what

we require is a transition period between the military withdrawal and the political solution. Not so that we can re-enter but so that we can let the people of Vietnam and other parts of Indochina determine their own fate . . . I have told the Prime Minister yesterday, and I am willing to repeat this, that if after complete American withdrawal, the Indochinese people change their governments, the U.S. will not interfere.

In plain English, the National Security Advisor to the President of the United States told a rival great power that the countries of South Vietnam, Laos, and Cambodia were being abandoned to fate. But not just any fate—anyone of Kissinger's intelligence could with great confidence predict that fate as military subjugation to a Communist Party. And so it was to be: in 1975 South Vietnam, Cambodia, and Laos would be taken over by Communist parties. In his meeting with Zhou Enlai, Kissinger committed the United States to washing its hands of responsibility for their well-being and to accepting whatever violations of international law and abuses of human rights that the peoples of those countries would suffer.

It is most notable that in these private conversations with Prime Minister Zhou, Kissinger imposed no condition on North Vietnam either to withdraw its forces from South Vietnam or to accept constitutional freedoms for the South Vietnamese.

At no time in these discussions with Prime Minister Zhou did Kissinger make any commitment to support the Vietnamese Nationalists or to legitimate their right to self-governance. He said only: "We will permit the political solution of South Vietnam to evolve and leave it to the Vietnamese alone."

Apparently, Kissinger's understanding of "political evolution" was rather Darwinian, where might makes right and only the fittest among "the Vietnamese" would survive.

By speaking to Premier Zhou of "the Vietnamese" as only one political community, not two, Kissinger, the adept student of Jean Sainteny, implied that Nationalist South Vietnamese had no rights—moral or legal—to self-determination as an independent national community. Or at least, he made no effort to defend their having any such rights, revealing yet again his disdain for his supposed allies.

On his return from Beijing, Kissinger drafted a long memorandum for President Nixon, dated July 14, 1971, recounting his discussions with Premier Zhou Enlai. Significantly, he did not report to his president 1) that he had presented to the Chinese leadership exactly what he had written down as "decent interval" for South Vietnam after the withdrawal of all American forces and 2) that the United States would not object to a subsequent conquest of South Vietnam by Hanoi.

What he memorialized to President Nixon about his discussions with Premier Zhou regarding the Vietnam War included little more than these cryptic observations:

- On Indochina, as on Taiwan, I noted the need for time for a political evolution and I re-emphasized the link between the two questions.

- especially after I explained the positions we had taken in Paris

- stressed Chinese interest in an "honorable exit" for the U.S.

- In addition, I reviewed the current situation in Paris and pointed out that the talks were blocked because of Hanoi's insistence on the overthrow of Thieu and its refusal to agree to a ceasefire. I warned that a breakdown in the negotiations would mean continuation of the war, with incalculable consequences.

In mentioning the "positions we had taken in Paris," Kissinger did not elaborate that those "positions" included his May 31 proposal that North Vietnam need not withdraw its forces from South Vietnam, once again leaving President Nixon in the dark as to that concession to Hanoi.[59]

Neither Haldeman in the diary he kept while devotedly serving Nixon in the White House nor Nixon himself in *The Memoirs of Richard Nixon* expressed awareness of a major compromise being made with the Communists by Henry Kissinger on behalf of the United States in late April or early May 1971. Nixon and Haldeman were more concerned at the time with prospects for a diplomatic opening to Mao Zedong in Beijing.

Similarly, Nixon's secretary of defense, in writing about the withdrawal of American troops from the Vietnam War, never mentioned a decision by Kissinger to give Hanoi a veto over the future independence of South Vietnam. Tellingly, Secretary Melvin Laird did remember Nixon's reluctance to withdraw American troops from combat prematurely: "Even Nixon, who had promised to end the war, accepted each troop-withdrawal request from me grudgingly."[60]

Later, when asked about Kissinger's modifications of Bunker's two-step negotiating proposal, President Nixon did not recall ever discussing the matter with Kissinger.[61] He then asked what difference such a discussion as proposed by Bunker would have made. When told that it would have brought up the right of North Vietnam to keep its forces inside the South and that Kissinger had abandoned the demand for such a withdrawal, Nixon's eyes lit up in intellectual recognition, but he seemed dumbfounded. He could find no words and sort of shrank back into himself, obviously a very lonely and regretful man. After a long moment, he changed the subject, no longer wanting to talk about Kissinger or Vietnam.

CHAPTER 4

PEACE WITH HONOR

NIXON'S PLAN TO WIN THE WAR

By the livin' Gawd that made you,
You're a better man than I am, Gunga Din.

—Rudyard Kipling, "Gunga Din"

Richard Nixon won a narrow victory in the 1968 American presidential election by capitalizing on angry divisions over Vietnam within the Democratic Party and by fending off a more strident nationalistic challenge from Alabama governor George Wallace.

Thanks to protests against the Vietnam War, America's contemporary cultural war began in earnest during that campaign. Cultural conflict between an old America holding fast to the virtuous certainties of its heroic past and a revisionist elite seeking liberation from such pieties boiled over from university campuses to heat up partisan politics across the nation. Nixon's campaign tactic to attract those voters increasingly mobilizing on the right around patriotism while keeping the support of moderates was to announce that he had a "plan" to win the war. Nixon was for "victory" in Vietnam and so he championed for the integrity and decency of the American self-image. He just didn't discuss how he would "win" where Johnson had "failed."

After the presidential election, along with all other presidential appointees, Ellsworth Bunker submitted his resignation as American ambassador to South Vietnam. On January 6, 1969, Nixon phoned from Washington, asking Bunker to stay on as ambassador. At first noncommittal, Bunker decided to stay until the spring of 1969 to provide a period of continuity for the new administration. Bunker was a Vermont Democrat but also prided himself on being a professional in service of his country. He had worked for Republican president Eisenhower as well as for Democrats when they were in the White House. His thoughts toward Nixon were positive; he felt that the new president would take a tougher position toward the Vietnamese Communists than the Johnson administration had shown in its concluding months. Bunker felt that to deserve greatness, powerful nations should not easily toss off past commitments to principle merely because such commitments had grown tiresome.

Intuitively sensing that the new administration did not have a Vietnam policy, that there was no substance to Nixon's "secret plan" to solve America's Vietnam dilemma, in late January 1969, Bunker asked that a senior person from the Nixon team come out to Saigon to get a "personal feel" for the situation on the ground. Bunker had two motives in making this suggestion: one, to impress the new administration with the real progress being made by the South Vietnamese since turning back the Communists' massive Tet Offensive of January 31, 1968, and, two, to present his own strategy of turning the war over to the South Vietnamese.

Melvin Laird, Nixon's secretary of defense, came out to Saigon. He arrived on March 7, 1969. The fourth Communist offensive against the city was still underway when Laird arrived. While Laird and Bunker were chatting in the small library in Bunker's house, some shooting started. Bunker's Marine guards rushed Laird and Bunker to the new secure bunker built in the house after the Tet Offensive. Called "Bunker's bunker," it was well appointed and filled with sophisticated communications equipment.

Bunker considered it a great improvement over the previous shelter—which had been the wine closet—even if the new bunker was "not so well stocked."

Laird wanted to call General Earle Wheeler, who had come out with him from Washington but was staying with General Abrams. Bunker tried to phone Abrams from the new bunker every way he knew how but failed. The next morning, he apologized to General Wheeler, but Abrams cut in, saying, "My phone was out of order. Not your fault."

Laird arrived with four preconceptions: 1) no solution to the war would be reached in the Paris talks, 2) the Nixon administration would not escalate beyond limited objectives of defending South Vietnam, 3) South Vietnam needed a capacity for permanent self-defense and self-reliance, and 4) Hanoi would not voluntarily abandon its aim of seizing political control over South Vietnam.

Bunker arranged for Laird to hear many straightforward presentations on all the aspects of the war effort, briefings giving the minuses and the pluses. Bunker himself pointed out where progress was solid and where serious problems remained. It was important to Bunker that Laird understand General Abrams's approach to tactical combat operations. Abrams had one strategic objective in mind: keeping Hanoi from taking the offensive anywhere in South Vietnam. Bunker liked the way Abrams approached the war. If Hanoi could not use its main forces for major attacks, then, Bunker knew, rural pacification would have a chance of success. Once pacification was successful, then the war would be transformed into one that the South Vietnamese could win on their own.

And by denying Hanoi opportunities to attack at will, Abrams was creating an invisible and intangible shield around American forces so that they might be withdrawn in carefully planned stages.

Abrams's new tactics had begun in the fall of 1968, after the third Communist offensive had sputtered to futile exhaustion. Abrams combined small-unit search operations with B-52 strikes. Constant small-unit operations kept the Communists from moving freely while the B-52s pounded their troop concentrations. Abrams thus kept the enemy away from populated areas, lowered American casualties, and opened up new areas for pacification efforts. Bunker described Abrams's tactics as the "application of force at a hundred points at once" to keep the enemy off-balance. The press called it a strategy of "maximum pressure."

Abrams's tactics had another advantage: they could be adapted for the needs and circumstances of local areas. In the flat Mekong River Delta with its canals and populous villages, building little mud forts everywhere to support village-based South Vietnamese forces took priority. In the rugged and mountainous Central Highlands, helicopter-assisted search-and-destroy missions were still necessary to beat back Hanoi's regulars coming out of Laos into South Vietnam off the Ho Chi Minh Trail. In Quang Nam and Quang Ngai provinces, long-cordon operations were mounted to clear and hold territory, sealing off villages from Communist penetration while identifying and arresting Viet Cong cadres living among the people.

The CORDS organization was coming off a highly successful Accelerated Pacification Campaign, activated in the fall of 1968 to bring South Vietnamese troops and officials back to many villages where control had been lost to the Communists in the Tet Offensive. Saigon had won the race to fill the vacuum of power in rural areas. CORDS stood for "Civil Operations Rural Development Support." It had been the brainchild of President Lyndon Johnson in the fall of 1966 after the allegedly brilliant Robert McNamara, then secretary of defense, admitted privately to Johnson that he had no idea how to successfully defend South Vietnam from Communist aggression. Seeking a better way to block Hanoi's strategy and tactics, Johnson turned to two civilians on his White House staff—Walt Rostow and Robert Komer. They came up with a plan to emphasize village-level counterinsurgency across South Vietnam rather than large-scale search-and-destroy operations seeking out conventional Communist units.[1]

Komer also insisted that low-level counterinsurgency programs be fully integrated into the military effort—both American and South Vietnamese. He wanted unity of command to ensure that the protection of villages and the people in towns and cities would get the same command attention as search-and-destroy operations. Thus, the CORDS organization was placed under General William Westmoreland's supervision as part of the Military Assistance Command Vietnam. Komer was appointed a deputy commander to William Westmoreland. Ellsworth Bunker was sent to be ambassador with overall supervision of all American efforts and the principal responsibility for working in daily collaboration with South Vietnamese leaders.

Johnson also sent to South Vietnam as Westmoreland's other deputy for military operations General Creighton Abrams. General Abrams was tasked with giving a priority to improving South Vietnamese military forces so that they could take over the defense of their country against Communist invaders from the North.

In a private meeting in 1967 when asking him to serve as the American ambassador to South Vietnam, President Johnson had instructed Bunker to turn the war over to the Vietnamese as quickly and efficiently as possible to permit the withdrawal of American combat forces. Bunker had previously served Johnson in that way in the Dominican Republic in 1965, when his diplomatic and political skills had drawn the Dominicans into collaboration on new elections, which permitted the withdrawal of twenty-five thousand American troops from that small Caribbean country. Johnson's long-term strategic vision of defending South Vietnam while withdrawing American forces was never made public.

In November 1967, General Westmoreland had announced at a press conference in Washington, DC, that the American strategy for winning the Vietnam War now included a "phase four"—the withdrawal of American combat forces. When asked when such withdrawals would begin, General Westmoreland estimated that they could begin in two more years, or in 1969.

In late 1968, Robert Komer had been replaced as head of CORDS by William Colby, also of the CIA. Colby had been CIA station chief in Saigon in the early 1960s, when he had worked closely with Ngo Dinh Nhu on the strategic hamlet program. Later in his career, Colby would become the director of central intelligence in Washington. Colby's grasp of the theory and practice of counterinsurgency was unsurpassed. Bunker gave him a very free hand in running the CORDS program. Under the Nixon administration, Colby would insightfully improve the CORDS effort by turning over power to village communities and so permitting the Vietnamese people to become the frontline troops in contesting the Communist insurgency.

During his stay in South Vietnam, Laird became convinced that Bunker, Abrams, and Colby were on a winning track. He arrived in Vietnam already supporting the idea of "Vietnamization." Laird later recalled,

> *Richard Nixon was elected in 1968 on the assumption that he had a plan to end the Vietnam War. He didn't have any such plan, and my job as his first secretary of defense was to remedy that—quickly. The only stated plan was wording I had suggested for the 1968 Republican platform, saying it was time to de-Americanize the war.*
>
> *By the time Nixon and I inherited the war in 1969, there were more than half a million US troops in South Vietnam and 1.2 million more US soldiers, sailors, and air personnel supporting the war from aircraft carriers and military bases in surrounding nations and at sea. The war needed to be turned back to the people who cared about it, the Vietnamese. They needed US money and training but not more American blood. I called our program "Vietnamization," and in spite of the naysayers, I have not ceased to believe that it worked.*
>
> *As secretary of defense, I took the initiative in the spring of 1969 to change our mission statement for Vietnam from one of applying maximum pressure against the enemy to one of giving maximum assistance to South Vietnam to fight its own battles.[2]*

In meeting with South Vietnamese president Nguyen Van Thieu, Laird put withdrawal of American forces out on the table. Without hesitation, Thieu accepted the concept. In fact, he had proposed it himself to President Johnson in Honolulu the previous July.

Laird put it to Thieu that the American people expected Nixon to disengage American forces from combat. Laird, therefore, wanted the burden of fighting to be shifted promptly and methodically to the South Vietnamese. The challenge to both governments, then, was improving South Vietnamese combat capability so that American forces could be withdrawn.

On his return to Washington, Laird sent a memo to President Nixon, saying in part that he assumed the following: 1) no breakthrough in Paris was likely in the near future to achieve a political resolution of the conflict, 2) we would not escalate beyond the limited objective of attempting to ensure for the South Vietnamese people the right to determine their own political and economic institutions, 3) self-determination required a capability for sustained self-defense and self-reliance, and 4) the North Vietnamese would not voluntarily abandon their aim to secure political control of South Vietnam.

Laird continued,

> *I recognize that the RVNAF modernization program had been designed to create an RVNAF capable of coping with insurgency that could remain if US/NVA forces withdrew. I am recommending that we advance our plans and furnish additional items needed to achieve full modernization for these indigenous forces. I am doing so, however, solely on the basis that this will permit us immediately to begin the process of replacing American forces in South Vietnam with better trained, better led, and better armed South Vietnamese military and para-military personnel.*
>
> *In the meantime, I believe it is essential that we decide now to initiate the removal from Southeast Asia of some US military personnel. The qualitative and quantitative improvement of the RVNAF to date, although perhaps less than desired, should permit us to redeploy from Southeast Asia between 50 to 70 thousand troops during the remainder of this calendar year. I am convinced that this will in no way jeopardize the security of the remaining US and Allied forces*

*and that such a move is necessary to retain US public support for
our continued efforts in South Vietnam.³*

This was the policy of "Vietnamization." President Nixon adopted it immediately on Laird's recommendation after his return from Saigon. It became
Nixon's plan to win the war to fill the policy vacuum of his 1968 campaign
for the presidency.

On March 14, 1969, Nixon set the new policy in motion. He laid down
three conditions for the withdrawal of American forces from South Vietnam: 1) the ability of the South Vietnamese to defend themselves, 2)
progress in seeking Hanoi's agreement to the continued independence of
South Vietnam, and 3) reduction in Hanoi's offensive capability.

The United States was now on its way out of the war. The objective set
for Bunker by President Johnson had been ratified by President Nixon.

Each of Nixon's criteria contained a risk for South Vietnam. It might
fail to field effective military forces. There could be a failure of will in the
negotiations, giving Hanoi a diplomatic victory. And Hanoi might be able
to sustain its offensive capability.

VIETNAMIZATION—THE BACKGROUND TO SECRET NEGOTIATIONS

Negotiating an agreement to end a war when the circumstances of the war
were constantly changing had its inherent instabilities. Each of the three
principal parties—the Communists in Hanoi and their southern dependents
in the National Liberation Front (NLF), the Nationalists in the Saigon government, and the United States—needed to consider terms in the light of
prospective probabilities. The weaker one party might become, the more
demanding another would be, and the stronger a party might become, the
more an opponent would want to lock them into terms based on their current prowess and stamina.

One reality in the calculation was the downsizing of American combat forces. The largest imponderable was the potential capability of the South Vietnamese. That potential, in turn, was to result from Vietnamization. Successful Vietnamization would produce a strong South Vietnam, to the detriment of the Communists. A botched Vietnamization—for whatever reason—would play into Hanoi's hands, especially in the long run. Negotiating strategies for Kissinger, Hanoi, and Thieu all revolved around the results of Vietnamization.

Successful Vietnamization, which Bunker took as the probable outcome of the war, would permit the Americans just to go home and not negotiate anything with Hanoi. This was the stance taken by Bunker in his proposal of April 17, 1971, with his two-step sequence of meetings with Hanoi—a tough-talking step followed by a possible second step offering minor concessions to the NLF.

For Thieu, successful Vietnamization would allow him to more easily agree to additional withdrawals of American forces and provide some access to political power for Hanoi's southern followers.

Successful Vietnamization would be Hanoi's nightmare. As American troops withdrew, the Communists would lose leverage over Nixon in domestic American politics. Hanoi's leaders knew from 1971 on that their greatest power over the American government was the antiwar movement in the United States. Thus, Hanoi had to extract concessions from the Americans that were harmful to South Vietnam while Nixon was still under great pressure from the antiwar movement and his Democratic Party opposition. Hanoi's fallback position in trying to minimize the success of Vietnamization would be to crush South Vietnamese military capabilities, which they would attempt with a massive invasion in 1972.

The more successful Vietnamization was, therefore, the less necessary it would be to concede to Hanoi the right to keep its forces inside South Vietnam. For Henry Kissinger to decide on making that concession on January 9, 1971, before the final results of Vietnamization were obtained showed lack of personal courage and an unbecoming preemptive disparagement of the Vietnamese Nationalists and their rights to freedom and independence.

Kissinger gave little credence to the strategy of Vietnamization. In his memoirs, he confessed he was in the beginning the most skeptical of the president's senior advisors. He perceived that withdrawals of American troops would cause Hanoi's need to bargain to gain American disengagement to evaporate. And if the South Vietnamese could not step up as American forces turned over combat responsibilities to them, "we hazarded not only the negotiating lever but South Vietnam's independence and the entire basis of our sacrifices."[4] He elaborated that Vietnamization was "inherently precarious."

> *If it were played out to the end, a delicate point would inevitably be reached where our withdrawals would create uncertainty about South Vietnam's political future, jeopardizing the whole enterprise at the final hour. A negotiated settlement that would give South Vietnam a fair chance to survive had always been far preferable; it would end the war with an act of policy and leave the future of South Vietnam to an historical process.*

In other words, an act of policy would give the Vietnamese Nationalists a decent interval during which they could walk in freedom along the road of history. And in still other words, an act of policy that would betray an American ally.

PHASES OF VIETNAMIZATION

The general pattern of Vietnamization followed the standard "oil spot" best practice in counterinsurgency. Starting as a few drops of oil surrounding secure cities, towns, and government bases, operations to deny the Communists control of territory and access to the people would spread in expanding concentric circles farther and farther out into once Communist-held zones of control. As the Communists were pushed back farther and farther from the people and security spread wider and wider, local residents all across South Vietnam could more freely live normal lives and promote their own livelihoods.

The progress of Vietnamization can be divided into four phases, one for each year.

1969

In 1969, all across rural Vietnam, power and resources were turned over to local village leaders. They were given budgets for development. Elections were held. Village leaders were brought to a national training center for instruction in administration and meetings with national leaders. Soldiers were drafted for the lightly armed Popular Forces (PF) and assigned to village platoons. They built mud forts and patrolled the villages and their surroundings. They prevented Viet Cong cadres from entering the villages, collecting money, and recruiting soldiers for Hanoi. Volunteers in village after village were asked to join self-defense teams. They were trained in weapons and tasked with static guard duties. Bit by bit, the Viet Cong guerillas and political activists were cut off from the people. More soldiers were recruited for more professional regional force companies. They would conduct search-and-destroy operations beyond village boundaries and maintain forts closer to Communist base areas. Army of the Republic of Vietnam (ARVN) battalions and regiments were asked more and more to take the lead in punching out from cities and their bases deep into Communist strongholds. The US Third Marine Division withdrew from South Vietnam's northernmost provinces, replaced by the First ARVN Division to fight back against invading NVA regulars. Brutal battles were fought in the Ashau Valley and around isolated base camps in the mountains near Laos.

1970

Mobilization of village communities continued. Village councils were reelected, bringing better-quality leadership to rural South Vietnam. A land reform program was commenced to give rice fields to those who did not own them. Decisions as to who would receive land and the provision of legal titles were decentralized to village governments. The rural people now had the ability to access public goods, such as security, education, and economic development, from officials they knew and trusted. Extensive outreach programs encouraged members of the NLF to leave Hanoi and support the government. More American forces withdrew. When a surprise coup d'état occurred in neighboring Cambodia, ousting Prince Sihanouk from power because of his supine acquiescence to Hanoi's demands to use Cambodia as a sanctuary from which to invade South Vietnam, American and South Vietnamese forces crossed the border and severely damaged Communist forces and supply depots. In general, American combat forces were used to "break up the enemy's system" and prevent attacks on South Vietnamese towns and cities. NVA forces were driven out of their traditional sanctuaries and pushed closer to the borders with Laos and Cambodia.

1971

Village governments were given more power and authority. Every village was given a credit program to make one-year low-interest-rate loans to villagers. Village governments were given powers to tax the local economy to raise funds for development projects like schools and roads and to invest in their credit program. Police officers were assigned directly to villages. To directly attack Hanoi's illegal use of Laos and the Ho Chi Minh Trail to bring men and supplies into South Vietnam, an ARVN-only task force crossed the border and cut Hanoi's supply lines for several weeks (Operation Lam Son 719). Hanoi's ability to use its main forces inside South Vietnam to disrupt the pacification/village development program was degraded substantially. More American combat units left South Vietnam.

1972

By 1972, most of populated South Vietnam was pacified. People throughout the country lived in peace and experienced economic growth. Some one hundred thousand former followers of the NLF had returned to loyalty to the Nationalist government. Really only North Vietnamese soldiers were left to fight Hanoi's war inside South Vietnam. Vietnamization was now a confrontation of ARVN regular forces against NVA regular forces. In the spring, for what was called the "Easter Offensive," or in Vietnamese, "the Summer of Blood and Fire," Hanoi sent its divisions against three targets: An Loc northwest of Saigon, Kontum in the Central Highlands, and Quang Tri and Hue cities along the northern coast of South Vietnam. After some initial failures and reverses, the ARVN forces held and then drove off the North Vietnamese invaders. Most of the North Vietnamese tanks sent south were destroyed. American air strikes were essential as a defensive weapon protecting dug-in South Vietnamese units and cutting down NVA troops moving in to attack a fixed position or caught out in the open.

PERFORMANCE METRICS

One basic measure of Vietnamization is casualty figures. How did the number of American soldiers killed in the war drop, and how did the number of South Vietnamese killed in combat increase? These numbers would reflect which forces were sustaining the hardships of combat, a proxy for the South Vietnamese taking over the military burden of defending their country.

The deaths for American forces and for the ARVN—but not for South Vietnamese local forces and civilian self-defense units—are known. They are as follows:[5]

	AMERICANS	SOUTH VIETNAMESE
1967	11,363	12,716
1968	16,899	27,915
1969	11,780	21,833
1970	6,173	23,346

	AMERICANS	SOUTH VIETNAMESE
1971	2,414	22,738
1972	759	39,587
1973	68	27,901
1974	1	31,219

The basic measurement of Vietnamization was the respective number of soldiers deployed for war fighting. Those numbers were as follows:[6]

	AMERICAN FORCES	TOTAL SOUTH VIENAMESE FORCES
1967	485,600	798,700
1968	536,100	820,000
1969	475,200	897,000
1970	334,600	968,000
1971	156,800	1,046,250
1972	24,200	1,048,000
1973	50	1,110,000

Another measure of successful Vietnamization was the declining strength of southern Vietnamese willing to fight for Hanoi. The weaker the NLF forces grew, the more Hanoi would need to send its own soldiers down the Ho Chi Minh Trail into South Vietnam.

The data from Hanoi's Ministry of Defense on North Vietnamese soldiers sent to South Vietnam are as follows (this schedule does not include an additional twenty thousand soldiers sent to Military Regions B3 and B4):[7]

	NORTH VIETNAMESE SOLDIERS SENT TO SOUTH VIETNAM
1967	94,243
1968	141,081
1969	81,092
1970	52,090
1971	49,321
1972	152,947
1973	75,600
1974	70,798
1975	117,293

This level of infiltration of soldiers from North Vietnam suggests Hanoi's inability to recruit sufficient fighters among South Vietnamese to derail Vietnamization.

For the Nationalist government in Saigon, security responsibilities were allocated to organizational structures with differing capabilities, each designed to counter different specific Communist threats. The ARVN was a conventional military force armed and organized in a manner that really started with Napoleon. The theory of how to organize and use such an army was most famously set forth by von Clausewitz in his treatise *On War*.[8] The purpose of such an army was to take the fight to the enemy and destroy its conventional forces, thus taking political power away from its civilian leadership. The focus of war when using such forces was on the "battle," violent engagements between mobile units on a battlefield. A large force with infantry, artillery, and armor units supported by specialized logistic and engineering units was divided into corps, each with three divisions. The combat force of a division was then subdivided into three regiments for more tactical mobility on the battlefield. Regimental commanders in turn supervised three subordinate battalions, each of which assembled its fighters into companies. Companies were further subdivided into three platoons, each of which managed the tactical prowess of three squads. Accordingly, the mission of the ARVN was, at first, to contest with Viet Cong companies and battalions in ground combat and then later with North Vietnamese battalions, regiments, and finally divisions sent south into the Republic of Vietnam. ARVN units were supported by airpower from the South Vietnamese Air Force and by ships from the South Vietnamese Navy.

In 1965, when Hanoi increased its military capability in South Vietnam with units from its army (the People's Army of Vietnam [PAVN]), Nationalist Vietnamese forces were at the edge of breaking. Thus, at the recommendation of General Westmoreland, American president Lyndon Johnson dispatched conventional American forces to South Vietnam as an interim expedient to hold the line against Hanoi until the Vietnamese Nationalists could reorganize and reequip ARVN units. The process of Vietnamization, therefore, was to bring that interim American effort to an end and have ARVN units take over the frontline fighting against Hanoi's armed forces. The missions for the Americans and the South Vietnamese were simply put in this saying: "As they stand up, we stand down."

But conventional forces—ARVN and American—were not designed or well adapted to counter and defeat another strategic avenue to victory employed by Hanoi's Communist leadership. This was the strategy of fighting a "people's war" or an insurgency. A people's war uses the people as weapons against a government. People are motivated and organized to take up arms and kill government officials, teachers, local leaders, and citizen supporters of the government. A people's war uses as tactics guerilla hit-and-run attacks, terrorist attacks, assassinations, economic sabotage of urban populations, infiltration of agents into government organizations to provide intelligence on government operations, sabotage, if possible, of successful government programs, organization of noncombatant citizens—old and young, male and female—into support activities under the direction of insurgent cadres, and political and cultural mobilization campaigns to win over supporters and dishearten those aligned with the government.

The central strategic power of a people's war was pithily put by Mao Zedong: "The guerillas are the fish which swim in the sea of the people."[9]

This strategy can be defeated only by 1) removing all the fish from the sea before they spawn or 2) drying up the sea so that the fish die from lack of oxygen. Military and police measures are needed to remove the fish by killing or capturing them. Different measures—political, cultural, economic—in addition to effective policing in local communities are needed to dry up the sea.

On the Vietnamese Nationalist side, local forces at provincial, district, and village levels were organized and deployed to defend local communities from attacks, harassment, and exploitation by the Communist guerilla units and their political affiliates. Provincial forces, called Regional Forces, or RF, were organized at the company level. Platoons of full-time, lightly armed fighters, the Popular Forces (PF), were recruited from villages and stationed in the communities from which they had been recruited. They were the face-to-face armed opponents of local Viet Cong guerilla formations. South Vietnam had, in addition, a very large police force in cities and towns and eventually in every village. After 1968, a very important innovation was introduced to provide more self-defense security to villages and urban neighborhoods. Citizen volunteers—men below and above the ages for salaried military service and women—were organized into self-defense groups for static guard duty. They were given old rifles as their weapons.

The process of Vietnamization was to insert a new level of security at the bottom of South Vietnam's political structures—in the villages. Then each level of Nationalist security capability could move up and take over responsibility for a more demanding tactical area of operational responsibility. Once villages could be defended by volunteer self-defense units and salaried PF, then the RF formerly responsible for guarding rural communities could shift their responsibility to searching out and fighting local Communist guerilla units. South Vietnamese divisions, which had previously concentrated on population security, could then turn that task over to the Regional Force companies and shift their operations to attacking regular North Vietnamese combat battalions and regiments. These refocused South Vietnamese divisions would be supported by South Vietnamese armor and artillery companies and airpower to hammer the invading North Vietnamese. The most proficient South Vietnamese combat units in the marine, airborne, and ranger battalions could then concentrate on providing penetration power to keep North Vietnamese army units away from the people—bottled up in the mountains, deep in the swamps of the Mekong Delta, or close to the borders of Cambodia and Laos. The South Vietnamese Navy would take over preventing North Vietnamese smuggling of men and supplies into South Vietnam by sea. And, finally, at the top level of combat capability, the American combat units supported by American armor, artillery, and airpower could go home.

Thus, winning the war against Hanoi depended most on making irreversible progress at the lowest level of South Vietnamese defensive capability through the counterinsurgency program directed by CORDS for the Americans and the Central Pacification and Development Council for the Vietnamese Nationalists. This was the priority for Ambassador Bunker—making South Vietnam work efficiently on its own behalf—in fighting, in economic development, and in politics.

The CORDS program was far more extensive than providing police protection to villages. It supervised the decentralization of power to village communities to enhance their community well-being with schools and teachers; more productive strains of rice and pigs; better feeder roads and bridges, giving easy access to local market towns; local elections; and land reform, giving farmers titles to the rice fields they worked.

The success of counterinsurgency and village development was the most important marker of how well Vietnamization would shift the fortunes of war against the Communists.

At the end of 1969, American analysts credited the Communists with control of only 3 percent of the population of South Vietnam and having intermittent influence over another 7 percent. Some forty-seven thousand soldiers had left the Communists and voluntarily come over to the Nationalists. ARVN battalions or larger mobile operations nearly doubled from 6,900 in 1968 to 11,400 in 1969. In the hamlets and villages, some 1,316,000 men and women had enlisted in the volunteer self-defense units protecting their communities. Another 1,750,000 were registered as providing support for the local self-defense units.

By the end of 1970, some four hundred thousand weapons had been distributed to self-defense units, and another thirty-two thousand supporters of the Viet Cong had left the Communists to return to their homes. Many now joined South Vietnamese local forces.

By the end of 1970, pacification was a solid success. The CORDS organization under Ambassador William Colby formed a small research unit—the Pacification Studies Group—to track the progress of village development. The group recruited and trained Vietnamese to meet with villagers and poll them on many dimensions of their lives for monthly Pacification Attitude Analysis Survey reports.[10]

The report for December 1970 revealed the following:

- Respondents rated South Vietnamese forces as more effective than American.

- Only 3.6 percent of respondents lived in insecure hamlets.

- 97.2 percent of hamlets had police posted.

- 46 percent responded that security was better than in the previous month.

- 6 percent responded that security was worse than in the previous month.

- Respondents believed that local forces were more effective than ARVN or American combat units.

- 69 percent believed that their local officials were of high quality and ability; only 9 percent thought that such officials were of low quality and ability.

- 83 percent believed that district and other government officials were capable and trusted; 13 percent believed such officials were not capable or trusted.

- 59 percent reported that their most serious problems were financial or higher prices; 21 percent pointed to security as the most severe problem they faced.

- 48 percent believed that the Nationalists would win the war, with 17 percent saying Hanoi would win.

A comment confirming the success of rural pacification and village development can be found in the summary of conclusions about the Vietnam War prepared by Hanoi's Vietnam Military History Institute in 1987. Referring to mid-1969, the summary concluded, "Even so, due to our having many difficulties, our attacks could not be sustained, were only small scale, stopping the pacification program was weak, unable to create power to attack the enemy in rural areas, and even worse, we were hit heavily by the enemy, and operations in the towns and cities were even less effective."[11]

The summary also noted: "But with changes during the two years of 1969 and 1970, faced with the ferocious counter-attacks of the enemy aimed at our oversight in not paying more attention to the rural areas, accordingly they achieved more than a few results, imposing on us long lasting losses and difficulties."

The Pacification Attitude Analysis Survey reported in June 1972 that not one respondent believed that Hanoi would defeat South Vietnam's army. In rural areas, 75 percent wanted to personally participate in defending their country. Very few thought there would be any political support for the NLF in their hamlet after a cease-fire went into effect.[12]

POLITICS AND VIETNAMIZATION

Starting in 1967, South Vietnam held many elections under a constitution adopted by a Constituent Assembly elected in 1966 at the insistence of President Lyndon Johnson. The constitution adopted by the assembly drew its decentralization and institutional checks and balances from the Tan Dai Viet Party and its uniquely Vietnamese theory of *Dan Toc Sinh Ton*. There was a presidential election in 1967 and elections that same year for the Upper and Lower Houses of the National Assembly. There were village elections, more elections for the Upper and Lower Houses in 1970 and 1971, and a second round of village elections and then a second presidential election in 1971.[13]

In the 1967 Upper House election, 480 candidates grouped in forty-eight different slates were certified to run. Most candidates resided in the capital city, Saigon. Turnout was 83.7 percent of eligible voters. A coalition slate with union support came in first. Two slates, each with their own Catholic following, came next. Fourth was a slate associated with loyalists to former president Ngo Dinh Diem. Fifth was another slate of conservative elders. The sixth slate to win was put forward by the Revolutionary Dai Viet Party from Central Vietnam.

The 1967 election for the Lower House saw 1,235 candidates contest the seats. Winners included fifty-nine from the southern provinces, forty-four from central provinces, and thirty-two refugees from North Vietnam. Also elected were forty-six Buddhists, thirty-five Catholics, thirteen Hoa Hao, six Theravada Buddhists, five Cao Dai, two Protestants, and four

Confucians. From a political party perspective, ten winners were aligned with General Tran Van Don, twelve were from the Southern Renaissance Movement, eight were militant Buddhists, and fifteen were militant Catholics.

The elections for the Upper and Lower Houses thus brought into office a range of Vietnamese Nationalist viewpoints.

In the 1970 Upper House elections, winners reflected the diversity of Nationalist viewpoints even more. Sixteen slates were certified: five Catholic, five Buddhist, one from the victorious 1967 coalition slate, and five composed of noted individuals, Tan Dai Viets, and Revolutionary Dai Viets.

The most popular slate was an opposition Buddhist one with support mostly from central provinces. The second-most popular slate was dominated by Catholics but included Hoa Hao and Cao Dai followers and an ethnic Cambodian. This slate won most of its votes in the southern delta provinces. Another Catholic slate recruited four Buddhists and one Confucian for its list.

In the 1971 elections for the Lower House, the political process continued to broaden engagement among Vietnamese Nationalists. There were 1,332 candidates vying for 159 seats. Many incumbents seeking reelection were rejected by the voters. The militant Buddhists in Central Vietnam elected twenty-five members. The Tan Dai Viet–affiliated Progressive Nationalist Movement won nineteen. The coalition Farmer-Worker Party won ten seats. Political insiders presumed that eighty-four of the Lower House representatives supported President Thieu's administration, sixty opposed it, and fifteen were independent.

The elections gave voice and power to a range of non-Communist Vietnamese whose aspirations were coalescing more and more around the fight to maintain South Vietnam as a democratic and independent country. This evolving political process thereby put a moral foundation under Vietnamization.

ECONOMICS AND VIETNAMIZATION

At the start of the CORDS program in 1967, agricultural production in South Vietnam was at 91 percent of the average from the years 1961 to 1965. But with pacification and village development in effect, by 1973, agricultural production had reached 115 percent of that 1961 to 1965 average.[14]

Rice production in South Vietnam during the years of Vietnamization was in thousand metric tons, as follows:[15]

1967	4,688
1968	4,366
1969	5,115
1970	5,716
1971	6,324
1972	6,348
1973	7,025

Under the Land to the Tiller program spearheaded by President Thieu as part of rural development, during the years of Vietnamization, some 2,700,000 acres of rice land were distributed free to some eight hundred thousand rural families. This land constituted about 60 percent of prime rice fields and 40 percent of all rice fields.[16]

In 1970, rubber exports began to revive, and lumber production in the hills and jungles grew by 10 percent. Tax collections were up by 37 percent over 1969. Government audits of taxpayers produced 187 percent more income for the government than had audits during the previous year. South Vietnamese put more money in savings accounts and invested US$24.4 million in new factories.[17]

By the end of 1971, agricultural output rose again, this time by 13 percent; exports increased again; and total GNP grew by 4 to 5 percent. Domestic revenue raised by the government increased by 32 percent.[18]

Human capital is always a factor of production partially responsible for economic growth. Educational achievement provides a rough measure of human capital formation. During the Vietnamization process, directly supported by the village self-government and self-defense efforts, enrollment in primary schools increased, as show in this graph:[19]

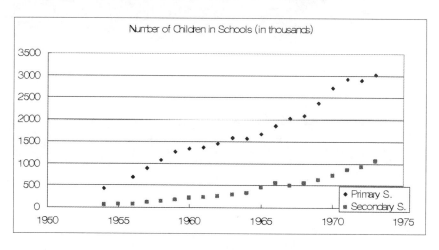

Number of Children in Schools (in thousands)

In Hanoi, a worried Le Duan told his colleagues that for the first time since the Communists had begun their struggle to seize total power over the Vietnamese people, Vietnam's bourgeoisie (*tu ban*) had the strategic initiative as well as sufficient organizational capacity to prevail over his Communist Party. He said, "If this trend is allowed to continue, victory for the revolution will be put off for 20 to 30 years."[20]

VIETNAMIZATION AND VIETNAMESE NATIONALISM

Confidence in the probable success of Vietnamization varied directly with an understanding of Vietnamese ethnic nationalism. From villages below to elite combat units at the top, the capability of Vietnamese Nationalists to hold off and defeat the Communists reflected their determination to persevere and suffer hardships and casualties. Nationalism in its many cultural expressions inspired opposition to Communism, an invasive species of politics that had no roots in traditional Vietnamese life.

Entering Vietnamese history from France via French education and politics, Communism needed to graft itself onto more authentic Vietnamese cultural patterns in order to root itself in a Vietnamese political dynamic. Vietnamese Communists found they could attach their ideology and their aspirations for governing Vietnam to the Neo-Confucian administrative state imported from China in the eighteenth and nineteenth centuries by the later Le and Nguyen Dynasty aristocrats, especially the latter. The appeal of Communism to Vietnamese was its promise of a share in political power to those who joined the party. Such power could, in addition, be shared with the extended families of party cadres.

Vietnamese left outside the mandarin class and state apparatus or whose values were more fundamentally grounded in Buddhism, spirit worship, yin/yang cosmology, or respect for family traditions made up the Nationalist community. The most vivid sign of respect the Communists showed to Nationalism was their refusal to make Communism their public cause. From 1945 to 1954, the Communist Party secreted itself behind the cause of anti-imperialism and winning independence from France. Starting in 1959 in the war to conquer South Vietnam, the Communists, under Le Duan's direction, never asked the South Vietnamese to submit to rule by Hanoi's Communist government but only to drive out the American "imperialists" and their purported lackeys governing in Saigon.

As Vietnamization started, really with the arrival of Ellsworth Bunker, General Creighton Abrams, and Robert Komer in the spring of 1967, the community of Vietnamese Nationalists consisted of the Buddhists, the Catholics, the Hoa Hao followers, the Cao Dai followers, the three main Dai Viet networks of activists, the various followings of the Viet Nam Quoc Dan Dang Party, and multitudes of ordinary Vietnamese who followed the ways of "mountains and rivers." In addition, numerous Vietnamese opposed the Communists out of their own interest—believing that their ownership of property had been ordained by heaven as a reward for their *phuc duc,* or merit virtue. And the million or so Vietnamese who had fled to South Vietnam in 1954 and 1955 to escape a Communist dictatorship were of no mind to let the Communists conquer their new homeland.

In short, there was a sizable quantum of psychological/cultural power among Vietnamese available to support Vietnamization.

At the village level, all the local leaders given opportunities through the pacification program to become important in their communities brought Nationalist values and motivations into the daily fight against Hanoi's ambitions. In the elite South Vietnamese units, political Nationalist officers were dedicated and heroic and more than a match for their Communist adversaries. The marines were dominated by Dai Viets born in North Vietnam. The airborne battalions drew officers from Dai Viets and VNQDD families in Central Vietnam. The armor units were mostly led by Dai Viets from the provinces around Saigon and in the Mekong Delta.

Perhaps most significantly, the entire theory and practice of decentralized, village-based pacification and rural development, centered on local elections and land reform, were provided by the Tan Dai Party. In particular, the formula proposed was to mobilize Vietnamese around their inherited values and aspirations, which had been belittled and marginalized by French colonialism.

Vietnamization, therefore, had to take its sustenance from Vietnamese Nationalism. It would stand or fall as a Vietnamese Nationalist movement. But because it had deep roots in Vietnamese identity and culture, South Vietnam's self-reliance could well survive and even thrive after the departure of its American allies. President Nixon's Vietnamization plan to successfully end America's war effort in Vietnam was made to work by Vietnamese Nationalists.

Le Duan and other Communist leaders in Hanoi knew this all too well. They needed help from the Americans in sabotaging the ability of the Nationalists to resist continued aggression from the North. In 1945 and 1946, they had needed similar help from Jean Sainteny to put down their Nationalist rivals.

An anecdote relayed by Tan Dai Viet leader Professor Nguyen Ngoc Huy told of Communist general Vo Nguyen Giap—on looking down from a window at French soldiers marching back into Hanoi after the March 1946 accord negotiated by Ho Chi Minh with Jean Sainteny—blurting out his disgust that the French were coming back to Vietnam.

Ho Chi Minh then asked him, "Junior Uncle, if you don't piggyback on their power to boost yourself up, whose power will you use?"[21]

In 1971, the Vietnamese Communist Party needed another Western power to again turn its back on the Nationalists. With help a second time from Sainteny, they fortuitously found a willing collaborator in their effort to install a Communist dictatorship over all their countrymen—Henry Kissinger.

Those Americans who lived in ignorance of Vietnamese Nationalism, especially members of Hanoi's fifth column inside American politics—the antiwar movement—had no confidence that the South Vietnamese could ever stand on their own. One popular slogan of the antiwar protests said all that needed to be said from this perspective: "Ho, Ho, Ho Chi Minh. NLF is going to win!" Based on their own narrative, antiwar leaders thus reasonably concluded in 1969 that there was nothing to be gained by fighting in South Vietnam for even just one more day. Their demand became "Out, now!"

CHAPTER 5

THE SECRET NEGOTIATIONS

AN OPPORTUNITY FOR BETRAYAL

If, drunk with sight of power, we loose
Wild tongues that have not Thee in awe,
Such boastings as the Gentiles use,
Or lesser breeds without the Law—
Lord God of Hosts, be with us yet,
Lest we forget—lest we forget!

—Rudyard Kipling, "Recessional"

The greatest threat to South Vietnam's survival came from secret negotiations between Washington and Hanoi where the Vietnamese Nationalists would have no control of what was said or done by the United States. The new Nixon administration, taking office in January 1969, inherited public negotiations with the Vietnamese Communists ruling from Hanoi and their subordinates in South Vietnam posing as an independent political movement, the National Liberation Front (NLF). Public negotiating sessions were held at the Hotel Majestic in Paris. Four parties were seated at tables in a face-saving compromise so that neither the United States nor the Republic of Vietnam in Saigon would have to accept the NLF as equal to the Saigon government and its constitution in authority and legitimacy. The sessions were primarily for making statements in public. There was no real negotiation conducted. Each party would issue or revise a "plan" for peace and answer questions from the press.

On the American side, the public Paris negotiations were under the jurisdiction of the State Department and its new secretary of state, William Rogers. Henry Kissinger, sitting in the White House as President Nixon's advisor for national security affairs, had no direct role in setting terms for the United States for how it would formally end its participation in the Vietnam War and arrange for the continued independence of South Vietnam and Laos and the withdrawal of North Vietnamese forces from Cambodia. Henry Cabot Lodge was appointed to lead the US delegation at the public Paris negotiations.

As the Nixon administration came into office, Hanoi proposed secret meetings between only itself and the Americans, cutting out the South Vietnamese from serious discussions regarding their future. On instructions from Washington, Bunker sought Thieu's consent to such private conversations.

Nguyen Van Thieu graciously presented no difficulty, saying, "We accept private talks. If they want to bring the NLF, that is OK with us. For us the important issue is the withdrawal of the North Vietnamese army."[1]

The first nonpublic meeting between Hanoi and Washington took place on March 17, 1969, after President Nixon had set out the framework for Vietnamization and withdrawal of American combat forces. Hanoi offered Nixon an olive branch if only Washington would turn South Vietnam over to the NLF.

On being told of this discussion, Thieu said,

> *They will not abandon the baby in the marketplace. The NLF seeks a coalition government because they know they can become a polit- ical party under the constitution. We offer the one-man, one-vote*

formula for an election with guarantees to NLF members after the North Vietnamese Army leaves. The NLF can participate in the commission which organizes the elections. But they worry over losing any election. Our real problem is how to prevent new North Vietnamese aggression after the Americans leave.[2]

Thieu was prescient. The Americans would leave South Vietnam in 1973, and thereafter Hanoi would launch a massive military offensive against the South Vietnamese government in 1975.

For his part, Thieu twice attempted to contact the NLF delegation in Paris, but there was no response from the Communists.

President Nixon had determined to bring home some American troops in 1969. Bunker wanted a studied program of steady American disengagement. That was the only way he saw to drain the cultural distemper of antiwar protest from American politics while at the same time giving the South Vietnamese confidence to stay the course against Hanoi's aggression largely on their own. Nixon saw things very much as Bunker did.

Bunker admired Nixon for his determination. But Nixon was certainly not admired at all by Bunker's Democratic and sophisticated friends and colleagues, including his wife, Carol. Serving Nixon loyally left Bunker more controversial and isolated than he liked, but he was a believer in his cause, a pilgrim making his difficult progress through temporary travails toward a higher goal. Bunker just didn't see any facts around him that spoke loudly enough to turn him away from unstinting support of democracy and independence for the South Vietnamese people.

Nixon reciprocated, trusting this blue-blooded, Yale-educated Yankee when he trusted so few—even in the circle of his close associates. Years later, Nixon would attend Bunker's funeral service in Brattleboro, Vermont, speaking to me then of what a steady hand Bunker had been under so much pressure.

Bunker was not a student of Vietnamese history or culture. He could not give a lecture on the Tran Dynasty or Buddhism. He was also not familiar with the ins and outs of the various Vietnamese Nationalist parties and uniquely Vietnamese religious sects. In fact, really no one in the American leadership—not even in the CIA—knew much about the Vietnamese Nationalists.

Americans saw Vietnam very superficially through the eyes of temporary visitors. They knew about Catholics and Buddhists, about Saigon notables and military leaders, and about protestors who made the press and thought of the Hoa Hao and Cao Dai faiths as Oriental curiosities. The news coverage of the failure of the Ngo Dinh Diem administration and the coup of 1963 painted the most vivid picture of Vietnamese in American minds—the scheming dragon lady stereotype of Madame Nhu, monks burning themselves in protest, student demonstrations.

Most Americans working in Vietnam or in Washington knew what little they did about the Vietnamese from journalists and the few scholars who wrote on Vietnam in the 1950s and 1960s, say Joseph Buttinger or Frances FitzGerald. French commentators like Bernard Fall and the British novelist Graham Greene had more influence on American thinking about the Vietnam War than any Vietnamese, such as Hoang Van Chi. No American official ever read Nguyen Ngoc Huy's Nationalist treatise *Dan Toc Sinh Ton*.

But Bunker relied on his instincts to sense intuitively where the strength of Vietnamese culture and society was. He was a gentleman of the old school who started with a premise of respect for others no matter who they were or what their station in life. He quickly perceived and absorbed as a moral reality the deep passion of the Vietnamese for their way of life and their individualistic fears of living inside a Communist social machine with its theocratic ways and police state terrors.

Bunker returned to Saigon from Washington in early 1969 after meeting with Nixon and immediately informed Thieu of Nixon's decision on the pace of American troop withdrawals, reassuring South Vietnam's president that General Creighton Abrams was already looking at how disengagement of American forces could proceed without increasing the danger to South Vietnam. Thieu replied that he had not been thinking about the problem because Nixon and Melvin Laird had indicated that the time had not yet arrived to bring the first American troops back home.

In the meantime, General Abrams, who had succeeded William Westmoreland as US commander, was starting the process of Vietnamization. Two artillery battalions—one of 105 howitzers and another of 155 howitzers—were turned over to Vietnamese soldiers. Five more South Vietnamese artillery battalions were in training. A-37 jets and UH-1 Iroquois helicopters were given to Vietnamese for their use in combat. Four South Vietnamese logistical battalions to support division-level operations were activated.

Thieu feared above all else that the Americans would leave with the Communists still in possession of base areas within South Vietnam. He was concerned that the United States would accept a partition of South Vietnam with some zones under his control and some given to the Communists to be ruled by them. This would come about if the United States accepted a cease-fire in place. The French had so accommodated the Communists in 1954. His big problem, he reaffirmed with Bunker, was how to prevent or inhibit future North Vietnamese aggression after the Americans had left South Vietnam.[3]

Regarding the details of Vietnamization, he wanted most to arm the people's self-defense forces and Popular Forces (PF) platoons in South Vietnam's 2,100 villages.

For its part, the Vietnamese Communist Party adopted Resolution 9, setting the party's objectives as smashing the American "will of aggression," forcing Washington to "end the war quickly and withdraw troops," and forcing the Americans to "accept a political solution." Hanoi had moved into a "fight while talking" strategy focused more on Washington than on Saigon. The Vietnamese Communist leadership knew that, while South Vietnam was getting stronger, Washington's will to persevere was getting weaker.

Every morning, members of Hanoi's Communist Party politburo awoke eager for news of what the American antiwar movement had accomplished the day before. Hope for a political victory in Washington kept Hanoi's leaders from accepting a compromise; Jane Fonda's visit to Hanoi had been a great shot in the arm for Communist morale.[4]

On June 9, 1969, the first withdrawal of American combat troops from the Vietnam War was announced. Thieu flew to the island of Midway to meet with President Nixon for the joint announcement. Midway's outstanding feature was the gooney bird, a hazard for planes landing and taking off and one that turned roads into obstacle courses for annoyed drivers.

The meeting was the most compact summit Bunker ever attended, but in some ways, it was more productive than most. Thieu and Nixon spent much time together, breaking briefly for a press conference in which they announced that twenty-five thousand American soldiers would soon be coming home. The two presidents seemed to get along well. Thieu made an excellent impression on Nixon.

Thieu proposed a further expansion of South Vietnamese armed forces to nearly one million men under arms. Nixon agreed to arm such a force. But American Defense Department plans rested on the assumption that all North Vietnamese combat forces would someday withdraw from South Vietnam. The military capability to be supplied to South Vietnam under Nixon's Vietnamization program did not include weapons for sustained combat against invading North Vietnamese regular divisions. The assumptions supporting this decision were that, pursuant to either a peace agreement or success in the ground war, North Vietnamese troops would leave South Vietnam and that Viet Cong guerillas would no longer be a threat to the Saigon government.

Thieu came back from Midway with the assurances he had asked for: 1) that the United States would not be a party to the imposition on South Vietnam of a coalition or any other form of government that would prejudge the results of free elections and 2) that American troop withdrawal would not proceed so rapidly as to undermine the stability or political viability of South Vietnam.

For his part, Nixon obtained Thieu's consent to steady troop withdrawals, tactics at the Paris negotiations, South Vietnamese flexibility in the negotiations, and a government for South Vietnam resulting from free elections.

On returning to Saigon, Thieu presented American disengagement to his people as a matter for national pride, as a sign that Vietnamese Nationalism was coming of age and shouldering at last the just obligations incumbent upon a sovereign people.

Bunker took no special pride in the launch of Vietnamization, even though it was the accomplishment of his vision for helping South Vietnam survive Communist aggression. There was still too much at risk. The pace of American disengagement had to be measured by an intangible yardstick—the self-confidence of the South Vietnamese. To withdraw American forces when the South Vietnamese had too little faith in the future would precipitate a debacle. To wait too long for American withdrawals would prevent the South Vietnamese from assuming their proper responsibilities. Bunker wanted to let the South Vietnamese test themselves, find their forces capable, and so gain the necessary self-confidence and self-respect before the Americans would withdraw critical deployments of combat troops.

Clark Clifford, who as Johnson's last secretary of defense had pressed for a unilateral American disengagement, now advocated in a widely read article that one hundred thousand American troops should leave South Vietnam in 1969 and the remainder in 1970. The American antiwar movement now entered the Washington political struggle to dictate the pace of Vietnamization.

Bunker wrote to Clifford in protest. The United States, Bunker argued, could achieve its goal best if Americans made their decisions quietly and avoided ultimata to their South Vietnamese ally. A rigid timetable for withdrawals would be self-defeating, Bunker wrote, only encouraging Hanoi to delay serious negotiations and discouraging too many people in South Vietnam. Bunker found it inconceivable that South Vietnamese would continue to make major sacrifices if the foreign support that made all the difference between ultimate victory or defeat was pulled away precipitously.

After the Midway meeting, Vietnamization picked up speed. At Nha Trang, Bunker turned over to the South Vietnamese Air Force a squadron of A-37s. He flew up from Saigon with Thieu. They were escorted by Vice

President and Vice Air Marshal Nguyen Cao Ky, flying a throttled-down A-37. Ky, loving the role of jet jockey, wore his black one-piece flying suit with a purple orchid–colored scarf around his neck.

After the ceremony, Thieu took Bunker to the coastal province of Phan Thiet. Thieu's principal objective seemed to be to mingle with and talk to the people. Large crowds turned out to see him. At the market, he was practically mobbed by the children, and all security arrangements broke down. Bunker was impressed with the political implications of his popularity with the people. Thieu spoke to a village council and the self-defense unit of citizens. Then lunch was served on a glorious beach. There were seven courses and cold beer. The heat of midday was relieved by the breeze off the ocean. An improvised latrine was set up. The wind made hitting the pot somewhat difficult, but Bunker joked that the surrounding sand absorbed all evidence of failure.

To begin American troop withdrawals, Bunker and Abrams agreed to pull American units out of combat first in those areas where the South Vietnamese had the best prospects of filling in effectively. In July, the First Army of the Republic of Vietnam (ARVN) Division, under the superb command of General Ngo Quang Truong, was given responsibility for search-and-destroy operations in the mountains near the demilitarized zone along the border with North Vietnam. Local Regional Forces (RF) and PF units took over from the First ARVN responsibility for village security along the coast. This assumption of new responsibilities by the South Vietnamese permitted the American Third Marine Division to stand down from combat. Then, as the security situation showed no deterioration, those US Marines went home.

By the summer of 1969, security in the Mekong River Delta had so improved that for the first time in years, one could drive during the day—unescorted—to every provincial capital in the region. Therefore, the next American division to be sent home was the US Army's Ninth Division, stationed in My Tho province along a branch of the Mekong.

The Communists reacted to the changing battlefield dynamics. Ho Chi Minh called on his forces to conserve manpower. General Vo Nguyen Giap called for a renewal of guerilla tactics. Infiltration from the North began to fall off. Nonetheless, the Communists were still losing 2,500 men a week, which some in the press called a "lull" in the fighting.

In June, Kissinger had approached "his old friend" Jean Sainteny to assist in opening private negotiations with Hanoi's leaders. Kissinger noted in his memoirs that Sainteny had provided him with his "first insights into the Vietnamese mentality."[5] Kissinger recommended to President Nixon that he meet with Sainteny; the meeting happened on July 15. Sainteny accepted the task of visiting Hanoi on behalf of the United States. Such a trip was rejected by Hanoi. But Sainteny was able to arrange a secret meeting for Kissinger with representatives of the North Vietnamese government in his Paris apartment on the Rue de Rivoli. The meeting would take place on August 4. Hanoi would be represented by Xuan Thuy and Hanoi's representative in Paris, Mai Van Bo. The secret talks, which would result in the betrayal of South Vietnam, would thus begin, appropriately, in the upscale apartment of the French colonialist who had been so helpful to Ho Chi Minh in 1946.

On July 30, President Nixon visited Vietnam. Only Thieu, Bunker, and Abrams knew of the visit in advance. Others were notified only one hour before Nixon's arrival. Bunker had flown to Bangkok to meet his president. Then they flew on Air Force One to Tan Son Nhut Airport to get a helicopter that would fly them to Thieu's office in the heart of crowded Saigon. The streets around the presidential palace had been closed to traffic since the morning, while troops were highly visible on guard around the palace. With a laugh, Thieu told the Americans, "The people thought a coup was coming!"

For two hours, Nixon, Thieu, Bunker, and Kissinger discussed the war. Nixon made three points: 1) he would make no new concessions in the peace talks, 2) there would be no hasty withdrawal of American troops, and 3) he would not agree to a peace that would result in turning South Vietnam over to the Communists in two or three more years.[6]

President Thieu expressed to President Nixon his concern that "if the US wishes to disengage, the best course would be to help South Viet-Nam grow strong." He added that "if you help us to resist and 'chase away the aggressor,' we can handle the rest of the problem."

The American president asked his South Vietnamese counterpart whether, if the North stayed out of South Vietnam, they could handle the Viet Cong. Thieu replied, "Yes, I believe we can. But we cannot imagine a permanent peace if North Viet-Nam remains in Laos and Cambodia."

Nixon gave Thieu confidence that the Americans would not disengage in a way that would endanger South Vietnam, that the Americans had the will to see the job through to the end. Nixon showed an incisive and comprehensive grasp of the situation. He expressed himself with great clarity and gave the Vietnamese a feeling that he believed in them. For Bunker, the American president struck just the right tone of partnership with all the Vietnamese he met.

As Bunker deftly understood, the success of Vietnamization turned on the capacity of the South Vietnamese. The American role was only secondary; it was principally not to sabotage South Vietnamese efforts. And South Vietnam's capacity turned on the quality of its leadership, above all on the skills of its president—the quietly intense, very proud, astute, but mistrustful Nguyen Van Thieu.

Hanoi came to the same conclusion regarding Thieu's importance to the war effort. Its principal demand of the Americans in the secret Paris negotiations became that the Americans should remove Thieu as president of South Vietnam. It wanted a repeat of how Sainteny had helped the Communists marginalize their Nationalist rivals in 1946.

As Vietnamization began, Thieu gave his government and people a strategy of national survival taken from Dai Viet political teachings, the theory called *Dan Toc Sinh Ton* (the people's life force). Thieu's strategy was centered on Vietnamese self-reliance. All government programs were to promote national survivability under the slogan "*Tu Luc, Tu Cuong*" (Self-Effort, Self-Strength). This Dai Viet political philosophy had come together in the 1930s first with a group of novelists who called for a new Vietnamese culture of individual self-determination, a culture that was post-Confucian and anti-French.

Thieu now assumed personal direction of the Central Pacification and Development Council to coordinate all his cabinet ministers, generals, and province and district chiefs behind the Civil Operations Rural Development Support (CORDS) pacification and rural development program. Thieu embarked on an ambitious land redistribution program. All those who tilled rice paddies would become owners of the land that supported them, and their families would be provided with a livelihood.

With certain exceptions, all land owned by absentee landlords was expropriated by the government. Landlords were given government bonds in exchange for their real estate. Large landlords, by and large, made no fuss about Thieu's reform, as they had long since shifted their wealth to commercial pursuits in the towns and cities. But small landlords—including many civil servants and junior and noncommissioned officers—looked to their modest inherited landholdings for valuable social prestige and for income to supplement their meager salaries. They opposed Thieu's Land to the Tiller program when it was sent to the National Assembly for approval.

Bunker strongly supported Thieu's sweeping and radical redistribution of rice fields to new owners. Giving farmers legal titles to land, making them small capitalists, would give them a dynamic stake in the future of a non-Communist South Vietnam. Bunker often said that self-reliant individuals like farmers were the best building blocks of pluralistic politics and representative democracy.

Farming is a life of measured tempo that encourages a sense of mastery over one's environment. Moreover, farmers are patient people when patience is democracy's necessary virtue. Farmers bide their time and get what they want in natural stages of a growing cycle without losing self-control to the rough human hurly-burly of winner takes all competition. Bunker once asked me whether one important cause of America's growing political and cultural divisiveness might not be the decline of its farming population.

But no matter how much Thieu and his colleagues achieved, it was never enough for American journalists and antiwar leaders. They fed on pessimism about prospects for Vietnamization and on finding flaws with Thieu and the South Vietnamese, of which, to be fair, there were more than a few. In this regard, the American antiwar movement and Hanoi were in alignment: both put Thieu in the crosshairs of their coldly calculated and sharply focused political attacks.

But as 1969 progressed, it became inescapable that Thieu was leading the most stable government South Vietnam had ever known. This was not good news for the Communists.

Hanoi had proposed ten points in the Paris negotiations as its terms for ending the war. Hanoi wanted an end to Thieu's government, while Washington wanted removal of North Vietnamese troops from South Vietnam, leaving all South Vietnamese to thereafter settle political affairs among themselves. The Americans had countered with eight different points of their own.

Kissinger constantly argued to Thieu that the South Vietnamese must agree to negotiating positions that would appear "fair and reasonable" to American public opinion, which was growing ever more tired of the war. To maintain day-to-day support for a measured program of Vietnamization, Kissinger bowed before criticisms of the war. Little by little he whittled away terms of settlement that were favorable to South Vietnam. Thieu's resistance to this process of escalating compromise put him in Kissinger's line of fire using targeted expressions of cutting annoyance and neocolonial condescension.

Thieu was asked by Kissinger to propose a political settlement with the NLF. Thieu responded with his position: South Vietnamese in the NLF could participate in a fair and free election after the NLF had renounced the use of force against other South Vietnamese. Thieu offered the NLF a role in devising the rules for such an election and promised to amend South Vietnam's constitution to give the NLF freedom to advocate its pro-Hanoi positions. The Americans reviewed a draft speech in which Thieu set forth his ideas. He gave the speech on July 11, 1969.

Hanoi's response was escalation: the formation of a Provisional Revolutionary Government intended to take over control of South Vietnam from Thieu. Known as the PRG, this supposed government immediately issued a ten-point peace program of its own.

Initially, both Thieu and Bunker welcomed this Communist initiative. Thieu thought that now Hanoi would accept an independent South Vietnam. Bunker briefly thought the negotiations might get down to meaningful agreement.

Not every South Vietnamese was happy with Thieu's offer of elections—Vice President Nguyen Cao Ky in particular. On July 22, Duong Van "Big" Minh, Tran Van Don, and seventeen other retired generals gave a lunch for the vice president. In his remarks, Ky took on Bunker as the "governor general" of South Vietnam. As Thieu accommodated the Americans, Ky sought to undermine him.

Thieu was angry at this intrigue, telling Bunker that "Ky rejects elections as an end to the war. He talks of coups. Before I made my speech proposing elections, he never objected. He is utterly dishonest."

Henry Kissinger now made the first of what would become a long series of compromises with Hanoi in the peace negotiations. This occurred at his August 4 meeting with Hanoi's Xuan Thuy and Mai Van Bo at Sainteny's apartment on the Rue de Rivoli in Paris. Kissinger affirmed that "in order to expedite negotiations, [his] President is ready to open another channel of contact with them. He is prepared to appoint a high-level emissary who would be authorized to negotiate a conclusion."[7]

While President Thieu was under the impression that the secret talks between his American ally and his Vietnamese enemy were to "explore" possibilities for a settlement of the war over who was to govern South Vietnam, Kissinger asked Hanoi to consider negotiating the final terms of that settlement only with him.

In this first session, Kissinger did, however, also affirm that the United States was willing to withdraw all of its forces without exception from Vietnam as part of a program for the removal of all outside forces from Vietnam.

Kissinger proposed mutual withdrawals of both US and North Vietnamese forces from South Vietnam consistent with the 1966 Manila proposal for ending the war. He indicated that the United States would not leave any residual forces in South Vietnam as it had in South Korea and

West Germany. And on the political side, Kissinger said that the United States would accept any decision by the South Vietnamese people about their political future. Kissinger proposed starting a special channel of talks apart from the public sessions.

Xuan Thuy countered that peace required the withdrawal of American forces and the removal of the Saigon administration, with its replacement being a coalition government including the NLF leadership, now called the Provisional Revolutionary Government (PRG). No withdrawal of North Vietnamese forces or any release of American prisoners of war was offered.

Kissinger's new secret channel was not used again until 1970. But its creation opened an opportunity for Kissinger to personally set the terms for ending American participation in the war.

But on October 15, 1969, Nixon experienced the first massive antiwar protest of his administration. Some 250,000 mostly white, middle-class Americans came to Washington to demand an immediate end to the Vietnam War. Hanoi's prime minister sent the demonstrators an open letter hailing their efforts and wishing that their "fall offensive" would "succeed splendidly."

Bunker took a short vacation to visit home. He was unprepared for the negative image of the South Vietnamese government held by so many Americans. Where he had seen so much progress and substantial development firsthand, Americans thought of South Vietnam in other terms—in harsh images of corruption, ineptitude, and repression.

Upon returning to Saigon, Bunker immediately saw Thieu and spoke bluntly: Thieu had a bad reputation in the United States. Americans worried about political prisoners, corruption, and a resurrection of Diem's Can Lao Party. Thieu listened politely, intellectually understanding Bunker's points but emotionally remaining unable to see their importance.

The Communists were not the only Vietnamese to notice the growing momentum of the American antiwar movement. Retired South Vietnamese general Tran Van Don had been in Washington during the big October demonstration. He now returned to Saigon and organized his own third force political movement to offer American antiwar leaders an alternative to Thieu. On October 31, Don held a splashy reception at his house. The next day, November 1, retired general and former chief of state Big Minh gave a similar reception to commemorate the coup against Ngo Dinh Diem, which he had led. Now he called for a national convention to create a "truly" representative government for South Vietnam, ignoring the constitution and elections. Big Minh complained that the democratic aims of the coup against Diem and his family had yet to be attained. He said, "It might be worth some confusion to save this nation."

Since the Communists in Paris had cleverly indicated that he was one South Vietnamese leader with whom they could treat, Big Minh became the focal point for dovish American hopes seeking a quick accommodation with Hanoi as the way to end the war.

That same day, Thieu gave a very emotional speech, during which he wept and promised to resign if his policies ever led to a loss of American support or to domination by the Communists. His Catholic wife attended a ceremony of mourning at the graves of Diem and his brother Nhu.

Nixon shifted South Vietnamese politics a few days later with a powerful speech on November 3. Rejecting calls to abandon South Vietnam to the Communists, Nixon refused to withdraw either irresponsibly or precipitously. He confidently affirmed that Vietnamization or negotiations, whichever succeeded first, would end America's Vietnam commitment with honor. He pledged to stand by America's Cold War strategy of defeating Communist aggression.

But not every observer shared Bunker's confidence. Maynard Parker of *Newsweek* told his readers that "Vietnamization is an illusion." The magazine predicted that South Vietnamese forces would not be able to withstand a full-force North Vietnamese invasion and that South Vietnam's future was fated to be an accommodation with the Communists. After all, opined *Newsweek*, "getting along with Charlie" was a well-established way of life in South Vietnam.

The strategic trends in place during 1969 continued over into the following year without interruption. More and more American troops left South Vietnam for home; the Communists grew weaker both militarily and politically. But still, Thieu could gain no footing with elite American opinion.

During 1970, the peace negotiations with Hanoi were conducted in great secrecy by Henry Kissinger. Kissinger would inform Bunker of his discussions with the North Vietnamese, and Bunker would then brief only Thieu on Kissinger's reports of the substance of the negotiations. Bypassing the normal channels of the State Department, Kissinger would send from the White House a long cable summarizing the points made by each side in the secret meetings. Later, a courier would fly out to Saigon with a more complete memorandum of the conversation between Kissinger and Hanoi's senior representatives. After reading these memos, Bunker would formulate five or six paragraphs containing the important points made by each side. He would then meet with Thieu alone and read those paragraphs to the South Vietnamese president. Thieu was told not to inform anyone in his government of the secret talks. He agreed to that restriction.

On January 12, 1970, Kissinger communicated with the North Vietnamese through an intermediary a desire for more private meetings to "produce the framework for a rapid solution of the conflict on a basis fair to all."[8]

Secret talks between Kissinger and the North Vietnamese were held again on February 21, March 16, and April 4. Kissinger had proposed the withdrawal of both American and North Vietnamese forces from South Vietnam. Hanoi had refused, demanding instead two agreements: one on military issues and another on who would rule in Saigon. No progress could be made on one until the other was resolved. Hanoi's strategy was to hold American forces hostage on the battlefield until Washington agreed to the overthrow of Thieu's government. Hanoi's strategy gambled on the growing strength of antiwar sentiment in the United States, a not-unreasonable calculation that, when push came to shove for Americans desperate for disengagement, Thieu would be thrown aside.

Kissinger had countered with the position that political issues should be left to the South Vietnamese to settle for themselves; Hanoi and Washington should concentrate only on the military issues.

The parties were deadlocked.

During the February 21 meeting, Kissinger stood his ground:

It is, of course, difficult for men who have shown your heroism and dedication to envisage an end to the war which doesn't guarantee all of your immediate objectives. It is not easy for us either, because we too have had over a period of time to adjust some of our thinking ...

The President has charged me with this responsibility of talking to you gentlemen because we thought this private vehicle would allow both sides to speak more frankly, and would make it easier to change positions already taken in the established framework.

Our basic approach is to deal with you on a basis of reciprocity and respect. On this basis, we believe we both might try to move the negotiations forward.

We could, for example, agree today on a time to meet again, and put as the first item on the agenda the withdrawal of forces, as I stated in my statement—not just of our forces, but of all non-South Vietnamese forces.

We understand that the arrangements for the withdrawal of your forces could be put in a special category. We would not insist that they be placed on the same legal basis as ours.[9]

In reporting on his meeting to President Nixon, Kissinger put down in passing his view that a settlement of the war would be reached between the Vietnamese Communists and the Americans. Subsequently, the NLF and the South Vietnamese would be maneuvered to "ratify" what the principal powers had already agreed to. Kissinger wrote to his president, "It was also implicitly agreed that, after we have discussed all the issues, and if we reach agreement, the other parties will be brought in to ratify it." This pulled the rug out from under Thieu by putting into play Sainteny's colonialist insistence that only the Communist Vietnamese deserved respect and deference.[10]

In a separate memo to President Nixon, Kissinger set forth his thoughts as to the future course of the negotiations with Hanoi:

> There are basically two issues involved in the talks: 1) mutual withdrawal of non-South Vietnamese military forces, which we have raised; and 2) political settlement in South Vietnam, which they have raised.

> Agreement with the North Vietnamese on a verifiable mutual withdrawal is in our and the GVN's fundamental interests, even if there is no political settlement. But the North Vietnamese will almost certainly not wish to withdraw their forces until they have a good idea of the shape of a political settlement, since the GVN seems at the moment to have the upper hand over the VC.

> As a general line of approach in the next meetings, therefore, I propose that I put forward a precise and fairly attractive proposal for mutual withdrawal, which could be negotiated with regard to timing but would necessarily include absolute reciprocity and devices for verification. I would seek to get from them a counterproposal on this issue and a new proposal on political settlement.

> Coordination with the GVN

> The lack of an agreed position with the GVN will require you to make decisions on our position which could, if later revealed, embroil us in difficulties with Saigon. This is risky, but I see no other way to proceed if we are to maintain momentum and secrecy.[11]

In the March 1970 secret negotiating session in Paris, Kissinger offered that the United States would withdraw all its forces from South Vietnam over sixteen months and that North Vietnamese forces should also with-draw from the South.[12]

At this time, Kissinger noted for President Nixon that

> *From our viewpoint, there is one issue to which all others are sub-ordinate—reciprocity in the withdrawal of non-South Vietnamese troops from South Vietnam (and foreign troops from Laos and Cam-bodia). Our first objective must be to reach agreement on reciprocity in principle or in fact. Once they have done so, they will have given up their claim to moral superiority and can no longer argue pri-vately that their forces are in South Vietnam on a different moral and legal basis than ours. This would be a quantum jump in the negotiations.[13]*

When Ellsworth Bunker returned to Washington for consultations on the now very important secret negotiations, he

> *specifically agreed with Mr. Kissinger's (1) stating our acceptance of the principle of total withdrawal, (2) presenting a schedule showing what a US withdrawal in 16 months would look like, (3) stating our understanding of their special problem with linking their with-drawals to ours, (4) asking them for a separate schedule for their withdrawal, (5) saying there should be means of verification and an exchange of POWs, and (6) stating that if there were agreement in principle the technical issues could be discussed at the [public sessions].*

Ambassador Bunker agreed with Kissinger's doubts about the wisdom of spreading knowledge of his meetings with the North Vietnamese. In addition to the dangers of leaks, knowledge of the meetings would lead to increased pressure for a flood of initiatives, such as cease-fire. They agreed, however, that at some point, they should bring in a select and very limited number of people. Kissinger said that he thought the secretary of state should be informed, perhaps after two more meetings.

Ambassador Bunker said that he had set up a special procedure for back-channel messages on this subject. Only one man in Saigon knew the code. Kissinger said that he would send Ambassador Bunker a brief account of the next meeting through this channel by the morning of March 18, Saigon time, and would then send him a full account by courier. He would probably use a code for names in these messages. (This code would be as follows: Kissinger = Luke, Xuan Thuy = Yul, Le Duc Tho = Michael, Mai Van Bo = Nestor, General Walters = Xerxes.)[14]

At the April 4, 1970, meeting, Hanoi refused to withdraw its forces from South Vietnam and demanded a new National Assembly and constitution for South Vietnam.[15]

But in July 1970, after successful operations in Cambodia against North Vietnamese forces and sanctuaries there but also after the escalation in antiwar sentiment occasioned by those operations and the killing of student protestors at Kent State, President Nixon decided upon a major new peace initiative. Bunker was called back to Washington for discussions as to what might be done in the negotiations. It was decided to put a new plan on the table with Hanoi—a cease-fire and a unilateral commitment by the United States not to leave a residual force in South Vietnam after peace was achieved. After the Korean War had ended in an armistice, American forces had remained in South Korea. And American forces still protected the western half of Germany from Soviet aggression. But now, in Vietnam, Americans would leave their allies at greater risk of future invasion. But it was also decided that these concessions would be offered in the context of President Nixon's speech of April 20, 1970, holding that they would go into effect only with the permanent withdrawal of all North Vietnamese forces from South Vietnam and upon assurances that such North Vietnamese forces would not return south.

In September, Bunker was instructed to obtain President Thieu's endorsement of the new American peace initiative. Nixon wanted to propose a more forthcoming negotiating position in a public speech. Thieu already had a position on offering the Communists a cease-fire. He had long feared one. His conditions were that any cease-fire be tied to North Vietnamese withdrawal and the holding of elections within South Vietnam. His plan called for the fighting to stop and military forces to regroup into zones and then move north if they were Communist. But with progress in pacification and success achieved in the Cambodian sanctuary operations, Thieu was now open to the principle of accepting an interim truce with the Communists while negotiations continued, looking for a permanent solution to the conflict. Since American forces were on their way home, he recognized that to ask Hanoi for mutual withdrawal was a "nonstarter," as Bunker put it in one cable to Kissinger. Nevertheless, Thieu insisted that the final settlement provide for a full North Vietnamese withdrawal from South Vietnam. Bunker suggested that Thieu think of a cease-fire not as an end in itself, like an armistice permanently fixing the position of two contending armies, but more as an interim step leading to a just and favorable solution of the dispute.[16]

Thieu was a hard sell. On September 19, Bunker asked Washington for more details about how a cease-fire would be implemented to discuss with Thieu. He reported very precisely that he had given Thieu assurances based on an assumption that Washington would hold to the principle of a final American withdrawal conditioned on a reciprocal North Vietnamese withdrawal. Bunker thought his superiors were proposing in the new peace plan only to subdivide the Paris negotiations into two phases—a preliminary one to achieve a cease-fire and a subsequent phase to formulate the terms of a final settlement. Discussion of North Vietnam's withdrawal was now being moved from the first phase to the second one but not being abandoned by Washington as a condition for a final and lasting peace.[17]

This understanding would later guide Bunker in drafting his April 1971 negotiating strategy, as requested by Henry Kissinger

Hanoi now put more political pressure on Nixon by adopting the peace plan of the American antiwar movement—the unconditional withdrawal of American forces as proposed by senators George McGovern and Mark Hatfield. A spokeswoman for the PRG announced that if the United States agreed to pull out its forces by the middle of 1971 and replace

Thieu's government with a coalition, then it could get a peace agreement with Hanoi.

Kissinger had held another secret meeting with the North Vietnamese on September 7. He had shortened the time during which all American forces would withdraw to twelve months.[18] No progress was made, and the channel for discussions was closed. On October 7, President Nixon went public with his new plan. Just prior to Nixon's speech, Bunker received a message informing him that President Nixon was concerned that nothing in the speech be interpreted as justifying the unilateral withdrawal of American forces. It was Nixon's position that American forces would leave South Vietnam only 1) as part of the Vietnamization process or 2) as part of an overall settlement. Bunker immediately passed Nixon's affirmation on to Thieu.

Thieu had been given an advance text of Nixon's remarks, and Washington reviewed the text of Thieu's proposed speech in support of Nixon's initiative. When the State Department instructed Bunker to seek certain changes in Thieu's speech, Kissinger sent him private instructions to ignore the State Department. It was becoming clear to Bunker that Kissinger had the dominant voice in Vietnam negotiations. Bunker's file of private communications with the White House began to grow, while important messages to the State Department became fewer and fewer.

On October 20, the House of Bishops of the Episcopal Church called for the United States to end its support of Thieu's government and withdraw its troops by December 31, 1971. Ending the war without regard for the South Vietnamese was now portrayed in the United States as a moral imperative.

In the spring of 1971, South Vietnamese forces with American helicopter support moved into Laos to cut the Ho Chi Minh Trail and deny Hanoi the ability to send more men and supplies into South Vietnam for the 1971 campaign season (Operation Lam Son 719). While South Vietnamese forces were pummeled hard by North Vietnamese battalions and artillery during their withdrawal back into South Vietnam, they did not break ranks. They were now largely the combat equals of North Vietnamese regulars, a step forward in Vietnamization.

The secret negotiations commenced again after the operation in Laos complicated Hanoi's prospects for winning an outright military victory. Hanoi responded favorably to Kissinger's proposals presented in Paris on May 31, along the lines which Bunker had drafted but which Kissinger had modified to allow the North Vietnamese to keep their army inside South Vietnam after a peace agreement.

A senior member of the politburo, Le Duc Tho, then arrived in Paris to lead Hanoi's diplomatic efforts. He brought with him the first concrete proposals for a settlement. In a meeting on June 26, the North Vietnamese put on the table a nine-point proposal in line with the framework which Sainteny had brought to Kissinger a month earlier on May 25. The proposal provided for the withdrawal of American forces from South Vietnam but not Hanoi's divisions. The sixth point presented by the North Vietnamese echoed Kissinger's language in his message to Bunker of May 25: the peoples of Indochina would discuss among themselves their disagreements. It promised a cease-fire with international supervision upon the signing of an agreement. After his secret trip to Beijing, in a July 12 meeting, Kissinger reached agreement with Le Duc Tho on all essential matters except the status of Thieu's government. True to his word, in these three meetings Kissinger did not raise the issue of Hanoi removing its army from South Vietnam. The North Vietnamese suggested that Washington could resolve the remaining open issue by manipulating South Vietnam's forthcoming election and so get rid of Thieu. Le Duc Tho even suggested assassination of Thieu as a means to this end.

In a July 26 meeting with the North Vietnamese, Kissinger sweetened his offer. He proposed an aid program for North Vietnam and a commitment that American troops would leave South Vietnam nine months after a cease-fire went into effect, not the twelve or sixteen months that he had previously put on the table.

On August 4, Bunker brought Thieu up-to-date on the secret negotiations. Neither man realized that withdrawal of North Vietnamese troops was no longer part of the plan to end the war. Thieu now proposed to

Bunker that Washington seek an understanding with Beijing so that both China and the United States might guarantee the peace in Indochina. Thieu's suggestion that Hanoi's close ties to Moscow might give rise to concern in Beijing was a shrewd insight on his part. In 1979, China would go to war with Hanoi over its imperialism in Cambodia.[19]

In meetings in Washington, Bunker reviewed a new draft of a possible peace agreement that was to be presented to Hanoi by Kissinger at his next meeting in the secret negotiations. Kissinger's able and dedicated assistant Winston Lord had combined Kissinger's seven points of May 31 with the nine points subsequently put forth by Hanoi into a single text that might serve as the basis for a final agreement. In its point five, Lord's draft said that among the problems to be settled after the cease-fire through discussions among the countries of Indochina was implementation of the principle that all military forces would remain within their national frontiers. Bunker pointed out that Thieu would insist on such a provision.

Bunker was not alert to the possibility that put in such a way, point five was actually of little help to South Vietnam. While the proposed future discussions about how best to implement the principle would go on between Saigon and Hanoi, Hanoi's troops would still be in Laos, Cambodia, and South Vietnam—free to do whatever they might wish on orders from their politburo commanders.

On August 16, Kissinger met in Paris with North Vietnamese diplomat Xuan Thuy only. Kissinger presented an eight-point proposal which he described as a merger of the earlier American peace proposal with Hanoi's new nine-point proposal. In his eight-point proposal, Kissinger included in elliptical wording his commitment not to contest a future Communist conquest of South Vietnam. His third point said: The political future of South Vietnam will be left for the South Vietnamese to decide for themselves, free from outside interference. The United States . . . will abide by the outcome of . . . any other political process shaped by the South Vietnamese people themselves.[20]

In a memorandum for his president, dated August 16, in his usual erudite way of using obfuscation and omission to deceive, Kissinger did not provide the wording of his eight-point proposal for obtaining a peace agreement. He sent a very similar report to William Rogers, the American Secretary of State, also without particularizing his eight points. Again President Nixon was left uneducated as to the specific concession Kissinger had made to Hanoi on May 31—that North Vietnamese forces could remain in South Vietnam after a peace agreement awaiting the first "opportune moment" in which to strike down their nationalist rivals.

Nor did Henry Kissinger share his eight-point plan with Nguyen Van Thieu, the freely and fairly elected president of the South Vietnamese. This refusal came after the American had perversely and presumptuously taken it upon himself to impose on those people an existential threat to their core values, their freedoms, and their right to national self-determination.[21]

On September 13, Kissinger met with only Xuan Thuy in Paris for a short two-hour session. Neither side gave way on the issue of how South Vietnam was to be governed and by whom. No date was set for another meeting.[22]

South Vietnam held an election for its presidency. Thieu campaigned for reelection based on his record of success in economic development, pacification, land reform, and standing up to Hanoi while the Americans withdrew their combat forces. He was opposed from the right by Vice President Nguyen Cao Ky and from the more pacifist left by former general Duong Van "Big" Minh. Thieu and his clique arranged for a law to be passed by the National Assembly making it hard for Ky to gain sufficient endorsements to qualify as a candidate. When Ky did not qualify, Big Minh refused to run as well, alleging that the election was "rigged."

With both Ky and Big Minh now out of the presidential race, the Supreme Court certified Thieu alone as a candidate. He then converted the election into a referendum, pledging that if the vote showed that the people had no confidence in his abilities, he would resign. Ky was angry, calling in members of the foreign press to say, "I am going to destroy [Thieu] and all his clique. I am a fighter. I will destroy him even if I have to sacrifice my life to do it."

Thieu promoted twenty-eight generals and named a new commander of the national police, further removing Ky from exercising influence over the military. Thieu made a few speeches, good in substance but too long, recounting his accomplishments. The militant Buddhists called for a boycott, and one of Big Minh's advisors organized some demonstrations against Thieu in Saigon. The militant Buddhists did not join the demonstrators. Ky put himself behind the boycott effort. On election day, October 3, 87.9 percent of the registered voters went to the polls. Thieu received 94 percent of the 5.9 million votes cast.

Even Thieu could see that he could have easily won a contested election. Bunker was rueful, for the election results showed that Thieu genuinely had substantial support among the people of South Vietnam, especially in the rural areas, where the farmers had never experienced such security and such good prices for their crops. Meaningful prosperity was blatant throughout South Vietnam. Bunker sensed that Thieu was embittered by the election, having let a chance to prove that he had popular support, that he had earned *uy tin*, slip through his fingers. After his reelection, Thieu seemed edgy and somewhat ashamed of himself.

Kissinger again whittled more away from his minimum terms for settlement with Hanoi. He sought to disassociate the United States from Thieu. In the secret talks over the summer of 1971, all issues had been conceptually resolved except the status of Saigon's government, which, after the one-man election, was tied up with the future of Nguyen Van Thieu. Kissinger now sought to propose to Hanoi a new presidential election in South Vietnam to be held within six months after a final settlement. Thieu was grossly unpopular in Washington. Convinced that Nixon's stock of political capital available to invest in pursuing peace "with honor" was rapidly dwindling, Kissinger did not want his president's remaining credibility squandered through unyielding support of a stubborn South Vietnamese general, albeit one just elected president of his people.

Kissinger had sent his deputy General Alexander Haig out to Saigon for discussions with Thieu. The two men met on September 23. Haig presented Thieu with the idea of a new initiative in the secret talks. Its central feature would be a promise by Thieu to step down as South Vietnam's president before the proposed new—postsettlement—presidential election would be held.[23]

Haig said President Nixon had concluded that South Vietnam's recent one-man presidential election had seriously complicated the administration's effort to help South Vietnam. The major obstacle to a peace agreement was Thieu himself. Without finding a way around this obstacle, Nixon feared that the US Congress would reduce funding or deployments of American forces for the war effort. Thus, Kissinger had already proposed, and Nixon had already accepted, creation of yet another new peace proposal. Washington now needed Thieu's concurrence with the new proposal. If Hanoi rejected this proposal, President Nixon would go public with the entire record of the secret negotiations. Such a revelation of the facts would boost support for the war and stall legislation seeking to disable American war efforts. Haig promised that the Americans would not present the new proposal to Hanoi before coordinating such a step with Thieu. The proposal for his resignation, Haig concluded, would help Thieu place peace for his people above his personal ambitions and thus "defang" his critics, who claimed him to be the last roadblock preventing a settlement.

Taken aback, Thieu replied that the United States could tell Hanoi privately of his personal willingness to step down as South Vietnam's president if that would lessen its resistance to terms of peace. If there were to be a real peace with the Communists, he would not run in any election after the fighting stopped. This he had already promised the people of South Vietnam.

Without Thieu's knowledge—much less his concurrence—a new eight-point proposal, including a provision for his resignation, was presented to the North Vietnamese on October 11.

On November 19, the National Conference of Catholic Bishops voted 158 to 36 that "it is our firm conviction . . . that the speedy ending of this war is a moral imperative of the highest priority."

Hanoi canceled a secret meeting in the negotiations scheduled for November 20. Thieu predicted that they would show "stubbornness" and await the results of President Nixon's visit with Mao Zedong the coming spring.

According to America's revolutionary founders, an appeal to arms is an appeal to heaven for vindication of one's rights. Defeat on the battlefield means that one's cause has been judged remiss by nature's God. In the spring of 1972, Hanoi threw its entire army into an attack on South Vietnam to seek from fate confirmation that the tides of history would carry the Vietnamese Communists to final victory over the Nationalists.

Furthermore, 1972 was a presidential election year in the United States, just as 1968 had been. Hanoi wanted to test the *the*—the dispositive circumstantial power—of the American antiwar movement when President Nixon needed votes for his reelection. This manipulation of *the* might create what North Vietnamese leader Le Duan called a *thoi co*, or opportune moment for seizing the advantage and winning power.[24] Both modern Leninism and traditional Vietnamese thinking combined in Vietnamese Communist thinking to fashion this strategic conception of total war without compromise.

Trained in Lenin's Soviet Union, Ho Chi Minh had once told his very first disciples that "because they do not understand the world situation, do not know how to assess the balance of forces, and lack tactics, people often act when conditions are not ripe and inversely they do not act when they should."[25]

In December 1971, Hanoi's army newspaper published an article pointing out that the withdrawal of American combat ground forces from South Vietnam had created a new balance of forces on the battlefield. "Main force attacks" were again a tactic of choice for the Communists. Large shipments of weapons began arriving in North Vietnamese ports in January 1972. Hanoi was preparing to send 153,000 men south into battle. As 1972 began, Thieu warned his countrymen of hard fighting to come, and Bunker warned his president that the Communists could not let the recent gains won by Saigon go unchallenged.

Two Democrats, Hubert Humphrey and Edmund Muskie, led off the American presidential campaign season with calls for an urgent end to the Vietnam War.

Bunker expected Hanoi to change its tactics, giving up the conservative economy-of-force raids coupled with standoff shelling of fixed targets that had been its fighting modus operandi since mid-1969. He expected further that Hanoi's offensive would begin in February, when President Nixon would be visiting China. Bunker also thought that the South Vietnamese would give a good account of themselves in standing up to the North Vietnamese offensive and that, with help from American tactical airpower, they would beat back the efforts of Hanoi's best troops.[26]

In 1972, the success or failure of American efforts in South Vietnam would rest on the will and capacity of the South Vietnamese.

But before Hanoi's offensive hit, another scene in the play that was more politely called "peace negotiations" was acted out. President Nixon wanted to go public about the Paris negotiations, steal the limelight from his Democratic rivals for the presidency, and pull the rug out from under his opponents in Congress. Bunker was sent to show Thieu the text of the peace proposal that Nixon wanted to use in his speech. Only then did Thieu learn that the offer of his resignation as president of South Vietnam had already been tabled with Hanoi. Haig had assured him the previous September that Kissinger's new initiative would not be presented to the Communists without his being informed of the move. Thieu was now put in the position of a department store mannequin being undressed by Henry Kissinger. Thieu felt betrayed.

Four days later, he sent Bunker a written memorandum of state objecting to Kissinger's plan. Nixon could now not go public without the rift between Kissinger and Thieu being exposed to common knowledge.

In his written response, Thieu asked for time to study the American proposal. It was the first time he had seen Kissinger's eight points and the first time he had seen a peace proposal in a form ready for signatures. He questioned why the withdrawal of North Vietnamese troops from South Vietnam was mentioned only in vague terms. Up to then, he wrote, both Saigon and Washington had publicly advocated the mutual withdrawal of all foreign forces from his country. Both governments should still hold to that position, he insisted. He asked for clarification of Washington's position on this point.[27]

Thieu also expressed reservations about Washington's use of the term "neutrality." It had two connotations to him: one acceptable and one not. The unacceptable use of the term implied a servile accommodation to Communism. He wanted a small committee of his top officials to consider the proposal, adding that if Washington went ahead and released the eight points to the public, he would not support them. In public, he would go no further than his July 1969 proposal for elections as a solution to the political conflict in South Vietnam.

Bunker went to see Thieu and review with him in person the concerns raised in his memorandum of state. Bunker first pointed out to Thieu that under Kissinger's eight points, mutual withdrawal of both US and North Vietnamese forces would have taken place prior to any final settlement and selection of a new government for South Vietnam through elections. Bunker also pointed to the provisions that made any North Vietnamese presence in the South contrary to the terms of peace, especially the requirement that all armed forces in the countries of Indochina remain within their national frontiers. Bunker was still unaware of Kissinger's change of heart and believed that the United States was still strongly pushing for withdrawal of North Vietnamese forces from South Vietnam.

Thieu wanted the fifth point on North Vietnamese withdrawals made more specific. Bunker assured him that the American eight points were only a statement of principles, not the final settlement of all issues. There was no need now, Bunker argued, to state fine points of implementation.

Nixon decided to delay making his speech on the secret talks to consider Thieu's objections. Bunker was asked to offer Thieu an apology and confirm that passing the eight points to Hanoi without his prior knowledge had been a mistake. Washington now confirmed what Bunker had assured Thieu: regarding withdrawals of North Vietnamese troops, such withdrawals would occur prior to any election in South Vietnam. The eight points envisioned two parallel schedules: on one, a clock would start running on American withdrawals and Hanoi's release of American prisoners of war when the peace agreement was signed; the second sequence of treaty obligations—including North Vietnamese withdrawals, Thieu's resignation, and a new presidential election—would be negotiated among the Vietnamese as the Americans were drawing down to their last troops. The clock on the second sequence would start to run when agreement on their particulars was reached and arrangements signed. Consequently, Washington assured Thieu that there would be no elections until a final agreement had been reached between Hanoi and Saigon.

Passed over by Washington in this reply was the possibility that after the Americans had left South Vietnam, Hanoi would not come to terms with Saigon while still keeping its forces in South Vietnam. The time after the departure of American forces while there was a stalemate or breakdown in negotiations between Hanoi and Saigon and resumption of Hanoi's aggression would be the decent interval left by Kissinger to the South Vietnamese.

Neither Thieu, suspicious as he usually was, nor the loyal Bunker, trusting the resolve of both President Nixon and Henry Kissinger, seriously considered this contingency.

Nixon revealed the history of the secret peace negotiations culminating in the American eight-point proposal on January 25, 1972. His domestic audience was stunned by the surprise. Overnight, Henry Kissinger became a political superstar for his efforts with the North Vietnamese. The pressure on Nixon to negotiate a quick end to the war lifted.

Everyone now waited for Hanoi's offensive to start. Washington augmented the airpower available to repulse Communist attacks. By mid-1972, the destructive power available to the tactical strike planes of six aircraft carriers and the bombs to be carried by two hundred B-52s would be ready for defensive action. The ARVN conducted preemptive sweeps in the southern Mekong River Delta, forcing the Communists to postpone attacks there.

In early March, B-52s were sent to bomb Communist troop concentrations along the border with Laos, where infiltration routes branched off the Ho Chi Minh Trail and entered the two northernmost provinces of South Vietnam. Simultaneously, ARVN divisions launched an operation into Cambodia to push North Vietnamese troops farther away from Saigon. Then, South Vietnamese moved into the mountains west of Hue in Central Vietnam to keep North Vietnamese troops from coming down into the coastal lowlands.

Hanoi's 1972 offensive opened in April, but it was limited to only three major drives into South Vietnam—each offensive thrust coming in from external sanctuaries. One thrust came south over the demilitarized zone, a second from Laos into the Central Highlands, and the third from Cambodia toward Saigon. The drives were uncoordinated, which allowed Thieu and his generals tactical flexibility to repulse them one after another. A fourth North Vietnamese effort used Communist forces already in South Vietnam to capture briefly the central coastal province of Binh Dinh.

Unlike 1968 in their Tet Offensive, the Communists could not attack widely throughout South Vietnam. Locations for three of Hanoi's offensive drives—one up near the demilitarized zone, one in the Central Highlands, and one in Binh Dinh—had even been predicted by Bunker's staff. The thrust in from Cambodia toward Saigon, however, did come as a surprise.

American troop strength was down to sixty-nine thousand men and dropping fast.

Nixon now ordered mines to be laid in the seaports of North Vietnam to prevent resupply of Hanoi by the Soviet Union and China in bulk. Having equipped Hanoi for the offensive, the Soviets were not helping Kissinger obtain a negotiated settlement either. Bunker's admiration of Nixon deepened to a new level of quiet loyalty. By ordering the mining— which his predecessor Lyndon Johnson had refused to approve—Nixon put in jeopardy his forthcoming visit to Moscow and his vision of a détente in the Cold War confrontation between rival powers overly armed with nuclear weapons, all to defend South Vietnam. Bunker thought this showed a proper determination, a respect for fundamental values, and considerable courage under a rather vicious political attack.

Nixon promised to pull all remaining American forces out within four months after a cease-fire and the return of American prisoners, incorporating into his terms part of what his critics were demanding.

Faced with Nixon's decision to stop Communist aggression at its source—the weapons of war sent to North Vietnam—*New York Times* columnist Anthony Lewis objected to such a course of action because "everyone knows [it] is morally outrageous and politically useless." He then quoted with much approval a British commentator who had written that the evils that would result from a Communist conquest of Vietnam are "'purely notional and arguable,' while 'the evils which are perpetuated in preventing it appear so actual and so evident that the "order" in whose name they are carried out stands . . . condemned'" and who had therefore concluded that "whatever the arguments may be about regional or global stability, about dominoes or deterrence, what the United States has been doing in Vietnam is wrong and ought to be stopped."[28]

In defending his decision to stand by South Vietnam under invasion, Nixon made reference to a "long night of terror" that would fall on the South Vietnamese if the Communists were to succeed. After their conquest in 1975, Hanoi's leaders would put tens of thousands of South Vietnamese into concentration camps in violation of the laws of war and international human rights. Economic gains made in South Vietnam prior to April 30, 1975, would be compromised as Communist regimentation was imposed on the people and much of their property, including all their savings accounts, was subordinated to Party and government regulations.

Thieu now addressed his people. He said that this was the last Communist offensive. There were only two alternatives, he thought, in the minds of Vietnam's Communist leaders: either South Vietnam would beg for mercy, or Hanoi would fight on until South Vietnam was crushed. His government would not surrender; rather, it would fight to deny Hanoi a military victory. Hanoi offered no alternative leading to a just peace. The war had to go on. Thieu declared martial law.

When Bunker met with Thieu after his speech, South Vietnam's president was almost ebullient. He asserted that now he would take strong economic measures to finance the war; more taxes would be imposed. All men from ages seventeen to forty-three would be drafted. Universities would be closed, and their students given military training. He would get special powers from the National Assembly to deal with the emergency. He had already met with the leaders of seventeen political parties seeking their support.

Hanoi's principal negotiator, Le Duc Tho, told some French Communists that Hanoi had not expected President Nixon's firm reaction to the offensive. Now, Tho said, the Communist offensive would "slow down," and diplomatic efforts would accelerate to win total victory over South Vietnam.

Kissinger proposed resumption of secret talks with Le Duc Tho. Thieu asked Bunker whether the United States planned to table any "new" proposals for the Communists to consider. Bunker quickly replied, "No," adding that the United States had no intention of conceding to the Communists in negotiations what they had been unable to win on the battlefield. Bunker was feeling pretty sure of himself now that ARVN soldiers had withstood a terrible pounding. As in Operation Lam Son 719 of the year before, South Vietnamese troops had proved to be no pushovers.

The drive to recapture Quang Tri City from the Communists began under General Ngo Quang Truong. His troops had been retrained and reequipped. They felt they could win. Necessary supplies were on hand. In a week, his troops reached the outskirts of Quang Tri City. By July 20, they raised the South Vietnamese yellow flag with three horizontal red stripes over part of the city, which was now mostly rubble.

Hanoi's massive Easter Offensive was beaten back. At the same time, South Vietnam's rural areas had held for the government. Provincial, district, and village forces had fought well against North Vietnamese regulars in Quang Tri, An Loc, Binh Dinh, and elsewhere. In the Mekong River Delta, losses were at the low level of 1971. But nearly one million new refugees had been created by the invasion. While the offensive had been underway, the United States had withdrawn nearly one hundred thousand men. The last American combat units left South Vietnam on August 12, 1972. Only forty-two thousand American soldiers remained in the country.

South Vietnam had now defeated a rural insurgency and had stopped a conventional cross-border invasion. The country's economy was productive, even in wartime, its political system was flexible and stable, its people were optimistic about their future.

George McGovern, a senator from South Dakota, had won the nomina-tion of his Democratic Party to challenge Richard Nixon for the American presidency in 1972. During the primaries in the run-up to the Democratic Party Convention, McGovern had promised that "I would go to Hanoi and beg if I thought that would release the boys one day earlier." His electoral platform pledged to withdraw all American troops from South Vietnam, terminate aid to the freely elected government of South Vietnam, and grant amnesty to American draft evaders.

CHAPTER 6

THE SELLOUT

It looked as if a night of dark intent
Was coming, and not only a night, an age.
Someone had better be prepared for rage.
There would be more than ocean-water broken
Before God's last Put Out the Light was spoken.

—Robert Frost, "Once by the Pacific"

Now, it is not good for the Christian's health to hustle the
Aryan brown,
For the Christian riles, and the Aryan smiles, and he weareth the
Christian down;
And the end of the fight is a tombstone white, with the name of the
late deceased,
And the epitaph drear: "A fool lies here who tried to hustle the East."

—Rudyard Kipling, *The Naulahka*

In May 1971, the politburo of the Vietnamese Communist Party had decided on one great big roll of the military dice to try to win the war hands down on their terms. If Hanoi's troops could crush the South Vietnamese on the battlefield, then the Paris Peace negotiations would become a mopping up operation for them. Thus, in 1972 Hanoi's leaders had mobilized forces and sent them into battle in three zones close to their sanctuaries—near the Cambodian border northwest of Saigon, in the mountainous Central Highlands not too far from the border with Laos, and just south of the demilitarized zone separating North from South Vietnam.

Their objective was to 1) smash and humiliate South Vietnamese forces and 2) exacerbate defeatism among Americans to give political momentum to the antiwar Democrats in a presidential election year. In the language of the politburo, Communist leaders developed their "strategic offensive posture in South Vietnam to defeat the American Vietnamization policy, gain a decisive victory in 1972, and force the US imperialists to negotiate an end to the war from a position of defeat."[1] To win on the ground, Hanoi used three or four infantry divisions in each attack sector. The divisions were supported by armor and artillery units. The tenacious and stalwart South Vietnamese lieutenant general Ngo Quang Truong would later write that for this offensive, Hanoi would commit its entire combat army, save one division (the 316th), which was fighting American and South Vietnamese allies in Laos, to a blitzkrieg kind of war in South Vietnam. Hanoi would send fourteen divisions, plus an additional twenty-six separate regiments, with supporting armor and artillery units, to the battlefield.

This was a force that Nazi general Erwin Rommel would have admired. In flagrant refutation of the delusional narrative held so dearly by the American antiwar movement, this was to be no spontaneous uprising of oppressed peasants seeking liberation from tyrannous landlords and greedy merchants. This was to be a very U. S. Grant/Robert E. Lee kind of warfare, a war of "big battalions" where firepower, not hit-and-run guerilla tactics, would be decisive in winning battles. Would the South Vietnamese troops be up to the fight?

Communist leaders planned to annihilate a number of South Vietnamese regiments and render entire South Vietnamese divisions ineffective. They planned to expand their base areas, moving their main force units into South Vietnam and providing "a firm foothold" for them there.

Gaining such a "foothold" inside South Vietnam would well prepare Hanoi to launch another offensive after American military power had completely disengaged and after the end of the "decent interval" they had given to Henry Kissinger in the secret negotiations, should such a future offensive become necessary for the conquest of South Vietnam.

As with the Tet Offensive of 1968, Hanoi failed to rout South Vietnamese forces. Vietnamization had succeeded.

South Vietnam's army held off the attacks and regained ground initially lost to the Communists. American combat forces continued to withdraw during the offensive. And Richard Nixon decisively defeated the antiwar candidate George McGovern at the polls in November 1972.

As North Vietnam's desperate offensive sputtered toward defeat over the summer of 1972, Thieu concluded that Hanoi's leaders would now seek a "leopard spot" resolution to the war. Some parts of South Vietnam—the "spots"—would host Communist troops and cadres. The leopard spots would provide Hanoi with secure base areas from which to carry on subversion after a cease-fire went into effect. Thieu told Bunker that Hanoi's politburo would wait until August or September before suddenly becoming tractable in the Paris peace negotiations. He thought they would wait until they could assess the probable results of the November presidential election in the United States.

Thieu, at least, was under no illusion that Hanoi desired a real peace. Again, he would be proved right by events.

Bunker right away sent off a warning to Washington of Thieu's apprehension over any cease-fire in place that would leave Hanoi in control over significant sections of South Vietnamese territory.

In Hanoi, the Communist Party politburo had met in continuous session toward the end of June to the beginning of July to make a comprehensive assessment of the balance of forces in the war.[2] The Communists decided, as one of their historians put it, to change "from a strategy of war to a strategy of peace." Both the Soviet Union and China, which had hosted President Nixon in precedent-shattering summits, wanted Hanoi to give the Americans an exit from the fighting. The American presidential election "put pressure" on Nixon and was therefore seen in Hanoi as providing an opportunity to make progress in the negotiations.

Hanoi also realized that Thieu was not a pushover. "With military forces clearly stronger than those of the revolution in South Vietnam, with modern weaponry, with all the cities, large and small, still under his control, with all strategic regions and main communications lines still in his hands, and with the majority of the population still living under his administration," Hanoi gave Thieu credit for winning the war on the ground up to that point in time.[3]

The politburo decided that its only strategic objective had to be the withdrawal of American military forces from South Vietnam. With their own troops remaining within South Vietnam to fight again another day, Hanoi's leaders concluded that letting the Americans withdraw would "change the relation of force on the battlefield to our advantage."[4] The politburo, therefore, gave up on its demand to have the South Vietnamese government overthrown in order to obtain its principal objective, which was an end to American military support for South Vietnam.

Hanoi had no interest in a real peace, only in shifting the form of struggle to different modalities and pushing final victory further off into the future. The Vietnamese Communists were now fully prepared to give Thieu's South Vietnam a "decent interval" of freedom and independence, the better to conquer the country at some later point when circumstances would permit. Hanoi and Henry Kissinger were now in full accord with one another.

On July 20, 1972, Bunker reported on a conversation with President Thieu. Thieu's analysis of Hanoi's intentions and considerations was astute, one Vietnamese mind assessing things from a generic Vietnamese point of view. He told Bunker,

> *In view of the changed situation which Hanoi now faced, it is being forced to develop a new policy for the future, is in the process of doing so, but has not yet reached a conclusion as to what it should be. They have been disappointed and embarrassed by the fact that*

the military situation on the ground has not worked out as they had expected. They do not want to call off the talks, yet know that their Seven Points are no longer an acceptable solution. Thus the Politburo is in the process of considering what course to follow and debating the problem among themselves.

Bunker added that in Thieu's view, this was confirmed by the fact that captured documents and prisoner interrogations reflected the fact that lower-echelon cadres were not receiving consistent instructions (e.g., the three points, destruction of the Army of the Republic of Vietnam [ARVN], imposition of a coalition government, and continuation of the war until after elections on the one hand and, on the other, instructions for preparation for a cease-fire, while other documents did not insist on Thieu's withdrawal).

Bunker continued,

In Thieu's view, the Seven Points were a carefully formulated proposal agreed to unanimously by the Politburo. Now they are faced with a new situation and have not yet reached conclusions on how to deal with it. In the meantime, he believes they will adopt a waiting posture. They will want to see what success they may have in a new offensive, which he thinks the enemy may initiate about mid-August and are in the process of moving troops to prepare for it. They also want to appraise the probable outcome of our elections. In other words, he thinks it will be another one or two months before we can expect them to come up with concrete proposals.[5]

On July 25, Kissinger had a conversation with his president that revealed his disdain for South Vietnam's constitution:[6]

Kissinger: Now, that one part about changing the constitution, we have to present without clearing with Thieu, because he'll just go into orbit. But, one of two things will happen: If they reject it, he won't give a damn that we offered it. If they accept it, then we have a little problem selling it to him. But—

Nixon: Changing the constitution how again?

Kissinger: Well, the constitu—what would happen is this: first, there's a statement to sign a dec—we sign a statement of principles—

Nixon: Um-hmm.

Kissinger: —that will—and that will produce a cease-fire. Then, three months—there'll be three months—that will be followed by three months of political negotiations to set up electoral commission. Six months after that, or nine months after the statement of principles, or in other words next August, there'll be elections, in which Thieu won't run. One year after this new government is put in, through elections, that new government will and we talk to PRG [Provisional Revolutionary Government] about drafting a new constitution, which means, in other words, that government has had two years to establish itself—

Nixon: [clears throat]

Kissinger: —and it has a veto because it doesn't have to accept any constitution that it doesn't want to. If the advantage—

Nixon: That'd be awfully hard to sell to Thieu, wouldn't it?

Kissinger: Well, but it has the advantage, Mr. President. It answers all the people who say: "Why should they run under—why should they live with a constitution imposed by the Americans in '67?"

On July 27, 1972, Thieu was again asked to approve yet another American modification of the proposed terms for peace. Kissinger now proposed that a cease-fire go into effect throughout South Vietnam immediately when a statement of principles was signed by all parties to the conflict. Such a cease-fire would give protection to Communist forces wherever they were, while real-time implementation of the principles was to be discussed and the Americans continued to disengage. Three months were proposed for South and North Vietnam to reach agreement on the political issues at the heart of the war. Four months after such an agreement had been reached, Thieu would step down as president of South Vietnam, and two months after that, a presidential election would be held.

Seeking assent to this new concession, Bunker suggested to Thieu that it might be good to explore such a line with Hanoi. Thieu asked for time to study the proposal.

Kissinger wanted to present the new proposal very quickly to the North Vietnamese on August 1. Bunker asked to know Thieu's response by July 29. In his response, Thieu was not very amenable to Kissinger's new concession. He did not want his resignation as president of South Vietnam offered to Hanoi as a concession. Rather, he wanted it presented only as a "suggestion" to preserve his resolve to bargain hard on behalf of his cause and country. He was uncomfortable committing himself to resignation from the nation's chief office because just then he was trying to rally his people to have courage and support their troops on the front lines as the ARVN was going over to the offensive. The proposal that he step down should be bargained out, not just thrown away gratis to Hanoi. To throw away such a card would encourage the Communists to bargain only with the United States over the political future of South Vietnam.

"Say only that Thieu can decide to step down as it is his personal contribution to peace," he added.[7]

Then Thieu presented Bunker with a written memorandum noting other concerns. He wanted any cease-fire to cover all the battlefields of Indochina—in Laos and Cambodia as well. He wanted international supervision of any such cease-fire, and he wanted withdrawal of North Vietnamese forces from South Vietnam. Otherwise, he said accurately to

Bunker, an end to the fighting would just allow the Communists to buy time on the cheap and thereafter to renew their aggression when more favorable conditions came into being.

Thieu said flatly that there would be no elections in South Vietnam that included Communist candidates as long as North Vietnamese troops remained in the South. Bunker reported Thieu's views to Washington.

Kissinger's meeting with Hanoi went ahead on August 1. Hanoi presented its own written set of terms as well. Now Hanoi's position differed from Kissinger's on only two points: Thieu and a coalition government. Hanoi proposed the immediate elimination of Thieu and the installation of a coalition government over South Vietnam.

Their offensive having failed, the North Vietnamese were in a much more cooperative mood, presenting for the first time substantive proposals.[8]

According to Kissinger's summary of his meeting with Hanoi's negotiators,

> Their positions reconfirm that all military and subsidiary issues are basically soluble and that the main problems remain the political question and the timing of an Indochina ceasefire in relation to the settlement of political issues. They made major moves on the political issue, including a willingness to deal with the GVN, including Thieu, on the details of political questions. Their overall plan, however, still contains unpalatable elements such as their insistence that we accept the principle of a three-segment government of national concord before talks between the Vietnamese parties themselves and that such government be established before a ceasefire . . . They dropped their demand that Thieu resign before a settlement, and essentially met our position that he would step down as part of a comprehensive settlement . . . They agreed to talk to the GVN, including Thieu, about the details of a political settlement once we had agreed on political principles.

Hanoi recognized that leaving its military forces inside South Vietnam was controversial and so put a fiction on the negotiating table to legitimate such an outcome. Kissinger described this rhetorical sleight of hand as follows:

> *This point restates their view that this problem will be resolved by discussions among the Vietnamese parties, though it specifies for the first time that the "parties" are the PRG and Saigon. From this it appears that the DRV envisages solution of this problem before an overall agreement is signed. The interesting point emerged in subsequent discussion that in the DRV view the North Vietnamese forces in the South will be considered for this purpose to be part of South Vietnam's "Liberation forces." It was astounding to hear Le Duc Tho claim with a complete poker face that the 12 NVA divisions now in South Vietnam are under indigenous Viet Cong control.*

Having lost on the battlefield, Hanoi now accepted the continued legitimacy—for a while at least—of South Vietnam's freely elected government. The Communist position was now in complete alignment with the concept that Hanoi had sent to Kissinger through Jean Sainteny on May 25, 1971—a US withdrawal, a small dollop of face-saving authority to the National Liberation Front (NLF), and a decent interval before the final conquest.

Kissinger proposed in reply to this new Communist offer the creation of a multiparty commission of reconciliation to organize a new election under South Vietnam's existing constitution. Kissinger's recommended council would have three parts: the pro-Hanoi PRG, Thieu's constitutionally elected government, and a neutralist component with half selected by the PRG and half by Saigon. The council would act only through unanimous agreement. It was only a device to restrain political conflict while the United States pulled completely out of South Vietnam.

In effect, Kissinger took a previous proposal from Hanoi for the composition of a coalition government to rule South Vietnam and changed the mission of the coalition from governing to running an election.

In reporting on his meeting with Hanoi to President Nixon, Kissinger, on August 2, sought to test the president's appetite for a "sellout" of South Vietnam.[9]

> *Kissinger: If you told me to sell out, I could make it look brilliant. I mean—I'm not ask—I'm not recommending it, Mr. President, but I'm saying—*
>
> *Nixon: Yeah.*
>
> *Kissinger: —that if we got up against a hard place—I do feel this, that a McGovern victory would be worse than a sellout in Vietnam.*
>
> *Nixon: Oh, Christ. Of course, of course. We know that for sure—*
>
> *Kissinger: But I also think we shouldn't do it.*
>
> *Nixon: Why?*
>
> *Kissinger: We shouldn't sell out, I mean, and fourth—*
>
> *Nixon: We can survive without it . . .*
>
> *Nixon: Yeah, what I mean—I guess that my question is then another one. Suddenly, we're ten points ahead and we are—and then, will we settle in October? The real question is whether, whether we settle at a cost of destroying the South Vietnamese.*
>
> *Kissinger: Well, we cannot accept this—*
>
> *Nixon: Yes, we cannot [unclear]—*
>
> *Kissinger: —present proposal.*

Nixon: We have to have something that would—

Kissinger: Uh-huh.

Nixon: I would like—frankly, I'd like to trick them. I'd like to do it in a way that we make a settlement, and then screw them in the implementation, to be quite candid.

Kissinger: Well, that we can do, too. See, they've given us—

Nixon: We could promise something, and then, right after the election, say Thieu wouldn't do it. Just keep the pressure on.

Nixon: —with the Communists. I don't see how far we can go in good conscience, not only—not because of South Vietnam, but because of the effect on other countries in the world—

Kissinger: But it will be more than murder for them, for them to have offered to us that they will talk to Thieu, which they have said for eight years they would never do under any circumstances. This will have a shattering effect on their guerrillas. I . . .

Nixon: See, I think with this that the—look, there's no question that—I don't know. I don't know. The real problem, which I guess you've got here on Vietnam—Vietnam poisons our relations with the Soviet, and it poisons our relations with the Chinese. We have suffered long and hard, and God knows how do we get out of it. All it is, is a question of getting out in a way that to other countries—not the Chinese or the Russians so much, they don't give a damn how it's settled, just that we're out—but to other countries, it does not appear that we, after four years, bugged out. That's all we have to do—

In this conversation, Kissinger did not point out to President Nixon that Hanoi would keep its forces inside South Vietnam after the peace agreement would be signed, and Nixon did not think to ask Kissinger about that contingency. Nixon, of course, was starting a campaign for reelection and would have had many things on his mind in addition to the particulars of Kissinger's complicated proposals for ending the Vietnam War.

The next day, August 3, President Nixon and his national security advisor again weighted the odds facing South Vietnam:

> *Nixon: Now, let's look at that just a moment again, think about it some more, but . . . let's be perfectly . . . cold-blooded about it. If you look at it from the standpoint of our game . . . with the Soviets and the Chinese, from the standpoint of running this country . . . I feel that the North Vietnamese are so badly hurt that the South Vietnamese are probably going to do fairly well. [Kissinger attempts to interject.] But also due to the fact—because I look at the tide of history out there—South Vietnam probably can never even survive anyway. I'm just being perfectly candid. . . .*

> *We also have to realize, Henry, that winning an election is terribly important. It's terribly important this year . . . but can we have a viable foreign policy if a year from now or two years from now, North Vietnam gobbles up South Vietnam? That's the real question.*

> *Kissinger: If a year or two years from now North Vietnam gobbles up South Vietnam, we can have a viable foreign policy if it looks as if it's the result of South Vietnamese incompetence. If we now sell out in such a way that, say, within a three- to four-month period, we have pushed President Thieu over the brink—we ourselves—I think, there is going to be . . . even the Chinese won't like that. . . .*

> *Nixon: But it'll worry them. . . .*

Kissinger: So we've got to find some formula that holds the thing together a year or two, after which—after a year, Mr. President, Vietnam will be a backwater. If we settle it, say, this October, by January '74 no one will give a damn.

Nixon: Yeah, having in mind the fact that, you know, as we all know, the—the analogy—comparison [to] Algeria is not on—is not at all for us. But on the other hand, nobody gives a goddamn about what happened to Algeria . . .

Kissinger: Mm-hmm.

Nixon: . . . after they got out. [chuckling] You know what I mean? But Vietnam, I must say . . . Jesus, they've fought so long, dying, and now . . . I don't know.[10]

Notoriously, Kissinger did not even then disclose to his president the terms of his agreement with Hanoi which was designed to ease the way for the Communists to "gobble up" South Vietnam in a year or two—just as Nixon feared.

For Kissinger, it seems that a "decent interval" of only two or three months would be a sellout but that a longer interval of one or two years would not be.

Sensing that climactic negotiating sessions were just around the corner, Kissinger asked Bunker for his personal view of "what the traffic would bear" in further compromises by Thieu. Bunker, also thinking that a compromise was at long last in sight, asked Kissinger to visit Saigon for a personal meeting with Thieu after the next meeting with Hanoi's negotiators.

Thieu was indisposed. Bunker did not see him until August 4 to report on Kissinger's most recent meeting with the North Vietnamese. Only on August 14 did Bunker give the South Vietnamese president the actual text of Hanoi's proposal.

That same day, Kissinger met with Le Duc Tho in Paris. Nothing was accomplished during a seven-and-a-half-hour meeting.

Kissinger now arrived in Saigon. He advised Thieu to be generous, not to get "hung up" on minor legal details.

Confronting Thieu's major concern, Kissinger offered assurances. He said, "We will do nothing behind your back. We will do nothing to betray you."[11] He added, though,

> First, we have a number of problems. We have an election—that is obvious. You know as well as I do the consequences of a victory by the opposition. Our opponents offer the North Vietnamese more than they even ask for, which is quite something. Therefore, it is essential for us to be always in the position that we can prove that we have made a serious and honest effort and that the only thing we refuse to do is to impose on the people of South Vietnam a government that they have not chosen. We always have to prove that it is not the person of Thieu that is the obstacle to a settlement but rather the demands of the other side to install a communist government. Our whole strategy is to put ourselves in a position where if the talks are published, we can prove that we have done all we can, and they have insisted that we install a communist government. And that we will never do. I can tell you that we will never do that.

To be fair to Kissinger, he was not completely disingenuous with his ally. In truth, he did not propose to have the United States install a Communist government in South Vietnam. Rather, he would let Hanoi do that by itself in its own good time. He would, however, give Hanoi time and favorable circumstances in which to accomplish the task.

Kissinger reported that Hanoi insisted that North Vietnamese forces in the South be under the command of the National Liberation Forces and should be counted as part of the South Vietnamese Communist forces. Thus, he said that the matter of North Vietnamese forces withdrawing from South Vietnam should not be raised in the statement of principles regarding the follow-on negotiations starting after the cease-fire but rather should be left to those subsequent negotiations. The withdrawal issue, Kissinger affirmed, was clearly dealt with by inference in a provision mandating the encapsulation of all Vietnamese, Lao, and Cambodian military forces within their national boundaries. Kissinger took the position that

> *since we know they will refuse to withdraw their forces from South Vietnam. It is better that the talks break down on this subject with you rather than with us. If the talks break down with us over this point, there might be many Americans who think the DRV position is reasonable.*
>
> *Should we agree in principle and then they say to you that they have a right to keep 11 divisions in South Vietnam, that is a good issue for a deadlock. Therefore since the issue [NVA presence in SVN] has never been raised before in our talks I recommend that it not be put in here.[12]*

He added, "It would be a mistake to mention the NVA specifically in point 5. It would produce an explosion in our talks inevitably leading to their breakup."

There was also a studied ambiguity about what the nation of Vietnam was. Hanoi took the position that there was only one Vietnam, not two. So, legally, if it left its forces in South Vietnam, they were still only within "Vietnam" and would not need to move from their bases in that "country."

On the issue of independent sovereignty for South Vietnam, Kissinger proposed presenting Hanoi with discussion forums to discuss and resolve such a political issue after a settlement agreement had been reached. In selecting members for the discussion forum on political questions, the GVN would have a veto. Thus, no Communist proposal could ever be accepted as compulsory for the South Vietnamese.

Suavely, Kissinger advised Thieu that if Hanoi accepted the proposal, Saigon would lose nothing because all matters would still be on the table for future negotiations. But, Kissinger continued, if Hanoi rejected his plan, Democratic Party presidential candidate George McGovern could not blame Nixon for being unacceptably stubborn.[13]

Kissinger explained Nixon's political problem to Thieu: With American elections coming in November, Nixon had to be in a position to make a serious and honorable settlement of the Vietnam War. Therefore, Washington had always to have on the table a reasonable peace offer that, if rejected by the enemy, would demonstrate that Hanoi, not Nixon, was obdurate and responsible for continued fighting. Nixon needed to be flexible with Hanoi to prove his sincerity about peace to the American electorate. George McGovern had made opposition to the war central to his campaign for the presidency. McGovern welcomed the prospect of a total Communist victory over South Vietnam and sent his press secretary to meet with the North Vietnamese in Paris. Kissinger argued that

> *If we can achieve what I propose to you and then if the President is reelected, there will be no Congressional pressures on us in the next congressional session. Their military situation will get worse over the next year, and we are determined not to let them do this to us again. That is why we are not withdrawing our air and naval forces now.*

> *But my view is that, if they reject the proposal, as is certain, then after November 7 we will go back to the May 8 proposal and say that we, the United States, will not discuss political issues any more . . .*

> *My nightmare is that they publish their plan. If McGovern has their plan, we would be in a terrible position.[14]*

Kissinger continued with assurances to Thieu that the South Vietnamese were in a strong military position:

> *In 1973 they will not be able to carry out any main-force activity of any significance and you should be able to make great progress*

in pacification. The dilemma for them is that, if they revert to protracted warfare, your position is unassailable. Their other alternative is to make a settlement. After the election we will interpret the provisions in the strictest possible ways, and I assume that although the war may not end the balance of forces will shift preponderantly in your favor.

Here Kissinger, in passing, revealed the fact that he knew the agreement he was negotiating with Hanoi would not be a "peace" agreement. Thieu, in a way, agreed, saying,

If we don't sign anything, the war will fade away and they will have less supplies, less manpower and less regular units in December 1973 than they had in December 1971 or March of 1972. If there is protracted warfare, they have no hope to win but they can try and continue to protract the war as long as they can because they cannot withdraw their troops; they cannot admit to their people that they have lost the war.

Thieu was misled by Kissinger's facile use of words. He and his assistant Nguyen Phu Duc, present for the discussion, understood Kissinger to mean by military forces "remaining" within national frontiers that Hanoi would have to pull its troops out of South Vietnam back into its national territory. Only later did they learn that to Kissinger the word "remain" meant only a prohibition on new troop movements from North Vietnam into the South. North Vietnamese troops already in the South could "remain" there as being already stationed in "Vietnam."

Damningly, Kissinger added his view that Washington and Saigon should not make any reference in the peace terms to four separate Indochinese countries—South Vietnam, North Vietnam, Laos, and Cambodia. Trying to do so would get nowhere with Hanoi. Kissinger remarked that the separate legal status of North and South Vietnam was only a "theological issue," forgetting for a moment how many people had died over the centuries in religious wars fought to settle supposedly unimportant and better ignored "theological issues."[15]

Kissinger asked Thieu to help Nixon get through the election without losing public support. He asked Thieu to approve a counterproposal to Hanoi's terms of August 1.

Thieu replied that he needed time to discuss Kissinger's plan with key South Vietnamese. He could not surprise the National Assembly and the armed forces with a complicated proposal that many would construe as a coalition government with the Communists. South Vietnam was not ready, Thieu insisted, psychologically or politically, for Kissinger's latest compromise.

Thieu gave Kissinger an assessment of Hanoi's August 1 proposal, pointing out its objectionable provisions. Hanoi wanted Washington to accept moral responsibility for the war by agreeing to pay "reparations" to North Vietnam, with Hanoi paying nothing to South Vietnam. Under Hanoi's proposal, the United States could not aid Saigon, but Moscow and Beijing could continue sending supplies to the Communists. The demilitarized zone was not considered to be a national legal boundary putting a southern geographical limit to the sway of Hanoi's sovereignty.

Kissinger noted that Thieu had only twelve days to consider his government's position before Bunker would meet with President Nixon in Honolulu to discuss the secret negotiations.

Thieu's staff responded to Kissinger on August 18. The American was told that Washington had no competence to resolve with Hanoi any issue between the elected Saigon government and other South Vietnamese in service to Hanoi through their participation in the PRG. Second, Hanoi had no right to interfere in the political affairs of South Vietnam. South Vietnam would make no claim that North Vietnam should change its form of government. Third, South Vietnam's constitution of 1967 should be respected, but a referendum could be held on whether to keep that constitution. This proposal was offered in place of Kissinger's demand for a tripartite reconciliation council to organize elections. And the South Vietnamese pointed out that even if Thieu resigned as president, Vice President

Tran Van Huong need not resign as well.[16]

The South Vietnamese worried that Kissinger's clever device of a reconciliation council nevertheless still closely resembled the coalition government long demanded by the Communists as a Trojan horse, facilitating their ultimate conquest of South Vietnam. Thieu had campaigned vigorously with the promise that he would never concede land or authority to the Communist aggressors. And the South Vietnamese knew that Nationalist members of the reconciliation council would never act in lockstep as the Communist members would, so the Communists would always have a tactical advantage in prying loose votes for their positions from wayward or undisciplined Nationalists. Instead of a reconciliation council, the South Vietnamese wanted a referendum to give the people of South Vietnam a voice in their political future. In that way, the Communists would have to confront the entire range of anti-Communist opinion among the South Vietnamese, including all the religions. In such a referendum, Thieu would not be the issue; Communist class struggle and proletarian dictatorship would. And it was well known in South Vietnam that the Communist Vietnamese had never sought free elections of any kind, fearing them as a kind of very noxious political pesticide.[17]

The next day, Bunker passed to the South Vietnamese Kissinger's flat rejection of their suggestions. Kissinger wrote from Washington that since Saigon would have a veto in all future discussions with Hanoi, it could afford to be flexible now over details. He rejected the idea of a referendum on the 1967 constitution. If Thieu accepted the current American proposal, including the tripartite council of reconciliation, no more concessions would be asked of him.

Kissinger's tough response to their thoughtful efforts shocked the South Vietnamese. They did not know what to say to their powerful ally. Thieu refused to meet with Bunker before the ambassador left Saigon for fateful discussions with President Nixon in Honolulu.

Later, Kissinger responded to South Vietnamese criticism of his draft proposal to present to Hanoi on September 15. On a key point, he instructed Bunker to inform Thieu that *we do not believe question of NVA forces should be raised in this document. This is a matter which will be discussed in the ensuing forums. You should point out that NVA forces were not repeat not mentioned in our January proposal and this would be a red flag to other side. The problem of NVA forces is clearly dealt with by inference in our point 7. Also it is better raised in a forum where the GVN has a veto.*[18]

Here Kissinger was clear that the Americans had dropped their demand that Hanoi withdraw its forces from South Vietnam.

From Washington Kissinger also rejected modifying his proposed point seven to have armed forces stay within the national frontiers of *four* nations of former Indochina. He wrote,

We cannot accept injecting idea of "four countries" into our formal proposal. Here again, we would be specifying separate North and South Vietnamese countries, a theological point not raised in our previous proposal and again a red flag for Hanoi. We believe our point as presently phrased deals adequately with GVN concerns and would again point out that GVN has ample room for maneuver on this issue in the negotiating forums which would open up.

Kissinger described his objectives in the negotiations as either an honorable settlement or, failing that, a clear record of reasonableness for the American people.[19] One wonders in retrospect what his idea of an "honorable" settlement included. Did Kissinger have in mind a successful defense of the independence of South Vietnam, or would something less than that suffice to meet his conditions for saving the "honor" of a purported great nation in keeping its word to an ally and in vindicating the sacrifices of its soldiers on the battlefield? One might also reflect on what Kissinger might have had in mind when his standard for success in the negotiations with Hanoi was what might be "reasonable" for the American people. Who was included in his personal definition of the "American" people—mostly the antiwar movement activists, the "silent majority" that supported President Nixon, his peers in academia and those of political and social prominence, or Americans in the future, who would look back on what America had achieved with its defense of the Vietnamese Nationalists?

When Bunker met with Kissinger in Honolulu on August 31, Kissinger asked Bunker's opinion: "Where do we stand?"

Speaking of "our problem," Kissinger said, "What bothers me most is, do you think we've made an unreasonable proposal?"

Bunker replied with New England reserve: "No, I do not think so."

Kissinger reassured him: "We haven't sacrificed all these years in order to sell out now. If you think this is unreasonable, we'll change it. And we'll pay whatever price we have to."[20] Bunker felt that his confidence in Kissinger's resolve was justified.

Meeting with President Nixon, the senior American strategists decided to accept Kissinger's proposal for a council of reconciliation over Thieu's suggestion for a referendum. But they amended Kissinger's proposal to incorporate a number of the changes requested by Saigon.

At Bunker's suggestion, President Nixon sent a personal letter to Thieu that Bunker carried back to Saigon. Nixon promised therein never to desert a brave ally and assured Thieu of meticulous and thorough consultations at every stage of the forthcoming negotiations. The United States, Nixon wrote, did not intend to undermine its friends in the homestretch after all the sacrifices that had been made by so many for so long.[21]

Thieu was very pleased with the letter.

Bunker then had long and difficult meetings with Thieu on September 6 and 7. Thieu was anxious and insecure. He feared the consequences if Kissinger's proposal leaked. He would be accused, he felt sure, of selling out his country. He also feared that Hanoi would reject Kissinger's proposal, and he would then be asked to make further concessions. He asked whether the United States would offer Hanoi more concessions if this proposal was rejected. Bunker assured him, "No."

Bunker reported,

I then talked with Thieu alone and, citing the reasons, impressed on him how essentially important it was for us to be in a position to table this proposal and assured him we would not ask anything more of him. I think he understands clearly all the considerations involved. He was in a cooperative mood and I hope to report substantial progress.[22]

Bunker, confident in Nixon's determination not to buckle as the election approached, assured Thieu that there would be no more concessions. Thieu's mood improved. He told Bunker that he was renovating his house in a military compound—just in case he had to suddenly resign as president and leave the presidential palace.

Bunker met with Thieu again on September 11. Saigon had sought further modifications of Kissinger's proposal. The South Vietnamese wanted the reconciliation council to include all political tendencies, with membership chosen by mutual agreement. Thieu was concerned that the tripartite nature of Kissinger's council gave reality to the concept of a "third force" in Vietnamese politics, a notion left over from the French Viet Minh war, looking then for an alternative to both colonialism and Communism. In the postcolonial struggle between two Vietnamese governments, seeking a middle or neutral position served mostly to undermine the Saigon government's legitimacy.

Thieu now formally replied to the letter Nixon had drafted in Honolulu. The United States had already made too many concessions to the Communists, he wrote. The American president had to remember that he, Thieu, could only make a peace offer acceptable to his National Assembly and the people of South Vietnam. He was unhappy with the proposal for a tripartite council, as it would remind the South Vietnamese of the "troika" government of Communists, neutralists, and rightists imposed on Laos in 1962, which had notoriously failed to bring peace to that country or even to end Hanoi's aggression there.

Kissinger and the North Vietnamese met on September 15 just as ARVN units under General Ngo Quang Truong recaptured Quang Tri

City. Hanoi produced different terms for a settlement. Now it asked for the division of South Vietnam into areas governed by separate administrations. This was Thieu's long-feared leopard spot proposal. The PRG would govern here, and Thieu would govern there. Above both the PRG and the Saigon government would be a tripartite entity holding some government functions but having subcommittees in every village and town of South Vietnam.

Hanoi also wanted to reach final agreement with Washington within a month—just before the American presidential elections were to be held.

Kissinger tabled his new proposal. Thieu's idea for a wide-open election was included in a minor way.

Kissinger felt that his strategy was paying off, that Hanoi was eager, even anxious, to settle. He planned now not to bring forth new positions but to force movement from the North Vietnamese with regard to their terms. Hanoi was not going public with its proposal, so Kissinger asked that Thieu also make no public comment. Bunker was directed to remind Thieu that it was not 1968.[23]

Saigon rejected the leopard spot proposal. Thieu and his colleagues felt that the secret talks were supposed to be no more than exploratory, but that Hanoi was treating them as a final negotiation of South Vietnam's future. Having lost on the battlefield inside South Vietnam, Hanoi was trying now to exploit Washington's domestic vulnerability due to the upcoming American elections. While Saigon "understood the Anglo-Saxon pragmatism which guides the US," the South Vietnamese objected to Hanoi's suggestion that it settle all issues in only bilateral talks with the Americans. To accept that approach would only confirm Hanoi's propaganda that Saigon was a puppet regime subservient to American policy whims. Therefore, Hanoi should negotiate directly with Saigon. If Kissinger went beyond the South Vietnamese position, Saigon would reject any agreement that he might reach in the secret negotiations.

Intelligence from the battlefields now indicated that the Communists planned to seize as much territory as possible just before the American presidential election. They were preparing for a cease-fire and a de facto leopard spot outcome of the war. Once again, Thieu knew what Hanoi was up to.

To whet American appetites for bilateral negotiations with Hanoi, the Communists, without prior notice, suddenly released three American prisoners of war on September 25.

In a two-day meeting in Paris on September 26 and 27, Le Duc Tho presented Kissinger with another proposal.[24] Kissinger reported,

> In this newest plan the Government of National Concord has largely advisory functions centered on implementing the overall agreement and mediating between the two sides. It would have no army, or police, or defined territory. And it would only "supervise" the foreign policy of the two sides. The GVN (and PRG) remain in existence with armies and police intact. They would administer the areas they control and conduct their foreign policy.
>
> This plan is still far from acceptable because elements like Thieu's immediate resignation upon signature of an overall agreement and the continued presence of the North Vietnamese army in the South, would all but ensure the psychological demoralization and political deterioration of the GVN.

Kissinger immediately wired Bunker word that the new Communist plan was for a coalition government between the PRG and Thieu, with each side having a veto. Hanoi was unwilling to put in a requirement that its troops would withdraw from the South, Kissinger reported.

Bunker was to tell Thieu that Kissinger would not just stop the bombing of North Vietnam in return for the release of US prisoners of war. Unless Hanoi suddenly caved, there would be no settlement prior to the American elections, Kissinger concluded. Kissinger was sending his deputy General Alexander Haig out to Saigon to discuss strategy for the period after the November election.[25] As Bunker relayed this information, Thieu took notes but made no comment. He had disengaged from Kissinger's negotiation process.

Alexander Haig came to Saigon on October 1, bringing with him yet another American negotiating proposal.[26] This time, the idea was to elect a new National Assembly to write a new constitution for South Vietnam.

Before he left Washington, Haig was given instructions on what to say to Thieu. Nixon advised him,

> *And he's—he's got to realize that. The other thing is that he's got to realize that this, this war has got to stop. I mean, that's all there is to it. [unclear] We cannot go along with this sort of dreary business of hanging on for another four years. It's been too long. It's been too long. I'm convinced of this. I'm convinced of it. If I thought—believe me, if I thought, if I was reasonably sure that immediately after [unclear] going all out—I mean after the election, the goddamn war would end, and the President's back and so forth, and you wouldn't be quite as concerned about trying to do something now. But I'm not sure . . . We've got to get the war the hell off our backs in this country. That's all there is to it.*

Kissinger added,

> *We've got to do it. If we can't end it this way, we've got to go all out after the election.*

Nixon followed up,

> *What you've got to say there is that this—you've got to point out that this President has stood by him with no support. The House is against him. The Senate is against him. The media has been against him. The students have rioted. All sorts of hell-raising loose. He's made these tough decisions. And, now, he's got to have something from him, in return. We've got to have [unclear], an agreement, an*

acceptable proposition that I think he can live with. That's really what you get down to.[27]

First, Haig had a private meeting with President Thieu, later reporting,

During the head-to-head, I covered in great detail our concerns about manifestations of growing South Vietnamese suspicion, reiterated the events of the past four years and noted the differences between the US domestic climate in 1968 and today. I layed [sic] out in the strongest terms the consequences of South Vietnamese threats for public parting of the ways as well as the consequences of unreasonable intransigence. I made it clear that our concerns for a forthcoming negotiating stance were dictated by long term considerations which involved our ability to support the GVN in the long haul and were not driven by immediate election needs. This portion of the meeting was emotional and even tearful on Thieu's part. However, it concluded by what I consider to be the reestablishment of mutual confidence and respect on both sides. Thieu appeared to accept both my admonitions and warnings with sincerity and good will. Despite the toughness and threatening nature of portions of my presentation, he was both docile and cooperative from the outset.

Haig stressed with Thieu that President Nixon and Henry Kissinger considered Hanoi's September 26 proposal to represent a major concession and that while it was still unsatisfactory in many details, the September 26 proposal demanded a forthcoming response from Washington and Saigon.[28]

Haig and Bunker met with the South Vietnamese again on October 4. Thieu confronted them with his National Security Council in the conference room of the presidential palace.

Haig began the meeting with yet another explanation of the reasons behind the proposal tabled by Kissinger on September 15.[29]

Thieu replied that now that the details of Hanoi's new terms for a coalition were in the open, it was clear that Kissinger had been "ambushed."

Thieu was close to tears; fear and anger were easily heard in his voice.

Vice President Huong stepped up to support his president. Hanoi's strategy, he spit out, was to get the United States to accept its demands—that the United States withdraw from South Vietnam as if it were an invader. Hanoi had deceived so many for so long; he continued, "How could the Communists ever be trusted?"

Huong said,

> *In 1968 the Communists demanded unilateral cessation of bombing and they obtained it. Furthermore, they got from the United States the acceptance of the installation at the Paris talks of the NLF. What is the NLF? It is an unknown force in South Vietnam. No one even knows where its headquarters are located. As a result of what the United States has done, it [the NLF] has gained international recognition.*

> *The North Vietnamese have made a number of unilateral demands of the United States. They demand the US withdrawal, that the US dismantle its bases, that it withdraw military advisors, technical personnel and so forth. I have a question, have the North Vietnamese done even any little thing to reciprocate? Now, since the cessation of the bombing, the United States has carried out the unconditional withdrawal of its forces while the North Vietnamese have done nothing. Their position is even more evident in that they call themselves "Vietnam" and not "North Vietnam." They do not make provision for the fact that, even though the country is just temporarily divided, there is legitimate provision for two separate sets of authorities to operate in each part of the country.*

> *As for Hanoi's agreement that the coalition government would act on the principle of unanimity, the Americans should not forget that similar provisions had not prevented Communist subversion of governments in Laos and Czechoslovakia.*

The blunt elder Vietnamese warned Haig not to be fooled by Hanoi's assent to a principle that sounded fair and equitable to all.

Haig answered mildly that the Nixon administration feared being seen as unresponsive while the Communists showed such rapid movement in their position. A settlement of the war through an agreement was necessary in Haig's mind in order to sustain continued support for South Vietnam in the US Congress.

Thieu asked, "Why didn't Kissinger present my proposal for a referendum to the Communists?"

Haig answered that such a proposal would have broken up the talks.

Thieu asked to know how many counterproposals Kissinger had and what Washington envisioned for the final terms for peace.

Haig replied truthfully but revealingly that Washington had no general concept of a future for South Vietnam, only an opportunistic strategy to keep public opinion behind Nixon's policy of supporting South Vietnam into the future, whatever that future may be.

Haig agreed that there had been a break in mutual confidence between Thieu and Kissinger, but that Kissinger always sought to maintain Saigon's survival as a regime.

Thieu complained that his government was given no notice of developments and had no staff to consider the implications of such momentous proposals coming from Washington and Hanoi.

Haig elaborated that Washington had rejected Thieu's proposal for a referendum because the Americans did not want to oppose the basic framework of Hanoi's offer now that the Communists had come so far toward acceptable terms of settlement.

Thieu said that there were basic differences between Washington and Saigon. He could accept only settlement terms that South Vietnam's National Assembly could support.

Prime Minister Tran Thien Khiem said that the Vietnamese remembered the Communist murders and betrayals of 1945 through 1947. Further, one reason for the decision to overthrow Ngo Dinh Diem was fear of betrayal occasioned by a rumor that he and his brother would try to save their government by making a deal with Hanoi.

Thieu added that if Kissinger acted as a middleman, he would confirm only that Saigon was an American lackey. He added, "As I said earlier, the Communists hold the position that they and the United States should agree on ten principles including a political solution and after that they will direct the GVN and NLF to implement the signed agreements." President Thieu later stipulated,

> *If Dr. Kissinger still plays the role of middle-man and keeps talking to the Communists on the political aspects, he will confirm the Communist theory that we are puppets even on the technical aspects [sic] of the fact that Kissinger is talking with the other side—there will be an endless deadlock in those talks. The Communists use these talks to place all responsibility for a settlement on the United States. This is a road without end. If once and for all the United States would say that the US and the DRV will only solve the military questions regarding Indochina while the political questions will only be settled if North Vietnam and South Vietnam talk to each other about relations between the two countries and the GVN and NLF will talk to each other about the internal problems, then the problems can be solved.*

Thieu added with personal emphasis, "I want to make a very frank statement. Dr. Kissinger does not deign to consider what we propose. He just goes his own way. Our August 26 memorandum was flatly rejected 24 hours later. That is my feeling; that is my impression." Thieu protested further,

> *We feel the Communists and the French have colluded to advocate a Government of National Concord with three components. We have further evidence in the fact of President Pompidou's press conference even though he said it was not for France to advocate any solution, he made two other statements which were ambiguous. Also Pompidou has been quoted as saying that the Americans are not*

discussing the principles of a solution with the North Vietnamese but the implementation of the principles. Moreover, Pompidou has affirmed that there are three political forces.

It is no longer a secret in the eyes of many politicians what the US and GVN are now discussing. Such politicians as Tran Van Tuyen, Nguyen Gia Hien, Big Minh, and Nguyen Ngoc Huy have all been discussing what we are talking about. I cannot tell whether this is a maneuver of the Communists or the French.

I think the French here are very active. They play an active role here and we wish to propose that the United States be careful in its rapport with the French Government.

Haig replied directly,

Now, if I return to the United States and tell President Nixon that we cannot work out a counterproposal to the North Vietnamese which will protect the Republic of Vietnam, we will be posed with a major crisis with a disastrous effect for your government and our government. We want an intelligent counterproposal that prevents Hanoi from breaking off the talks and going public. And above all, we want to enable the United States to be able to go through next winter and next spring and continue to provide the essential support to you.

If I go back and say that you are holding to your September 13 memorandum, then we will have a major problem with President Nixon.

Thieu answered back,

Another serious problem is that you only give us 24 to 36 hours to work on these proposals. As far as the talks are concerned, I recognize that Dr. Kissinger is entitled to set the date and the schedule for his talks with the North Vietnamese but I want to make a point and that is that prior to the meetings and after the meetings you give us very short notice, sometimes 12 hours, sometimes 24 hours. In the case of these counterproposals, you only give us 36 hours. Moreover, these proposals have a Top Secret/Sensitive character and you insist that I must limit the discussion within my National Security Council so I can't even get other people's ideas. Dr. Kissinger has a large staff. He knows what is ahead. He has ample time to analyze what the North Vietnamese are saying. Our staff and our time is limited. Our assessment that we have given you today is on basic principles. We can't possibly decide the details in the time you have given us.

In my letter to President Nixon of September 16th, I set forth my views clearly on how forthcoming our proposals were. I made clear that any proposals he made should be justifiable to the internal opinion of the South Vietnamese people and National Assembly, and must meet the basic objectives of self-determination and should reflect the existing political structure. Otherwise, there would be three risks: first, instability; second, loss of morale on the part of our troops; and third, a loss of confidence on the people in the US and the GVN.

Thieu's advisor Nguyen Phu Duc interjected,

I have two questions, why does the US think that North Vietnam has the competence to discuss political matters affecting South Vietnam? Secondly, in August, Dr. Kissinger presented a communist proposal and the US counter-proposal. And he said he would ask no more concessions from us. Since then, there have been two more counter-proposals. In view of the successive Communist counter-proposals, I would like to ask whether the United States has developed a concept of final settlement or do we simply react to their proposals, each time trying to embody as much of their language as possible.

General Haig tried to answer the question:

> *I will answer your second question first. As to whether there is a concept of an outcome which would visualize a settlement, frankly I have not, but we do feel that there are a number of pressures on Hanoi now which are not permanent in character and which could put them in a position—to bring them to change the character of the conflict they could change their tactics, not their intentions, their tactics. We have an obligation to explore each Hanoi initiative in an honest and constructive way. First, because there might be an outside chance of settling. Secondly, we must establish a negotiating record of having been as reasonable and forthcoming as possible. I don't think any man at this table is naive enough to think that the realities of power are not the determining factor in the outcome of this conflict. We will explore every opportunity for peace. We have an obligation to do so. What we want is first of all to keep the support of the United States people behind President Nixon's action on behalf of South Vietnam.*

President Thieu said with evident pain,

> *We agree that any political solution should be based on the right of self-determination and political reality. The US has the right to explore a political solution between the GVN and the NLF and serve as the go between. But a political solution must, in the final analysis, be between the GVN and the NLF and between the GVN and Hanoi, and the US should use its pressure to influence Hanoi. You should not be caught in the dilemma of acting on our behalf. Whatever plans are made and whatever policies are followed should be for the survival of the whole Vietnamese nation and not for the sake of President Nguyen Van Thieu. In the proposal you have suggested, our Government will continue to exist. But it is only an agonizing solution and sooner or later the Government will crumble and Nguyen*

Van Thieu will have to commit suicide somewhere along the line. I will send a letter to President Nixon.

He continued,

In 1967 when I was asked by Ambassador Lodge how to absorb the NLF, I said we were a sick man, please don't give us another spoon of microbes. It will kill us. We must get better first. Now we are prepared to take the risk, a great risk, in fact, and let the NLF participate in the future government, and in the Committee of National Reconciliation. We have answered the question as to how to absorb the NLF. It is certain that the NLF will be represented in a Presidential election and after that they will be represented proportionally in the future government. It will be an elected coalition government. Furthermore, with our proposal for proportional representation, we have answered former Ambassador Harriman's question about how do we reach a coalition government. This will, in essence, be an elected national coalition government.

Duc jumped back in: "You have not answered one of my earlier questions. What right does the DRV have to talk about a political solution in South Vietnam?"

Haig agreed that the two governments were on divergent courses. The United States would continue to see whether Hanoi was in a mood to make concessions.

Thieu replied, "We are on the edge of an abyss."

The meeting ended with the exchange of cold formalities. Neither Haig nor Thieu could afford public exposure of these differences. Bunker realized that matters were out of his hands and that Kissinger held the high cards in the negotiations regardless of Thieu's entreaties. He was loyal to Kissinger but knew that there was much merit to Thieu's concerns and objections.

The anger of the South Vietnamese toward their ally and protector, the United States, which dominated their meeting with General Haig, pointed to a powerful reality. In his negotiations with the Vietnamese Communists and in his private discussions about negotiation strategy, Henry Kissinger often remarked on the dependence of diplomacy and negotiations on the balances of forces on the fields of contest. A position of imbalance encouraged the strong not to yield and the weak to acquiesce. As Thucydides had put it, "The strong do what they can, and the weak suffer what they must."

While this probable law of human nature was working away against Hanoi on the battlefields of Vietnam, it was also making itself felt in the United States. Haig's plea to the official leaders of South Vietnam to give President Nixon cover against the antiwar movement and the Democrats in Congress responded to political power realities in the United States. Through the antiwar movement and the Democratic Party, Hanoi had power (*the*) in the United States. Not power of its own that it could command but circumstantial power that it could apply in its negotiations with Henry Kissinger.

Hanoi's power to frustrate and check Kissinger and drive him to one compromise after another was a kind of "associative" power wherein many Americans associated themselves with the interest of Hanoi in taking over South Vietnam and communizing it with a dictatorship of one-party rule. And it must not be forgotten that the conceptual source of that willingness of some Americans to associate themselves with Hanoi's aims and methods had arisen out of French colonialism. The American antiwar movement was the intellectual child of French colonial parents such as Jean Sainteny.

There is a second lesson to be drawn from General Haig's meeting with Thieu and his closest civilian advisors. At no time did Henry Kissinger seek to have a frank and fully open discussion with the South Vietnamese about the risks they would run if Hanoi were to leave its forces inside their country. Representing the dominant partner in the Washington/Saigon alliance, Kissinger did not act appropriately for having such a fiduciary position of stewardship. He behaved as if he and the South Vietnamese had to hold themselves apart from each other, at arm's length, like rival third parties separated by different values and interests. Kissinger's view of the American–South Vietnamese relationship was transactional—a momentary meeting of minds on the price of the deal and then separation, with each going its own way.

An alliance, however, is a partnership. In law, every partner has fiduciary duties to the others in the joint venture. As Judge Benjamin Cardozo famously wrote in an opinion for the New York Court of Appeals, being a partner demands good faith and more. He wrote that "a trustee is held to something stricter than the morals of the marketplace. Not honesty alone, but the *punctilio of an honor the most* sensitive, is then the standard of behavior . . . the level of conduct for fiduciaries [has] been kept at a level higher than that trodden by the crowd."[30]

Ellsworth Bunker understood that morality. He had been in business and had acted with honor always. Bunker's central perception about serving as a diplomat was that the position demanded acting from trust and building trust. He once said that a British diplomat during the Renaissance had quipped that a diplomat is a person sent abroad to lie for his country. Smiling, Bunker would add that the man was never again asked to serve abroad for England. It was Bunker's personal character of being an upstanding New England Yankee that empowered him to get along with Thieu and make a success of Vietnamization.

Ambassador William Colby and General Creighton Abrams had similar character and therefore also won the trust of Vietnamese and thereby contributed to the evolution of South Vietnamese capability under the intense pressures and stresses of Vietnamization.

Unlike the emotionally sturdy and self-effacing Bunker, Kissinger was a novice in negotiations. Kissinger's standoffish intellectual and emotional stance toward the South Vietnamese had disastrous consequences for their country and for his, contributing to the ultimate loss of South Vietnam to the Communists.

One instance of his fundamental lack of concern for Vietnamese Nationalists was telling. About this time in the negotiations, Kissinger discovered that the US Department of Defense had not delivered high-performance jets to the South Vietnamese air force but mostly propeller-driven planes. This put the South Vietnamese at a serious tactical disadvantage in using airpower to stop attacks by North Vietnamese battalions and regiments. Once American airpower would leave Vietnam after the peace agreement, the South Vietnamese would be largely unable to frustrate North Vietnamese ground attacks from the air, especially against isolated South Vietnamese positions in the mountains and along the border with Laos. Just such a shortfall in airpower would contribute to the fall of South Vietnam in 1975.

Kissinger's response to learning about this increased future risk to the South Vietnamese was to blame Secretary of Defense Melvin Laird for malfeasance.[31] But Kissinger had never opened up with Laird or the Joint Chiefs of Staff about the need to help the South Vietnamese counter over the long haul the presence of North Vietnamese forces in their country. Kissinger kept his negotiating positions as secret as possible from other Americans, even those in the Nixon administration tasked with helping the South Vietnamese defend themselves.

Also worthy of note was Kissinger's careful use of silence and evasion when talking with his president about the likely impact of the peace proposal under discussion with Hanoi:[32]

> *Kissinger: You see, Mr. President, this is all baloney. Because the practical consequence of our proposal, and of their proposal, is a cease-fire. There'll never be elections. The election would be run by a committee, or in their case by a Government of National Concord, which makes decisions by unanimity. There'll never be an electoral law. They'll never agree on an electoral law on the basis of unanimity. Therefore, there'll never be elections. In either case—*
>
> *Nixon: That's right.*
>
> *Kissinger: This is—*
>
> *Nixon: Then what happens? Do we just resume the war later on?*

Kissinger: There'll be a cease-fire.

Nixon: But we'll be gone?

Kissinger: Yes. This is their face-saving way. We've always said: "Will they ever separate military from political issues?"

Then Kissinger continued by blaming President Thieu for not wanting peace and so not deserving Nixon's support:

Kissinger: Of course, Thieu doesn't want a cease-fire—

Nixon: Um-hmm. He's gonna get one—

Kissinger: —and he doesn't want us out. I mean, let's face it.

Nixon: He wants us to stay, huh? I guess that's it.

Kissinger: The real point is that our interests and his are now divergent. We want out. We want our prisoners.

Nixon: Yeah—

Kissinger: We want a cease-fire. He wants us in. He thinks he's winning. And he wants us to continue bombing.

Nixon: And for another two or three years.

Kissinger: For as long as needed.

Later in this conversation, Kissinger spoke, but Nixon quickly cut him off:

Kissinger: That's why I'm so much—

Nixon: Interested in pushing Thieu?

Kissinger: You know, next to you, I've been the hardest guy on Vietnam.

Nixon: I know that. South Vietnam, at least, of course, we just know how much is at stake and not doing something [unclear]—

Kissinger: But, I—but we can't have a Communist government.

After his January 9, 1971, concession to Ambassador Anatoly Dobrynin, was Kissinger misleading his president by presenting himself as "the hardest guy on Vietnam"?

That same day, Nixon had a different conversation with Henry Kissinger. This time, Nixon's chief of staff, Bob Haldeman, was present as well. Of interest is Nixon's resolution that he did not need to abandon South Vietnam in order to win the upcoming presidential election:[33]

Kissinger: See my worry, Mr. President, isn't the election. My worry is that—

Nixon: Oh, I know, I know. That's just what I—just what—Bob agrees with me, and I said exactly that I was prepared, that I'm prepared, and I know we have to end the war. I know that now, but when we really decimate the place, you've got pretty serious problems. But nevertheless, the real question is, it's the old—the old irony: if we don't end it, end it before the election, we've got a hell of a problem. But, if we end it in the wrong way, we've got a hell of a problem—not in the election. As I said, forget the election. We'll win the election. We could—Bob, we could surrender in Vietnam and win the election, because who the hell is going to take advantage of it? McGovern says surrender, right?

Haldeman: Yeah—

Nixon: But the point I make—

Haldeman: It doesn't affect the election; it affects—

Nixon: It affects what we're going to do later. It affects our world position.

On learning about Haig's meeting in Saigon, Kissinger instructed Bunker to see Thieu immediately and tell him that the Americans were very disappointed in his behavior, that now, Kissinger had no alternative but to proceed to another meeting with Hanoi on October 8 since antiwar Americans would not understand their government adopting South Vietnamese principles.

This comment from Kissinger revealed exactly what, in his mind, was driving his conduct in the negotiations. It was not the principle of defending democracy and the rights of the South Vietnamese people. Rather, his mind was preoccupied with the ignorance and narrow-mindedness of the American antiwar movement. Kissinger was largely a supplicant seeking to appease dissident Americans. He had no warmth toward the South Vietnamese and little respect for Thieu. Kissinger found the South Vietnamese to be a "difficult, stubborn, and suspicious people." He saw no American interest connected with any aspect of the Vietnam conflict except to exit with "dignity."[34]

Kissinger looked to Bunker to keep Thieu in line while the negotiations came to their conclusion. Bunker was instructed to urge Thieu not to bring about a confrontation between the two allies. However, to assuage Thieu, Kissinger also promised to "deal very specifically with provisions with the intention of obtaining from Hanoi reciprocal assurances of North Vietnamese troop withdrawals from Laos, Cambodia and South Vietnam."[35]

Kissinger's sincerity in making this commitment is unknown, but Thieu was led by this assurance into a more cooperative stance. The commitment also encouraged Bunker in holding to his conviction that Kissinger was still hanging tough on behalf of American war aims.

On October 4, Hanoi sent instructions to its negotiators in Paris. They were to end the war through an agreement with the United States prior to the November election in America. Hanoi recognized that Nixon would be in a stronger position after he had won reelection. Hanoi's primary requirement was to end what it called "the US war" in South Vietnam. Withdrawal of US military power would lead, so the Communists calculated, to the de facto recognition of the existence of two administrations, two armies, and two areas in South Vietnam. If that could be done, it would "create a new balance of forces to our great advantage," concluded Hanoi. The instructions went on to say, "To concentrate the brunt of the struggle on using the electoral opportunity to put pressure on Nixon and to obtain the aforesaid requirement before the election, we should, for the time being, set aside some other requirements regarding the internal issues of South Vietnam."[36]

Just as Thieu had understood it to be, Hanoi's policy was always focused on conquest. The Communist negotiators were told, "However, if we succeed in ending the US military involvement in South Vietnam, we will have conditions to obtain these objectives later in the struggle with the Saigon clique and win bigger victories."[37]

On October 5, Bunker passed on to Thieu Kissinger's disappointment in the South Vietnamese president's recalcitrance and obstinacy during his meeting with Alexander Haig, along with Kissinger's pledge to press for the withdrawal of Hanoi's troops. Bunker pointed out to Thieu that a public confrontation between Saigon and Washington would lead to a unilateral American disengagement over complete impatience with the pace of the negotiations. Bunker reminded the South Vietnamese president that previously, Nixon had taken great risks to support South Vietnam, and now the American president needed Thieu's help.

Thieu replied that up to now he had been making decisions alone regarding the negotiations. Now he needed to consult others. But he assured the ambassador that Saigon and Washington would work closely together, promising that he would not provoke any public disagreement with the Americans.

Nixon sent another personal letter to Thieu, giving personal reassurance that no settlement would be arrived at, the provisions of which had not been discussed with Thieu beforehand. This commitment applied specifically, the letter said, to the next round of secret talks in Paris. Thieu was pleased.[38]

Bunker replied to a request from Nixon for advice on how to best work with Thieu. Bunker reported that, in his judgment, South Vietnam's president was worried by five contingencies. First, the tripartite formula for the reconciliation council bothered him. Second, Washington was moving too fast. Third, he was intensely suspicious of Kissinger. Fourth, he didn't trust the Communists. And finally, he resented being placed by Washington in a junior position in the negotiations.

Bunker asked that Washington slow the pace of negotiations to give the South Vietnamese more time to consider events and the Americans more time for persuasion and argument. While Washington couldn't let Thieu call the tune, Bunker noted that the Americans needed not to give him the impression that they were forcing things along against his will and best interests. Washington should help the South Vietnamese avoid painting themselves into a corner, as had happened in 1968. Calm explanation, not hysterical pressure tactics, Bunker affirmed, would do the trick.[39]

Kissinger took Bunker's advice. He agreed not to table with Hanoi the new American idea about electing a new constituent assembly to write a new constitution for South Vietnam.[40]

Kissinger then left Washington for Paris and the final round of negotiations on the future of South Vietnam.

Hanoi came prepared with cosmetically more acceptable terms. Le Duc Tho tabled a simple "decent interval" scenario:

> First, on the basis of our 10 Points and on the basis of your 10 Points, the Democratic Republic of Vietnam and the United States will agree on and sign an agreement on ending the war and restoring peace

in Vietnam as you have once proposed. This agreement is aimed at the settling of the military questions, such as the question of US troop withdrawal, the question of handing over captured people of the parties during the war, the question of the ceasefire under international control and supervision in Vietnam, including the question of US responsibility to heal the war wounds and to rehabilitate the economy of Vietnam. As to the political and military questions of South Vietnam, we shall only agree on the main principles. After the signing of this agreement a ceasefire will immediately take place . . . The people of South Vietnam shall decide themselves their political system through genuinely free and democratic general elections under international supervision . . . The armed forces of the two South Vietnamese parties shall remain in place in the regions respectively controlled by them.[41]

Le Duc Tho elaborated on the need to keep North Vietnamese forces inside South Vietnam:

Now regarding the question of Vietnamese armed forces in South Vietnam. Regarding the so-called withdrawal of North Vietnamese troops, we have repeatedly expounded our point of view to you. We have expressed our views on that question over the four years of our negotiations. It is not the first time that we have said this. If this question is posed, as I told you last time, this question cannot be settled. So your proposal on the withdrawal of North Vietnamese troops is utterly unacceptable. We propose the following provisions. We propose the following formulation: "the question of Vietnamese armed forces in South Vietnam will be settled by the South Vietnamese parties themselves in a spirit of equality and mutual respect, in keeping with the post-war situation and with a view to lessening the people's contributions." We have proposed such a formulation; you have proposed the same too. If an agreement should be reached

between us, we propose to record this principle: "The South Viet-
namese parties will discuss and settle this question."[42]

Kissinger never challenged Tho's intransigence by actually asking for the
return of those forces to North Vietnam:

Now, with respect to your forces. We have not asked for the with-
drawal of all your forces. We have said that on the day of ceasefire
there be an exchange of [lists of] the units that are in place in each
area, which is required in any event. We would hope that such a list-
ing on your side would show that some of the units that have entered
South Vietnam after March 25 had returned to North Vietnam. Of
course, it would also mean that some of your units remain in South
Vietnam. We simply would like the de facto situation on the day of
the ceasefire to reflect some movement.

Kissinger was not naive. He knew full well that Hanoi could resume its
aggression against South Vietnam. He said candidly to Le Duc Tho:

Now I know, speaking frankly, and the Special Advisor knows, that
if you are determined to move supplies through Laos you will find
a way of doing so. You always have. Or am I wrong? [Le Duc Tho
laughs.] On the other hand, we rely on the fact that you will consider
this inconsistent with our long-term relationship and that therefore
you will look at problems henceforth in a different way.[43]

Later, he volunteered a similar pious hope:

Now let me tell you how I see your forces in the South. I recognize it
is a question of principle for you. I recognize also that if you observe
this agreement in my judgment some of these forces will have to be
withdrawn. For your own reasons, not because you're obliged to
do it. Because if you cannot introduce any equipment, supplies, you

*cannot keep all these forces there. So as a practical matter that is
actually not a matter whose outcome will be very different whatever we decide at all. Yet in the American mind the first question
that I shall be asked at a press conference, where I will be the chief
advocate of this agreement in America, will be about your forces.
And you will see that when we make an agreement I will be the
person who will put it over with public opinion. Just as I did our
agreements with the Soviet Union in Moscow on strategic arms. So
the first question I will be asked is about your forces.*

*As far as I'm concerned, speaking realistically, I believe that the
guarantee for peace in South Vietnam will depend on the relationship you and we will develop and the relationship that I hope to start
when I come to Hanoi. If the agreement breaks down, because you
feel you have been cheated, you have demonstrated amply your ability to bring your forces back into South Vietnam. So our long-term
objective in dealing with you would be to create such a relationship
between the Democratic Republic of Vietnam and the United States
that you will not want to start the war again.*[44]

Kissinger here spoke knowingly of the exact scenario Hanoi would use
to bring about its conquest of South Vietnam. Kissinger may have been a
false friend of South Vietnam, but he was no fool.

In general, Kissinger's attitude toward the Vietnamese Communists
as opposed to his feelings for the Vietnamese Nationalists was reflected
in this comment:

*Mr. Special Advisor, Mr. Minister, I first of all want to say I share
completely the sentiments you expressed at the end of your presentation. Our two countries must make peace and they must start a
new relationship and they must pursue that relationship with the
same energy and the same dedication with which we have been
adversaries before. This is our solemn intention.*

Kissinger also made a gift of a regimental tie to Xuan Thuy.[45] The record does not indicate whether he ever gave a personal gift to South Vietnam's President Thieu.

After long hours haggling with Hanoi's representatives in Paris, Kissinger sent Bunker only two short messages. One advised Thieu to seize the maximum amount of critical territory as possible. The second reported that the Communists had tabled new proposals very similar to their earlier version so as not to warrant further elaboration. Mostly military matters had been discussed by the two sides.

The agreement reached with Hanoi on October 8 was acceptable to Kissinger. He considered it rather proudly as a fine outcome to the war. He flew back to Washington to report the negotiations' results to President Nixon.

The following conversation occurred between them:

> *Kissinger: I have to—I have to go up—out—here is what we have to do: I have to go to Paris on Tuesday [October 17] to go over the agreed things word-for-word with Le [Duc Tho].*

> *Nixon: You could then get it?*

> *Kissinger: No problem. I think we have an agreed text. I've left a man behind to go over it. Except, but I've—you know, just in case there's any last-minute treachery. Then I go to Saigon to get Thieu aboard. Then I have to go to Hanoi if they're willing [unclear]—*

> *Nixon: Won't it totally wipe out Thieu, Henry?*

> *Haldeman: Yeah.*

> *Kissinger: Oh, no. It's so far better than anything we discussed. He won't like it because he thinks he's winning, but h—*

Kissinger: We've done just about everything we can do, but this is a deal, Mr. President, that telecon could go along with. So we have no problem. I mean this is—if—if you went on television and said you're going to make this as an American proposal, the New York Times, the Washington Post, and even moderates would fall all over themselves, foaming at the mouth, swearing that this couldn't—that you were indeed out of—

Nixon: Henry, let me tell you this: it has to be with honor. But also it has to be in terms of getting out. We cannot continue to have this cancer eating at us at home, eating at us abroad. Let me say, if these bastards turn on us, I—I am not beyond [unclear] them. I believe that's, that's what we're up against.

Nixon: They're leaving Thieu in. They're in. And they're supposed to negotiate a National Council? Thieu will never agree, they'll never agree, so they screw up, and we support Thieu, and the Communists support them, and they can continue fighting, which is fine. Right, telecon? Do you see it that way, Al—?

Nixon: Let me come down to the nut cutting, looking at Thieu. What Henry has read to me, Thieu cannot turn down. If he does, our problem will be that we have to flush him, and that will have flushed South Vietnam. Now, how the hell are we going to come up on that?[46]

Thieu was laid up with a fever from a bad reaction to a tetanus inoculation. Bunker could not meet with him to report on Kissinger's Paris talks until October 10. Thieu then told Bunker that documents recently captured from the Communists indicated that Communist units were preparing for a "solution." Communist cadres were being told by their superiors that there would be a coalition government running South Vietnam, with the PRG in full control of many local areas. North Vietnamese soldiers would become members of the southern NLF, posing as citizens of South Vietnam.

A third, and equally brief, message arrived from Kissinger for Bunker. Kissinger was extending the talks. Negotiations had become sufficiently complex for him to come to Saigon to brief Thieu on the discussions.

The next cable from Kissinger instructed Bunker to ask Thieu to think about what political terms he was prepared to accept and to again ask him to make a maximum effort to seize territory. Kissinger planned to arrive on October 18.

Bunker quickly cabled back asking whether, before his arrival in Saigon, Kissinger could give Thieu a written amplification of the developments that had occurred during the recent Paris meetings. With so little substance to report after four days of discussions, Thieu's apprehensions, not to say suspicions, would be aroused, Bunker advised Kissinger.

Back from the former Harvard professor of international relations came only general guidance:

> *F.Y.I.: In posturing him for my visit hopefully you can strike a balance which on one hand reassures him that we are not about to accept any political demands which would result in his overthrow and on the other hand keep sufficient heat on him so that he cannot adopt the frame of mind that he has faced us down and that he can afford to fend off successfully whatever solutions may emerge from our discussions with the other side. I recognize this is a difficult task but suspect that at this juncture Thieu may think that he alone can set the terms for a final settlement.*[47]

By these figurative words was Bunker forewarned that whatever deal Kissinger had struck with Hanoi would be crammed down Thieu's political throat. Still trusting Kissinger, Bunker was not worried by what this haughtiness portended.

What Bunker did not know was that Kissinger had already agreed with North Vietnam's Le Duc Tho not to give Thieu any opportunity to obtain changes or modifications in the terms of the agreement reached by Hanoi and Washington. As North Vietnamese negotiator Luu Van Loi has written:

"With regard to Saigon, the US would see to it."[48]

Thieu was again not feeling well, this time from an overdose of laxative. He was most surprised to learn that Bunker and his staff would be working on a Friday the thirteenth. Tongue in cheek, Bunker confided in Thieu that he had cleared the risk of doing so with his own astrologer.

While waiting for Thieu to feel better, Bunker reread his memorandums of the November and December 1968 deadlock with the South Vietnamese over starting peace negotiations in Paris. He then cabled Kissinger his fear that the Americans were now heading into a similar confrontation with their ally. Bunker said he would try to convince Thieu that such a course was unacceptable. While Thieu might agree with the Americans rationally, in his heart, he would not welcome their imposing on his destiny as well as on the destiny of his people.[49]

More guidance from Kissinger arrived on October 13. Kissinger was back in Washington. He mentioned the possibility of a settlement containing a "fig-leaf political arrangement," requiring much less of Thieu than Alexander Haig had suggested just ten days before. However, Thieu would be expected to show reasonable flexibility on the "modalities" of a cease-fire in place in return for Hanoi's concessions on the political issues.

Kissinger reported that President Nixon was determined to seek settlement on a cease-fire now—with or without Thieu's agreement. The United States would not sell Thieu out, Kissinger continued, but he must be under no illusion that he could stare Washington down. A good deal was to depend, cabled Kissinger, on the "spadework" Bunker was to do with Thieu before Kissinger arrived in Saigon after one more round of meetings with the North Vietnamese.

Later that day a second but still less than fully revealing cable from Kissinger arrived at Bunker's desk. In it, Bunker was asked what he could get Thieu to concede with respect to some thirty thousand civilian prison detainees, some ten thousand of whom were being held for collaboration of one kind or another with the Communists. Kissinger repeated that Thieu must be made to see that the period ahead could not be a replay of 1968. The United States would never drop Thieu; the only person who could do

that was Thieu himself. Within this framework—that is, his personal survival as president of South Vietnam—Thieu could be expected to cooperate
to "solidify his position" and "demonstrate flexibility on the modalities of
a ceasefire arrangement."

The cable instructed Bunker to "see Thieu immediately and commence
the posturing now."[50]

Bunker saw Thieu the very next day. They discussed a cease-fire. Thieu
reported that he had instructed General Nguyen Van "Little" Minh, com-
manding the military region around Saigon, to show some drive and expand
his zones of control. Bunker had yet to see Little Minh perform with any
efficiency. Bunker told Thieu only that Hanoi had agreed to make the proposed coalition an administrator of the agreement and not a government.

Back in Washington, Nixon was reflective. He impressed upon
Kissinger that a peace agreement was not needed to help him win the
forthcoming presidential election against George McGovern:

> *Nixon: The making of a settlement is not going to hurt us in the
> election, and it isn't going to help us significantly. You know, who
> can tell? But the main point is what could hurt, really, is to go down
> the road and then—and then fail.*

> *Kissinger: Right.*

> *Nixon: That is why I think even before going to Saigon, I would—I
> think we have to be fairly, fairly sure that—that, well, not fairly
> sure, but at least have a pretty good chance of making it go. If you
> go to Saigon, and it doesn't go, of course, then—I mean, you can't
> even really consider going to Hanoi, because if you do, it escalates
> it to a point where we just couldn't, we just couldn't—*

> *Nixon: Yeah. And I, incidentally, the—on the other side, I don't—
> there need be no concern about the political effect. We just can't
> think in the terms of the fact: "Well, gee whiz, it'd be better not to*

> *have this politically." Sure, it's risky. We don't need it. We're going to win without it, and very heavily. But the point is that you've got to take a risk to get the damned war over. And if there's more, if there is—if this is the best settlement we can get—which I think it is—and if this is the best time, when the forces will be the strongest to get it, then the thing to do is to push it and get it. That's my attitude.[51]*

On October 16, Bunker was finally sent a brief synopsis of the terms that Kissinger had agreed to in Paris. Thieu was meeting with his associates and the cabinet. He was unavailable to meet with Bunker. Bunker now awaited Kissinger's arrival with some foreboding of the worst.

Privately, Nixon instructed Kissinger to obtain Thieu's willing consent to the proposed agreement. General Haig informed Kissinger that "our leader is adamant about next leg not repeat not taking place unless a firm agreement with full support by Thieu is assured."[52]

President Nixon had not overlooked the flaw in Kissinger's peace proposal—allowing Hanoi to keep its army inside South Vietnam. He concluded that continuous American determination to enforce the agreement with military measures would be the only worthwhile protection provided to the South Vietnamese after the proposed agreement went into effect. With Hanoi's divisions within South Vietnam ready to fight at any time, only a credible threat of retaliation for any violation of the agreement by those troops would ensure the peace. In his *Memoirs*, Nixon would write,

> *I sympathized with Thieu's position. Almost the entire North Vietnamese army—an estimated 120,000 troops that had poured across the DMZ [demilitarized zone separating North from South Vietnam] during the Spring invasion—were still in South Vietnam, and he was naturally skeptical of any plan that would lead to an American withdrawal. I shared his view . . . I knew, as he did, that [the Communists] would observe the agreement only so long and so far as South Vietnam's strength and America's readiness to retaliate forced them to do so.[53]*

While worried over its shortcomings, Bunker nevertheless accepted the agreement as negotiated by Kissinger. America's cause had been vindicated. Hanoi had been forced by allied victories in the field—in pacification, political development, and hard fighting—to formally acknowledge South Vietnam's authenticity and autonomy. American defense of South Vietnam had prevailed over Communist aggression. The American justification of helping the South Vietnamese defend their independence as a nation-state would now be ratified by Hanoi.

The final agreement signed on January 27, 1973, would require North Vietnam to implement the following provisions:

THE EXERCISE OF THE SOUTH VIETNAMESE PEOPLE'S RIGHT TO SELF-DETERMINATION

Article 9 *The Government of the United States of America and the Government of the Democratic Republic of Viet-Nam undertake to respect the following principles for the exercise of the South Vietnamese people's right to self-determination: (a) The South Vietnamese people's right to self-determination is sacred, inalienable, and shall be respected by all countries. (b) The South Vietnamese people shall decide themselves the political future of South Viet-Nam through genuinely free and democratic general elections under international supervision. (c) Foreign countries shall not impose any political tendency or personality on the South Vietnamese people.*

But like Nixon, Bunker knew that only continued American resolve, vigilance, and support for the Saigon government would guarantee real peace for an independent Nationalist South Vietnam. Bunker was confident that such resolve, vigilance, and support would be forthcoming. After all, expensive American forces remained in West Germany and South Korea to deter Communist aggression there.

CHAPTER 7

THE BETRAYAL IS CONSUMMATED

*Things are in the saddle
and ride mankind.*

—Ralph Waldo Emerson, "Ode, Inscribed to William H. Channing"

Henry Kissinger came to Saigon to inform South Vietnam's leaders of the terms of peace with their Communist enemy that he had just reached on their behalf. It was not Kissinger's intention to give Nguyen Van Thieu and his colleagues any significant role in determining how the United States would end its participation in the war to defend South Vietnam.[1]

Ellsworth Bunker, however, retained admiration, even some affection, for Kissinger. In a world where many spoke airily with ease and where even more lacked both convictions and courage, Bunker looked upon Kissinger as a man who used power well. Bunker judged others by the results of their undertakings. Kissinger's intensity and quick mind were always focused on getting what he wanted. Bunker felt his spirits rise in Kissinger's dynamic presence. With so many others acting from minimalist or even defeatist expectations, Bunker found Kissinger's vitality a refreshing alternative.

Bunker's South Vietnamese counterparts had no illusions about Kissinger. What Thieu had always feared most—that Washington would permit North Vietnamese troops to stay in South Vietnam—was now a reality. Accordingly, Thieu and his associates felt keenly that the American national security advisor had willfully betrayed them. They were understandably angry and bitter over this. In their minds, his peace agreement was nothing to celebrate. It was, from their point of view, a fatuous piece of worthless paper, only a photo opportunity, boosting him up personally to strut about on the world stage indulging in great intellectual condescension at their great expense.

Thieu had also not been consulted as promised before Kissinger had reached this understanding with Hanoi. Thieu had told the Americans that they were on their own in the negotiations, and Kissinger had gone ahead on his own without Thieu's consent. What could the South Vietnamese do now to protect themselves? They could not alienate the Americans, but they didn't want to accept Kissinger's terms for a temporary truce in their war with Hanoi, a truce that left Hanoi with impressive strategic advantages.

The reality was that Kissinger could easily have consulted with Thieu and even sought specific guidance from President Nixon after October 8, when Le Duc Tho had presented new and conciliatory proposals in Paris. Then, there had been time for Kissinger to ask for an adjournment of the negotiations to confirm that his president really wanted a peace agreement on such terms and to give Thieu a meaningful say in the negotiations.

Having negotiated only a "decent interval" for South Vietnam, Kissinger now found himself very much on the defensive. He now proceeded to maneuver to extend the interval of "decency" that Hanoi might provide for the Nationalists to be free of Communist dictatorship. He was caught between Hanoi and Saigon. He had to gain concessions from Hanoi to give more length to the "interval" while convincing the South Vietnamese that the interval he was providing for them to live freely according to their nationalist values would last and last.

Upon his arrival in Saigon, Kissinger and Bunker met with Thieu and his National Security Council. Bunker stepped back to let Kissinger carry the burden of persuasion. Kissinger presented a letter from Nixon affirming that Kissinger spoke for the president of the United States. General Creighton Abrams had been sent along with Kissinger to describe the vast quantities of weapons and munitions the United States would now suddenly ship to South Vietnam before the cease-fire would go into effect. The Vietnamization program was not as far along with providing South Vietnam with airpower and artillery as it was with augmentation of naval vessels and ground combat battalions.

Kissinger noted first that his objective was not to assist President Nixon's reelection but to prevent Hanoi from publicizing its terms for peace, which would be used by the American antiwar movement to undermine congressional support for South Vietnam. Kissinger emphasized strongly that under the peace agreement, Thieu would not have to resign as president of South Vietnam. The proposed Council of National Reconciliation and Concord was a nullity as far as holding real power was concerned. The agreement as a whole, Kissinger concluded, represented a "disintegration" of Hanoi's position even though the Communists would not agree to the withdrawal of their troops from the South.[2]

Important, in Kissinger's mind, was the impact that the peace agreement would have on defusing the American antiwar movement. With that political sentiment on the wane, continued American financial support for South Vietnam would be assured. But to assist in achieving that result, Thieu had to make clear to public opinion that he was not an obstacle to peace. He had to accept, said Kissinger, an agreement that contained unfavorable provisions from his perspective. Kissinger would stay in Saigon for three days and wanted Thieu's reaction to the peace agreement within that time.[3]

Kissinger had arrived in Saigon with a completed peace agreement substantially along the lines of his September 15 proposal. There were, however, two significant changes, both contained in an Article 9.

First, after a cease-fire was declared, the proposed peace agreement now called for the establishment of a limited administration to supervise elections by the two contending South Vietnamese parties (the Saigon government on one side and the Provisional Revolutionary Government [PRG]/National Liberation Front [NLF] on the other). This entity would be called the Council of National Reconciliation and Concord and would consist of three subgroups. There was no requirement for Thieu to step down as president of South Vietnam. Saigon and the PRG would meet to determine whether this council would organize lower-level entities in the provinces and the districts. In addition, Saigon and the PRG would meet to seek solutions to the internal problems of South Vietnam, and the National Council would subsequently promote implementation of any solutions so agreed upon.

Thus died Hanoi's demand that Washington overthrow its South Vietnamese ally as the purchase price of peace. South Vietnam's defeat of Hanoi's invasion had brought about a diplomatic dividend. The Republic of Vietnam in Saigon, with its constitution, National Assembly, president, supreme court, laws and regulations, army and police, political parties, land reform programs, and village governments, remained in full force and effect as the legitimate government of South Vietnam.

But this Article 9 of Kissinger's peace agreement rested on a lie—the falsehood that the PRG/NLF in fact represented some meaningful segment of South Vietnamese opinion.

But more in line with reality, the draft peace agreement in its Article 9 also recognized the right of the South Vietnamese people to self-determination and in its Article 10 provided that North Vietnam could not unify all of Vietnam under its rule through coercion or annexation.

Second, however, and more treacherously, Kissinger's peace agreement contained no mention of the principle that all armed forces of the countries of Indochina would remain within their national frontiers. There was no requirement or even the implication of any requirement that Hanoi withdraw its army from South Vietnam, Laos, or Cambodia.

Article 9(h) obligated the two South Vietnamese parties only to settle among themselves the issue of Vietnamese armed forces in South Vietnam in a spirit of national reconciliation. The two parties were to discuss between themselves steps to reduce military numbers on both sides and to demobilize the soldiers so taken out of service. Hanoi was under no unilateral obligation to demobilize its forces either in South or in North Vietnam.

Correspondingly, Article 15, on the independence, sovereignty, and territorial integrity of the countries of Indochina, did not refer specifically to South Vietnam. The peace agreement mentioned by name only Vietnam, Laos, and Cambodia. After the agreement would come into effect, Hanoi could claim that its activities in South Vietnam did not constitute impermissible interference in the internal affairs of another sovereign people.

Kissinger had agreed to obtain Thieu's immediate acceptance of these terms. Then he was to fly on to Hanoi to finalize and—surrounded by smiling Communist leaders—sign the peace agreement, denying Thieu respect and importance in the eyes of the American people and in world opinion.[4]

Kissinger had thus even accepted Hanoi's demand that the United States ratify its conceit that it was the government most fit to speak for all Vietnamese.

Explaining exactly why he had given in to Hanoi on the pivotal point of letting North Vietnam leave its divisions in South Vietnam, Kissinger later told Bunker that the only way to get the agreement that he believed the American people so desperately wanted was to surrender to Hanoi's intransigence.[5]

So just as, twenty-six years earlier, the influential French colonialist Jean Sainteny had turned his back on the Vietnamese Nationalists in order to accommodate the ambitions of Ho Chi Minh, now the very powerful American Henry Kissinger had similarly taken the knee before Ho Chi Minh's colleagues and turned his back on Nguyen Van Thieu and his Nationalist compatriots.

Where Sainteny had sought to take advantage of what he perceived to be Ho Chi Minh's political stature, Henry Kissinger hoisted himself upon the political power of the American antiwar movement conjoined with the militant forcefulness of the Vietnamese Communists.

In meeting with President Thieu to obtain his consent to the agreement, Kissinger revealed that the American negotiating strategy had been designed primarily to minimize the political appeal of the antiwar movement, Hanoi's fifth column in the United States:

The President and I have had to spend enormous time and have produced an enormous amount of expedients from month-to-month in order to maintain support. We have had the imperative of always being in the position to make clear that we are not the obstacle of a settlement, even on terms which would have been very difficult for you to accept. When I was here last time, President Thieu pointed out to me very profoundly that his problem and ours are exactly the opposite. He had to demonstrate to his populace that he was firm. We have to point out to our populace that we are flexible. This was a correct description of the state of affairs.

I have gone into so much detail because I wanted to show you gentlemen that our problem is not in the next two weeks but in the next six months. Our fear is that if we do not move in the direction I will describe to you, we may be forced into a position where all support may be cut off by Congressional action. We have financed the additional operations produced by the Communist offensive, which have now reached $4.1 billion, by means and procedures that are at the very margin of legality and which will have to be submitted to Congress in January. This is the situation in which we find ourselves, and this is what President Thieu and his colleagues should keep in mind in assessing our imperatives.

We have maintained support for the war in Vietnam for four years by a combination of drastic military measures and the demonstration to the American people that we were pursuing a peaceful course. Therefore, our general strategy at these meetings, as during the four years, was to accept enough of the North Vietnamese proposals to enable us to show that we have been reasonable, but not enough to achieve the objectives of the Communists. In this respect, our tactics were bound to be different. Our tactics were different, but our strategy was not different from yours.

But they will not give up the struggle. The question is how many years is it before they can really start again, and what can you do in those years.[6]

Kissinger was thus open and explicit that what he had brought Thieu was really only a chance for a decent interval of survival for South Vietnam.

Thieu then became formal, correct, aloof, and cool to his visitors. He queried Kissinger, "What does Hanoi expect from this agreement? Does President Nixon need this agreement for his re-election?"

Dr. Kissinger: I can answer you best by reading to you in part what the President delivered to me on the plane when I was leaving. This is indiscreet but it is better than anything I could say. [Reading from the president's handwritten note] "Dear Henry, as you leave for Paris I thought it would be useful for you to have some guidance that we were talking about on paper. First, do what is right without regard to the election.

"Secondly, we cannot let a chance to end the war honorably slip away. As far as the elections are concerned, a settlement that did not come unstuck would help among young voters, but we do not need it to win."[7]

(Reading between the lines of President Nixon's guidance to his subordinate, I think, lets us conclude that the president was cautioning Kissinger not to surrender to the narrative of the American antiwar movement. In his *Memoirs*, Nixon made an explicit point of telling us that "I wanted to make sure once again that Kissinger understood my feelings about not rushing to reach a settlement before the election and about not forcing a break with Thieu by pushing him too fast.")[8]

Mr. Duc: I would like to ask Dr. Kissinger a small point. There is to be no further infiltration of the NVA after a ceasefire. How do you think this can be effectively controlled, and implemented?

Dr. Kissinger: We have elaborate provisions, more elaborate than efficient. I will be quite honest. Since they managed to get down 100 tanks to An Loc without being found by our intelligence, I'm not sure that they can't infiltrate against Polish, Indonesian and Canadian inspectors. I do not wish to delude you.

If, on the other hand, you act with confidence and assurance, we may not know if they infiltrate 5,000, but we should know if they infiltrate 25,000. At that point you and we have to decide what measures are to be taken. I tell you candidly, speaking for myself, I rely more on unilateral intelligence than on the inspectors.

In my judgment there are two possibilities. One, they are planning the whole operation to get us out and start another offensive next spring. Against this contingency, certainly, almost certainly, if they do, we will reinforce again like last year and the President, who has just been reelected and had the political triumph of this settlement, in the first year of his second term is almost certain to do again what he did in an election year when all the odds were against him.

One other thing in the confidence of this room. We approached both the Chinese and the Russians, because they were told about this by the North Vietnamese, and we told them that we understand military support for an ally at war, but we would not understand military support to a country that had just made a peace settlement. We do not have a formal reply. I just made this approach on Sunday on behalf of the President. I am reasonably certain the Chinese will not continue their present scale of military supplies because Chou En-lai told me that when I was there in June. This fact is not to be repeated. The Soviets have not yet replied, and therefore I can't say.[9]

Thieu then asked for a copy of the peace agreement in Vietnamese. Kissinger did not have one. He promised to get one to Thieu. The meeting adjourned.

Kissinger reported calmly that the South Vietnamese had "objections and questions, none of them capricious, centered on North Vietnamese forces remaining in the south; clarifications on the infiltration and replacement provisions; questioning of the three equal segments for the Council; and probing for US response if the agreements were to break down."[10]

He also realized that "it was clear from the sober, somewhat sad, mood of the session that they are having great psychological difficulty with cutting the American umbilical cord. They probably realize that the deal is a good one by American standards, but their focus is on remaining North Vietnamese forces and the likelihood of violations of the agreement."[11]

The senior Americans and South Vietnamese gathered again in the afternoon.[12] Thieu and his aides asked questions. Thieu especially wanted to know whether the agreement was needed to help President Nixon win reelection. The South Vietnamese wanted to know what the United States would do if Hanoi violated the agreement in the future.

The South Vietnamese went to work assessing the fine points of the agreement. The next morning, they requested that Kissinger obtain twenty-three changes from Hanoi.[13]

The South Vietnamese wanted North Vietnamese regular and irregular troops to withdraw from South Vietnam concurrently with the remaining American withdrawals. Just as the Americans were to dismantle their bases, the South Vietnamese wanted Hanoi to dismantle its bases in the South under the supervision of a joint military commission. They wanted a provision that neither South nor North Vietnam would accept outside military aid. They wanted the Council of National Reconciliation and Concord to be composed of two parties, not three. They objected to the wording of Article 9(h) on the demobilization of military forces in South Vietnam because it seemed to refer only to South Vietnamese forces and not to North Vietnamese units. They wanted the text to require the four—not three—countries of Indochina to respect each other's independence and sovereignty.[14]

Nguyen Phu Duc, advisor to President Thieu, asked the advisor to President Nixon why the proposed agreement did not mention South Vietnam. Kissinger replied that "this is an error in the text. The number of states has to be removed. For the United States, there are four states in Indochina."

Duc followed up: "Why not make a specific mention of four states in Indochina in the text?"

Kissinger replied, "It would be difficult."

Duc later wrote in his memoirs: "There was a silence after this answer of Kissinger which gave to the [Vietnamese] the impression that Kissinger had made to Hanoi a major concession which implied the recognition of Hanoi's ultimate jurisdiction over all of Vietnam."[15]

Kissinger refused to budge on seeking withdrawal of North Vietnamese troops and on modification of the Council of National Reconciliation and Concord so that it would become a bilateral entity. Kissinger admitted that Hanoi's troops in the South had become part of the PRG structure.[16] The meeting ended with the Americans leaving to consider South Vietnamese demands.

That afternoon, Thieu refused to meet with Kissinger. Bunker was quite put out by what he considered to be unprofessional lack of cooperation on Thieu's part.

Late that night, Thieu called Bunker at home. Thieu was very emotional and very agitated, accusing members of Kissinger's staff, along with other American officials, of leaking details of the peace proposals to various political personalities in Saigon.[17]

In Washington, President Nixon instructed General Alexander Haig to send a message to Henry Kissinger saying in part:

As you continue discussions with Thieu, I wish to reemphasize again that nothing that is done should be influenced by the U.S. election deadline. I have concluded that a settlement which takes place before the election which is, at best, a washout has a high risk of severely damaging the U.S. domestic scene, if the settlement were to open us up to the charge that we made a poorer settlement now than what we might have achieved had we waited until after the election. The essential requirement is that Thieu's acceptance must be wholehearted so that the charge cannot be made that we have forced him into a settlement which was not in the interest of preventing a Communist takeover of a substantial part of the territory of South Vietnam. As I outlined yesterday, we must have Thieu as a willing partner in making any agreement. It cannot be a shotgun marriage.[18]

The next morning, Sunday, October 22, Kissinger and Bunker met with Thieu at eight in the morning.[19] Still in high emotion and sitting forward on the edge of his chair, Thieu spoke in Vietnamese. His private secretary and trusted younger cousin translated. As the group explored the alternatives before them, Thieu grew calmer. Bunker developed the impression that he and Kissinger were making a breakthrough in their relationship with Thieu, overcoming his resistance. Bunker was mistaken.

Kissinger started by stating his amazement that Thieu felt that the United States would try to undermine his position. Then Kissinger objected to the cold treatment he had received during the past few days as the personal representative of the president of the United States. He read a message from Nixon asserting that, in Nixon's view, the peace agreement was in the best interests of both countries and should be accepted as it was.[20]

Kissinger said he had moved at an accelerated pace in Paris only to prevent Hanoi from presenting publicly a peace plan that Washington would then have to accept without making changes. He had judged that making an agreement on a date for signing the peace agreement would induce Hanoi into making compromises favorable to South Vietnam. Now, given Thieu's concerns, there were only two courses open in his mind: work on those changes that Hanoi might accept or return to Washington empty-handed.

If he did return to Washington without Thieu's acceptance of the agreement, Kissinger concluded, Hanoi would go public with the text as it stood.

Thieu replied that the local Communists already knew of the agreement; opposition politicians were spreading word of its essential points. Even worse, North Vietnam's prime minister, Pham Van Dong, had just given an interview to *Newsweek* magazine in which he had described Thieu as having been "overtaken by events" and the Council of National Reconciliation and Concord as a "three-sided government of transition." Thieu concluded from this that Hanoi's commitment in the peace agreement to respect South Vietnam's independence was fraudulent.

Thieu continued: his National Security Council could not accept two points in Kissinger's agreement. First was the continued presence of North Vietnamese troops in the south. Second was allowing the Council of National Reconciliation and Concord to have three political components. They could accept the role and purpose of that council but not its composition. The issue raised in these South Vietnamese concerns was the life or death of South Vietnam.

Kissinger said that Thieu could deal with North Vietnam's units in the South since the Army of the Republic of Vietnam (ARVN) outnumbered them. As for the Council, advised Kissinger, arguing over its composition was pointless. The Council was irrelevant to the distribution of power over the country. Kissinger had obtained Hanoi's agreement to pull out from Cambodia, which would be of great advantage to Saigon in the future. Further, Kissinger went on, Thieu did not have to resign.

Kissinger warned that once the peace agreement became public knowledge, the Congress of the United States would cut off aid to South Vietnam if Thieu did not sign. South Vietnam had won, but Thieu was acting as if he had lost, Kissinger concluded somewhat sharply.

For himself, Bunker found Kissinger's arguments sound and the peace agreement an acceptable risk for South Vietnam to take, though he did not like leaving North Vietnamese troops in the South.

Thieu replied only that he must report to his National Security Council. He was not yet in a position to accept Kissinger's peace agreement. Furthermore, the National Assembly, not himself as president, had to ratify any peace settlement.

Kissinger now offered Thieu something in consolation. While there was no possibility of doing anything about a North Vietnamese withdrawal, Kissinger said the United States would offer a unilateral declaration that it recognized Saigon as the only government of South Vietnam. Then Thieu could visit President Nixon after the peace agreement was formally signed.

In the meeting, Kissinger notably did not disclose to either Ambassador Bunker or President Thieu his 1971 private proposal presented to Soviet Ambassador Dobrynin, which had been accepted by Hanoi and then shared with Zhou Enlai, that the Vietnamese Communists were free to resume their war against South Vietnam in "a couple of years" after the signing of the very peace agreement that had just been revealed to President Thieu and his colleagues.

Kissinger had to leave for Phnom Penh so that he could inform Cambodia's leaders of the peace terms. The group agreed to meet again in the afternoon after Kissinger's return to Saigon.

In the interim, Bunker took time to report to Washington that Hanoi's attempts to seize territory just before any agreement was signed had been repulsed by South Vietnamese forces.

In Washington, President Nixon asked to meet with General William Westmoreland to learn his opinion of the terms negotiated by Henry Kissinger.[21]

General Westmoreland stated that in his view the major difficulty with the settlement was the cease-fire in place and the lack of any mention of specific commitments with respect to the North Vietnamese divisions in the South. He pointed out that the political framework provided for a cease-fire in place without withdrawal commitment, and this amounted to a de facto cessation by Thieu of sovereignty over substantial portions of South Vietnamese territories.

The president stated that in his view no control mechanism would ever provide assurance against cheating if the will existed to do so. General Westmoreland agreed but stated that he was concerned that the plan was not adequate for the realities of the situation. In effect, the United States was now in a strong position that had been brought about by the president's courageous decision to bring the war to the North. Had it been done six years earlier, the war would have been long since over. Now that the North was hurting, we should not move precipitously to take their first proposal.

President Nixon emphasized that he had no intention of being stampeded in this situation and that he recognized the strength of our position. Above all, he would do nothing that would dishonor the sacrifices of all the Americans who had given their "the last full measure of devotion" to the defense of South Vietnam against illegal aggression. However, he had reviewed the plan, and if President Thieu could wrap himself around it with confidence and in an air of optimism and victory, he felt it offered a fair chance for the people of South Vietnam to retain their freedom. Within this framework, the United States would do all that was necessary by way of support, including strong military action if required, should violations occur.

Nixon recognized the possibility that the proposed peace agreement might bring only a decent interval, but he was feeling cornered and without options to reject out of hand what Kissinger had brought back from Paris. Thus, Haig informed Kissinger during his negotiations with Thieu:

> The President believes, and I agree fully, that this latest concession if made public by the North along with the rest of the negotiating record will pose the most serious difficulties for us. Consequently, he wants you to use your best judgment in pushing Thieu up to the limit of not forcing him to break publicly with us before November 7. On the other hand, he should understand clearly that if he persists in resisting all efforts to settle the conflict in what we consider to be just

to both sides, we will be forced to work out bilateral arrangements with the Democratic Republic of Vietnam which could risk all that we have worked so diligently to achieve.[22]

A letter from Nixon to Thieu was included in the telegram:

Dear Mr. President:

I have studied with utmost care all of the provisions of the proposed agreement as they now stand, including the most recent concessions by Hanoi concerning Laos and Cambodia. Based on my study, I consider this agreement to be acceptable in all its ramifications and therefore urge your most careful consideration and acceptance of it.

Were you to find the agreement to be unacceptable at this point and the other side were to reveal the extraordinary limits to which it has gone in meeting demands put upon them, it is my judgment that your decision would have the most serious effects upon my ability to continue to provide support for you and for the Government of South Vietnam.

I can assure you that if you proceed with us under the conditions which now have been outlined, you will continue to have my fullest support.

This would include whatever military actions might be necessary in the event of an abrogation of the agreement by the other side.

Sincerely,

Richard Nixon

After Kissinger returned from his briefing of the Cambodians in Phnom

Penh, the Americans met again with President Thieu.

Thieu had not been intimidated by Kissinger's warnings. The stubborn South Vietnamese president began the next meeting of the allied leadership with new requests.[23] He and his National Security Council had three requirements that must be reflected in the peace agreement, Thieu announced. First, the peace agreement must confirm that there are two Vietnamese states and that the demilitarized zone line should be used to show that Hanoi could not violate the territory of the southern Vietnamese nation-state. Second, there could be no North Vietnamese forces left in South Vietnam. Third, the composition of the Council for National Reconciliation and Concord must not denigrate the Saigon government's claim to legitimacy.

In short, the South Vietnamese rejected Kissinger's peace agreement.

He presented new language to describe the Council for National Reconciliation and Concord. He also called for a provision requiring North Vietnamese units to at least leave South Vietnam's first military region around Hue and the demilitarized zone.

In no mood to compromise with Thieu, Kissinger pointed out that if he returned to Washington without reaching agreement with the Saigon government, some delay in signing the peace agreement could be justified, but, in the end, Washington would have to cave and accept the terms he had worked out with Hanoi in Paris.

Thieu retorted sharply, "We feel we are being sacrificed after being faithful to you. The proposed agreement is worse than the 1954 Geneva Accords, for now the United States acknowledges that there are only three Indochinese countries—not four—and so in time South Vietnam will collapse."

How right Thieu was.

Importantly, in the afternoon meeting, Thieu said: "I was correct to have expected that you would connive with Beijing and Moscow. You recognize the presence of the North Vietnamese within South Vietnam. The South Vietnamese people will assume that they have been sold out and that Hanoi had in reality won the war." Thieu grew emotional:

Dr. Kissinger said the other day that Le Duc Tho had burst into tears, but I can assure him the South Vietnamese people are the ones who deserve to cry, and the man who should cry is I.

There are three problems which I discussed with the NSC [National Security Council] this morning, and we came to the conclusion that there was no way out. The three problems are:

Viet-Nam was separated as a result of the 1954 agreements, and now is the time to officially confirm that there are two separate states pending reunification as recognized by the 1954 agreements; and that the DMZ divides the states in order to ensure that North Viet-Nam cannot violate South Viet-Nam.

That we cannot accept the presence of the North Vietnamese army in the South. As a soldier, I have been fighting Communism for 25 years. As a soldier and as President, I cannot accept it. The North Vietnamese have broken down their forces into small units so as to South-Vietnamize their army. I do not believe that North Vietnamese forces in South Viet-Nam number less than 300,000.

The political solution. I have reaffirmed my position that a tripartite [Council for National Reconciliation and Concord] CNRC is totally unacceptable.

If the President and Dr. Kissinger think they can help us, we welcome it. But if the US wants to abandon the South Vietnamese people, that is their right.

My last comments concern my own person. Ever since the US asked me to resign and bargained with me on the time of my resignation, had I not been a soldier I would have resigned, because I see that those whom I regard as friends have failed me. However great the personal humiliation for me I shall continue to fight. My greatest satisfaction will be when I can sign a peace agreement. I have not told anyone that the Americans asked me to resign, since they would share my humiliation, but have made it appear voluntary on my part.

Kissinger confronted Thieu's mistrust by saying that while he admired President Thieu's speech, he deeply resented the suggestion that the Americans had connived with Beijing and the Soviets. When President Nixon had mined North Vietnam's ports, he had risked his political future to assist South Vietnam. American principles were preserved in the proposed peace agreement. No American would understand Thieu's contention that Kissinger had undermined his position as president of South Vietnam. The American government looked on the peace agreement as a major defeat for the Communists.

Kissinger argued:

When we talked with the Soviets and Chinese, it was to pressure them to exert pressure on Hanoi. We genuinely believed that the proposed agreement preserved South Viet-Nam's freedom—our principles have been the same as yours and we have defended them. You have only one problem. President Nixon has many. Your conviction that we have undermined you will be understood by no American, least of all by President Nixon.

As to specifics: We have not recognized the right of North Viet-Nam to be in the South. We have used the language of the Geneva Accords, since we thought this the best way to work out a practical solution. Had we wanted to sell you out, there have been many easier ways by which we could have accomplished this. We do not regard the agreement as embodying a coalition government, but as a major Communist defeat.

With respect to the DMZ we may be able to add another sentence which would clarify this point.

We are faced with a practical problem. Concerning the immediate situation, it is imperative not to have a confrontation. Should the US withdraw, it will affect all of your neighbors.

The longer-term problem is what happens to our relationship? I do not see how the US can justify to the Congress what it is we are fighting for. We have not destroyed your government; we have obtained better terms than any American would have believed possible. Concerning your resignation, we think that the January 25 speech got us through this Congressional period and enabled us to get appropriations in an election year. It is impossible to say that President Nixon who risked the summit meeting with the Soviets could conceivably undermine you. It is clear now that we cannot continue with the present negotiations. I would like to know how you view that we should proceed from here.

Thieu replied,

The US has been negotiating on our behalf. If you now tell North Viet-Nam that they have to talk to us, that will be very good. Recently the PRG has wanted to negotiate directly with the US and Pham Van Dong has spoken of us and of me in very derogatory terms. This has been a great humiliation. If I can negotiate with North Viet-Nam, I will do so in the spirit of reconciliation.

Perhaps we have two different concepts. Let me ask you, if you were a Vietnamese, would you accept the fact that the Geneva agreements have not been restored in the agreement in a clear manner? Would you accept the fact that the North Vietnamese can have 200,000 to

> *300,000 troops in the South and can you accept the fact that the*
> *CNRC should be composed of three segments?*

"If we accept the document as it stands, we will commit suicide and I will be committing suicide," said the president of South Vietnam.

Thieu expressed his gratitude for President Nixon's decisions. But he added, just as the American president had acted for the best interests of his people, now he, Thieu, had to act for the best interests of the South Vietnamese. "I have been the object of organized slander in the US press as an obstruction to peace, and I resent it," Thieu said.

Kissinger said that Thieu's course was suicidal, adding that the United States had fought for four years and had mortgaged its entire global foreign policy to the defense of one little country. "What you say has been a bitter thing to hear," Kissinger said with a tone of anger. Kissinger went on, saying that, had Thieu spoken openly at the start of these four days, we could have made plans on how to proceed; now we are totally on the defensive. Kissinger then concluded that he must return to Washington and try to prevent publication of the proposals by Hanoi. He asked to see Thieu briefly before his departure the following morning.

It was the end of the discussion. The Americans left Thieu's office with little ceremony.

Kissinger later reported to Washington,

> *Thieu has just rejected the entire plan or any modification of it and*
> *refuses to discuss any further negotiations on the basis of it. He*
> *insists that any settlement must contain absolute guarantees of*
> *the DMZ, total withdrawal of North Vietnamese forces, and total*
> *self-determination of South Vietnam without any reference as to*
> *how this is to be exercised.*[24]

Kissinger then added in a subsequent telegram to the White House,

It is hard to exaggerate the toughness of Thieu's position. His demands verge on insanity. In addition to the points I mentioned in my previous message, he stated that we have been colluding with Moscow and Peking for months against him and that there has been an organized press campaign in America against him. He insisted that he would settle for nothing less than a document which legally recognizes the two Vietnamese states with the DMZ as their border. He is totally oblivious to the score of DRV concessions, the massive amount of equipment we are moving for him, the various Presidential guarantees, or the ramifications of the course he has chosen.[25]

Of course, if Kissinger had come to Saigon with a provision for the withdrawal of North Vietnamese forces, Thieu would not have been so recalcitrant in withholding his support.

Later, Thieu recalled that "Kissinger had come not as a comrade in arms, but to advocate the North Vietnamese cause. He gave me the impression that he was a representative of Hanoi, not of America . . . I didn't understand for whom he was working. Was it for us or for the North Vietnamese?"[26]

Kissinger and Bunker called on Thieu early the next morning.[27] Kissinger said that President Nixon had received a full report of Thieu's feelings but did not agree with his characterization of the peace agreement. Thieu had been apprised fully of every development as it had occurred and had been consulted on every move, with the single exception of the September 15 meeting, when Kissinger felt it had been necessary to move before hearing from him. Now, said Kissinger, we must let no disagreement show between us if the other side goes public, although Washington cannot disavow the text already agreed upon.

Kissinger had canceled his trip to Hanoi and would ask for another meeting in Paris to seek changes in the agreement.

Thieu noted that he would not publicly acknowledge any difference between President Nixon and himself. He left open what he might say about his differences with Henry Kissinger.

Kissinger now retorted with some force, "You must understand how it seems to an individual who had stood against 300,000 demonstrators, against bureaucratic and congressional opposition and against public opinion and the press. That is why I spoke as I did yesterday. But the course you are following is suicidal."

"After fifteen years of fighting, it is not much to ask for two changes," Thieu replied. "If I am forced to accept, I will feel that I have been pressured by North Vietnam. If the United States plans to support South Vietnam, it should seek two changes," Thieu added. Hanoi could agree to withdraw its troops without any public announcement of that commitment, he offered. Then Thieu said firmly that he would always strive to help the United States support the South Vietnamese people and that if he himself became a hindrance to that support, he would step down. He proposed forgetting what had been said.

The South Vietnamese had in addition raised a touchy point about the legal authority of the Council for National Reconciliation and Concord: Was it to be a "*hanh chanh*" (administrative structure) or a "*chinh quyen*" (governing structure)? Hanoi had called it a "*chinh quyen*," which implied that it would replace the Saigon government in ruling South Vietnam. Now Kissinger said that he could not judge the meanings of words in Vietnamese but that to the Americans, the term meant something insignificant. Had he been allowed to go to Hanoi, Kissinger continued, he could have sought modification of the agreement on the Council and the withdrawal of North Vietnamese troops from Military Region 1.

He did not consider Thieu's demands unreasonable, but if the war went on at its present rate, funds would be cut off by Congress at the end of six more months. He was telling this to Thieu in anguish, he said. Had the draft agreement been presented to the world as a surprise, it would have been seen as a great triumph and would have enabled Nixon to obtain continuing support from Congress. He was leaving Saigon, he said, with a sense of tragedy.

Thieu agreed with Kissinger's prediction of the American reaction in six months if the war continued. He did not know, he said, how he would explain to his people the difficulties that had to be faced. He suggested that Kissinger use Moscow and Beijing to influence Hanoi.

Kissinger responded that "we must dominate events." He said he would hold a press conference and ask Hanoi for changes, though not all of what he would ask for could be achieved. He had no intention, he affirmed, to ask Thieu to resign, but if Thieu became an obstacle, Washington could no longer support him.

Thieu acknowledged that, in retrospect, the November 1968 breakdown between Saigon and Washington should have been avoided. The problem now in South Vietnam, he said, was that unless the agreement contained the points he brought forward, the morale of the South Vietnamese military and people would collapse. If they ever concluded that they had been abandoned without any hope of survival, he meant, they would panic, and their will to resist would rapidly collapse.

Kissinger left Saigon having failed to bring Thieu fully into the process of reaching agreement. Thieu had stood up to Henry Kissinger.

In Washington, General Alexander Haig also stood up to Kissinger, sending him a message saying,

> Hanoi has made political concessions in return for an improved de facto security situation on the ground which would enable them to maintain a strong presence in South Vietnam backed up by their divisions from the North. This is combined with the figleaf of an agreement in principle recognizing the reality of two governments, two armies, and an ultimate coalition which would be representative of that reality . . . And the degree to which we are willing to undermine Saigon in the interest of a settlement is a matter of the gravest concern which will require the most careful, detailed and unemotional consideration.

> It would be inconceivable to me that the American people would support President Nixon if he agreed to an option which unilaterally terminated the bombing of the North and reduced further military pressures in the South—all this combined with a public open break with Thieu. Were we to pursue the course outlined, we would forever

destroy those forces here in America which have provided the basis of support needed to do what has been right about our policies in the past four years. This course of action would have an equally devastating effect on all of the countries in Southeast Asia which depend on our reliability and consistency for their future.

I urge you to rethink again the essence of this problem.[28]

Haig, with apparent disparagement, used the word "figleaf" to describe the outcome of Kissinger's secret negotiations with Hanoi and put him on notice that undermining our South Vietnamese allies should not happen.

Separately, he told Kissinger: "I have been, however, from the outset concerned about the North Vietnamese forces in the South and have expressed those concerns to you repeatedly both during the meetings in Paris and subsequently."[29] Apparently, Kissinger did not disclose to Haig that, actually, it was he—Henry Kissinger—who had proposed such a possibility to Soviet ambassador Anatoly Dobrynin on January 9, 1971.

In another message, Haig faulted Kissinger's approach to the negotiations for putting our ally in a vicious dilemma:

It is inconceivable to me that we could ask the Congress to fund $700 million of aid to a government which has refused to accept the most reasonable of peace terms. Thus, we will have in the long run set upon a course which gives Thieu two options: either personal or national suicide. The outcome of either, as our best analyses have already confirmed, would be to ease a way for a Communist takeover. It appears to me that we are focusing too intensely on not losing the achievements that we have made at the negotiating table and on the immediate requirement to maintain an essential credibility and trust between ourselves, Hanoi, Peking, and Moscow.[30]

General Haig's advice to Henry Kissinger was to back off the negotiation track which had put the South Vietnamese in an untenable position and to consider the application of military pressure on Hanoi:

> *I believe we now have no alternative but to avoid sharp over-reaction to what is a devastating disappointment to all who have worked so tortuously over the past eight weeks. Above all, we cannot lose perspective of the realities of our relative strengths. There may be some hope for a purely military solution. Certainly if Hanoi were willing to abandon the main outlines of its political demands, it may be in the final analysis equally susceptible to paying the price to obtain a cessation of U.S. actions against the North. Any course of action which you consider will have to give appropriate weight to this remaining bluechip which is the only viable pressure-point we have to obtain the release of our prisoners and the honorable extraction of our remaining forces.*[31]

When Kissinger complained on October 23 that a letter to Thieu drafted by Haig was insufficiently threatening, Haig shot back at him, "I am sorry you did not find the letter to Thieu up to your standards of toughness."[32]

Bunker now found himself just where he had been in late October 1968. Once more, American political pressures had led to an American agreement with Hanoi contrary to the best interests of South Vietnam remaining free and independent. Twice now South Vietnam's President Nguyen Van Thieu had quietly but firmly stood up to his American patron and had refused to go along with the demands of American diplomacy. It had been in 1968 as it was now again in 1972, principally for Ellsworth Bunker to bring about a convergence between Thieu and Washington. On one side in Saigon, he had the face-to-face relationship with Thieu and could win his confidence. And in Washington, Bunker could guide Nixon and Kissinger in the nuances of just how to obtain Thieu's concurrence with what Kissinger had independently agreed to with Hanoi.

With the negotiations moving forward, the Americans presumed that a cease-fire with the Communists was a likely probability. In addition, the proposed peace terms would limit the American ability to supply the armed forces of South Vietnam. Thus, Operation Enhance Plus was authorized to quickly ship large quantities of military equipment and supplies to South Vietnam, especially for its air force. The transfer was completed by November 17. Delivered were 22 AC-II9 and 32 C-130 transport aircraft, 90 A-37B fighter jets, 277 UH-1 helicopters, and 116 F-5A tactical support jets.

On October 24, Bunker received a cable. Moscow had just advised that Kissinger should go to Hanoi for the next round of talks; prospects for settlement would be better if he went there than if he met the North Vietnamese in Paris. Kissinger wanted Bunker's advice on that point: How would his going to Hanoi affect the South Vietnamese situation?

Bunker advised that he not go to Hanoi. Thieu would resent being marginalized in the negotiations. Kissinger's trip would be evidence that the United States was determined to make a deal at Saigon's expense, and it would look like a McGovern ploy—going to Hanoi to beg for the return of our prisoners of war. If Hanoi had a mind to compromise, Bunker said, it would do so in Paris just as well as at home.

But Bunker, ever astute in seeing matters from the perspective of his superiors, noted the possible benefit of getting a faster response from the North Vietnamese if Kissinger indeed went to Hanoi.

The next day, Kissinger cabled that he would not go to Hanoi. He would try to meet with the North Vietnamese again in Paris on October 29. He said that there was no hope of further aid being appropriated for South Vietnam if the peace negotiations broke down over Thieu's obstinacy. Bunker was to see Thieu every day at President Nixon's direction and get the South Vietnamese to develop alternatives. Kissinger wanted Thieu stripped of his illusions but wanted to avoid a public break with him before the November 7 election in the United States. The Americans couldn't brutalize Thieu, wrote Kissinger, to the point where he undertook a public confrontation with Washington. But after November 7—election day in the United States—Kissinger promised, full leverage would be applied to Saigon.

Kissinger shared his thinking with Bunker:

Between now and November 7, we are posed with a most delicate problem. Before November 7, we cannot brutalize Thieu to the point that he will kick over the traces and undertake a public confrontation and break with us. We should, however, impress upon him the impracticality of his failing to plan for the contingency of ultimately having to accept a settlement along the lines which have been currently worked out. Therefore, in your discussions with Thieu you should impress upon him the urgent need to plan intensively for the contingency of a cease-fire in place in the very near future and perhaps as soon as mid-November. Concurrently, and also in the contingency context, we should move jointly to ensure that the expedited flow of equipment and matériel is undertaken so that the additional matériel will be in South Vietnam by mid-November. We have instructed Defense and State to proceed with the shipments, with General Abrams serving as the Secretary of Defense's and the President's executive agent in the theater. In pressing Thieu vigorously to proceed with this kind of contingency planning, you should at the same time make it very clear to him that he may be faced with absolutely no alternative but to accept the broad outlines of the current proposal. You will have to employ a degree of vigor which is strong enough to strip him of his current illusions but at the same time avoid forcing him to kick over the traces and break publicly with us before November 7. After November 7, full leverage will be applied.[33]

Hanoi now published the draft agreement. Kissinger responded with a press conference saying to the American people especially just before a presidential election that "peace is at hand."

Alexander Haig had a different take on the former's choice of words and their effect. In his memoirs, he wrote, "It is hardly possible to imagine a phrase, so redolent of Neville Chamberlain and the effete 1930s cult of appeasement, more likely to embarrass Nixon as president and presidential candidate, inflame Thieu's anxieties, or weaken our leverage in Hanoi.

The president regarded Kissinger's gaffe as a disaster."[34] In a subsequent account, Nixon appeared to agree more with Haig than Kissinger, writing, "When Ziegler told me that the news lead from Kissinger's briefing was 'Peace is at hand,' I knew immediately that our bargaining position with the North Vietnamese would be seriously eroded and our problem of bringing Thieu and the South Vietnamese along would be made even more difficult."[35]

But in reality, Kissinger was under no illusions that genuine peace was at hand. He told his president that Nixon should not describe the agreement with Hanoi as a "lasting peace or a guaranteed peace because this thing is almost certain to blow up sooner or later."[36]

Bunker did not want Thieu driven into desperation. Now Prime Minister Tran Thien Khiem passed on to Bunker's embassy a conversation with Thieu where the South Vietnamese president compared himself to the famous nineteenth-century martyr Phan Thanh Gian, who, beset by a powerful French army in the Mekong River Delta, surrendered his provinces without a fight but then committed suicide. In so surrendering to the enemy, he had betrayed his emperor. For a proud people like the Vietnamese, martyrdom has appealing features. In 1963, Buddhist monks had famously immolated themselves in protest over Ngo Dinh Diem's administration.

Bunker knew that Thieu was a realist and no fool. Bunker had learned that Thieu had instructed his military commanders to prepare for a cease-fire. Bunker thought it likely that South Vietnam's president was holding out for a while to see how many changes he could get in the proposed peace agreement. Bunker also understood that Thieu wanted Hanoi to deal with him, if only through an intermediary.

Bunker called on Thieu. Given Hanoi's disclosure, the world knew the terms that Kissinger had accepted. Bunker told Thieu that Saigon and Washington had no choice but to work within the framework of the proposed peace agreement—namely that the Republic of Vietnam (GVN) would remain the legitimate sovereign authority for South Vietnam and that Hanoi's divisions would remain inside South Vietnam. Bunker wanted to cut off attempts to perform major surgery on the agreement. Thieu's cousin had already leaked to the press Thieu's alternative of a referendum.

Thieu told Bunker that the Communists would now approach the cease-fire in two stages. First, they would seize as many hamlets and villages as possible right as the cease-fire went into effect. Then they would continue fighting in a "half-dark, half-light" phase of struggle. Thieu added some intelligence on Hanoi's plans: on October 25, province-level cadres had been told that the ultimate objective of the NLF's guerilla war had not been attained and that "the puppet government in South Viet-Nam was not destroyed" but that the "US war of aggression" was brought to an end and favorable conditions had been created for the elimination of the "puppet government in South Viet-Nam."[37]

Thieu told Bunker that he had only just learned from Radio Hanoi of Kissinger's agreement regarding the dates for signing and of the letters of assurance to Hanoi from President Nixon. Those revelations were just further evidence of Kissinger's duplicity vis-à-vis South Vietnam.

Bunker replied that no matter what Hanoi said, the allies couldn't now develop significant alternate settlement proposals, as that would create new confrontations in the negotiations.

Thieu sent to Bunker a memorandum that the ambassador forwarded to the White House. In it, Thieu argued that the peace agreement's deficiencies were important issues, not linguistic difficulties, as Kissinger had described them in his "peace is at hand" press conference.

On October 29, President Nixon sent Thieu a personal letter affirming that no distinction could be drawn between Kissinger's views and Nixon's own position.[38] He had sent letters to Prime Minister Pham Van Dong of North Vietnam, as revealed by Radio Hanoi, but Hanoi had yielded to the United States on the points raised in those letters. Nixon affirmed yet again that he had a personal commitment to South Vietnam and would demonstrate his stand by having a meeting with Thieu after the peace agreement was signed. Unity between Saigon and Washington was needed, Nixon wrote. He asked that Thieu give him a base of public support in the United States. Both countries had to achieve peace on the terms that he, President Nixon, decided would be workable.

And, Nixon added, Kissinger had used the phrase "linguistic ambiguity" in his press conference only to give all parties a way out of an impasse. Nixon warned against any rift between Saigon and Washington and that Thieu should harbor no illusion that Nixon's position on peace terms would change after the November election. Bunker felt that exactly such firmness was needed at that moment.

In presenting Nixon's letter to Thieu, Bunker stressed first the facts about Saigon's military strength. The ARVN had destroyed most of the Communist units seeking to capture territory just before the date for a cease-fire accepted by Kissinger in Paris. Then Bunker spoke to the point that the Council for National Reconciliation and Concord was not a government. Accordingly, Thieu could tell the people of South Vietnam honestly and firmly that the constitutional government in Saigon had not been dissolved.

Bunker advised Thieu to take the political and psychological initiative and inform the people of South Vietnam of the agreement's terms. Silence on his part would exacerbate the impact of uninformed, apprehensive fears of its provisions. Saigon had won, Bunker asserted; Hanoi had given up its political demands after four years of brutal warfare.

With some emotion and leaning stiffly over to get closer to Thieu, Bunker asked to speak as a friend and an admirer. Bunker noted his concern over the drifting apart between the allies. Thieu's wisest course was to wait for Kissinger's new round of talks with Hanoi.

Thieu replied that, in fact, his greatest fear was of another massive North Vietnamese offensive coming after the Americans had left.

Bunker observed that any such attack would violate the agreement, and the United States would react strongly in that case, as President Nixon had assured him.

Hanoi then agreed to resume negotiations with Kissinger on November 20, after the American elections.

The CIA's senior analyst of the war, George Carver, weighed in with a critique of Kissinger's decent interval deal. Carver concluded,[39]

There is a basic imbalance: the responsibilities and performance obligations of the allied side, particularly US, are spelled out with far greater clarity, precision and rigor than the Communist side's responsibilities and performance obligations, especially Hanoi's. In all key areas (e.g., troop withdrawal, non-interference, acceptance of future political developments), our commitments are explicit and reasonably concrete. Hanoi's commitments, by contrast, are generally couched in broad language that is allusive or elliptical, vague and often ambiguous.

Here are four areas in which the language of the present draft would cause (and clearly has caused) legitimate concern to the GVN and should cause similar concern to us. These areas are the ones covering (1) North Vietnamese Army personnel and units now in South Vietnam, (2) the role and nature of the tripartite "National Council of National Reconciliation and Concord," (3) South Vietnam's right to existence as an independent sovereign state, and (4) the arrangements for monitoring both sides' compliance with the provisions of any final agreement once the latter is signed.

Hanoi will, of course, strongly resist any endeavor to incorporate any reference to the 195,000-odd North Vietnamese Army troops—including twelve NVA line divisions—now physically present in South Vietnam. For one thing, Hanoi has never been willing to admit, formally or publicly, that there are any NVA troops in South Vietnam. Furthermore, Hanoi's whole political position and its pursuit of its basic political objectives are keyed to the concept that "Vietnam is one," hence NVA troops in South Vietnam are, by definition, not "foreign." The GVN, however, simply cannot ignore the presence on what it insists is its sovereign territory of close to 200,000 hostile troops that, by the definition of political reality essential to Saigon's vital interests, are part of an invading army that is unarguably "foreign." The GVN also can, and will, contend that both its description of NVA forces as foreign invaders and its opposition to their continued presence on South Vietnamese territory are completely consistent with the heretofore unvarying policy of the United States Government, frequently and forcefully enunciated by President Kennedy, President Johnson and President Nixon. The GVN, therefore, would find it almost impossible to acquiesce in a comprehensive peace agreement which turned a blind eye to the presence of NVA forces in South Vietnam. Inevitable GVN sensitivities in this sphere also will be intensified and reinforced by the current draft's provisions in the other three key areas of concern here discussed.

The GVN, with reason, will probably regard the present language as a cunningly baited trap; for if strictly and literally interpreted, that language eliminates any South Vietnamese government's right to exist. The unamplified endorsement of reunification as an ultimate goal (Article 1) by itself may do little damage; but when taken in context with the current draft's language at two other places, the picture becomes quite different. First there is the explicit endorsement of the language of the 1954 Geneva Accords holding that the 17th Parallel is a temporary truce line, not an international boundary (Article 10). Then there is the express reference (Article 15-d) to the three countries of Indochina.

It could be, and has been, argued that the draft's silence with respect to these NVA forces in the South has little practical significance since other portions of the agreement will deprive these forces of their Laotian and Cambodian sanctuaries and, above all, their Ho Chi Minh trail lifeline of support through Laos. Given the record of the past eighteen years, however, and particularly given North Vietnam's flagrant and systematic violation over the past decade of the similar provisions of the 1962 Laos "Declaration," the GVN has considerable legitimate ground for considering any such line of argument as transparent sophistry.

There is no mystery or secret about Hanoi's goals and basic objectives. They have often been spelled out, always consistently, most recently in that very 26 October statement which publicized Hanoi's version of the current peace agreement. These basic goals and objectives of the DRV, toward which all DRV policies are oriented, are (in Hanoi's own 26 October words): "to liberate the south, to defend and build the socialist north, and to proceed to the peaceful reunification of the country."

Now among senior Americans there could be no illusion about the probable impact of Kissinger's path to extricate the United States from the Vietnam War. But as the coming weeks would show, President Nixon was so hemmed in by anti-war opposition that he could not withhold his support for Kissinger's plan of disengagement so favorable to Hanoi but not to Saigon.

Bunker asked his deputy Samuel Berger to meet with Prime Minister Khiem and go over the peace agreement's terms with him. Bunker wanted to build support for the agreement among Thieu's close associates. Khiem was not concerned with the terms. His view was that Thieu was being most influenced by a small coterie of his most intimate advisors. Berger met with the minister of economy, who was equally sanguine. He reported no fiscal panic in business circles over the recent developments in seeking a peace agreement.

Thieu met again with his National Security Council on November 6. He announced that a cease fire was inevitable—Nixon could not be reversed on that score—but that Saigon's government would survive under the proposed peace agreement. He expected Kissinger now to obtain a reference to "four" Indochinese states, a symbolic North Vietnamese withdrawal, and confirmation that the Council for National Reconciliation and Concord was not a government. He expected to sign the agreement in December so that the American prisoners of war would be home by Christmas 1972. A peace agreement would be his holiday present to President Nixon.

Bunker sought to allay Kissinger's fears that Thieu was acting irrationally, noting that Thieu had

> not highlighted the fact that our previous proposals had always provided, however phrased, for the withdrawal of North Vietnamese troops from South Viet-Nam. The fact that North Vietnamese troops are to be withdrawn from Cambodia and Laos adds to his suspicion that Hanoi will maintain that their troops have the right to be anywhere in Viet-Nam, North or South. Thieu has asserted that in addition to the 143,000 North Vietnamese troops in North Vietnamese units, there are at least 100,000 more fillers in VC [Viet Cong] units who cannot be identified and will remain in country in any event.

Bunker went on to inform Kissinger of growing popular support for Thieu in his unyielding opposition to North Vietnamese demands, reporting, "In fact, there is greater unity in political and religious circles than I have seen here since November 1968. Mass meetings have been held in various parts of the country and resolutions passed by many political and religious elements in support of the GVN position."[40]

On November 7, Richard Nixon won reelection to the presidency of the United States in a landslide. George McGovern's policy of abject surrender to Hanoi was repudiated by the American people.

General Alexander Haig then arrived from Washington. He brought yet another letter from Nixon for Thieu. Nixon and his aides had realized that since Thieu's distrust of Kissinger was so firm and intense, Haig would be more fitting as a White House representative with South Vietnam's president.

Nixon's letter confirmed for Thieu that the Americans would indeed seek certain changes from Hanoi. He confirmed that the Americans had never used the term "*chinh quyen*," or governing structure, to describe the Council for National Reconciliation. The problem of North Vietnamese

troops, he said, would be addressed with a requirement for the demobilization of forces in South Vietnam and their return home.

In a conciliatory letter, President Nixon affirmed,

*We are in any event resolved to proceed on the basis of the draft
agreement and the modifications which we are determined to obtain
from the North Vietnamese which General Haig will discuss with
you. With regard to these changes in the agreement, I wish to make
clear what we can and cannot do:*

*With respect to the political provisions, we will weaken the Viet-
namese translation of the phrase "administrative structure" to make
even clearer the fact that the National Council is in no way a governmental body. As you know, we never agreed to the North Vietnamese
use of the phrase "chinh quyen" and we will do our utmost to see
that the phrase "hanh chanh" is substituted. In Article 9(f) we will
also press for a sentence that makes clear that the membership of
the Council is appointed equally by both sides. And in Article 9(g)
we will attempt to dilute the already weak functions of the Council.
In any event, as we have explained to you on numerous occasions,
it is obvious that the Council has no governmental authority.*

*With respect to the demilitarized zone, we will press in Chapter V
for language that says it will be respected by the parties.*

*With respect to North Vietnamese forces in South Vietnam, we will
treat this problem in two ways. First, we will press for the de facto
unilateral withdrawal of some North Vietnamese divisions in the
northern part of your country. Secondly, we will introduce wording at the end of Article 9(h) which stipulates that troops should be
demobilized on a one-to-one basis and that they should return to
their homes.*

In Article 15(d) we will insist on deleting the inadvertent reference to "three Indochinese countries" and substituting "the Indochinese states."[41]

Here President Nixon attempted to roll back the fundamental concession that Kissinger had officially made on behalf of the United States government on May 31, 1971, allowing Hanoi to keep its forces inside South Vietnam without protest. But his effort was too little too late.

Then Haig requested Thieu's trust and cooperation in a new round of talks with Hanoi. Haig reported back to the White House that "the meeting was tense but never emotional and despite the frankness of the discussion it never lost cordiality. Thieu seemed much more controlled and confident than during the October discussions."[42]

Haig added that he had reasoned with Thieu along the following lines:

It is now apparent that the United States and the GVN have fundamental differences on the issue of the North Vietnamese troops in the South with a fundamental disagreement of this kind it was now apparent that the President would have to consider alternate courses as outlined in his letter. More importantly, I stated that it was very obvious that Thieu would surface very quickly as the obstacle to what most analysts consider a reasonable agreement. This being the case, the essentially Democratic Senate can be expected to promptly cut off the provision of further aid and assistance to the Government of South Vietnam.

I pointed out that his uncompromising and unconditional demand for the immediate withdrawal of North Vietnamese forces could not but have this effect, even if the executive branch were inclined to agree with this principle. Thieu and his associates were obviously shaken by my response, not so much because they accept the assurances that we had provided in the agreement for the means to reduce the threat of the North Vietnamese forces but rather because they understand that their position could have the effect of depriving them of further US support. Thieu then softened his stance considerably with respect to the North Vietnamese forces, stating that his real problem was that he could not accept the ambiguous statement in the President's letter with respect to the one-for-one withdrawal. In a somewhat emotional way, he asked that we give him some specific clarification. He stated he must have the answers to the following questions:

—If the North Vietnamese forces will go home, when will they do this?

—How will they go home? And how will we verify that they have done so? And how many do they admit are in the South?

—Will they take their weapons with them or bury them to use later?

Thieu then shifted to tougher argumentation and stronger demands, being joined by the Vice President, the Prime Minister and Mr. Duc. There is no question in my mind however that he was attempting to arrive at a compromise which would preclude a total break with us. We then went on at great length and I attempted to achieve additional concessions from him on the troop issue.

In the discussion that followed, Thieu stated that he would immediately release all prisoners as soon as his had been released, including the political prisoners if they would go North. Thieu stated that he had no problems with an agreement that kept the South Vietnamese Communist forces in South Vietnam but could never accept the principle that the North Vietnamese had the right to permanently station forces in South Vietnam. I told him that this is precisely what the additions described in the President's letter were designed to preclude. He replied that we then had something to work with providing he could have the answers to the questions cited above and providing that there were provisions in the agreement that were clear with respect to these obligations. He stated that he could not accept secret understandings on this issue. The principle must be clearly provided for in the agreement.

Thieu then replied in writing to Haig's points. Thieu insisted that a peace settlement indicate unambiguously that North Vietnam had no right to invade South Vietnam and, therefore, should withdraw its troops back into its own territory. "If a settlement allows North Vietnam to maintain its forces in South Vietnam, then our struggle and the sacrifices we made during so many years would have been purposeless. Our allies would then be portrayed as aggressors, the South Vietnamese troops would be placed in this case in the position of mercenaries fighting for an erroneous cause," Thieu wrote.[43]

Thieu continued that it was not fair for President Nixon to accuse him of distorting the peace agreement when Nixon had earlier made a similar observation about the consequences of leaving North Vietnamese troops in the South. His seeking withdrawal of North Vietnamese troops contrary to Henry Kissinger's wishes also had a very "practical purpose for preserving the moral and psychological balance in the political contest in South Vietnam," he observed. Thieu could not see, he wrote, how free elections could be held as long as Hanoi's troops remained in the South. He agreed with the changes President Nixon now sought from Hanoi and proposed a joint working group to work on finalizing a text.

Bunker set up a joint task force to review the peace agreement closely. He asked an embassy Vietnamese language officer to comment on the Vietnamese version of the text.

He advised Kissinger that

the one fundamental difference remaining between us is that of the withdrawal of NVA troops from South Viet-Nam. This, I think, has always been Thieu's major concern. As long as NVA troops remain in South Viet-Nam he sees "real peace" as impossible to attain,

rather a continuing state of turmoil, a fact which he feels is con-
firmed by intelligence we are getting on the other side's intentions;
he believes that as long as the NVA remain in the South the NLF
will be compelled to do their will, and that this will prevent a solu-
tion which he is convinced could be readily worked out between the
GVN and the NLF. He believes that if it is just and correct that the
US and other allies are compelled to withdraw troops from South
Viet-Nam, those who have invaded the country should likewise be
compelled to withdraw.[44]

Thieu's continuing difficulty with the terms of peace negotiated by
Kissinger was that the agreement gave South Vietnam only a "decent interval" for its likely future. Thieu objected to the concession Henry Kissinger
had secretly put forward nearly two years before in his January 9, 1971,
meeting with Soviet ambassador Anatoly Dobrynin.

Nixon replied to Thieu with another letter expressing great plea-
sure in the common understanding Thieu had reached with Haig.[45] Now,
Nixon wrote,

But far more important than what we say in the agreement on this
issue [North Vietnamese troops in South Vietnam] is what we do in
the event the enemy renews its aggression. You have my absolute
assurance that if Hanoi fails to abide by the terms of this agreement
it is my intention to take swift and severe retaliatory action. With
this attitude and the inherent strength of your Government and
Army on the ground in South Vietnam, I am confident this agree-
ment will be a successful one.

Toward the end of his message, President Nixon reiterated his determination: "I repeat my personal assurances to you that the United States will
react very strongly and rapidly to any violation of the agreement."

The letter was dated November 15, 1972.

Nixon realized the sound grounds Thieu had for objecting to the continued presence in South Vietnam of North Vietnamese combat divisions tied to a secure rear area through the Ho Chi Minh Trail. Continued and determined defensive vigilance, concluded Nixon, would be needed to make an inadequate agreement "essentially secure."

Nixon had been outfoxed by Kissinger. Nixon didn't like the agreement as negotiated by his national security advisor, but once its terms were known to the public, he had to live with it. His tactic was to supplement the flawed agreement with additional American commitments to South Vietnam.

Personally, Nixon was emotionally moved by the plight of the South Vietnamese. He recalled his 1957 visit to South Vietnam:

> *I was there in 1957. I went down to the Delta and visited an American-Vietnamese Hospital with both Americans and Vietnamese shot up. I saw the children's ward—the little Vietnamese children—a beautiful child of 12 who lost one leg and one arm. The next day the doctor was going to amputate the other leg. I've thought of that often. The point is that killing children and women is a deliberate policy for them.[46]*

Thieu continued to prepare for a cease-fire, enjoying an immense outpouring of public support in South Vietnam for his resistance to American demands. The Lower House supported him without question. The Senate voted to support his stand on the peace agreement. On October 30, some ten thousand people had rallied in Danang in his support. Provincial councillors met in Saigon to voice their approval of Thieu's stance. On National Day, November 1, the yellow and red South Vietnamese flag flew everywhere in the country. Much of this display of support was orchestrated by government activists, but it was heady and effective nonetheless.

The PRG contacted the militant Buddhists, seeking mutual cooperation after the cease-fire. The monks curtly replied that there would be no politics in their pagodas. Those administering those pagodas were told by Buddhist leaders not to fly the Viet Cong flag. Leading militant Buddhist monks even agreed that "Communist domination of South Vietnam would be the extinction of Buddhism." These monks offered to cooperate with Thieu even if his administration in their eyes was corrupt and too self-regarding. A senator supported by the militant Buddhists said, "We must have the army; we must have the government. We will persuade Thieu to change his ways."

On November 23, Kissinger met with Hanoi's representatives in Paris. He reported that

> We have just completed a six-hour meeting with the North Viet-namese which proved to be every bit as difficult as predicted. After granting some improvements, including a more satisfactory state-ment on the status of the demilitarized zone, the other side held rigidly firm that there would be only minor changes in the political chapter, and no improvements whatsoever in the text of the agree-ment with respect to the issue of their troops in South Vietnam.[47]

On November 24, President Nixon sent a personal note to General Haig, who was in Paris and about to meet with the North Vietnamese along with Henry Kissinger. Nixon was definitive: the "decent interval" deal with Hanoi had to be accepted:

> Because of expectations that have been built up in this country that a settlement will be reached, we face a very difficult situation if the talks collapse. Consequently you should inform the Saigon repre-sentatives that all military and economic aid will be cut off by the Congress if an agreement is not reached. Inform them also that, under these circumstances, I will be unable to get the Congressional support that is needed.
>
> In my view the October 8 agreement was one which certainly would have been in our interest. You should try to improve it to take account of Saigon's conditions as much as possible. But most

> *important we must recognize the fundamental reality that we have*
> *no choice but to reach agreement along the lines of the October 8*
> *principles.*[48]

Then on November 24 Nixon sent instructions to Kissinger with regard to his new round of meetings with the North Vietnamese. A copy was sent to Bunker to share with Thieu. Nixon said,

> *If Saigon becomes the only roadblock to the October 8 deal, then it*
> *will get no support in Congress. Tell Thieu that the fat is in the fire;*
> *it is time to fish or cut bait. What counts is not the agreement but*
> *my determination to take massive action against North Vietnam in*
> *the event they break the agreement. NVA troops in the south mean*
> *nothing in that eventuality. Thieu must trust me, and what I decide,*
> *we will sign.*[49]

Nixon was giving Thieu reasons to go along with Kissinger's peace agreement even though the agreement itself did not deserve such support.

Now the decent interval scenario had become American policy. The betrayal of all those who had believed in and had died for the cause of a free South Vietnam was consummated.

In Paris, Kissinger threatened to break off the negotiations, quoting Nixon to the North Vietnamese:

> *The President is very disappointed at the tone as well as the substance*
> *of the last meeting with Le Duc Tho. Under the circumstances, unless*
> *the other side shows the same willingness to be reasonable that we*
> *are showing, I am directing you to discontinue the talks and we shall*
> *then have to resume military activity until the other side is ready to*
> *negotiate. They must be disabused of the idea they seem to have that*
> *we have no other choice but to settle on their terms. You should inform*
> *them directly without equivocation that we do have another choice*
> *and if they were surprised that the President would take the strong*

action he did prior to the Moscow Summit and prior to the election,
they will find now, with the election behind us, he will take whatever
action he considers necessary to protect the United States' interest.[50]

Tho replied that Hanoi desired peace, but if peace was impossible, the war would continue.

Tho explored a compromise on the issue of North Vietnamese troops in South Vietnam, saying that the Communists had agreed to the relocation of forces in the northern part of South Vietnam.

Kissinger replied that unless this figure were very large, it could not help.

Le Duc Tho asked how large it should be—total withdrawal?

Kissinger said that if it were in the neighborhood of one hundred thousand, then he thought one could solve the political prisoner issue.

Le Duc Tho said this amounted to wishful thinking and was hardly different from demanding total withdrawal.

On learning of Le Duc Tho's inflexibility, Nixon communicated his willingness to use bombing of the North as pressure to get better terms from Hanoi:

> *Would be prepared to authorize a massive strike on the North in the*
> *interval before the talks are resumed. I recognize that this is a high*
> *risk option, but it is one I am prepared to take if the only alternative*
> *is an agreement which is worse than that of October 8 and which*
> *does not clear up any of the ambiguities which we and Saigon are*
> *concerned about in the October 8 draft.*[51]

Though he tried through various wordings, Kissinger could not get Hanoi to give up the advantages it had secured. On November 24, Kissinger reported that he had secured only minor revisions:

- *In several articles, including the first one, we have removed*
  invidious references to the US by changing purely American

obligation to ones required of all foreign countries. This includes respect for the independence, etc. of Vietnam and not imposing a political solution on South Vietnam. Thus, the document has a better tone and the obligations are made on both sides.

• *In the political chapter we have made a very slight improvement by deleting from the tasks of the National Council the "maintenance of the ceasefire" and "preservation of peace," thus marginally reducing the Council's prerogatives. We have also improved the tone of the article dealing with South Vietnam's future foreign policy.*

• *We have achieved significant improvement in the chapter on reunification and the demilitarized zone, based partly on GVN suggestions. There is now a specific obligation for North and South Vietnam to respect the DMZ.*

On the troop issue, the GVN does have a case. However, I am convinced from years of negotiations with Hanoi and study of Vietnam, that the North Vietnamese will never agree to handle this issue directly in a document. We have built into the present agreement conditions which would effectively take care of this problem; the North Vietnamese forces in South Vietnam could not be maintained if the agreement's provisions on the DMZ, Cambodia and Laos are satisfactorily implemented. If they are not carried out, we would, of course, be vulnerable. But if these provisions are not carried out, adding another unenforced provision will not help matters much.[52]

Kissinger was trapped in a cage of his own making. His more likely option was to press Saigon to accept the "decent interval" deal. He met with South Vietnamese diplomats in Paris.[53] He had in hand another strong message from President Nixon:

I have checked today as to the attitude of the leading Democrats and Republicans who support us in the Senate on Vietnam. In preparing them for the consultation which must take place once agreement is reached we have informed them of the key elements of the October 8 agreement: the return of our POWs, a ceasefire, and a formula under which Thieu remains in power and all South Vietnamese have an opportunity to participate in a free election to determine what government they want for the future. The result of this check indicates that they were not only unanimous but vehement in stating their conclusions that if Saigon is the only roadblock for reaching agreement on this basis they will personally lead the fight when the new Congress reconvenes on January 3 to cut off all military and economic assistance to Saigon. My evaluation is that the date of the cut-off would be February 1. They further believe that under such circumstances we have no choice but to go it alone and to make a separate deal with North Vietnam for the return of our POWs and for our withdrawal.

I personally want to stand by Thieu and the South Vietnamese Government but as I have told him in three separate messages, what really counts is not the agreement but my determination to take massive action against North Vietnam in the event they break the agreement. The North Vietnamese troops in the South mean absolutely nothing in that eventuality. If they had no forces there at all and I refused to order air retaliation on the North when infiltration started to begin, the war would be resumed and the outcome would be very much in doubt.

You must tell Thieu that I feel we have now reached the crossroads. Whether [Either] he trusts me and signs what I have determined is the best agreement we can get or we have to go it alone and end our own involvement in the war on the best terms we can get. I do not give him this very tough option by personal desire, but because of the political reality in the United States it is not possible for me, even with the massive mandate I personally received in the election, to get the support from a hostile Congress to continue the war when the North Vietnamese on October 8 offered an agreement which was far better than both the House and the Senate by resolution and directive to the President during this last session indicated they thought we ought to accept.

Tell Thieu that I cannot keep the lid on his strong supporters in the House and Senate much longer. They are terribly disturbed by what they read and hear out of Saigon. It is time for us to decide to go forward together or to go our separate ways. If we go separate ways, all that we fought for, for so many years, will be lost. If, on the other hand, he will join us in going forward together on the course I have laid out we can, over the long pull, win a very significant victory.

The third option of our trying to continue to go forward together on the basis of continuing the war is simply not open. The door has been slammed shut hard and fast by the longtime supporters of the hard line in Vietnam in the House and Senate who control the purse strings.

Here Nixon makes reference to the real power driving the negotiations from the American side: opposition to the war fostered by a political movement deriving its core beliefs from French colonialism.

Bunker held a meeting with Thieu on November 27. He concluded finally, "It seems to me we have reached that point where we have given the Vietnamese the resources to do the job, that the draft agreement you have worked out gives them the opportunity, and that we have discharged fully our responsibilities. It is up to them now to make it possible for us to support them."[54]

For his part, Thieu tried to get a hearing of his concerns with President Nixon himself in person. Thieu's aide Nguyen Phu Duc was sent to

Washington to meet with the American president. They met on November 26. Duc brought with him a long letter from Thieu to Nixon. Kissinger had advised White House Chief of Staff H. R. Haldeman that Nixon should be "brutal" to Thieu's emissary.[55]

In his letter to his American counterpart, Thieu argued that the fate of his South Vietnamese people turned, first, on the issue of North Vietnamese troops returning home and, second, on the issue of the composition of the Council of National Reconciliation and Concord. In the agreement, Hanoi had neither renounced its illegal objectives of conquest nor put an end to its aggression. At a later stage, it would attempt a general uprising in South Vietnam, waiting only until the Americans fully disengaged their military power.[56]

But, Thieu argued, if Hanoi's troops were to leave South Vietnam, the PRG would then be free of North Vietnamese domination and both South Vietnamese political parties could quickly settle their dispute over who should have political power in the South. Not all members of the PRG shared Hanoi's objectives of conquest and imposing Communism, Thieu reported. More than two hundred thousand former Viet Cong supporters who had come over to the government had demonstrated the truth of this conclusion. Hanoi was aware of growing resentment among its southern followers and so had placed its own cadres more and more in command of PRG military and political units.

Thieu wrote that he faced two choices: to accept an agreement leading to the eventual death of his country or to refuse it, in which case the United States would cut its aid and South Vietnam would quickly die on the vine.

He presented the Vietnamization program as an argument for Nixon not to cut South Vietnam off from American support. In 1969, he had told Nixon in Saigon that the Vietnam War had been America's longest, and that South Vietnam would become self-sufficient militarily and economically to alleviate America's Cold War burdens. At the time, he had asked for full US air support through the end of 1973 until the full "Vietnamization" of South Vietnam's air force had been completed. He recalled for Nixon that he, Thieu, had then explained that the years 1972 and 1973 would be very crucial for South Vietnam because the Communists would launch a big offensive prior to the US elections and that after the elections there would be a decisive confrontation between the two Vietnamese armies. The United States had agreed with him then. Now his predictions had been proved true by events. By the same token, both nations could be proud of the success of Vietnamization. The settlement needed now should guarantee to the people of South Vietnam freedom from fear and coercion.

Or must he be resigned to a settlement that would have wasted the efforts and sacrifices of his soldiers and citizens and would place more than seventeen million people under Communist tyranny after some interval had passed?

One paragraph of Thieu's letter was rather poignant:

> *I wish to recall here that in the past four years, you and I have put forward many peace proposals and peace initiatives. On those occasions, I personally took heavy risks of serious internal instability. In each instance, you told me that this was the last mile and that we should go no further. During all that time Communists maintained their stubborn attitude and systematically prepared for their general offensive, which was spearheaded by many infantry divisions, thousands of tanks and sophisticated artillery swarming across the DMZ. Faced with their ruthless enmity, I think that we put ourselves at a great disadvantage by imposing deadlines upon ourselves. I venture to say here that this would seem unwise in such an important and complex endeavor as that of establishing a lasting peace.*

Haldeman reported that Nixon "softened a little bit" in his meeting with Thieu's emissaries.[57]

Thieu was holding firm to his position, suggesting that Saigon and Washington might go their separate ways: the United States would trade its residual military presence in South Vietnam for the return of its prisoners of war, and South Vietnam would stay the course of fighting for its independence.

Bunker now told Washington that Thieu would go along with the American terms for a peace agreement and a cease-fire when he realized that he had no other alternative. Thieu was playing his old game of waiting until the last minute to jump, but as always, when the right time came, he would opt for survival.

On November 30, the president met with the Joint Chiefs of Staff of the American armed forces to report to them on the negotiations, the stalemate with Hanoi, and the probability of future bombing of Hanoi.[58]

That same day, Kissinger made a passing comment about Vietnamese in a conversation with President Nixon: "Well, I'm seeing the North Vietnamese Monday. They are having a message for us now, too. Maybe they are going crazy. They're both nuts. I mean, that's the trouble with these Vietnamese, they're—" He also said in exasperation that, to his mind, the South Vietnamese were "acting out a Wagnerian drama. I mean, I must say when I went through the agreement this morning, I told Haig afterwards, when you listen to these guys you begin to doubt your sanity."[59]

Kissinger was under strain in trying to find his way forward, having put his country in the exhausting position of trying to please both Hanoi and Saigon. This was noticed by President Nixon and General Haig:[60]

> *Nixon: Henry cannot take the—this heat much longer. You know what I mean? He's—you know what I mean? It's—it's been hard for him. But—an emotional pattern here is . . .*

> *Haig: It's worse. Well, I, this past—well, he had three weeks where I thought he lost touch with reality. It started out in Paris, the first round in October. He drove that thing despite all the counsel, all I could give him—*

> *Nixon: Well, and I was trying telling him that, you know, I didn't want the goddamn thing. But you know why he did that? He wanted to make peace before the damned election. There isn't anybody to do it after the election.*

Haig: That's right.

Nixon: For Christ sakes don't do that. Then what happened?

Haig: Then in Saigon he really lost touch because here he was sending two messages to the North Vietnamese, agreeing to the [unclear], knowing that Thieu was not on board, and it was going to take some careful working. That's what caused our problem. Now, this week he started to regain himself. And I think he did a very fine job last week.

In Hanoi, the politburo of the Communist Party had responded with modest resolve to Thieu's refusal to accept the peace agreement as negotiated by Kissinger and to the American failure to sign the draft agreement before the American elections (as Kissinger had promised). The politburo sought to reach an early cease-fire according to the terms agreed to on October 8 and at the same time to prepare for eventual resumption of hostilities.[61]

On December 4, Kissinger met with North Vietnam's Le Duc Tho and his assistants again in Paris. Kissinger did not ask for changes in the composition of the Council of National Reconciliation and Concord. He did ask that the Vietnamese text of the agreement refer to that Council as a *hanh chanh*, or administrative structure. He asked for reduction in Hanoi's forces in South Vietnam and a requirement that Hanoi "respect" the territory of South Vietnam and the demilitarized zone.

Le Duc Tho was not accommodating. He refused to respect the territory of South Vietnam and wanted Vietnamese language for the Council of National Reconciliation and Concord that referred to it as a governing authority. And he wanted the United States to confirm that it respected the independence, sovereignty, unity, and territorial integrity of only one Vietnam, not two. When Kissinger objected to these firm demands by Hanoi, Le Duc Tho proposed sticking with the peace agreement as originally drafted earlier, in mid-October. Kissinger and Nixon privately discussed the advantages and disadvantages of breaking off the talks.

Kissinger met with Le Duc Tho again on December 6. He found the North Vietnamese still refusing to compromise.[62] Kissinger reported to his president with considerable realism that, if Hanoi accepted the changes to the October agreement now required by the United States,

> the outcome would be that we would have improved the October agreement, by strengthening the DMZ, reaffirming the Geneva Agreements with respect to Laos and Cambodia, making easier military aid replacements, improving the tone of the document with respect to U.S. obligations, deleting the reference to only three countries in Indochina, making clear in Vietnamese that the Council is not a government, adding a three-month target date to the demobilization provision, a faster ceasefire in Laos, international machinery in place at the time of the ceasefire and some other technical changes. We will have also bought the GVN several weeks to get ready for the ceasefire and given them over a billion dollars in sophisticated military equipment. Nevertheless, and despite our consultations and guarantees over the past weeks, we can be certain that even this modified agreement will be rejected by Saigon, which has dug itself into the position of demanding what amounts to surrender by the other side.

But now Kissinger admitted to President Nixon, in effect, that his efforts to separate the "military from the political" as a way of truly ending the Vietnam War had not been all that successful from the point of view of the United States:

> The eventual outcome of any settlement will essentially turn on the confidence and political performance of the two sides. Having seen the total hatred and pathological distrust between the Vietnamese parties, and knowing as well that Hanoi has no intention of giving up its strategic objectives, we must face the reality that this

agreement may lack the foundation of minimum trust that may be
needed. Thus it could well break down. It will certainly require from
us a posture of constant readiness and willingness to intervene.

Nixon sent a message to Kissinger: "If the negotiations are to be broken
off, it must be absolutely clear that they were responsible for breaking off
the negotiations rather than we."[63]

After his December 7 meeting with the North Vietnamese, Kissinger
finally admitted to his president that his handiwork would not bring peace
to South Vietnam.

As for the North it is now obvious as the result of our additional
exploration of Hanoi's intentions that they have not in any way
abandoned their objectives or ambitions with respect to South Viet-
nam. What they have done is decide to modify their strategy by
moving from conventional and main force warfare to a political and
insurgency strategy within the framework of the draft agreement.
Thus, we can anticipate no lasting peace in the wake of a consum-
mated agreement, but merely a shift in Hanoi's modus operandi.
We will probably have little chance of maintaining the agreement
without evident hair-trigger US readiness, which may in fact be
challenged at any time, to enforce its provisions.[64]

Kissinger's realism was supported by analysis from the Defense Intelligence Agency. On December 8, its experts concluded that South Vietnam
did not have great prospects of resisting Hanoi's continued assaults over
the long term.[65]

The agency went on record that

a cease-fire in the Vietnam War is unlikely to affect Hanoi's princi-
pal goal in Indochina—control of a unified Vietnam. Strong North
Vietnamese forces will presumably remain in control of areas they

occupy in the South. Some will be retained as integral units; others may be "camouflaged" in various ways.

Under the cease-fire, however, the communists will shift from conventional to "clandestine" warfare. Primary emphasis will be on political, psychological, propagandistic, and subversive efforts to weaken the support for and the influence of the well-entrenched Saigon government. These efforts will be time-phased over a year or two to accommodate to changing circumstances and opportunities. During the first several months, Hanoi will probably have compelling reasons to avoid major cease-fire violations, but later on will almost certainly undertake a more intensive campaign to demoralize the South Vietnamese government, induce massive civilian and military defections, and show the people that their only means of survival lies in casting their lot with the communists.

Hanoi's objectives are likely to be at least partially achieved by these means. Should the North Vietnamese regime be dissatisfied with the results, however, it would retain the option of resuming conventional military operations. In this event, without continued direct external military aid and support, South Vietnam's chances of successfully resisting would probably be, at best, only even.

Over at the Central Intelligence Agency, George Carver, one of the most insightful and knowledgeable Americans following Vietnamese developments, had similar views. He wrote a memorandum critical of Kissinger's negotiating strategy and sent it to Kissinger.[66]

Carver was blunt:

At the risk of being rude, I must here be brutally frank. Thieu does not like you nor does he trust you. He is convinced that you are much more interested in getting a piece of paper signed amid fanfare and panoply than in protecting what he considers South Vietnam's

legitimate vital interests. Though appearances may indicate other-
wise, there is really nothing personal in Thieu's attitude. He sees you
as a symbol not an individual, and you have become what T. S. Eliot
would have called an "objective correlative" for many of Thieu's
emotions about the United States. As you know, the Vietnamese have
an ingrained penchant for explaining situations or developments
in terms of personalized conspiracy theories—the more complex,
the better. Thieu may not totally accept but is nonetheless obvi-
ously taken with the (to us) [far] fetched theory that there is or
at least may be a Soviet-US deal afoot to establish a Vietnamese
buffer against Chinese expansion and, further, that Washington and
Moscow have mistakenly decided that China can be better contained
by a unified Vietnam under Communist rule—ergo South Vietnam
is in danger of being sold down the river.

Thieu has another conviction about the US to which he also makes
clear reference in his speech, though in language that tries to be con-
siderately delicate. He believes (along with many South Vietnamese)
that our understandable concern—laudable from a humanitarian
point of view—for several hundred prisoners has distorted our
perception or appreciation of Vietnamese reality and made us vul-
nerable to Hanoi's "cunning and crafty trick" of extracting major
military and political concessions from us in return for these pris-
oners, and little else.

There is, however, one issue over which I am quite sure Thieu
will not compromise and, indeed, being who he is and what he is,
cannot compromise—psychologically or politically. There is a deeply
rooted aspect of all Asian cultures, including the Vietnamese, that
imposes a limit on Asian pragmatism: form can be conceptually
distinguished from substance only up to a certain point. Beyond
that point, form becomes substance, and any attempt to distinguish
between them becomes meaningless in the sense of being (literally)

incomprehensible or unthinkable. Thieu would be personally and politically destroyed if he were to sign an agreement that eliminated the GVN's legal right to existence, and he would have the greatest difficulty (real, not just rhetorical) in signing any agreement that did not specifically endorse and sanction that right. In Thieu's eyes, probably the most important sentence in his [recent] speech is the one that reads: "As for the Communists, they seek to elude, or refuse to accept this important basis: South Vietnam and North Vietnam are two separate zones which must be temporarily considered as two separate states among the four Indochinese states."

What is notable about both the Defense Intelligence Agency (DIA) and the CIA analyses is that neither evinced any awareness of Vietnamese Nationalism as a moral and political force among Vietnamese, as an explanation of the thinking and decisions on the part of Thieu and his generals.

As the discussions continued in Paris, Bunker again argued with Thieu that the South Vietnamese leader need not worry so much. His forces would contain the invading North Vietnamese, he would win any election, and he could rely on assurances of a strong American reaction to any violation of the cease-fire by Hanoi.[67]

A well-informed Vietnamese told Bunker that Thieu was holding out for more American commitments. The respected conservative, anti-Communist Saigon newspaper *Chinh Luan* now accepted the proposed peace agreement.

On December 12, Thieu gathered one hundred political leaders to hear his concerns. He told them that he was discouraged. South Vietnam either had to accept Hanoi's forces within its territory or forfeit continued American aid. Thieu told them he was very proud to have been the first chief of state to stand up to President Nixon in a period of dazzling summitry among the world's three superpowers. Thieu then addressed the National Assembly in the same spirit.

Kissinger was angry and manic. He had no leverage over either Hanoi or Saigon: "We now find ourselves in an increasingly uncomfortable position. We have no leverage on Hanoi or Saigon, and we are becoming prisoners of both sides' internecine conflicts. Our task clearly is to get some leverage on both of them."[68]

Nixon too was frustrated, saying, "We can no more—we can no more just say, 'Well, because he [Thieu] won't take this we're going to continue this war then.' There's no way I could."

General Haig replied to him: "And I also think he's—he's playing for the big stakes, and he's going to push us right up to the goddamn brink, which he's doing now. And we can't—we can't back down there anymore than we can back down to Hanoi. We've got to—"

Nixon retorted: "Back down to him? Never. And back down in Hanoi? Never. Neither one."

Nixon later realistically put the state of the war to Haig: "Russia and China cannot allow North Vietnam to lose; we cannot allow South Vietnam to lose. That's where this war is at the present time."[69]

But pressure was growing on President Nixon. His secretary of defense and the chairman of the military Joint Chiefs of Staff sent him a terse memorandum recommending acceptance of the agreement that Kissinger had procured from the Vietnamese Communists.[70]

Nixon was feeling the pressure. Haig then informed Kissinger, who was in Paris, about Nixon's state of mind:[71]

> As to the President's mood, I believe he is genuinely concerned and somewhat uncertain as to where we go from here. He appeared to be fully in agreement with your analyses with the single exception of the tactics on bombing. On one hand, he is opposed to miniscule escalation and on the other is very leery of undertaking any additional bombing at all. At the same time, he recognizes that we are likely to be faced with continued stalling from Hanoi unless we can find a manageable way to apply additional pressure on them. With respect to Thieu, I believe he is in a genuine dilemma. He is extremely miffed at Thieu's performance but understands cold

*bloodedly that the US, certainly the executive branch, cannot be the
vehicle for crushing Thieu.*

Kissinger, having, so to speak, thrown Humpty Dumpty off the wall with
his January 9, 1971, "talking out loud" proposal to Soviet Ambassador
Dobrynin, was now helpless to make things right in the long run for South
Vietnam and the United States. And he had exposed his president and
his South Vietnamese allies as well to the dangers of being overtaken
by events.

Yeats put quite poetically the tragedy of such hubris:

*Things fall apart; the centre cannot hold;
Mere anarchy is loosed upon the world,
The blood-dimmed tide is loosed, and everywhere
The ceremony of innocence is drowned;
The best lack all conviction, while the worst
Are full of passionate intensity . . .
And what rough beast, its hour come round at last,
Slouches towards Bethlehem to be born?*[72]

Stiffening Kissinger's resolve before his next Paris meeting with the North
Vietnamese, President Nixon sent him these instructions:

*Prior to your departure for Washington for consultations on
Wednesday, December 13, I want you to be aware that the United
States will under no circumstances participate in a precipitous
settlement which is unsound and which offers no hope of implementation or the ultimate achievement of an honorable settlement.
I want you to express my disappointment in the outcome of this
round of discussions which have been characterized by repeated
delays and procrastination on the part of the Government of the
Democratic Republic of Vietnam. In this type of negotiating environment, the United States can not nor will it make more concessions.*

I remain genuinely interested in achieving a negotiated settlement of the conflict and I am convinced that the time has come to turn a new page in our relations with the Democratic Republic of Vietnam. Your counterpart should be aware that I stand ready to consummate an honorable settlement at any time that Hanoi is prepared to join with us in a spirit of goodwill and reciprocity. Until that time arrives, however, the understandings which have governed the conduct of both sides during these talks will no longer apply and until there has been measurable progress in resolving the current impasses the U.S. side intends to act in accordance with its own interest.[73]

Reporting from Paris, Kissinger told the president that the North Vietnamese were not cooperative. Le Duc Tho was stalling, opening up issues that had been resolved.[74]

Kissinger said that

their international ceasefire supervision and military commission protocols are outrageous and I formalized our objections of major principle. Predictably they wish to make international supervision so ineffective as to make it impossible to ask a self-respecting country to participate, while giving extensive powers to the military commissions, especially the two-party one, so as to give the Vietcong a country-wide presence and right of intervention. The ceasefire supervision paper reopens all kinds of political issues such as giving the National Council and lower level councils a significant role in supervising the ceasefire. It injects many other political elements, such as using Communist terminology and area designations to describe the regions in South Vietnam; unnecessary repetition of the PRG's title; and referring to Cua Viet [river estuary] as a point of entry, thus implying the DMZ has moved southward. As for the functions of the supervision commission itself, it would be largely paralyzed by stipulating numerous liaison officials from the parties; making investigations conditional on the concerned

*party's agreement; making the commission dependent for its com-
munications and transportation upon the party in whose area the
commission is operating, etc. They propose a total of 250 members
for the entire commission, compared to our 5000, and inadequately
distribute teams around the country. Furthermore, the parties
would agree on the location and activities of the teams; the ICCS is
not authorized to submit separate or dissenting reports; and no link
is established with the international conference.*

*The military commissions would be as strong as the supervision
commission is weak. Their basic approach to the ceasefire is to
define areas of control, rather than identifying and locating military units as we propose. The almost hopeless function of agreeing
on areas of territorial control is given to the two-party commission.
There would be a total standstill, including flights by combat aircraft or movement by ships. It gives wide scope to meddling for the
joint commissions around the country and provides for investigations at the request of any one of the parties. There are also some
pejorative political references. The sum total would be to legitimize
Vietcong interference down to the district level without any effective
restrictions on investigations.*

Le Duc Tho had brought up new issues and proposed very one-sided sup-
plementary agreements for international and joint military commissions
that would supervise the cease-fire and resolve future disputes. Hanoi thus
put any quick settlement out of reach.

On his return from Paris, Kissinger met with President Nixon.

In passing he remarked how the previous November he had presented
the North Vietnamese with sixty-nine requested changes to the draft peace
agreement:

First of all, let me give you my assessment of how these negotiations went. . . . We gave them 69 changes, of which many of them were crap, just to go through the motions of supporting Saigon. . . .

Later in the conversation, Kissinger spelled out just how unyielding Le Duc Tho had been in the just concluded December meetings:

The way they phrase it, we would not just leave their troops there, we would abolish the dividing line between North and South Vietnam, after which they would have an unlimited right of intervention. They would be the only legitimate government in Vietnam, while there were severe restrictions on the South Vietnamese. That—then, we might just as well overthrow Thieu. I mean, we've got to keep Thieu—not sovereignty . . . Sovereignty's not the issue, because he can have sovereignty with a cease-fire.[75]

While Kissinger was being ignored by Le Duc Tho in Paris, Bunker reported some better news about Thieu, saying that the Vietnamese president "realizes he faces a dilemma—not to sign the agreement and risk a cut off of aid by Congress; or to sign and risk political reaction and deterioration in South Viet-Nam."[76]

Thieu said that the worst he had hoped for was disengagement by the United States, withdrawal of all US troops, cessation of all US military action, and exchange of prisoners but provision of aid, which would allow the GVN to fight on alone and try to work out political arrangements with Hanoi and the NLF. This would be difficult for the GVN but would provide a chance for survival.

Here Thieu made the same proposal as Bunker had back on April 17, 1971. In Bunker's recommendation to Kissinger, the ambassador had proposed a two-step exit for the United States from the Vietnam War. In step one, the Americans would just leave—withdraw their forces and continue aid to South Vietnam. That way, there would be no illusion of peace as a finite end to the conflict. The South Vietnamese would just continue fighting to drive the NVA out of their country. But if Hanoi wanted something for its southern supporters, it would have to pay a price. That price would be a withdrawal of its forces back to its own territory. Was it coincidence that both Bunker and Thieu had the same sensible idea that had escaped Kissinger's strategic genius, or were they just two men each with sound judgment looking at the same facts?

This alternative "ending" to the Vietnam War for Americans would have had a very salutary side effect for the Vietnamese Nationalists. The longer they stood on their own against the movement associated with Ho Chi Minh in the minds of American antiwar activists, the more they would come to be seen as Nationalists with their own self-generated, moral legitimacy. In that way, the Nationalists could bring about intellectual and emotional rejection of the caustic French colonial "misinformation" that they did not exist.

Bunker then told Thieu in a private meeting that the crux of the question before Saigon and Washington was not what he or we want but what we can negotiate. Reality needed to be acknowledged over the appeal of ideals. The problem, Bunker told him quietly, was to end the war and do it in a way that would assure the GVN of US support. Without that support, there was no chance for GVN survival; therefore, it was essential to find a solution that would provide it. Clearly, we wanted him and the GVN to survive, but he would have to make this possible. If it was going to be possible, there must be an end to the kind of confrontation between us that had taken place. Negotiation involves compromise, and obviously, we were not going to be able to get all we wanted.[77]

As Hanoi backed away from agreement on an end to the war, Nixon started to perceive that what Kissinger had negotiated with the Vietnamese Communists was something less than "peace with honor."

On December 14, a frustrated Kissinger let slip from his mouth a truth about what he had accomplished: "It seems to me, to sign an agreement which leaves whatever number they've got there—let's say 150,000, which we think, plus the unlimited right of movement across the border, and, indeed, not just the right to movement across the border, but abolishing the border—that I think is close to a sell-out."[78]

A few minutes later, Nixon focuses on that reality:

> *Nixon: They were using these negotiations solely for the purpose, not of—that is not [unclear] not for the purpose of ending the war, but of continuing the war in a different form. . . . And not of bringing peace, but of having—continuing war in this terribly difficult part of the country. War in South Vietnam; peace in North Vietnam. Well, that was their proposal: peace for North Vietnam and continuing war in South Vietnam.*

> *Kissinger: So, we have come to the reluctant conclusion that—you have expressed it very well right now, Mr. President—that this wasn't a peace document. This was a document for perpetual warfare, in which they create . . .*

> *Nixon: Perpetual warfare in South Vietnam . . .*

> *Kissinger: That's right.*

> *Nixon: . . .and peace in North Vietnam. That's the way to put it.*

> *Kissinger: That's right . . .*

> *Nixon: Peace in North Vietnam and perpetual warfare in South Vietnam, with the United States—and the United States cooperating with them in . . . imposing a Communist government on the people of South Vietnam against their will.*

Nixon then reflects on what he really wanted:

> *We are the party that wants peace in Vietnam, for both sides. And let the future of this poor, suffering country be determined by the*

people of South Vietnam and not on the battlefield. That's what our
proposal is. We call on the South and we call on the North to agree
to this kind of thing. Call on them both to agree.

After this, Nixon—in his private, recorded White House conversations—never lauds Henry Kissinger as a remarkable diplomat or great peacemaker. He is not effusive with Kissinger or generous with thanks and praise.

In 2022 Kissinger would flatly assert that "With the Paris Accords, Nixon had brought his country to an outcome that merged honor and geopolitics, . . ."[79] But the "geopolitics" he refers to degraded that agreement and drained it of all claims to honor, just as Thieu predicted.

On returning from Paris, Kissinger met with his president and General Haig. They decided on a very heavy bombing campaign on Hanoi itself. Bunker was informed on December 14 that President Nixon was considering forceful measures against North Vietnam to counter Hanoi's stalling in the Paris discussions.

The next day, Thieu finally agreed with Bunker that South Vietnam could handle Hanoi's troops in the South. He noted that their withdrawal could not be enforced, as had been the case in 1962 in Laos, when Hanoi signed an agreement to withdraw its forces from that country but then refused to do so. Thieu would accept American assurances of retaliation in lieu of a treaty commitment on the part of Hanoi. But, he told Bunker, he still objected to the agreement because he feared political deterioration among all the Nationalist political parties and groups if he signed the agreement and so created a Council of National Reconciliation and Concord.[80]

Bunker replied that Saigon and Washington together had to win the war in a way that ensured continued American financial support for his government.

Renewed American bombing of North Vietnam commenced on December 18. B-52 bombers hit Hanoi and the port of Haiphong with precision and great military effect. Antiwar leaders in the United States were apoplectic in rage and opposition.

Upon his failure to obtain agreement with Le Duc Tho, Kissinger had returned to Washington angry at and dismissive of South Vietnam's President Thieu for putting the American national security advisor to a President in such a jam—trapped between irreconcilable Vietnamese Nationalists in Saigon and Communists in Hanoi. On December 20, Kissinger would castigate Thieu to President Nixon in harsh terms: ". . . if Thieu were not a cheap, self-serving son-of-a-bitch, because that's really what's involved. That bastard can't figure out how he's going to stay in office in a free political contest"; "All he wants is total withdrawal of North—[coughs]—North Vietnamese forces and two other insane conditions. And—he has to be insane. . . . the one thing in which [Averell] Harriman was right, unfortunately, is that Thieu is an unmitigated, selfish, psychopathic son-of-a-bitch."[81]

Alexander Haig returned to Saigon for meetings with Thieu the day after the bombing of Hanoi began. He presented the American position on moving forward with the peace agreement in a manner Thieu could not take offense to.[82]

General Haig handed to President Thieu another letter from President Nixon, which President Thieu read very carefully, obviously somewhat shaken by its contents.

The letter said that Nixon "was now more determined than ever to proceed with an agreement if Hanoi again demonstrated the reasonableness which it had shown in October. Were President Thieu to view the current state of affairs from any other perspective it would be a grave mistake." Thus, as President Nixon's letter confirmed, General Haig advised President Thieu to

> *take no comfort from the present turn of events [in Paris and the bombing]. There will be even greater domestic pressure upon President Nixon because of the military escalation. When combined with the letdown which had already occurred due to the peace stalemate, it was likely that a hue and cry would develop for an early settlement at any cost, including the termination of support to President Thieu.*

President Thieu nodded and agreed that he felt confident the GVN could indeed easily stamp out a guerrilla insurgency. General Haig continued that what was important for President Thieu to remember was that President Nixon was not naive about Hanoi's intentions. There were, however, considerations that President Thieu must understand if the United States and Saigon were to prevail. The facts were simple. For the past four years, General Haig, Kissinger, and President Nixon had been the principal personalities in the US government who had worked against a majority consensus to discontinue the struggle and terminate support for President Thieu. As early as October 1970, President Nixon was uniformly counseled by his cabinet and his congressional leadership to cut US losses in Southeast Asia and to withdraw from the conflict. Despite this counsel, President Nixon rallied the American people to continue the struggle and justify the sacrifices of the then forty-nine thousand American dead.

The facts were indeed simple. President Thieu could not rationally deprive President Nixon of the platform he must have to continue to support President Thieu. Were he to do so, the outcome would be inevitable and prompt a total cutoff of US support. This was not the desire of President Nixon and was not presented to President Thieu as a threat but merely as a recitation of simple objective reality.

President Thieu stated that he understood General Haig's concerns and pointed out that General Haig had to understand that President Thieu had the responsibility for the security of the people of South Vietnam and, therefore, had an obligation to improve the agreement to the degree possible.

President Thieu stated that in his view, guerrilla warfare would last for many years and this agreement would not settle the problem. Nevertheless, this would be an acceptable risk. It took twelve years in Malaysia to stamp out guerrilla warfare with a troop ratio of ten to one. He noted that it was obvious to everyone that the warfare would continue. The GVN's difficulty involved signing an agreement that recognized that Hanoi had a right to be in South Vietnam. As the president of South Vietnam, Thieu saw that everything must be done to ensure continued US support to permit South Vietnam to survive. It was important that the president do everything possible to get as many favorable changes as could be achieved in the draft agreement. It now appeared that South Vietnam had two choices:

- First, to sign the agreement and thereby receive continuing US support but with the full knowledge that the war would not end and guerrilla conflict would continue.

- The second alternative was not to sign the agreement and thereby to lose US support.

President Thieu stated that given the realities of the situation, what he was being asked to sign was not a treaty for peace but a treaty for continued US support. There would be no peace, but North Vietnam would not be able to take over South Vietnam, even with the agreement. However, Hanoi would have the capability to wage war for a long time. Under the provisions of the treaty, Hanoi would never take an action that would provoke a US response. Nevertheless, the agreement would not provide a lasting cease-fire. If Hanoi were to abide by the prohibitions against infiltration, it would be tantamount to suicide for Hanoi.

Again, the power of the American antiwar movement over South Vietnam via the Nixon administration was openly acknowledged. It had put Thieu and the Nationalists under duress, in some limbo between independence and subjugation for the foreseeable future.

Thieu then met with his top advisors and associates. They agreed to accept the Council for National Reconciliation and Concord but still held out for more on the issue of North Vietnamese troop withdrawal. It was a sad, somber meeting, Bunker learned.[83]

After Christmas, Hanoi accepted a new round of discussions with Kissinger. Nixon stopped the bombing.

In response to a query from Washington, Bunker resisted the suggestion that economic pressure be brought to bear on Thieu. Taking such measures was premature, he counseled. Only when Thieu understood that Washington would definitely go ahead with signing the peace agreement would he decide to follow his American allies, advised Bunker.[84]

But to help bring Thieu along with the least bitterness and friction, Bunker now suggested adding to a letter that President Nixon wanted to send Thieu on January 5, 1973, a final sentence promising continued assistance in the postsettlement period and that the United States would respond "with full force" should the terms of settlement ever be violated by Hanoi. Washington agreed with Bunker's recommendation, and the letter was revised to include that commitment.[85]

Bunker then met with Thieu on January 6.[86] Thieu was now relaxed and smiling but still fearful that Hanoi's troops would renew the war if the PRG won only a minority position in the government in any postsettlement elections. Using his emergency powers (which were about to expire), Thieu took steps that he felt would minimize the ability of the PRG to manipulate and seduce so-called third force elements within South Vietnam's political elite in any such postsettlement election.

On January 7, Thieu replied to Nixon, confirming his reliance on American support in the event Hanoi would ever violate the peace agreement:[87]

> I value very highly your assurance of continued assistance in the post-settlement period and that you will respond with full force should the settlement be violated by North Viet Nam. We consider that we should not take the risks of a new aggression if we sign this agreement. Consequently, we believe that to avoid the occurrence of a new aggression by the Communists the agreement should at least create minimum conditions for the peaceful exercise of the political solution in South Viet Nam, that is the question of the North Vietnamese troops should be resolved satisfactorily.

The principal negotiators of this curious "peace" agreement met in Paris two days later. The agreement was actually finalized five days thereafter. The final terms were an improvement over the October 17 draft and even over what had seemed possible in mid-December. Nixon's decision to bomb Hanoi and Haiphong had paid off in the negotiations. Now the Council of

National Reconciliation and Concord was not composed of three elements. It was not even called an "administrative structure" in Vietnamese. The demilitarized zone as originally provided for in the 1954 Geneva Accords and supporting documents had been reaffirmed, creating two independent zones protected from one another by a demilitarized strip of land. The peace agreement made no mention of only "three" Indochinese countries. Infiltration of soldiers and supplies into South Vietnam was prohibited.

Thieu did not obtain withdrawal of any North Vietnamese forces from his country, but he was allowed by the agreement to receive extensive military aid from the United States.

Thieu now asked the South Vietnamese National Defense College to study the implications of the agreement. Haig flew out again from Washington to ask for Thieu's acceptance of the agreement. He brought with him another letter from Nixon, which was something of an ultimatum. The American president told his South Vietnamese counterpart that he, Nixon, would sign the peace agreement as it stood. Nixon wrote that he was convinced that the alternative course of action would lead to a congressional cutting off of funds to support Saigon.[88]

Nixon wrote Thieu,

> *I have therefore irrevocably decided to proceed to initial the Agreement on January 23, 1973 and to sign it on January 27, 1973 in Paris. I will do so, if necessary, alone. In that case I shall have to explain publicly that your Government obstructs peace. The result will be an inevitable and immediate termination of US economic and military assistance which cannot be forestalled by a change of personnel in your government. I hope, however, that after all our two countries have shared and suffered together in conflict, we will stay together to preserve peace and reap its benefits.*

Nixon had a historian's sense of destiny about his situation in trying to end the war. He was being carried forward by events. An illusion of peace was all that he could get. He told Kissinger, "Sometimes the war situation becomes—it's almost like mobilization which leads to war. Once it turns on—World War I even though they tried to stop it, it was too late. As so it is in this case—the mobilization leading to peace may be just too great for them to resist."

Kissinger, a professional historian, replied, "Mr. President, the fact is that we are now doomed to settle."[89]

British prime minister Harold Macmillan was once asked what was most likely to blow a government off its course. His reply was telling: "Events, my Dear Boy, events."[90]

Once again, General Haig was sent for personal diplomacy and suasion with President Thieu.[91] Haig reported,

> *I have just finished one hour meeting with Thieu. He was emotional and extremely despondent. He explained that he felt this was the most serious period he had faced in his six years as President and handed me a sealed reply to the President's letter of January 14. He noted that I would probably open it but when I asked him if I could do so he suggested that I wait until later. He then went through his lengthy exposition to the effect that the agreement would be viewed by the people of South Vietnam as a defeat but constantly repeated the theme that nevertheless he understood he had to maintain US support. Upon reading the letter after the meeting, it is quite evident that Thieu was trying to soften in conversation what was brittle and uncompromising in writing. I am convinced, based on our intelligence readouts of his meetings earlier today, that Thieu believes that he can afford one more stalling round in an effort to either get further improvements in the agreement or as a minimum to buy more time. We know from his discussion with the NSC [National Security Council] today that this was his strategy. We also know that he told the NSC that if the US remains firm he will collapse.*

Thieu had once joked with Kissinger that as a general rule, Vietnamese will haggle over pennies in every purchase. They have no idea of a fixed take it or leave it price. Further, it could be well said by insiders who know the Vietnamese that their unwillingness to trust the good faith and constancy of others encourages them to seek control in relationships. Kissinger had denied Thieu any control over the future of his country and his cause, so, naturally for a Vietnamese person, Thieu was inclined to bargain hard for every even very tiny advantage he could get from someone whom he felt did not deserve his trust.

Many Vietnamese, like Thieu, believe that human actions are forced by circumstances, a kind of natural law that moves the will in predictable directions. The calculation derives from yin/yang cosmology, the moving forces of which could be interpreted, for instance, by analysis of *I Ching* hexagrams. Thus, it is most often considered advantageous by Vietnamese to wait until the last minute to see how far the other person will be guided or pressured into giving way.

A successful countervailing strategy in bargaining is studied indifference—a sort of Buddhist detachment—which takes one out of the pressure cooker of circumstances and so discourages others from playing brinkmanship at the last minute of dealmaking. For an American, Bunker's character was rather like this.

Bunker did not try to control Thieu in their relationship. He was too mature for that—and comfortable with himself. He approached Thieu with facts first and foremost, giving his considered opinion, not colored by emotions about the realities. He offered choices to Thieu but choices informed by the relevant facts as he saw them. Thieu responded well, trusting Bunker and always in the end working out a position more or less aligned with Bunker's preferred approach.

On learning of Thieu's continued contumacy, Kissinger offered Nixon this interpretation of the Vietnamese president's motivations: "No, I think the problem is that none of these military guys there can really face the problem of any free political process." At another time, Kissinger had said about Thieu to President Nixon, "Well, I think the basic problem, Mr. President, is that this group that is now governing Vietnam cannot imagine peace time conditions. He is a great leader when he is a sort of a dictator."[92]

Kissinger did not see his ally as having any cause except self-interest. Such a fundamental misunderstanding of Thieu was the logical consequence of Kissinger seeing Nationalist Vietnamese only through Sainteny's eyes.

Not surprisingly, during his private lunch with Kissinger on May 25, 1971, Sainteny had described South Vietnamese leaders contemptuously:

> *The extensive corruption in South Vietnam gives the non-corrupt North Vietnamese an advantage with the South Vietnamese people. The GVN is so tarnished that it would be better from the [US] standpoint to see it replaced. There are good people in South Vietnam and Paris; for example, "Big" Minh, who, while not brilliant, is popular.*[93]

Here again Bunker was different from Kissinger. Bunker had never been exposed to French colonial presumptions about the Vietnamese and their values. He took the Vietnamese as he found them on their own terms. He sensed French condescension toward "les Annamites" and was well aware of how the Vietnamese with whom he worked resented and mistrusted their former colonial masters. Bunker shared an American prejudice against colonialism, that it was not well intentioned and not so good for those under its rule. He saw himself and his country, idealistically perhaps but in a constructive way, as a friend of the Vietnamese Nationalists. His moral obligations to them, as Aristotle and Cicero had recommended, were like those of a fiduciary, using power in the best interest of others. Bunker's mind, therefore, was unsullied by the convictions of a Jean Sainteny.

Yet another letter came from Nixon, this one dated January 17, bluntly telling Thieu that his rejection of the agreement would destroy America's ability to assist him.[94] Nixon was prepared to send Vice President Spiro Agnew to Saigon to reassure Thieu publicly that, in the American view, Saigon was the only legitimate government of South Vietnam, that no foreign troops had a right to remain on South Vietnamese soil, and that the United States would react vigorously to any violations of the agreement. Thieu could then come to San Clemente in California and meet with Nixon personally to reaffirm these guarantees.

Thieu would not go down without a final effort. He asked for more changes in the text concerning Hanoi's forces in the South. Nixon then had passed on to Thieu comments from the very conservative Senators Barry Goldwater and John Stennis that South Vietnam's president had better sign the peace agreement along with the Americans.

But Thieu had met with his military commanders and other senior officials on January 17 to tell them he was prepared to sign the agreement as negotiated by the Americans and that they should prepare for a cease-fire.[95] Alexander Haig, now vice chief of staff of the army, was again sent to Saigon to meet with Thieu. On January 20, Thieu presented to Haig yet another letter to President Nixon reiterating the need to make more changes in line with South Vietnamese needs.[96] Bunker and Haig noted for Kissinger that

> both were in full agreement with following assessment. Thieu will unquestionably sign the agreement. We know he has so informed his entire bureaucracy and the word has now been disseminated down through division level that a ceasefire will take place on the morning of January 28. A careful reading of Thieu's letter clearly indicates Thieu's intention to do so while he at the same time makes a final effort to improve the agreement and protocols. It is important that we view Thieu's response in the context of Oriental pride and face. [However] the General [National] Assembly could be another problem because it contained political opponents. It is for this reason that Bunker and I believe that Thieu is going to make a fight right up until the last possible minute so that he can take the position with factual evidence to support it that he has done his absolute utmost to get the best possible deal for South Vietnam and its people.[97]

Nixon now asked for Thieu's answer by January 21 in order to inform congressional leaders of the peace terms. Nixon specified all the terms now included in the peace agreement, which had been negotiated since October to minimize the deleterious effect of letting Hanoi retain its forces inside South Vietnam. Nixon agreed to provide Thieu with a formal diplomatic note containing the assurances previously stated only in presidential correspondence.[98]

When Bunker handed over the last letter from President Nixon, President Thieu said calmly, "I have done my best and all that I could for my country."[99]

Thieu appeared resigned but not unfriendly as Bunker walked out of his office for the short drive back to the American embassy. Bunker immediately cabled the White House that Thieu had finally crossed the bridge of fear, doubt, and resentment and would sign the peace agreement as requested.

Then, quickly, Thieu delivered to Bunker a letter for President Nixon. It said, in part, "However, for the sake of unity between our two governments, and on the basis of your strong assurances for the continuation of aid and support to South Vietnam after the cease-fire, I would accept your schedule for the paraphrasing of the principal agreement on January 23.[100]

But even after that, Thieu held out for more changes in the Vietnamese text of the agreement and in a provision of an ancillary protocol regarding the right of South Vietnamese police to carry and use rifles.[101]

The next day, January 23, almost brought for Bunker a last-minute hitch in getting Thieu to finally agree to his government's signature on the peace agreement. Thieu's astrologer told him not to sign any agreement prior to the upcoming Tet Lunar New Year. But Thieu ignored his astrologer, kept his word to Nixon, and had South Vietnam sign Henry Kissinger's peace agreement.

And so did Henry Kissinger finally get to impose on the people of South Vietnam an indecent interval between 1) their having won genuine independence at great sacrifice and 2) their military subjugation under Communist tyranny.

As we watch the decades pass us by,
we see justice and destiny adroitly at cross-purposes;
Watching the tides of history ebb and flow,
everything we see brings pain to our hearts.

—Nguyen Du (1765–1820)

CHAPTER 8

IT ALL FALLS APART

THE CONQUEST OF SOUTH VIETNAM

There is a tide in the affairs of men,
which taken at the flood, leads on to fortune.
Omitted, all the voyage of their life is bound
in shallows and in miseries.

—William Shakespeare, *Julius Caesar*

For the Vietnamese Communist Party leadership, the 1973 Paris Peace Accords—negotiated for the South Vietnamese by Henry Kissinger and then imposed on their government by Richard Nixon—opened the door to victory. Hanoi's leaders described the Peace Accords as "a big victory for our people and a big defeat for the United States and its lackeys."[1]

Though the words of the agreement guaranteed the independence and freedom of South Vietnam, from Hanoi's perspective, such words were of no effect. In Vietnamese Communist morality, such as it is, circumstances, not ideals, control our decisions. For Vietnamese Communists the course of life ebbs and flows with the vagaries of power. Selfishly taking advantage of opportunity was always their main criterion for decision-making. To them, there was no truth, no honesty, no keeping of promises, only the advantages to be enjoyed from an unscrupulous opportunism. Communist cadres devoted much time to the task of *danh gia tinh hinh*, or evaluating circumstances.

Anything could be said or done to enhance one's power and so improve the odds of winning in the end. Lies, murder, deceit, betrayal, misrepresentation, incarceration, intimidation, false friendship, economic advantage, promises—everything that would or could change a situation in one's favor was right and good. The more clever and manipulative, cruel and unscrupulous a cadre could be, the more respected he or she became within the party. As Le Duan insisted, morality for Communists is whatever the party line requires at any given time.[2]

There was only one criterion for restraint and discipline on the part of a cadre: loyalty to the party and to higher authority. According to Le Duan, the "Party constitution has adequately and strictly defined all criteria and fundamental requirements for a party member." One could be a person outside the organization—but not a cadre—a cadre must live in a definite organization that "determines who will do what, what position and function he should hold in the apparatus of activity. It defines beforehand the direction and objective of man's actions. It directs man and obliges him to act one way instead of another."[3] He firmly insisted that "organization in its activity, brings forth in man definite characteristics and qualities." It trains man so that a "man's strength is his organization." The party is a monolithic bloc, a combat instrument forged out of many individuals.[4] The party must always "create a single, organic system which will enable it to utilize and mobilize all the material and spiritual potential of society."[5]

A cadre, therefore, had to be *nhat tri* (of one mind) with party decisions. Individualism, personal initiatives, lone-ranger-ism, innovations, and deviations were all forbidden, as they would erode the power of the party.

Le Duan, after 1958 the center of power and direction in Vietnam's Communist Party, once wrote that "concern for the common objective, the common interest, the common cause, must be manifest first of all in the full execution of his personal responsibility."[6] He insisted that all party cadres "place all their energies and talents at the service of the collective and society" because he worried that "even the slightest slackening of discipline suffices to create a fissure for the enemy to thrust his hands into."[7]

The Vietnamese Communist Party doctrine of opportunism centers on the concept of the *thoi co*, or opportune moment. Le Duan wrote the party's most important essay on this approach to life.

Le Duan instructed readers that the first step in planning action is to ask "How are the various social forces aligned? What are the enemy's strong and weak points? How is he maneuvering, and what are his aims? . . . One must be able to foresee, at least in a broad outline, the results of forthcoming actions and all possible trends of development of the objective situation."

Accordingly, from 1936 through 1939, the Vietnamese Communists could use political trends created by the left-leaning Popular Front government in Paris to expand their activities and membership in Vietnam. And in 1945, when the Chinese defeated Japan's Kwantung Army, that change of circumstance created a political vacuum in Vietnam, then under Japanese control, into which the Communists could thrust themselves by staging a coup in Hanoi, just as Lenin had done in the October Revolution in St. Petersburg.[8] Then the Communists were able to "smash the enemy's key structures in the capital and other cities and liquidate his entire administration, divide and isolate the enemy, even though armed units prestige far outstripped their numbers."

Le Duan advised that a *thoi co* could arise "either [from] revolutionary forces or conditions abroad." Boldness to act was then necessary. Once the *thoi co* was unfolding, actions would precipitate new possibilities, and trends would reveal themselves.[9] He added, "Nothing succeeds like success and each success in a given field stimulates the struggle in other fields."

So the permission given to Hanoi by Kissinger's diplomacy to leave its forces in South Vietnam created the probability that a *thoi co* would happen, one that would permit the Vietnamese Communists to conquer

South Vietnam. That *thoi co* would come about when the Americans refused to come to the battlefield assistance of Saigon's army.

After signing the Paris Peace Accords, Hanoi's leaders turned to the task of setting in motion events and developments that would lead up to the happening of that favorable—for them—*thoi co*. Le Duan was the leader of the Vietnamese Communists and shaped programs and policies according to his vision of how to seize total power.[10]

Hanoi then had about two hundred thousand North Vietnamese soldiers inside South Vietnam supplemented by a negligible number of Viet Cong loyalists. Le Duan began augmenting that military strength day by day in order to bring about a *thoi co* permitting the conquest of South Vietnam.

To those initiated into the Vietnamese Communist cult, the Paris Peace Accords were cleverly designed to facilitate the achievement of a *thoi co* favorable to Hanoi's leadership after the Americans withdrew their support from the Vietnamese Nationalists. The agreement contained no commitment by Hanoi's government to withdraw any of its forces from South Vietnam. The agreement further had created no objective obstacle to Hanoi sending supplies and more troops into South Vietnam. The Ho Chi Minh Trail running from North Vietnam through Laos into South Vietnam was open twenty-four/seven to Hanoi's troops. The Paris Agreement only bound Hanoi's proxy, the nominal Provisional Revolutionary Government (PRG), from accepting military support from outside South Vietnam.[11]

This provision was of no effect because the PRG had no authority and no control over military units. It could mount only a stage performance of a fiction, something imaginary and unreal, with the script it was to follow written by the Communist Party in Hanoi. The only authority over Communist military forces inside South Vietnam with any decision-making power was the politburo of the Vietnamese Communist Party, controlled by Le Duan and his allies and the Central Military Commission subordinate to that political leadership.

If Hanoi had, as President Nguyen Van Thieu had demanded, withdrawn its combat forces from South Vietnam in January 1973 when the

Paris Peace Accords were signed, the balance of forces between the Communists and Nationalists would have been this:[12]

- In Military Region 1 (the five northernmost provinces): 145,000 to 170,000 GVN ground combat troops; three thousand Viet Cong troops.

- In Military Region 2 (twelve provinces in the central mountains and along the central coast): 145,000 GVN ground combat troops; six thousand Viet Cong troops.

- In Military Region 3 (ten provinces around Saigon): 155,000 to 175,000 GVN ground combat troops; five thousand Viet Cong troops.

- In Military Region 4 (sixteen provinces in the Mekong River Delta): 246,000 to 257,000 GVN ground combat troops; eleven thousand Viet Cong troops.

- In addition, the Saigon government had an air force and nearly a million armed village self-defense volunteers.

Under that balance of power, the Nationalist government in Saigon would have never fallen to the Communists. Only the presence of Hanoi's regular divisions, regiments, artillery and armor units, engineers, and transportation/logistics commands inside South Vietnam made the 1975 Communist conquest of South Vietnam possible.

As it was, in January 1973, under the Paris Peace Accords, Hanoi had in South Vietnam 16 division commands, the GVN only 13; the Communists had 94 regimental commands, the GVN 48; the Communists had 424 maneuver battalions, the GVN 264.[13] The North Vietnamese units in the South could bring some 219,000 troops to battle. On its side, the GVN could deploy 192,000 to 229,000 similarly capable main force units in the defense of its territory. Additional GVN military units were only lightly armed regional and local forces and volunteer village self-defenders.

Hanoi's units could be thought of as a blowtorch and the Nationalist defense forces more as plywood covering the roof and sides of a house—all-encompassing but thin.

PREPARING FOR THE *THOI CO*

After the Paris Peace Accords were signed, preparing for the coming assault on the Nationalists became a major undertaking for Hanoi.

Thanks to Henry Kissinger's generosity in the secret Paris negotiations, in 1973, Hanoi had inside South Vietnam more than enough combat troops to prepare the battlefield for the expected *thoi co*. South Vietnamese forces were pushed back, and supply lines for Communist forces were opened up—all the better for Hanoi to seize the tactical advantage when the *thoi co* arrived.

Hanoi's allies sent 2.8 million metric tons of commodities and supplies to its forces in 1973, 50 percent more than in 1972, and 3.5 million metric tons more in 1974. Its allies also gave Hanoi $1.7 billion in 1974.[14]

A document prepared by Hanoi's Ministry of Defense reported that in 1973, Hanoi sent 75,600 new soldiers into South Vietnam. In 1974, 70,798 more soldiers were sent south. And in the crucial year of 1975, when its final offensive against South Vietnamese Nationalist forces was launched, Hanoi sent an additional 117,293 soldiers south to join the fight.[15]

Hanoi organized mobile commands to better hammer South Vietnamese defensive strongpoints.

During 1973, Hanoi launched four division attacks to capture strategic operational centers. They took the coastal port of Cua Viet and failed to capture the port of Sa Huynh and a base in the Central Highlands but did capture Tong Le Chan near the Cambodian border northwest of Saigon.[16]

Toward the end of 1973, the Communists began a comprehensive effort to "nibble away" at GVN defensive lines surrounding populated areas. One by one, they massed and overwhelmed isolated outposts.[17] President Thieu's strategic option was "no retreat; no surrender of any post; hold everything." He would not authorize abandonment of any GVN territory to defend the maximum amount of territory at all costs.

Hanoi then sent tanks, rockets, long-range artillery, and antiaircraft guns to the front. Starting in 1973, with thirty thousand troops, Hanoi's engineers built a new road south inside South Vietnam. It was eight meters wide so that trucks could drive it in both directions. A five-thousand-kilometer-long oil pipeline was built to end up at Loc Ninh, just eighty miles northeast of Saigon, to provide fuel for Hanoi's trucks and tanks threatening South Vietnam's capital city.[18]

Hanoi increased its shipment of supplies into South Vietnam by 64 percent in 1974 over 1973. Communist forces stockpiled sixty-six thousand tons of ammunition inside South Vietnam, enough for a full year of intense combat. The ports of Dong Ha and Cua Viet just inside South Vietnam behind the cease-fire line of 1973 were fully used to bring supplies into the northernmost province of South Vietnam. An average of ten Chinese ships a day delivered supplies to North Vietnamese forces at Cua Viet.[19]

By 1974, Hanoi had sent into South Vietnam six hundred tanks, five hundred heavy cannons, two hundred antiaircraft weapons, and many SA-7 rockets. Every week, 1,500 trucks moved up and down the Ho Chi Minh Trail and the new roads bringing supplies to NVA units in South Vietnam.[20]

None of this could have happened if Hanoi had withdrawn its army from South Vietnam just as President Nguyen Van Thieu had demanded as a condition for peace but as Henry Kissinger had refused to pursue diligently with Vietnamese Communist negotiators.

During 1973, Hanoi added five divisions to its strategic reserve. The 316th Division was moved from Laos back to North Vietnam; a new division, the 341st, was raised, and the 338th division was converted from a training division to a combat unit.[21] By early 1975, Hanoi had seven divisions in its strategic reserve that could be sent south to overwhelm South Vietnamese forces stationed in a thin line of defense.

Hanoi's dramatic escalation of its military capability in 1973 and 1974 was made possible by Soviet Russia and Communist China. North Vietnam did not produce rifles, machine guns, B-40 rocket propelled grenades, tanks, heavy artillery, trucks, and SA-7 rockets. Without the provision of such armaments, Hanoi could never have subdued the South Vietnamese Nationalists. However, since 1971, both Soviet and Chinese Communist leaders could quite rationally presume that there would be no serious retaliation against them from the United States for their arming their Vietnamese Communist ally. Kissinger had been explicit in his communications with the Soviets and in his meeting with Chinese leader Zhou Enlai in setting out such a specific expectation of a negligible, passive reaction from the United States should Hanoi resume its war against South Vietnam.

It is very important to notice that the PRG and NLF (Viet Cong)—the South Vietnamese followers of Hanoi—played no significant role in the military buildup.

In October 1973, the 21st Plenum of the Central Committee of the Vietnamese Communist Party adopted a resolution preparing for the desired *thoi co*, which would permit the conquest of South Vietnam. The resolution affirmed that "the revolutionary road for the South is the road of revolutionary violence. Whatever the situation, we must firmly seize the opportune moment, maintain a course of strategic offensive, and give active guidance to advance the revolution in the South."[22]

So much for a peaceful ending to the Vietnam War. So much for international law.

On the sixteenth of that same month, October 1973, the Nobel Peace Prize Committee in Oslo, Norway, awarded the 1973 Nobel Peace Prize jointly to Henry Kissinger and Le Duc Tho. Neither man came to Oslo on December 10 to attend the award ceremony and personally accept the award. Henry Kissinger apologized that his new position as secretary of state for the United States required his presence in Washington. He did, however, much later make this pretentious comment about receiving the prize: "There is no other comparable honor. A statesman's final test, after all, is whether he has made a contribution to the well-being of mankind."[23]

Le Duc Tho refused to accept the prize. In his letter to the Nobel Peace Prize Committee, Tho wrote, "Peace has not yet really been established in South Vietnam." He added, "In these circumstances, it is impossible for me to accept" the prize, stating that he would be able to "consider acceptance only when the Paris accord is respected, the arms are silenced and real peace is established in South Vietnam."[24]

For many Vietnamese, Nationalist and Communist, Tho's decision to reject acceptance of a world-famous prize for making peace happen was a very dark portent of more fighting to come in South Vietnam. In his refusal, however, Tho at least offered some honesty instead of complete deceit. He needed to signal to his forces in South Vietnam and the citizens of North Vietnam the truth that the war was not over, that they still needed to gird themselves for more fighting in the South.

Ironically, many years earlier, Henry Kissinger had described in his PhD dissertation the very situation Tho was masterminding from his side: "Whenever peace—conceived as the avoidance of war—has been the primary objective of a power or a group of powers, the international system has been at the mercy of the most ruthless member of the international community."[25] Indeed, in late 1973, South Vietnam and the United States were at the mercy of very ruthless men in Hanoi thanks to Kissinger's 1971 concession to their cruel and unrelenting ambition, which had no place for either law or morals. Yet again must we realize that the ancient truth of realpolitik is with us still: the strong do what they can; the weak suffer what they must.

On March 31, 1974, Hanoi's politburo decided to open the "final strategic battle." That month, the Central Military Commission adopted an implementing resolution, ordering Hanoi's armed forces to "advance" toward final victory.[26] The commission affirmed that the revolution in the South must hold firmly to the concept of an offensive strategy.

Then the general staff coordinating the North Vietnamese military began planning for a general strategy across all of South Vietnam and for independent combat campaigns in each separate territorial command sector. "They spelled out preparation and maintenance plans, and . . . directed all battlefields to step up activities, carry out offensives and uprisings, preserve and develop the strategic initiative, and change the situation on all fronts, thereby creating conditions for widespread, large-scale offensives in 1975."[27]

In October 1974, Hanoi's military general staff presented to the party's politburo and Central Military Committee a strategic plan to violate the Paris Peace Accords with large-scale aggression against the Nationalist government of South Vietnam designed to conquer that country.[28] For Hanoi's leaders, there was only one serious open question: Would the Americans reengage with troops or airpower? The discussion turned on an evaluation of the situation using Le Duan's formula for strategic thinking on the flow of power and events—*danh gia tinh hinh*, or evaluating circumstances. Le Duan himself put the conclusion in a resolution: "It will be hard for the US to jump back in. No matter how they intervene, they cannot rescue the Saigon Administration from its disastrous collapse."[29]

Also as a result of their analysis of the balance of forces in South Vietnam, the Communist leadership agreed that the principal battlefield for the coming campaign of conquest would be in the mountainous Central Highlands of South Vietnam, where the GVN had stationed only two divisions in isolated bases difficult to reinforce and resupply. Using the basic tactic of guerilla warfare, Hanoi's leaders planned to strike where their chosen enemy was weakest.

Vietnam War critic Frances FitzGerald was visiting Hanoi as the Communist leaders were preparing to renew their war against South Vietnam. She met the editor of the Community Party newspaper, who said that some in North Vietnam's Politburo believed that they had lived up to their "decent interval" deal with Henry Kissinger and were now free to do as they pleased with South Vietnam. The editor explained that Kissinger had agreed to a two-year interval between the withdrawal of U.S. forces and a Communist victory in South Vietnam, adding: "The two years are over."[30]

COLLAPSE OF AMERICAN MILITARY SUPPORT FOR SOUTH VIETNAM

While Hanoi, with help from the Soviet Union and the People's Republic of China, was gaining battlefield prowess every day, Saigon was getting weaker and weaker. As politburo member and Vice Chief of Staff Van Tien Dung would later write, "Thieu had to fight a 'poor man's war.'"[31]

US aid fell from $1.614 billion in fiscal year 1972/1973 and $1.926 billion in fiscal year 1973/1974 to only $700 million in fiscal year 1974/1975 out of $1.6 billion requested by the Ford administration.[32] Colonel William Le Gro, a military attaché in the US embassy in Saigon, would later write:

> In Washington Congress reduced military assistance to South Vietnam to below operating levels, a decision that seriously undermined South Vietnamese combat power and will to continue the struggle. While in Hanoi, taking fresh heart from the political fall of Richard Nixon [in the Watergate scandal] and waning Congressional support for the war, Communist leaders decided that 1975 would be the year of final victory.[33]

The United States had planned to support the defense of South Vietnam after the Paris Peace Accords were signed only at a level commensurate with a cease-fire remaining in effect. In other words, the United States did not plan to provide South Vietnam with funds, munitions, and equipment to withstand a major violation of the cease-fire by Hanoi. Only the letters from President Nixon to President Thieu in the fall of 1972, written as an inducement for Thieu to sign the proposed peace accords, foresaw a major future breach of the accords by Hanoi. Should that happen, Nixon had, in effect, promised his counterpart that the United States would dispatch B-52 bombers to smash North Vietnamese divisions on the move or on the attack.

In the past, Hanoi had respected neither the 1954 armistice agreement with the French not to use North Vietnam as a base for attacks on South Vietnam nor the 1962 agreement to withdraw from Laos. Making promises and keeping them were always only temporary tactical accommodations for the Communists, used whenever necessary to advance closer to final victory.

In December 1973, Kissinger met with Le Duc Tho in Paris. Kissinger postured that Thieu and his government were nearly invincible so that Hanoi's best alternative was to compromise with Thieu in a political settlement. Kissinger pledged that he would encourage Thieu to reach a suitable political accommodation. Le Duc Tho was inflexible.

In May of 1974, Kissinger again met with Tho. He also asked the Soviet Union to reduce its aid to Hanoi.

But then the US Department of Defense accountants charged to the 1975 budget year some $300 million in equipment that should have been charged to fiscal year 1974. The authorized support for the South Vietnamese military in 1975 was therefore only $400 million. Inflation in fuel costs and other items reduced the real value of those dollars even more.

By 1975, the South Vietnamese air force had lost 281 aircraft and had received eight little spotter planes in replacement. Flying squadrons had been reduced from 66 to 56, and 224 aircraft were placed in storage, including all C-7 cargo aircraft and 34 C-47 and C-119 gunships vital for the defense of fixed defensive positions under attack. The navy had lost 58 ships, and none had been replaced.

In 1975, no Army of the Republic of Vietnam (ARVN) infantry battalion had more than four hundred men present for duty. Mobile ranger battalions had only three hundred. Military hospitals were overcrowded and short on medicines, especially antibiotics and plasma needed to treat combat wounds. Bandages and surgical dressings were washed and reused. Ambulance units were so short on fuel that they had to use a 2.5-ton truck to tow four ambulances in a row away from the battlefields. Medivac helicopters were in short supply as well. One wounded soldier often had to wait for others in his unit to be hit as well before an evacuation by ambulance could be justified.

Soldiers were limited in the bullets allocated, getting two hundred rounds instead of four hundred. Mortars and artillery pieces were similarly on small rations of munitions. The monthly allocation of ammo usually ran out by the twenty-fifth day of the month.[34] The GVN was spending only about a dollar per day per soldier, not enough to hold off an onslaught.

By summer 1974, the ARVN had 35 percent of its tanks and 50 percent of its armored personnel carriers, and aircraft idled for lack of spare parts; because of a fuel shortage, only 55 percent of vehicles were in operation.

Battle-damaged M48 tanks and armored personnel carriers had to be sent to the United States for repair and rebuilding, taking them out of combat for months at a time.

By 1975, helilifts were down by 70 percent, and regular airlifts were down by 50 percent.[35] Only four to eight C-130 aircraft out of thirty-two were serviceable daily, too few to bring necessary reinforcements and supplies to ARVN units under attack. The airborne and marine mobile reserve units could not be quickly moved around the country to counter specific NVA assaults.

South Vietnamese airplanes were very vulnerable to Soviet SA-7 missiles. They could not perform at their best in close support of ground troops under attack.

During its 1973 war, Israel had received $2.2 billion in US aid.[36]

THE FIRST STRIKE: PHUOC LONG

In December 1974, Hanoi launched its first blow in the remote provincial capital of Phuoc Long, up near the Cambodian border. Diversionary attacks were made in the more important provinces of Tay Ninh and Binh Tuy, forcing the South Vietnamese local commander to concentrate troops in those tactical zones. Phuoc Long was defended by only four battalions of regional forces, posted in isolated garrisons around the town. Hanoi attacked with two divisions, a tank battalion, two regiments—one artillery and one antiaircraft and several local-force sapper and infantry units. President Thieu refused to transfer the airborne division protecting Hue in Military Region 1 to defend Phuoc Long. The ARVN regional units defending the small, very isolated city fought tenaciously but could not hold out against overwhelming numbers. NVA artillery fire was devastating, with nearly three thousand rounds per day crashing in on ARVN positions. On January 6, the remaining South Vietnamese fled the town.

One ARVN survivor of the battle said, "The enemy troops were not so good and so courageous as we might have thought. There were simply too many of them. Enemy tanks had something new and strange. Our M-72 rockets were unable to knock them out. We hit them; they stopped for a while then moved on. Our air support was not very effective; the planes flew too high. If only we could have had B-52s!"[37]

As the battle for Phuoc Long played out, the politburo met from December 18, 1974, to January 8, 1975.[38]

Le Duan concluded on January 8: "Now the Americans have withdrawn, we have our troops in the South, and the spirit of the masses is rising. This is what marks an opportune moment (*thoi co*). We must seize it firmly and step up the struggle on all three fronts: military, political, and diplomatic . . . We must strike the strategic blow in 1975 . . . The year will open with attacks on the Tay Nguyen."[39] The politburo adopted a resolution affirming that "never have we had military and political conditions so perfect or a strategic advantage so great as we have now."[40]

In Saigon, ARVN chief of staff Cao Van Vien and Prime Minister Khiem, for their part, had seen the future of South Vietnam, as had Le Duan: the Nationalists were in grave peril. So in December 1974, at a meeting of South Vietnam's National Security Council, they proposed to President Thieu a concentration of South Vietnamese divisions for the defense in depth of a smaller territory, abandoning much of Military Regions 1 and 2. Such a retreat would conserve ammunition and other supplies for a last stand. Thieu listened but then in January 1975 refused.[41]

On January 13, 1975, the US State Department filed an official protest with the International Commission of Control and Supervision, given responsibility for policing and maintaining the cease-fire agreed to in the Paris Peace Accords.[42] Kissinger's State Department wrote,

> *The United States deplores the Democratic Republic of Vietnam's turning from the path of negotiations to that of war, not only because it is a grave violation of a solemn international agreement, but also because of the cruel price it is imposing on the people of South Vietnam. The Democratic Republic of Vietnam must accept the*

full consequences of its actions. We call upon the Democratic Republic of Vietnam to halt its military offensive and join the Republic of Vietnam in re-establishing stability and seeking a political solution.

Who were these American diplomats kidding? Maybe only themselves, or maybe they were just pretending to care.

The United States did not send B-52s to stop Hanoi's military offensive. It just asked politely for Hanoi to relent. President Gerald Ford made no mention of Vietnam in his January 15 State of the Union address to Congress. On January 21, he said in a press conference that he could foresee no circumstances in which the United States might actively reenter the Vietnam War.[43] Sic transit gloria mundi.

In February, a congressional delegation came to Saigon to assess the situation.[44]

In February 1975, the Nationalists had some one million men in their armed forces, but most were in territorial defensive units. Hanoi now had 356,000 soldiers inside South Vietnam, mostly in mobile divisions with armor and artillery support. Importantly, however, the South Vietnamese were dispersed over a wide expanse of territory in static defensive positions protecting 95 percent of the population. The Saigon government did not have sufficient military assets to defend every important area in depth. In addition, the South Vietnamese lacked mobile reserve units to throw quickly against any single localized Communist offensive.

THE SECOND STRIKE: BAN ME THUOT

In December 1974, General Pham Van Phu was appointed to command Military Region 2, including both the mountainous Central Highlands and a narrow strip of coastal lowlands. General Phu convinced himself that Hanoi's attack would come in the northern part of the Central Highlands, where the Ho Chi Minh Trail in Laos afforded the Communists easy access to supplies and reinforcement. He, therefore, did not deploy his best units to the southern part of his military region.

That was where Hanoi decided to strike—where the GVN was weakest. In contrast to Hanoi's tactic in its 1972 invasion, attacks were not made on the major cities of Pleiku and Kontum, which Phu had defended heavily. General Phu had only two regiments in the southern half of the Central Highlands and no reserve forces to send to their aid once they were attacked. He also had no reserve forces to deploy to reopen the major highways should the NVA block them with troop deployments, shutting down passage.[45]

The capture of Ban Me Thuot, a small city in the southern part of Military Region 2, would smash GVN defensive deployments in the entire Central Highlands.[46] So three NVA divisions—the 320th, 10th, and 968th—were moved south to assault Ban Me Thuot from three directions. The 316th Division was also moved into the South from North Vietnam to support attacks in the southern part of the Central Highlands.[47]

The 316th Division could easily move south over very passable roads and bridges in five hundred trucks. This logistics capacity was new for Hanoi, a consequence of the very favorable terms given the Vietnamese Communists in the Paris Peace Accords.[48]

In the coming battle for Ban Me Thuot, Hanoi would have a 5.5 to 1 advantage over the South Vietnamese in infantry on the ground, a 1.2 to 1 advantage in tanks and armored vehicles, and a 2.1 to 1 advantage in heavy artillery firepower.[49] Only one South Vietnamese regiment with some supporting local forces was in place to hold off and defeat three NVA divisions.

General Van Tien Dung ordered some attacks to the north around Kontum and Pleiku as diversions to keep General Phu focused on his defense obligations far from Ban Me Thuot. General Dung also had his forces cut in two the strategic highway that ran from Pleiku up in the mountains down to the coast, trapping some of General Phu's best soldiers in their tactical area of responsibility around Pleiku.

By March 9, General Dung's three divisions had surrounded Ban Me Thuot and cut the north-south road over which any reinforcements sent from Pleiku would have to come. At two in the morning on March 10,

NVA sappers moved onto the Ban Me Thuot airfield, and tanks entered the town.[50] Defense of the town collapsed the next day.

From the March 10 attack on Ban Me Thuot, it would be only twenty days to the March 30 fall of the great city of Danang on the coast, which would precipitate the final collapse of Nationalist South Vietnam.

After the loss of Ban Me Thuot, Thieu ordered a counterattack, so General Phu sent a regiment in by helicopter, but it could not hold its ground.

THIEU'S FATALISTIC BUT STILL FATAL DECISION

On March 12, the headquarters of Military Region 1, the northernmost provinces of South Vietnam, received orders to return the airborne division to Saigon. The Communists were pressing hard on Tay Ninh northeast of Saigon, so Thieu needed reinforcements to counterattack there. The next morning, President Thieu informed his top associates that South Vietnam could no longer defend all its territory. Strategic withdrawals had to be made to better defend the most important parts of the country.

On March 13, South Vietnam's President Nguyen Van Thieu called General Ngo Quang Truong, his commander of Military Region 1, down to Saigon for a private meeting in the presidential office. Years later, I met with General Truong in his house in the Virginia suburbs of Washington, DC. We spoke in Vietnamese.[51]

He told me,

> We were in his presidential office, just Thieu and myself. He walked over to a big map of South Vietnam hung on one wall. Saying "This will be the new boundary of South Vietnam," he passed his hand from Binh Long province on the Cambodian border diagonally up to the right ending at Phan Rang on the coast.
>
> He said, "Chu [younger uncle], bring the main force divisions from I Corps south to defend the new border."

I asked, "Anh em nghia quan, nhan dan tu ve, thi sau?" [What about the village defense forces?]

Thieu replied, "Ke" [Ignore them].

Hearing this, I was stunned. He had given me an order I could not obey. I knew I was a ruong cot [pillar holding up a roof] of the country. My duty was to be trung hieu [loyal to those below and obedient to those above]. Now if I were trung to the people of I Corps, I would not be hieu to my president. But if I were hieu to my president, I could not be trung to the people. I had no way to go. I was broken as a leader and a commander. I returned to my headquarters in Danang with no enthusiasm left.

Later in 1982, General Truong would write: "I was bitter and angry because the order was so sudden, beyond anything I ever anticipated or desired. . . . although the situation in Hue, Quang Ngai, and Danang was rather serious because of the enemy's continuous attacks, I had sufficient strength to resist and planned to send the Airborne and Marine divisions to those areas to regain a position of superiority. I meticulously explained my ideas and my plans to the President and the Prime Minister but these ideas and plans were rejected."[52]

The next day, on March 14, President Thieu and his top subordinates flew to Cam Ranh Bay on the central coast to meet with General Pham Van Phu, the commander of Military Region 2. Thieu instructed Phu just as he had ordered General Truong: withdraw the heavy combat forces (the 23rd Division, the rangers, and the armor brigade) out of the highlands down to the coast and leave everyone else to their fate.

This decision by President Thieu to abandon Military Regions 1 and 2 to Hanoi's divisions precipitated the very rapid collapse of South Vietnam. On April 30, 1975, North Vietnamese forces would enter Saigon, leading to the unconditional surrender of the Nationalist government.

On a deeper, more emotional level, Thieu's decision resonated very well with his 1972 prediction to Henry Kissinger that imposing a "decent interval" on South Vietnam would lead to the suicides of South Vietnam and Nguyen Van Thieu.

(Forty-six years later, in Afghanistan, similar feckless American decision-making and diplomacy would precipitate the sudden collapse of the secular government in Kabul and abandon the Afghan allies of the United States to a dictatorship of the Taliban.)

The shortcoming in Thieu's thinking was to put out of his mind the social-psychological reality of South Vietnamese (ARVN) divisions. They were not mobile forces to be moved here and there from one battlefield to another as American divisions had been in World War II. Only the marine division, the airborne division, and the ranger battalions had incorporated into their approach the culture of mobile warfare. The other South Vietnamese divisions were at heart really only territorial forces—to be sure, much better armed than provincial, district, and village troops but just like them emotionally tied to a local social structure.

For instance, the First ARVN Division, the best division of the Vietnamese Nationalists, was based in Hue. Nearly all its soldiers and officers came from Hue. Their families lived there. When they fought the invading North Vietnamese, they were defending their homes and their families. Were they to leave their homes and families to go fight at Thieu's order far to the south, they would have less reason to endure combat. Moreover, they would abandon their families to the Communists for revenge and oppression, something not permitted by their ancient ethical code of *trung hieu*.

Wives, children, and family members most often lived in and around military encampments. To move the soldiers would have made them abandon their families.[53]

In addition, Thieu's order violated the moral norms of the defensive war against the Communist Party. The war had been fought to protect good Vietnamese values from abuse at the hands of ethical primitives, exploiting rent seekers, and murderers. Just as General Truong understood, not to defend the common people would be to turn against the moral principles justifying war and sacrifice and so strip the Saigon government of legitimacy.

To violate the norms of *trung hieu* would cause the government and its leaders to lose their *duc* and so their *uy tin*.

After Thieu's orders to withdraw the regular divisions from Military Regions 1 and 2 were put into effect, morale collapsed all across South Vietnam. Why fight on, and for what? The common cause flipped from stalwart defense to "let the last ones to leave put out the lights."

One general later said, "What good did it do to resist when the defeat was inevitable? To prolong the war by several months, or several weeks, could only cause Vietnamese blood to be shed in vain, be it Communist or Nationalist blood."[54]

Responding to his president in their March 14 meeting in Cam Ranh, General Phu proposed using an old, poorly maintained alternate route for the evacuation of ARVN forces down to the coast. The main highway down to the coast was blocked by North Vietnamese regulars. Thieu approved. General Phu returned to Pleiku and did his duty. He gave orders to his subordinates to start the retreat to the coast using the old road. Then he flew out of Pleiku. In early May, two days after the final collapse of South Vietnam, General Phu, humiliated and abandoned, took his own life.[55]

The ARVN units in Pleiku, accompanied by panicky families and civilians, scrambled to move along the designated escape route. General Van Tien Dung had no trouble sending his mobile forces over the hills to cut off the fleeing mob. Trapped on the road, the ARVN soldiers surrendered.

One of the ranger battalions ordered to withdraw from the Central Highlands to the coast took a detour on its way down from the hills. It went to the village of Tri Thuy, the family home of President Thieu. There, in the late 1950s, on the advice of a geomancer, Thieu had relocated the grave of his grandfather to a more auspicious location at the foot of a hill. (I saw it there in 1971.) The move was to bring upon Thieu better fate and so accelerate his career up army ranks. He did become president of the country.

To punish Thieu and all his descendants, the rangers destroyed the grave and allegedly dug up the grandfather's bones and smashed them. When this desecration was reported to Thieu in his presidential office, he fainted.

In the Central Highlands, after Hanoi's quick-moving mobile units had cut the road on which ARVN divisions had chosen to flee down from their strongholds in Pleiku and Kontum, other North Vietnamese divisions and regiments took control of those cities.

General Cao Van Vien, the ARVN chief of staff, later wrote, "Psychologically and politically, the self-inflicted defeat of MR II [Military Region 2] in the Highlands amounted to a horrible nightmare for the people and armed forces of South Vietnam. Confusion, worries, anxieties, accusations, guilt and a general feeling of distress began to weigh on everybody's mind."[56]

Hanoi's politburo and the Central Military Committee had already considered the consequences of an ARVN retreat from the Central Highlands. They concluded that it would be a "strategic error" by Thieu that would provide them with an "extremely favorable opportunity to annihilate a large enemy force and completely liberate the Central Highlands."[57]

Hanoi simultaneously moved quickly to encircle Hue and Danang and the large ARVN base at Chu Lai in Military Region 1. Its objective was to destroy the combat capacity of ARVN units in the region and so render them completely inoperative in war fighting. Hanoi's military strategists also wanted to tie down and immobilize South Vietnam's mobile reserves constituting the airborne and marine divisions, then fully deployed in Military Region 1.

Use of roads was preempted by Hanoi's forward units, ARVN units abandoned their positions, and civilians panicked and fled for Danang to find some way by plane or boat to flee farther south.

General Truong was in no state of mind to respond with decisive speed and agility and the fierce determination he had shown in repelling the previous massive Communist offensives of 1968 and 1972. South Vietnam's most compelling general officer, his confidence had been broken, and his emotions were flip-flopping around inside his head. He fled from Danang in a US Navy ship.

I am not aware that President Thieu ever fully explained his reasons for ordering withdrawals from Military Regions 1 and 2, even to his closest confidants. There was a slogan bantered about to "lighten the top and keep the bottom." Thieu did know that he had no strategic reserves to throw against Hanoi's local offensives, which were happening seriatim all over the country. After the Paris Peace Accords had been imposed on him by the Americans, he had made a policy decision to spread his forces—regular, regional, and village—across all of South Vietnam, defending every square meter that they could reasonably hold. Even the South Vietnamese marine and airborne divisions had been used for territorial defense. Thus, Thieu left himself no heavily armed, combat-seasoned reserve forces to send in as reinforcements wherever Hanoi might launch large attacks.

I infer that Thieu also knew from staff reports that his forces were short of fuel for their vehicles and airplanes and ammunition for their rifles, machine guns, mortars, and large artillery pieces—105s and 155s. Under such circumstances, he could not hold all of South Vietnam. Something had to be given up. So under pressure, perhaps panicked, at the last minute abandoned by fate, he gave up Military Regions 1 and 2.

Though he never said so, one can also infer that his only hope was for the Americans to send B-52s to take out NVA divisions as they marched south in the open, just as Nixon had promised to do—respond to any major violation of the peace accords with "full force."

He reportedly said, "If they [the US] grant full aid we will hold the whole country, but if they only give half of it, we will only hold half the country."[58]

What Thieu is reported to have said to his senior commanders was a reversal of the decision to hold all territory. Thieu pointed out that with severe cuts in US aid and no hope of American B-52 strikes against North Vietnamese divisions on the march, his only option was to consolidate his main forces, conserve his supplies, and play for time.[59]

Some Vietnamese later would accuse Thieu of acting *nhong nheo voi My*—throwing a temper tantrum to provoke the Americans. Vietnamese children act out this way to extract favorable attention from their often distant or overbearing parents. (Vietnamese girls as well sometimes demand attention this way with unresponsive boyfriends.) In being petulant, the more vulnerable party in a relationship takes the moral high ground. With his decision to give up Military Regions 1 and 2, Thieu psychologically was being self-destructive in order to shame the Americans into coming to his rescue.

There was a decisive difference in character between South Vietnam's president, Thieu, and North Vietnam's dictator, Le Duan, a difference shaped by opposing aspects of Vietnamese culture. Thieu was a fatalist. He very much believed in the power of fortune to determine the events of our lives. He consulted fortune-tellers regularly, trusting people based on the coincidence of their birth date with his. Thieu's psychological posture was to wait and respond as the moment required. He had no confidence that he could shape events very much. He lived according to the Vietnamese saying about success: "Heaven sets the time for success or not, earth provides advantages or not, and people provide willing support or not."

Le Duan, in contrast, was a driver of events. He was not a fatalist but was always scheming about how to amass powers and forces to turn events to his advantage. Each man in his own way was an opportunist, Thieu on a small scale and Le Duan on a large one. As a fatalist, Thieu was more accommodating to circumstances, while as a Nietzschean *Übermensch*, Le Duan lived to impose his will on his times.

In Vietnamese terms, Thieu's inclination was to *cho thoi*, to wait for the time, while Le Duan applied the practice of *tao the*, creating opportune moments in which circumstances had no choice but to play out in his favor.

Both Thieu and Le Duan played off of whatever the Americans would do. But Thieu would fold and collapse if, in extremis, American power would not carry him forward, while Le Duan would instead lay plans to force the Americans into a corner from which climbing up over a wall and running away to escape their predicament was their only realistic option.

But Thieu's response to adversity, if you ask me, was far from heroic. It might even be considered cowardly, a formalistic response to an impending disaster, a posture of leadership but not the thing itself.

I can only infer that his psychological recoil from Kissinger's betrayal intensified his fatalism and sense of hopeless passivity and so forced his decision to abandon the people of Military Regions 1 and 2. His paranoia and mistrust of others must have escalated in the fall of 1972 when he learned that the future of the Vietnamese Nationalists—after all their suffering and sacrifices—had been thrown to the mercies of the Communists and when he had been forced to accept that consequence. Such acceptance had resulted from good faith nationalist Vietnamese reliance on American determination and goodwill. Feeling betrayed, Thieu had given up hope for South Vietnam's survival but was too proud to admit that to his people.

Kissinger's brutality toward him only confirmed Thieu's sense of dependence on what the Americans wanted and his belief that, in the end, Americans, like fate itself, were fickle. He thus avoided assuming personal responsibility for the fate of his country.

After the war, Tran Van Don, a former general, politician, and rival to Thieu, commented that "in 1974 Thieu had decreased capability. Not tired; physically he was in good shape. But he seemed not to believe . . . The summer of 1972 he was on top of his power . . . He was on top in 1972 and 1973. After that he was decreasing."[60]

From the 1969 start of Kissinger's secret negotiations, Thieu's one condition for an acceptable negotiated outcome always had been removal of Communist soldiers from South Vietnam. He knew his enemy well, and he knew strategic military realities. He knew what it would take to save South Vietnam from conquest. But Kissinger had never taken him seriously. Bunker had.

Thieu was not alone in his perceptions. Interviews with leading Nationalist generals and officials revealed an unquestioning faith in US help in an emergency . . . holding fast to a conviction that the United States could and would 'do something' if Hanoi were to undertake cease-fire violations which would seriously endanger their national existence.[61]

I only met Thieu once, in his house in Boston in the mid-1990s. He was gracious, relaxed, and self-satisfied, saying he had done better than others could have done under the circumstances. I did not take him to task for his failures.

THE AMERICAN RESPONSE

The response of the Ford administration to Hanoi's aggression and violation of the Paris Peace Accords was to ask Congress for more money for the defense of South Vietnam and the Vietnamese Communists and the Soviet Union to cease and desist in their violations of the agreement.

On January 28, 1975, the administration sought a supplemental appropriation from Congress to restore military aid to South Vietnam to the $1 billion level, which was lower than that provided in the years before Hanoi's multidivision assault.[62]

On March 12, the House Democratic Caucus voted 189 to 49 to reject the Ford administration's request for an additional $300 million supplement. Democratic Party opposition to South Vietnam was stridently led by Bella Abzug, a prominent antiwar activist.[63]

On March 13, 1975, the House Foreign Affairs Committee rejected a compromise proposal for more aid for South Vietnam.[64] There was a perception that reducing aid to the Saigon government would force Thieu out of power and thus open the way to a political solution that would bring Communists into the government of South Vietnam, presumably what Hanoi wanted.[65]

On Sunday, March 30, I was in our newly purchased home at 755 Union Street in Brooklyn scraping old lead paint from window frames. We had the radio on. The station interrupted the rock and roll music playing with a news flash that the city of Danang had fallen to the Communists. I knew then that South Vietnam was lost. All the sacrifices of so many would now be in vain. My country had lost its first war, a noble one to defend a small people of a different race far, far away, and, accordingly I predicted, would henceforth suffer a tormenting cultural crisis of self-doubt. My thought then turned to refugees. I had family on my wife's side in Saigon, and we now had to plan to get them out. Her brother was an army officer. They might suffer punishment and discrimination because of her marriage to me should they have to live under the Communists. I thought of my friends there who were officials, village chiefs, intellectuals, officers, politicians, good people all.

I recalled the Hungarian refugees from 1956. My sixth-grade class-mate and friend Peter Batzell had a crush on Judith Szatmari, a refugee from Hungary, who was staying with her mother temporarily in a house on Lowell Street in Washington, DC, around the corner from ours. What we had done then to help those Hungarians seeking freedom, I thought we could well do again to help similarly threatened South Vietnamese.

The next day, Monday, I went to Washington—and not to work at the Wall Street law firm of Simpson, Thatcher, and Bartlett—but to volunteer to help out in the crisis and to start a refugee program for those Vietnamese Nationalists who could get out.

Yet consider these words from George Packer's article "The Betrayal" from the *Atlantic* in January 2022:

> *On April 14, 1975, as North Vietnamese divisions raced toward Saigon, the 32-year-old first-term senator from Delaware was sum-moned to the White House. President Gerald Ford pleaded with him and other senators for funding to evacuate Vietnamese allies. Biden refused. "I feel put-upon," he said. He would vote for money to bring out the remaining Americans, but not one dollar for the locals. On April 23, as South Vietnam's collapse accelerated, Biden repeated the point on the Senate floor. "I do not believe the United States has an obligation, moral or otherwise, to evacuate foreign nationals" other than diplomats, he said. That was the job of private organizations. "The United States has no obligation to evacuate one, or 100,001, South Vietnamese."*

Very much in my mind that Monday morning was a resolve that my country would not, on my watch, become contemptible in the history of humanity for its squalid treatment of defeated allies.

When I arrived in Washington that morning, I called my friend Parker Borg, a foreign service officer then working for Secretary of State Henry Kissinger as one of his two staff assistants. Parker and I had been in the same 1968 training class at the Vietnam Training Center before our assignments to the Civil Operations Rural Development Support (CORDS) pacification and rural development program in South Vietnam.

When he picked up the phone, I said, "Parker, I need your help. We have to have a refugee program for Vietnam."

"Sorry, I can't help you," Parker replied. "I just resigned on Friday as Kissinger's aide. I couldn't stand working for him anymore."

Stunned, I could say only, "Parker, you can't do that. I need you. Too many people will suffer once the Communists take over. They relied on us. We can't just turn our backs and run away."

Parker went on, "Nobody here cares. The president wants it over and done with. Kissinger has no interest in saving a single Vietnamese."

Then he said, "Let's talk with Lionel tonight." Lionel was Lionel Rosenblatt, another colleague from Vietnam, then working as the assistant to the deputy secretary of state. So that night, Parker drove me to Lionel's house in Cleveland Park in Washington. Lionel brought out three snifters of brandy, and we plotted. Lionel was both skeptical that anything could be done and emotionally open to the need to help those who had depended on us in a just cause.[66]

He perked up. "There's a small group of us meeting once a week following the deteriorating situation in Vietnam. You know many of them. They work for senior people at State, Defense, and CIA. Come by the State Department at noon tomorrow, and make your case."

The next day, as I walked out of the elevator on the seventh floor of the State Department, Parker and Lionel came out of Kissinger's office tense and upset.

"Steve, you can't participate. Al Adams [then Kissinger's other staff aide] won't sit in if you are there. You no longer have a security clearance; you're just a civilian, not part of the government. We need Al's support if anything is to be done."

Taken aback but sympathetic to Al's position of talking about top secret matters in front of one not cleared to hear them, I said, "OK, we need Al's support. I'll be back in an hour, but you know what needs to be done. I trust you two to get it done—a refugee program."

I returned after walking around the Lincoln Memorial, thinking about his trials in the Civil War and reading his words: "With malice toward none, with charity for all, with firmness in the right as God gives us to see the right, let us strive on to finish the work we are in, to bind up the nation's wounds, to care for him who shall have borne the battle and for his widow and his orphan, to do all which may achieve and cherish a just and lasting peace among ourselves and with all nations."

Parker and Lionel came out from Kissinger's suite of offices energized and full of obvious determination. "Done," they said. "Ken Quinn [another colleague from CORDS and then on the staff of the National Security Council] will move the idea in his shop. The other guys will all forward memos to their seniors recommending a refugee program."

(It might not be immaterial to note that Ken Quinn, Al Adams, and I each had married Vietnamese women and so had family ties to Vietnamese Nationalists.)

And it got done. An item on refugees was added to the agenda of the next National Security Council meeting. When it was tabled for discussion, no one argued for abandoning our allies in their hour of extreme distress.

Parker was assigned to start the program. Later, Julia Taft was made administrator, and Congress approved funds for resettlement.

I came back to Washington a week later to check in on progress. I walked into Lionel's office, as he was on the phone with a senior staff aide to Senator Edward Kennedy, chair of the Senate Judiciary Committee. Refugees would not have visas granting them permission to enter the United States. Another procedure was needed to give them the legal right to live here. Under the Constitution, Congress is given authority to set rules for immigration. To deal with refugees—say, in 1956 from Hungary or in 1965 from Cuba—a process was established where Congress would permit the administration to admit a set number of refugees under the parole authority. After their arrival, they could apply for permission to be residents and then become citizens.

As I stepped into his office, Lionel cupped his hands over the phone and asked, "Steve, how many refugees will we have to take?"

Not yet knowing why he was asking the question, I stumbled for an answer. I said, "One million fled the Communists in 1954, and years later, they have children and grandchildren. There are one million soldiers in the ARVN, a couple hundred thousand civil servants and teachers, thousands of village leaders and self-defense fighters; there are intellectuals, priests, monks, members of nationalist political parties."

I told him we would need to take at least one million people. Lionel shook his head and looked at me with a bit of disdain. He went back to his phone call. After he hung up, he said to me, "Kennedy will accept the same number of Vietnamese as we took Cubans from Castro in 1965. That is 150,000 only."

And so it was.

With the quick collapse of South Vietnam and the withdrawal of American airlift capacity and ships, only some 130,000 South Vietnamese were able to escape.

But that was better than what we did for the Cambodians. We had no refugee program for them. They were left to live and die under the Khmer Rouge.

Watching my friends scramble to save Vietnamese Nationalists from oppression, hardships, even death, and sensing how our American leadership was desperate not to be held responsible for a crushing and ignoble defeat, our first ever as a nation, I easily concluded that the United States had never written a field manual for defeat—for offense, yes, for victory, yes, but not for defeat. We have no contingency plans for such a case and no experts to throw at the embarrassment to minimize its consequences. We are reduced to flailing around as if our thoughtless, aimless actions and superfluous words would do some good. That very same observation came back to me in August 2021 when the United States went through similar haphazard and ad hoc responses to defeat when our allied government in Afghanistan collapsed and those Afghans who had depended on our resolve and good faith were left to their own devices as the Taliban swept into power.

COLLAPSE

As the ARVN withdrawal from the Central Highlands turned into a calamity, Hanoi launched punishing attacks in Military Region 1. On March 18, Route 1, the escape road south from Hue, was cut. Hue was sealed off with the famous First ARVN Division and some marine units trapped inside. Around the city were the 304th, 324th, and 325th NVA divisions. On March 2, the men of the First Division broke ranks and scattered.

Other North Vietnamese forces isolated the Second ARVN Division in its base in Quang Ngai province, to the south of Danang.

Troops and people flooded into Danang seeking escape from the North Vietnamese. General Truong gave up its defense on March 30. There was chaos in the streets. Ships and planes were sent to take desperate people and soldiers out for passage to safer southern locations.

As Vietnamese Nationalist units disintegrated in Military Regions 1 and 2, no defense against Hanoi's divisions could be organized. Hanoi's Military History Institute later affirmed that Thieu's decision to order retreats from Military Regions 1 and 2, as precipitated by mobile Communist forces, had created a "new situation" and that a *thoi co* had arrived.[67] Meeting on March 31, the politburo evaluated the situation in South Vietnam, concluding, "The revolutionary war in South Vietnam is now growing by leaps and bounds and the time is now ripe for the launching of the general offensive into the heart of the enemy's lair. Our final strategic battle has begun." The politburo was confident that North Vietnamese forces in the South were of sufficient strength to "overwhelm the enemy's army." The politburo issued guidance to Hanoi's forces in South Vietnam: "Lightning speed, daring, surprise, certain victory!"

The wished-for *thoi co* promising total victory for their party had arrived at last after hundreds of thousands of Vietnamese had been killed at the instigation of one Communist leader or another, for nothing other than ideological vainglory. There wasn't even a polite nod by the Communists in recognition of the claims to leadership and authority by the PRG or the National Liberation Front (NLF) of South Vietnam, the widely touted independent vanguard of the South Vietnamese people allegedly rising up in resistance to American imperialism. The *thoi co* was for Hanoi to exploit and enjoy alone. Its Military History Institute later wrote: "Our army swept forward like a river; trucks, trains, aircraft, and ships seemed to be pointed in only one direction—Saigon."[68]

President Ford sent General Frederick C. Weyand to Saigon to observe and make a report designed to convince members of Congress to approve additional funds for South Vietnam.[69] On March 26, Kissinger spoke at a news conference, stating that the administration would welcome a compromise with the Democrats on the requested supplemental appropriation.

Under the War Powers Act of 1973, limitations had been placed on the power of the American president to undertake acts of force without congressional approval. President Ford was reluctant to confront Congress with a decision to send B-52s to the defense of South Vietnam, even though Hanoi's divisions were moving south along roads and would be sitting ducks for American bombing runs. Ford's conclusion was that "I do not have the authority to do some of the things President Nixon could do."[70]

Arriving in South Vietnam, Vietnamese Communist leader Le Duc Tho, who had negotiated with Kissinger for the "decent interval" that his party would give the people of South Vietnam and who had declined to accept a Nobel Peace Prize, brought to his leading cadres the most recent resolution of the politburo in Hanoi. Overjoyed, Le Duc Tho wrote a few lines of poetry for Hanoi's paramount leader and his close comrade for decades: "Such good news on the road to the front! Glad cries of victory are everywhere, urging haste to my steps on the long road; the *thoi co* has arrived."[71]

In its March 31 meeting, Hanoi's politburo discussed a campaign to attack Saigon and bring about the end of South Vietnam as an independent country. The meeting concluded that "a great opportunity" was before them and that they must rise to the occasion and seize it. The plan was to strengthen their forces to the west of Saigon, send more forces to the southwest of the city, close in from the northeast, and cut Route 4, closing the city off from access to the Mekong Delta provinces. In the final confrontation, Hanoi would have fifteen divisions of troops to deploy, the Nationalists only five.[72]

The month of April was largely a mopping-up operation for Hanoi's forces. Some ARVN units doggedly fought doomed but heroic final battles, while others evaporated as officers and soldiers deserted to seek out and be with their families.

Only one division of the North Vietnamese army, the 308th, was left in North Vietnam as a strategic reserve. Hanoi had no fear of American retaliation against its home territory.[73]

On April 1, Le Duan sent new instructions to his subordinates in the South that the politburo had decided to successfully end its war of conquest in the shortest time.

On April 3, the US Defense Intelligence Agency (DIA) gave South Vietnam thirty more days of independence.[74] An interagency report of the CIA, the DIA, and the State Department affirmed that South Vietnam would collapse. "The North Vietnamese have recognized South Vietnam's vulnerability and appear determined to take rapid advantage of it."[75]

On April 4, Thieu asked Khiem to resign as prime minister. He appointed a new one with instructions to form a broad-based government to rally the people and offset their despair.

On April 8, Le Duc Tho himself arrived at the command center in lower South Vietnam to present the new orders. A new command was established to coordinate the final push on Saigon. All its leaders were Communists sent from Hanoi.

General Vo Nguyen Giap sent a poem as his personal contribution to troop and cadre morale:

> *Speed, ever greater speed*
> *Daring, ever greater daring*
> *Exploit every hour, every minute*
> *Rush to the battlefront, liberate the South*
> *Resolve to fight to secure total victory.*[76]

The ARVN commander of Military Region 3 around Saigon concentrated forces around the town of Xuan Loc, a major road junction north of Saigon facing the south-moving tide of NVA forces. There, the 18th ARVN division would face the 6th, 7th, and 341st NVA Divisions—some forty thousand troops supported by armor and artillery.

The first NVA assault on Xuan Loc northwest of Saigon was soundly repulsed. Then, on April 9, the 341st NVA Division began a second assault with tanks and shock and awe artillery fire of some four thousand rounds.[77] The ARVN held. On the third day, Hanoi resumed the attack using three regiments. Again, they failed. On April 15, Hanoi sent its 325th Division into the battle. After another week of relentless fighting, the battered 18th ARVN Division finally had to give ground and fall back.

By this time, NVA divisions were moving toward Saigon proper from the south, west, and northeast. The plan was to rush into the city to capture buildings from which the GVN provided leadership. General Dung wanted to "cut the snake at its head," judging that no capable, heroic leader would arise to rally the South Vietnamese Nationalists for an improbable military counteroffensive.[78] General Dung believed that a *thoi co* consisted of force and power—making an offer that could not be refused.[79]

But inside the city of Saigon, with its population of 3.5 million people, the Communists had only a handful of supporters, only three hundred armed civilians with some followers.[80]

Thus, a new government of Communists was formed to run Saigon after its capture. Nguyen Van Tran, secretary of the Central Committee, and other trusted bureaucrats were sent from Hanoi. Top Communist leaders Le Duc Tho and Pham Hung took direct charge of the incoming administration.[81] It was the end of the line for the Viet Cong and the nominal PRG.

General Frederick C. Weyand returned to Washington and recommended $722 million in aid for South Vietnam.

On April 14, the US embassy received parole authority to accept for travel to the United States alien relatives of US citizens.

On April 18, the coastal provinces north of Saigon, Ninh Thuan and Binh Thuan, were overrun by NVA units. The United States ordered its officials to begin evacuation of South Vietnam.

The battlefields around Saigon were quiet from April 20 through 26. Hanoi's forces were getting orders and targets from headquarters.[82] The final attacks on Saigon would come from five directions. Tactical units and supplies had to be moved to their proper positions in time for the assault.

South Vietnamese politicians scrambled to accept a coalition government and negotiations with the Communists in order to stave off the collapse of their regime from a military assault. This naivete was actively abetted by the French ambassador, who talked up a coalition government as the future for South Vietnam.

On April 21, Thieu resigned as the defense of Xuan Loc was abandoned.

On April 23, President Ford said, "The Vietnam War has ended as far as America is concerned." In effect, the antiwar movement had won the struggle for the hearts and minds of Americans. French President Charles de Gaulle (1890-1970) might have said with a wink: *Merci!*—"Thanks."

Now, at the end of the Vietnamese Nationalist struggle for the right to govern just half of their own country, the French again took sides with their Communist rivals. Paris sought to arrange the installation of a coalition government in South Vietnam to prevent a complete Communist conquest.[83] In a reprise of Jean Sainteny sponsoring a Vietnamese government in 1946, Jean Merillon, French ambassador to South Vietnam, now contacted retired ARVN general "Big" Minh and Tran Van Tra, the nominal commander of NLF forces in South Vietnam, to propose a "coalition" government for South Vietnam. The Vietnamese personage used by the French in pushing for a coalition government between the Nationalists and the Communists, just as they had attempted in December 1963, was General Duong Van "Big" Minh, widely looked upon as a French protégé since his formative years as an officer in the French colonial army of Indochina. In late 1963 the Dai Viets had rightfully suspected de Gaulle of promoting "Big" Minh as the leader of a coalition between non-Communists and the allegedly independent and autonomous NLF. Hanoi, cooperating with Moscow, gamely ran a disinformation campaign to convince the South Vietnamese and the Americans that negotiations, a coalition government, and a cease-fire were just around the corner, the better to lull the South Vietnamese into relaxing their defense of Saigon.

On April 25, the US embassy received parole authority to accept fifty thousand high-risk Vietnamese.[84] C-141 jets arrived at Saigon's huge Tan Son Nhut airport to pick up what refugees came out to the tarmac. On April 29 and 30, another 11,600 would leave Saigon by barge down the Saigon River. Nearly 1.5 million Vietnamese Nationalist soldiers and civil officials (not including more loyalists in politics, religion, and culture), along with their extended families, were left to live under Communist diktat and oppression.

Thieu and former prime minister Tran Thien Khiem flew out of Saigon on an American aircraft for exile in Taiwan.[85]

Others fled as best they could to US Navy ships waiting offshore in the South China Sea.

On April 26, the Communists began artillery fire on Saigon.

On April 27, Vice President Tran Van Huong resigned, and the National Assembly elected "Big" Minh to be the new president. He immediately offered the Communists negotiations and a coalition government. The Communists outfitted some captured GVN aircraft and bombed Saigon's Tan Son Nhut airport. They didn't bother replying to President Minh's plea for compromise.

On April 29, heavy bombardment of Tan Son Nhut airport began, and a North Vietnamese military noose of force and violence choked democratic Saigon to death.

On April 30, the last Americans left by helicopter, and President Minh surrendered as Hanoi's troops captured the various headquarter buildings and the Tan Son Nhut airport.

And so South Vietnam disappeared from human history and a Communist tyranny was militarily imposed on Vietnamese Nationalists, all just as Kissinger had validated with premeditation with his 1971 affirmations to Ambassador Dobrynin and to Premier Zhou that the Vietnamese people would be left alone to sort out their "political" differences among themselves. And those exact outcomes of the Vietnam War were intentionally facilitated by Kissinger in his negotiation of the Paris Peace Accords of 1973.

TO THE VICTOR GO THE SPOILS: THE CHARADE OF "LIBERATION" ENDS, AND THE MASKS COME OFF AT LAST

Truong Nhu Tang, a senior member of the PRG of South Vietnam, attended Hanoi's victory parade in Saigon on May 15, 1975. He grew more and more anxious in the reviewing stand on not seeing Viet Cong units march in victory. Finally, a few companies of unkempt men in ragtag array came walking along under the flag of North Vietnam. Tang, reeling from physical shock, turned to North Vietnamese general Van Tien Dung, who was standing next to him, to ask, "Where are our Divisions 1, 3, 5, 7, and 9?"

Dung replied sardonically, "The army has already been unified."

Tang objected, "Since when? There's been no decision about anything like that."

Dung turned away without speaking. Tang now knew he had been used by the Communists and was to be only a cipher in their ruling hierarchy.[86] That quickly came to be. Security for the PRG leaders was provided by cadres from Hanoi. Other such cadres became their staff and handled every item of business. The Military Management Committee, run by Communist Vo Van Kiet, a member of the party's Central Committee, acted as the government.

As a student in France in 1946, Truong Nhu Tang had been seduced into collaboration with Ho Chi Minh's Viet Minh front by Ho's adroit skill in playing the role of a genuine Vietnamese nationalist. At that time in the summer of 1946, Ho was in France to finalize his agreement with Jean Sainteny. He was on his best behavior, trying to impress all and sundry as an apparent representative of the Vietnamese people with his warmth and also his dedication to working things out between the Vietnamese and their former colonial rulers. Truong Nhu Tang later recalled that, when Ho met with him and other Vietnamese students from various provinces north to south, Ho said: "Voila, the youth of our great family of Vietnam. Our Vietnam is one, our nation is one. You must remember. Though the rivers may run dry and the mountains erode, the nation will always be one."[87]

Finally, on that May 15th of 1975, the long, internationally marketed fictional narrative of an independent revolution by Southern Vietnamese against a corrupt Saigon administration installed and managed by American imperialism was abandoned. Such a narrative was no longer needed by Vietnam's Communist Party, which now had South Vietnam under its complete and very airtight military and police control. All the actors retained to impersonate leaders independent of Hanoi's ambitions and the propaganda poured forth for years about an independent southern political movement—all fabricated to create belief in the NLF—were now revealed as just that, actors and propaganda. It had been just a stage play full of sound and fury, with only a pretense of reality. It had all been a lie—just as the American government had insisted from 1961 on.

The Vietnamese quip about how the Communists behave is *"Vat chanh, bo vo"* (Throw the rind away after you squeeze out all the juice).

In 1978 Truong Nhu Tang fled his homeland as a Boat Person to live more freely but in exile.

The antiwar leaders in the United States and elsewhere were shown to have been easily duped. To demonstrate their deep complicity in promoting falsehood, as Hanoi incarcerated tens of thousands of Nationalists in concentration camps for years of "reeducation" after 1975, only Joan Baez among the well-known antiwar movement leaders raised her voice in protest. No one in America listened.

What the documents that I reviewed for this book do not answer is the question "Why?" Why did Henry Kissinger, with seeming insouciance and lack of remorse, abandon the Vietnamese Nationalists? One possible answer that, at least superficially, conforms to what the documents reveal is a personality profile that falls within the spectrum of antisocial personality traits—the needs and behaviors of a sociopath or a psychopath. Such a personality, we are told, brings forth charm, intelligence, and charisma, coupled with manipulation and deceit—the better to exploit others and control their behaviors. But such people have little empathy, they are cold and callous, and they do not experience remorse. They easily rationalize actions that negatively affect others. Their self-promotion and narcissism are unchecked by a strong moral compass.[88]

Kissinger once described himself to journalist Oriana Fallaci in quite grandiose terms. He said: "The main point arises from the fact that I've always acted alone. Americans like that immensely. Americans like the cowboy who leads the wagon train by riding ahead alone on his horse, the cowboy who rides all alone into the town, the village, with his horse and nothing else." This self-assessment came on November 4, 1972, during a tense, crucial time in Kissinger's crusade to impose on presidents Richard Nixon and Nguyen Van Thieu his very own ideal of a "decent interval" for South Vietnam.[89]

In his 2022 book *Leadership*, Kissinger deflected away from himself responsibility for creating the conditions which empowered the Vietnamese Communist Party to conquer South Vietnam. He placed responsibility on the American people:

"The [Paris Peace Accords] had always depended on the willingness and ability to enforce its provisions. It was based on the assumption . . . that, in case of an all-out attack, American airpower would be available. Amidst the Watergate investigation, an exhausted public would not support additional conflict in Indochina. . . . In these circumstances, enforcement of the limitations of the Vietnam Agreement became impossible, and restraints on Hanoi disappeared."[90]

In an August 2022 interview, Kissinger also said: "I do not torture myself with things we might have done differently."[91]

He then defined success in negotiations as arriving at an equilibrium—"a kind of balance of power with an acceptance of the legitimacy of sometimes opposing values." And he easily accepted sacrificing his values in order to gain such a balance of power: "Because if you believe that the final outcome of your effort has to be the imposition of your values, then I think equilibrium is not possible."

Such a mind had no capacity either to defend the Vietnamese people in their hour of desperate struggle or to honor the moral integrity of the United States.

Let me give the last word to Vietnam's great poet Nguyen Du—three lines from his epic poem *Kim Van Kieu*:

> *Don't reproach Heaven for being too near or too far;*
> *The source of good-heartedness is in all of us,*
> *One good heart can do more than great talent and ability.*

AFTERWORD

The current travails of Americans—here at home and overseas—arose from the failure of our effort to make good on our promise to the people of South Vietnam to defend them from Communist aggression.

The loss of the Vietnam War brought us the shame of dishonor and a loss of self-confidence. Defeat broke our morale, unnerved us, and caused us to turn against our traditions, ideals, and our trust in ourselves and in each other.

Our veterans were ostracized, which caused them a vicious kind of posttraumatic stress disorder, one not experienced in combat but only after they returned home to rejection and stigma. Many then self-victimized, blaming their government for exposing them to Agent Orange herbicides or not seeking the return of our prisoners of war.

The unwritten foundational contract of America to honor those citizens who served in its wars was abandoned after our loss in Vietnam. It was a contract that began with the Revolution and was honored through the Civil War, two World Wars, and the Korean War.

To this day, the greeting of one Vietnam veteran to another has been "Welcome home!" Yet it rings hollow.

Filling the cultural vacuum left by the collapse of confidence in ourselves, our leaders, and our cause was the narrative of those opposed to the war in Vietnam—a divisive repudiation of America as a moral exemplar, the "city upon a hill."

This was the first time that the professoriat, supported by journalists and other intellectuals, came up with its own narrative about what America was doing wrong in a foreign war, a false story about the Vietnamese and the origins of the war. Then they imposed it upon the American people through control of critical elite cultural institutions. It would not be the last time that this would happen.

As I write this afterword, the results of a March 7, 2022, poll from Quinnipiac University show that 38 percent of those Americans asked replied that they would leave the country rather than fight for it. The responses tracked the cultural differences that have divided Americans since the 1960s, when the antiwar movement started to oppose the war in Vietnam: 68 percent of Republicans said they would fight, while—to the contrary—52 percent of Democrats replied that they would leave the country.

Antiwar protestors, picking up the narrative, chanted, "Ho, Ho, Ho Chi Minh. NLF is gonna win!" Of course, when South Vietnam was conquered by North Vietnam's army in April 1975, the NLF did not win. That organization of South Vietnamese was cannibalized by its creator, the Communist Party of Vietnam, just as Cronus ate his children.

Antiwar protestors expressed their regard for their country with chants like "Hey, hey, LBJ, how many kids did you kill today?"

Young men of draft age who did not want to serve in Vietnam had an emotional need to find a narrative that would justify their refusal. The antiwar narrative filled that need precisely and passionately. The antiwar movement quickly attracted many followers, especially on college campuses and among elite families.

Men of draft age then who did not serve in Vietnam and later became prominent political leaders include William Jefferson Clinton, George W. Bush, Dick Cheney, Mitt Romney, Donald Trump, and Joe Biden. In 1989, Dick Cheney told the *Washington Post* that he had other priorities in the 1960s than military service.

In my 1967 class of perhaps more than 1,200 young, well-educated men at Harvard College, not many more than fifty served in their country's armed forces, and, I believe, fewer than twenty-five served—as I did—in Vietnam.

In 1969, President Nixon canceled enlisting draftees for the months of November and December. In January 1973, he ended the duty young American men had to serve their country in its armed forces.

The failure to achieve our national purpose of successfully defending the South Vietnamese people gave traction to a new cultural narrative that exposed masculinity to disdain and belittlement and proposed a feminine yin power, as the Chinese *I Ching* expresses it, as its replacement. *The Feminine Mystique*, calling into question traditional social roles for women, was published in 1963. Erica Jong's *Fear of Flying* was published in 1973.

In 1968, the Baez sisters made a poster to encourage American men to avoid military service. The poster affirmed that "GIRLS SAY YES to Boys who say NO."

The academic narrative that the Vietnam War was both immoral and unwinnable divided Americans from one another in a way that has never healed. The divisiveness started by the antiwar critique of America has metastasized, year in and year out, until today, when we have separated ourselves into five incompatible tribes living in two Americas—one red and the other blue.

The polarization started with the success of the antiwar movement in capturing the organizational structure of the Democrat Party in the 1972 presidential campaign. When the Supreme Court announced a woman's right to abortion in 1973, our culture war began in earnest.

Once American ideals and goodness were mocked and denied and the incapability of America was revealed by the failure in Vietnam, false narratives were pushed by the progressive left to dominate American culture and politics. These narratives built on the foundation first laid by the antiwar movement, starting in 1965 with the import of French colonial ideas about the Vietnamese. Under militant and unforgiving advocacy from the left and resistance from the right, our culture unraveled; mass narcissism took the helm; leadership atrophied into grifting, self-serving mediocrity; and our politics became dysfunctional.

The cultural changes set in motion by our Vietnam failure have been impressive and long lasting. By 2022, we had sunk into an abyss of systemic irrationality in many of our socially constructed narratives, such as "follow the science," a Green New Deal, intersectionality, the reverse racism of critical race theory, and other modes of self-victimization. To champion a new kind of America and new kinds of Americans—ones much less traditional—a new elite came into power, with laptops and smartphones as their weapons. The elite sought to subjugate culturally and politically those it considered "deplorable."

Today we live constantly beset by that censorious elite composed of those ashamed of being American, seeking only their own self-actualization and advocating a democracy that seemingly can't recognize rights of free thought and free expression.

Ironically I suppose, Kissinger has affirmed my assessment of the harm done to Americans as a people of pride and constructive purpose, and so also, the damage inflicted on the United States as a remarkable constitutional democracy by Hanoi's conquest of South Vietnam. In *Leadership*, he wrote, "The Vietnam War initiated an internal division of American society that has torn it to this day. The conflict introduced a style of public debate increasingly conducted less over substance than over political motives and identities. Anger has replaced dialogue as a way to carry out disputes, and disagreement has become a clash of cultures. In the process, Americans have stood in danger of forgetting that societies become great not by factional triumphs or the destruction of domestic adversaries, not by victories over each other, but by common purpose and reconciliation."[1]

Observing events from the Kremlin, Vladimir Putin decided that such an America was a lost cause, self-incriminating and in the painful throes of being marginalized by history. Such an America could not and did not deter him from invading Ukraine.

If, on the other hand, South Vietnam had prevailed over Communist North Vietnam—as South Korea stood up to North Korea and West Germany refused to fall to Soviet might—and we were successful in our defense of a free people, few, if any, of our destructive domestic cultural and political misadventures would, in all probability, have happened.

Internationally, if we had prevailed in our defense of South Vietnam, our military would, in all probability, have learned best practices to apply in our subsequent wars against Islamic terrorists and in Iraq and Afghanistan. We would have won our "forever wars."

But when South Vietnam was conquered, our military turned its back on what had worked there to defeat the Viet Cong guerillas and help the South Vietnamese hold off the 1972 invasion by North Vietnam's army. As goes the saying, "Success has a thousand fathers; defeat is an orphan." Once your efforts fail, people turn their backs on you. When this happens, some might say it's best just to forget what is embarrassing, say "never mind," and move on with no baggage to carry. But we often pay a price when we forget too much too quickly.

As an example, Robert McNamara never accepted personal responsibility for failure. Even though he had been secretary of defense to Presidents Kennedy and Johnson and supervised for them until the end of 1967 the strategy and tactics deployed by the United States in South Vietnam, he failed to dissuade Hanoi from pursuing the conquest of that country. In McNamara's case, it was failure to master the strategy and tactics of successful counterinsurgency—of working with the Vietnamese Nationalists in their villages.

In particular, the successful program of Vietnamization begun by Johnson (after McNamara privately admitted to his president that he had no idea how to win the war) and extended and completed by President Richard Nixon was not repeated in either Iraq or Afghanistan.

In Iraq, the Sunni Awakening—when Sunnis came to the assistance of American forces and the Baghdad government—stabilized the conflict in our favor. But Sunni clan leaders started that initiative on their own. It was not the result of any intentional American strategy.

In Afghanistan there was no application of the lessons learned in Vietnam—ground your programs in the norms of local cultures; organize villages for their own self-governance, self-defense, and self-development; and create a unified civilian/military command for American and NATO efforts.

The COIN tactics that our generals devised and applied in Iraq and later in Afghanistan were not informed by the sophisticated combined political and military Civil Operations Rural Development Support (CORDS) program we had deployed in South Vietnam from 1967 to 1972.

By putting the loss of Vietnam in the rearview mirror and not looking back, our national security leaders could not prevail in either of our twenty-first-century "forever wars."

The Biden administration's feckless abandonment of Afghanistan in August 2021 after twenty years of inadequate performance in counterinsurgency was noticed by the world.

On February 4, 2022, Russia and China signed a pact of mutual support to impose their values on the United Nations, and each pledged to oppose efforts by the United States to uphold crucial ideals of world order, such as international law, democracy, and human rights.

On February 24, Russia invaded Ukraine while dismissing pleas from the United States to cease and desist from acting on its aggressive ambition of living up to the age-old mythos of the "third Rome"—Russian Orthodoxy categorizing Russians as a "chosen people."

In May 2022, the American special investigator for Afghanistan reconstruction concluded that the fall of Afghanistan to the Taliban followed Henry Kissinger's playbook for ending the Vietnam War. The special investigator said without the slightest equivocation that "the single most important factor in the [Afghan National Defense and Security Forces'] collapse in August 2021 was the U.S. decision to withdraw military forces and contractors from Afghanistan through signing the U.S.–Taliban agreement in February 2020 under the Trump administration, followed by President Biden's withdrawal announcement in April 2021."

America did not, with honor and fidelity, stand by the South Vietnamese—who were faithful to their ancient Nationalist values and who, therefore, rejected the Western creed of Communist dictatorship.

Had we been more honorable and more faithful then, we would be a happier people today. Moreover, our world would be more stable and more just.

POSTSCRIPT:

WHEN CONFRONTING EVIL,
WHAT SHOULD ONE DO?

"What evil lurks in the hearts of men? The Shadow knows."
—*The Shadow* radio program, 1937

"The difficult we do immediately; the impossible takes a little longer."
—U.S. forces, Pacific theater, 1944

"Here I stand. I can do no other . . ."
—Martin Luther, Diet of Worms, 1521

In 1978, the effects of Communist rule over the countries of former French Indochina—Vietnam, Laos, and Cambodia—were apparent, though "mainstream" American media, leaders of the antiwar movement, and most political leaders looked the other way. Vietnamese were fleeing their homeland in small boats, chancing a rendezvous with a cargo ship in the South China Sea or landfall in Thailand or Malaysia.

A tiny number of Cambodians were in camps in Thailand, safe from the massacres of the Khmer Rouge who sought to "cleanse" the country of unworthy persons. Hmong tribespeople from the mountains of Laos who had sided with the United States during the Vietnam War against the North Vietnamese invading their enclaves were swimming across the Mekong River to seek sanctuary in Thailand.

In the United States, Leo Cherne, of the International Rescue Committee, formed a Citizens Commission on Indochinese Refugees. He asked me to join the group. He and William Casey, later campaign chairman for Ronald Reagan and then director of the CIA in the Reagan administration, were the co-chairs. The noted African American civil rights leader Bayard Rustin was another in our small group, along with Reverend Kenneth Cauthen. We flew to Thailand to visit the refugee camps there, intending to return with a report on the need for a special immigrant program to welcome these victims of political tyranny to the United States.

I remember most a visit to the camp of Cambodian refugees in Chanthaburi on the Thai border with Cambodia. Leo asked me to go alone as the others were visiting other camps. The drive to the camp was long and arduous. An interpreter, Im Vin, accompanied me.

The camp was a collection of about a thousand thatch huts at the foot of some hills. Khmer Rouge soldiers loyal to Pol Pot patrolled the ridgeline above the camp. I walked around for a while, looking at listless people sitting around with nothing to do. Their hopelessness was driven home to me by their blank stares and their dead eyes.

I then saw to my left a small house off on its own. A man in orange robes sat on a covered porch in front of the house—a Buddhist monk. I quickly walked over with Im Vin to interview him.

I asked: "How many monks are left in Cambodia?"

He replied: "They are all dead."

I asked: "What about the temples?"

He replied: "They are all abandoned or used for government schools."

I asked: "What happened to the books of scripture and Buddhist philosophy?"

He replied: "All burned."

Ah yes, I thought, a Communist paradise—no monks, no religion: taking advantage of the inherent perfectibility of humanity.

On the drive back to Bangkok, Im Vin opened up about his life under the Khmer Rouge. As a speaker of English, he was classified as part of the "new population"—those incurably infected with bad thinking. He and his family were moved to the countryside to live and work under the supervision of Khmer Rouge cadres.

One day all the people—men, women, and children—in the hamlet were ordered to gather at the schoolhouse. After a while, a truck drove up. People were loaded on. The truck drove off. Sometime later it returned empty. Everyone in the school then knew what was happening: it was their day to die. The rule of the Khmer Rouge cadres was "if you live, we gain nothing. If you die, we lose nothing. So why not kill you today?"

Im Vin pulled his wife close. He said "I will not let them kill me like a dirty dog. I am going to run away. Let them kill me while fighting back." He hugged his wife and children. She said only: "Tell me the truth: If we meet again on the other side, will you marry me again?" He said yes.

Then he crawled out a back window and ran into the woods without looking back. He started walking north towards Thailand. After many days, he crossed the border, having avoided mines and Khmer Rouge patrols. He knew how to speak English and found work with a refugee agency helping others who had also escaped the Killing Fields.

Upon returning to Washington, our Citizens Commission accomplished our mission. The Carter administration, led by Secretary of State Cyrus Vance and Assistant Secretary of State for Human Rights Patricia Derian, worked with the Congress to pass the Refugee Act of 1980.

And so America opened its doors to the Vietnamese boat people, the survivors of the Killing Fields in Cambodia, the Hmong from Laos, and other Lao nationalists—several hundred thousand people. In 2018, when the median family income for White Americans was $65,902, the median family income for Hmong families was $67,372. For Vietnamese families, it was $67,331.[1] In 2019, the median family income for Cambodian families was $66,000.[2]

In later years, tens of thousands Somalis would also come to America, as authorized by this statute. Our Citizens Commission had made a difference for good.

In 1979, the Vietnamese Communists invaded Cambodia to overthrow Pol Pot's heinous regime. China retaliated with an invasion of Vietnam. The Vietnamese ably defended their border.

The horrific ideology imposed on the Cambodian people starting in April 1975 had been learned in French colonial schools and in Paris. When they had been students in Paris, the most senior Khmer Rouge leaders had been throughly exposed to French revolutionary thinkers like Jean Jacques Rousseau and Gracchus Babeuf, the first so-called "Communist."

Civil war in Cambodia ensued. The Communist Chinese supported and armed Pol Pot's faction while the Communist Vietnamese sent troops to succor their own faction of Cambodian Communists, which they provided with arms and supplies. The killings went on and on.

In 1989, the Council of Foreign Relations in New York City sponsored a study of the continuing tragedy in Cambodia. Retired General John Vessey, former chairman of the Joint Chiefs of Staff and President Reagan's special representative to obtain cooperation from the Hanoi government on seeking information on Americans missing in action during the Vietnam War, was selected to chair the group. Vessey had asked my advice on his negotiations with the Vietnamese Communists. Now he asked me to be a member of the study group. I had been a member of the council as a young lawyer practicing in New York City and later as an assistant dean at Harvard Law School. It would prove important that Congressman Stephen Solarz was also a participant in our discussions.

My thoughts turned to ending the war between Beijing and Hanoi over who would dominate Cambodia—China or Vietnam. Normal diplomatic negotiations over sovereign rights under international law would get nowhere, I concluded. Until there was a victory on the battlefield, Beijing would never yield to Hanoi, and—vice-versa—Hanoi would never yield to Beijing.

The fighting in Cambodia was very much a zero-sum rivalry, with the winner to take all. This polarization, minimizing the opportunity for compromise, was exacerbated, I thought, by the reality that it was a struggle for sovereignty under the modern Western system of international law governing nation-states.

After the Treaty of Westphalia in 1648, European governments evolved into nation-states where the power to rule was concentrated and centralized in a "sovereign"—be it a king, a parliament, or a president. Sovereignty was hard to share; it was indivisible. Either you had it or you didn't. In the new nation of the United States, the mantra was e pluribus unum—"from many, one." The American Civil War, triggered by slavery in the southern states, implicated sovereignty. The southern states argued that they were defending their sovereignty against outside interference, while the northern states argued that the federal government was sovereign and therefore had superior authority over the states.

In the polities of Southeast Asia before the arrival of Western powers, the authority of rulers was elastic, flexible, and porous. Kings would negotiate the terms of fidelity and alliance with other kings, princes, or communal leaders. The less powerful would subordinate themselves to some degree to the more powerful in various forms of feudal submission or tributary dependency.

Thus, I surmised and confirmed with various Vietnamese and Thai friends that the international law structure of exclusive sovereign authority was in the way of a peaceful resolution to the question of who would rule Cambodia—a Chinese client or a Vietnamese client.

I concluded that if sovereignty could be taken off the table as the outcome of war, then reaching a peace agreement between Beijing and Hanoi would become more probable. The way to remove sovereignty as the bone of contention was to create a trusteeship administration. Installing a trustee as an interim administrator of Cambodia would permit China to back down without losing to Vietnam and, simultaneously, Vietnam to back down without losing to China.

The introduction of a third party into the power equation would add new options for the allocation of powers within Cambodia while saving face for all concerned. The international law precedent for such an interim trusteeship was provided by the Charter of the United Nations in its creation of the Trusteeship Council, formed to facilitate the peaceful evolution of Western colonies into independent nations.

I ran this idea by General Vessey, and he thought it was sensible. I then presented the idea to our study group. Congressman Solarz picked it up and made it his own initiative.

Coincidently, in Australia, former Ambassador Malcolm Booker was thinking along similar lines. Booker had been Australian ambassador in Bangkok when my dad was the American ambassador. The two men were quite close in their thinking. Australian foreign minister Gareth Evans listened to Booker and responded favorably to the idea put forward by Congressman Solarz.

In the meantime, I called up retired president Nixon to run the idea by him and get his reaction. He agreed with my analysis of sovereignty as a big pothole on the road to ending the war in Cambodia and suggested I present it to Larry Eagleburger, then Deputy Secretary of State. Eagleburger kindly agreed to see me. I gave him my reasons for seeking a trusteeship for Cambodia.

He grew emotional, telling me that in April 1975 he had taken the last phone call from Cambodian nationalist leader Sisowath Sirik Matak, refusing the American offer to evacuate him as Khmer Rouge troops were entering Cambodia's capital of Phnom Penh (see Matak's farewell letter to American ambassador John Gunther Dean in the Documents section at the back of the book). Matak said he preferred to die in his country rather than flee. Thus, the American leadership was open to adopting Congressman Solarz's proposal.

By coincidence, in 1990 I was in Hanoi working on a behind-the-scenes rapprochement between the Vietnamese Communists and the Nationalist enemies along the lines used by Nelson Mandela in South Africa. One evening I was supposed to meet with Vietnamese prime minister Do Muoi.

I was in the reception room in the prime minister's office when a deputy foreign minister, Nguyen Dy Nien, entered with apologies. He said the prime minister had returned to Hanoi from a day trip to the port city of Haiphong. The road was bad and the ride uncomfortably bumpy, and so the prime minister was tired. Nien had been asked to meet with me and hear me out.

We spoke in Vietnamese. After a while, I asked what he thought of the proposal to have an interim United Nations administration take power in Cambodia to end the fighting among all factions.

Nien immediately sat up straight, looked me directly in the eyes, and said: "Yes, we have heard of that. But we don't know who is behind the idea and what their secret agenda is."

I said: "Well, you may not believe it, but you are looking at the person who came up with the idea."

He was visibly surprised and skeptical. I then described in detail my thinking, the Council on Foreign Relations and its study group, my friendship with General Vessey (whom he knew), Congressman Solarz liking my suggestion, and my private meeting with Larry Eagleburger.

With a bit of well-intentioned exaggeration, I lowered my head a bit and said with some emotion that I had expressly taken Vietnam's interest into consideration in coming up with an innovative solution to ending a war. I noted that my wife was Vietnamese and that I had come to Hanoi offering my good offices in bringing Vietnamese together to seek greater national concord.

I also explained the law of trusteeship, with its fiduciary duties of loyalty and due care to those who are to benefit from the trust—a practice that had been unknown in Chinese and Vietnam law and history. In this case, the Cambodian people were to be the beneficiaries of government power and authority.

I said that Hanoi's problem was how to get out of a war it did not need—and that was getting in the way of economic development and better relations with the United States—without losing to China. If a UN trusteeship were established in Cambodia, Hanoi could say to the Vietnamese people and to the world that it had successfully stopped Beijing from taking over Cambodia.

He was thoughtful, nodding in agreement, and relaxed. He concluded our chat and warmly walked me to the car, which took me back to my hotel.

Later, the Hanoi government accepted the trusteeship proposal. And then so did the Chinese. The UN secretary-general and his staff happily accepted the challenge of organizing an interim trust administration for Cambodia. An international conference was held in Paris in 1991, and the United Nations Interim Administration was established.

The Killing Fields came to an end. The Khmer people began to recover their self-confidence, overcome their post-traumatic stress disorders, restore their Buddhist religion, and rebuild their culture and economy.

Stephen B. Young

ENDNOTES

CHAPTER 1

1. This letter was written for President Eisenhower by Kenneth T. Young Jr., director of Southeast Asian affairs in the Department of State and my father; Foreign Relations of the United States, 1952-1954, Indochina, Volume XIII, Part 2, Presidential Correspondence, Lot 66 D 204.

2. Truong Nhu Tang, *A Vietcong Memoir* (New York: Harcourt Brace Jovanovich, 1985)

3. Nguyen Trai, *Gia Huan Ca*; Huynh Sanh Thong, ed., *The Heritage of Vietnamese Poetry* (New Haven, CT: Yale University Press, 1979)

4. Nguyen Ngoc Huy, Ta Van Tai, and Tran Van Liem, *The Le Code* (Athens, OH: Ohio University Press, 1987)

5. Nguyen Du, *The Tale of Kieu*, trans. Huynh Sanh Thong (New Haven, CT: Yale University Press, 1983)

6. Quang Minh, *Dai-Viet Quoc-Dan Dang* (Westminster, CA: Van Nghe, 2001)

7. Ibid., 350–362

8. Ibid., 357

9. Nguyen Ngoc Huy, conversation with author, 1975

10. Kenneth Todd Young Jr., *The Southeast Asia Crisis* (Dobbs Ferry: Oceana, 1966) 112, 113; conversation with author, 1966

11. Jeffrey Race, *War Comes to Long An* (Berkeley: University of California Press, 1972), 83

12. Military History Institute of Vietnam, *Victory in Vietnam*, trans. Merle L. Pribbenow (Lawrence: University Press of Kansas, 2002), 47, 48

13. Ibid., 50

14. Ibid.

15. Agreement on the Cessation of Hostilities in Viet-Nam, July 20, 1954, Avalon Law Archive, https://avalon.law.yale.edu/20th_century/inch001.asp

16. Military History Institute of Vietnam, *Victory in Vietnam*, 62

17. Ibid., 73

18. Nguyen Thi Lien Hang, *Hanoi's War* (Chapel Hill: University of North Carolina Press, 2012)

19. Van Kien Dang and Toan Tap, Collected Party Documents, ed. Trinh Nhu, vol. 21 (Hanoi: National Political Publishing House [Nha Xuat Ban Chinh Tri Quoc Gia], 2002); Merle L. Pribbenow, translator; translation provided to author by George Veith

20. Military History Institute of Vietnam, "History of the Vietnamese People's Resistance War against the Americans to Save the Nation" (unpublished manuscript, 1987), copy presented to PAVN General Vo Nguyenj Giap, later given to author by PAVN Colonel Bui Tin, 28; Truong Nhu Tang, *A Vietcong Memoir*

21. Military History Institute of Vietnam, *Victory in Vietnam*, 68

22. Ibid.

23. Ibid., 76; 455, note 6

24. Nguyen Ngoc Huy, conversation with author, 1970

25. Military History Institute of Vietnam, "History of the Vietnamese," 125, 126

26. Pham Thai, member of the central leadership of the Dai Viet Party, conversation with author

27. Robert McNamara, *In Retrospect* (New York: Times, 1995), 112

28. George Veith, *Drawn Swords in a Distant Land* (New York: Encounter, 2021), 139

29. Ministry of Defense, Democratic Republic of Vietnam, Quan So MB Tang Cuong Cho Mien Nam, 19551975 [Number of Soldiers Sent from the North to the South 1955–1975]; provided to author by PAVN Colonel Bui Tin

30. John Hill Brinton, *Personal Memoirs of John H. Brinton, Major and Surgeon U.S.V., 1861–1865* (1914), 239. Statement to John Hill Brinton at the start of his Tennessee River Campaign, early 1862

31. Mark Bowden, *Hue 1968* (New York: Atlantic Monthly Press, 2017)

32. Stephen B. Young, *The Theory and Practice of Associative Power: CORDS in the Villages of Vietnam 1967–1972* (Lanham, MD: Hamilton, 2017)

CHAPTER 2

1. Dang Thi Hoai, *Vietnamese United States Negotiations During the Vietnam War (1965-1968)* dissertation, Ludwig Maximilian, University of Munich; https://edoc.ub.uni-muenchen.de/22796/1/Dang_Hoai_Thi.pdf; Kissinger, *White House Years*, 52

2. Henry Kissinger, *White House Years* (Boston: Little, Brown, 1979), 277

3. Henry Kissinger, "The Viet Nam Negotiations," *Foreign Affairs*, January 1969

4. Kissinger, *White House Years*, 274, 276

5. Thurston Clarke, *Honorable Exit* (New York: Doubleday, 2019), 97

6. Kissinger, *White House Years*, 284

7. Ibid., 286

8. Joseph Buttinger, *The Smaller Dragon* (New York: Praeger, 1958)

9. Alexandre de Rhodes, *Cathechismus* (Saigon: Tinh Viet, 1961)

10. My instructor in geomancy was Duong Thai Ban. I also read the manual of Ta Ao. Ban also taught me how to cast the *I Ching*. I studied face reading with Dien and read the popular books of Vu Tai Luc on how to learn a person's character as revealed by the arrangement of his or her facial features.

11. Nguyen Ngoc Huy, Ta Van Tai, and Tran Van Liem, *The Le Code*

12. Nguyen Trai, *Gia Huan Ca*

13. Stephen B. Young, "The Law of Property and Elite Privileges under Vietnam's Le Dynasty, 1428–1788," *Journal of Asian History* 10 (1975): 1–48

14. Gerald Hickey, *Village in Vietnam* (New Haven, CT: Yale University Press, 1964); Pham Tuong and Viet Hoang, *Nguon Coi Van Hoa Than Minh Dai Viet* (Ho Chi Minh City: Van Nghe, 2006); Le Quang Liem, *Phat Giao Hoa Hao Yeu Luoc* (Hoa Hao, 2003); Do Van Ly, *Tiem Hieu Dao Cao Dai* (Perris, CA: Cao Dai, Hai Ngoai, 1989); Nguyen Dang Thuc, *Tu Tuong Viet Nam* (Saigon: Khai Tri, 1964); Kim Dinh, *Viet Ly To Nguyen* (Saigon: An Tiem, 1978); Nguyen Thuy and Tran Minh Xuan, *Tinh Than Viet Nam* (San Jose, CA: Mekong-Tynan, 1992); Kim Dinh, *Triet Ly Cai Dinh* (Saigon: Nguon Sang, 1971)

15. Phan Huy Chu, *Lich Trieu Hien Chuong Loai Chi* (Hanoi: Khoa Hoc Xa Hoi, 1992)

16. P. Philaster, *Le Code Annamite*, (Paris: Ernest Leroux, 1909)

17. J. L. De Lanessan, *L'Indo-Chine française* (Paris: Felix Alcan, 1889)

18. Phan Boi Chau, *Chu Dich Thuong Kinh*, (Saigon; Khai Tri 1969); a study of the hexagrams in the *Yijing*

19. Georges Coulet, *Cultes et religions de l'Indochine annamite* (Saigon: C. Ardin, 1929); see also Édouard Jacques Joseph Diquet, *Les Annamites: société, coutumes, religions* (Paris: A. Challamel, 1906); Édouard Jacques Joseph Diquet, *Annam et Indo-Chine française* (Paris: A. Challamel, 1908)

20. Coulet, *Cultes et religions*, 63–65

21. John McAlister and Paul Mus, *The Vietnamese and Their Revolution* (New York: Harper & Row, 1970), 116

22. Jean Lacouture, *Ho Chi Minh* (New York: Random House, 1968), 119

23. Ibid., 122

24. Jean Lacouture, *Vietnam: Between Two Truces* (New York: Random House, 1966), 38

25. Duong Thu Huong, *The Zenith*, trans. Stephen B. Young and Hoa Young (New York: Penguin, 2012)

26. To Huu obituary, *Telegraph*, December 19, 2002, www.telegraph. co.uk/news/obituaries/1416538/To-Huu.html

27. Frantz Fanon, *The Wretched of the Earth* (New York: Grove, 1963), 21, 218, 223

28. McAlister and Mus, *The Vietnamese*, 112

29. Ibid., 1

30. Jean Sainteny, *Ho Chi Minh and His Vietnam* (Chicago: Cowles, 1970), 43; Jean Sainteny, *Histoire d'une paix manquée* (Paris: Amiot-Dumont, 1953)

31. Archimedes Patti, *Why Vietnam?* (Berkeley: University of California Press, 1980), 152

32. Author conversation in 1983 with Robert Maynard (who worked with Patti in Kunming in 1945), 1983

33. Studies in Intelligence 62, no. 2 (June 2018); Patti, *Why Vietnam?*; William Duiker, Ho Chi Minh (New York: Hyperion, 2000)

34. Sainteny, *Ho Chi Minh,* 47

35. Duiker, *Ho Chi Minh*, 301

36. Ibid.

37. Ibid., 372

38. "Truong Chinh," Wikipedia, accessed July 15, 2022, https://vi.wikipedia.org/wiki/Truong_Chinh; see also Huong, *The Zenith*

39. Sainteny, *Ho Chi Minh*, 48; Patti, *Why Vietnam?*, 209

40. Patti, *Why Vietnam?*, 370–374

41. Sainteny, *Ho Chi Minh*

42. Sainteny, *Ho Chi Minh,* 50; Hoan Van Dao, *Viet Nam Quoc Dan Dang: Lich Su Dau Tranh Can-Dai* (Saigon: Giang Dong, 1957)

43. Sainteny, *Ho Chi Minh,* 56

44. Duiker, *Ho Chi Minh*, 353

45. Sainteny, *Ho Chi Minh,* 52

46. Lacouture, *Ho Chi Minh*, 118

47. Ibid.

48. McAlister and Mus, *The Vietnamese,* 278; Bernard Fall, *Ho Chi Minh on Revolution* (New York: Praeger, 1967), 56

49. Sainteny, *Ho Chi Minh*, 57

50. Le Duan, *This Nation and Socialism Are One* (Chicago: Vanguard , 1976), 165

51. Ibid., 19

52. Quang Minh, *Dai-Viet,* 350

53. Duc Huynh Giao Chu, *Sam Giang Thi Van* (Saigon: Hoa Hao Buddhist Association Committee on Spreading the Teachings, 1965), 467–472

54. 1947 documents from French security service given to author by Nguyen The Anh

55. Hoang Van Dao, *Viet-Nam Quoc Dan Dang* (Saigon: Thuy Phuong, 1964); Bui Diem, *In the Jaws of History* (Boston: Houghton Mifflin, 1987), chap. 7

56. McAlister and Mus, *The Vietnamese,* 76

57. John Hall Stewart, *A Documentary Survey of the French Revolution* (Toronto: Macmillan, 1969), 528

58. McAlister and Mus, *The Vietnamese*; see also Paul Mus, *Viet-Nam: Sociologie d'une guerre* (Paris: Editions du Seuil, 1952)

59. Ibid., 1, 2, 31

60. Ibid., 89

61. Ibid., 49

62. Ibid., 64

63. George Kahin and John Lewis, *The United States in Vietnam* (New York: Dial, 1967), 114; quoting Lacouture in *Le Monde*, April 15, 1965; Lacouture, *Vietnam,* 54, 55

64. Philippe Devillers, "The Struggle for the Unification of Vietnam," *The China Quarterly*, Jan-March 1962; George Chaffard, *Indochine:dix ans de'independence*, (Paris: Calmann-Levy, 1964)

65. Truong Nhu Tang, *A Vietcong Memoir*

66. Lacouture, *Vietnam: Between Two Truces,* 58

67. Bernard Fall, *The Two Vietnams* (New York: Prager, 1963), 357

68. Neil Sheehan, "Not a Dove but No Longer a Hawk," *New York Times,* October 9, 1966

69. Hans Morgenthau, *Vietnam and the United States* (Washington, DC: Public Affairs, 1965), 14, 40

70. Ibid., 44

71. Arthur Schlesinger, *The Bitter Heritage* (Boston: Houghton Mifflin, 1967), 17

72. Ibid., 31

73. Ibid., 34, 35

74. Howard Zinn, *Vietnam: The Logic of Withdrawal* (Boston: Beacon, 1967), 74

75. Ibid., 104

76. Frances FitzGerald, *Fire in the Lake* (New York: Vintage, 1972)

77. Ibid.

78. Ibid., 7

79. Ibid., 14, 15

80. Ibid., 48, 51

81. Ibid., 71

82. Ibid., 75

83. Ibid., 290

84. Ibid., 590

85. Kahin and Lewis, *The United States,* 114, 120

86. Robert Brown, Abraham Heschel, and Michael Novak, *Vietnam: Crisis of Conscience* (New York: Association, 1967)

87. Arthur Schlesinger, *Robert Kennedy and His Times* (New York: Ballentine, 1978), 788

88. Ibid., 793

89. Ibid., 824

90. Ibid., 829

91. Susan Sontag, *Styles of Radical Will* (New York: Bantam Doubleday Dell, 1978), 271

92. For antagonistic ideological dispositions among intellectuals, see Norman Mailer, "The White Negro," *DISSENT,* 1957; Students for a Democratic Society, "The Port Huron Statement" (1962), http://www2.iath.virginia.edu/sixties/HTML_docs/Resources/Primary/Manifestos/SDS_Port_Huron.html

93. Author's 1973 conversation with Prof. John Roche (former assistant to President Lyndon Johnson), conversation with author, 1973

CHAPTER 3

1. Kissinger, *White House Years*, 802

2. Edward C. Keefer, C. Geyer, and Douglas E. Selvage, eds., *Soviet-American Relations: The Détente Years, 1969–1972* (Washington, DC: US Government Printing Office, 2007), document 110, 258

3. Luu Van Loi and Nguyen Anh Vu, *Le Duc Tho—Kissinger Negotiations in Paris* (Hanoi: The Gioi, 1996), 165

4. Kissinger, *White House Years*, 515

5. Kissinger, "The Viet Nam Negotiations"

6. Ibid.

7. Ibid.

8. Kissinger, *White House Years*, 436, 437

9. Foreign Relations of the United States, 1969–1976, volume XIII, Soviet Union, October 1970–October 1971, document 90, January 9, 1971

10. Richard Nixon, "Address to the Nation on the Situation in East Asia," April 7, 1971, https://millercenter.org/the-presidency/presidential-speeches/april-7-1971-address-nation-situation-southeast-asia

11. E. Mabry Rogers and Stephen B. Young, "Public Office Is a Public Trust: A Suggestion That Impeachment for High Crimes and Misdemeanors Implies a Fiduciary Standard," *Georgetown Law Review* 63, no. 5 (May 1975): 1025–105

12. Richard Nixon and Henry Kissinger, "Richard Nixon and Henry A. Kissinger on 7 April 1971," conversation 001-010, Presidential Recordings Digital Edition, Nixon Telephone Tapes, 1971, ed. Ken Hughes, University of Virginia Press, Charlottesville, http://prde. upress.virginia.edu/conversations/4001626

13. Winston Lord, memorandum, Vietnam negotiations, April/June 2017, box 853, volume 7, folder 3, National Security Council Files, Nixon Presidential Library; Kissinger, *White House Years*, 1015

14. "Agreement on the Cessation of Hostilities in Viet-Nam," July 20,1954, Avalon Law Archive, https://avalon.law.yale.edu/20th_century/inch001.asp

15. Foreign Relations of the United States, 1969–1976, volume VII, Vietnam, July 1970–January 1972, document 180

16. Foreign Relations of the United States, 1969–1976, volume VII, Vietnam, July 1970–January 1972, document 184, April 17, 1971

17. Richard Nixon, Address to the Nation—Vietnam, May 14, 1969; https://www.nixonfoundation.org/2017/09/address-nation-vietnam-may-14-1969/

18. H. R. Haldeman, *The Haldeman Diaries* (New York; Putnam, 1994) 281

19. Foreign Relations of the United States, 1969–1976, volume VII, Vietnam, July 1970–January 1972, document 131, February 18, 1971

20. Foreign Relations of the United States, 1969–1976, volume VII, Vietnam, July 1970–January 1972, document 185, April 17, 1971

21. Foreign Relations of the United States, 1969–1976, volume VII, Vietnam, July 1970–January 1972, document 188, April 17, 1971

22. Foreign Relations of the United States, 1969–1976, volume VII, Vietnam, July 1970–January 1972, document 190, April 23, 1971

23. Foreign Relations of the United States, 1969–1976, volume VII, Vietnam, July 1970–January 1972, document 191, April 26, 1971

24. Foreign Relations of the United States, 1969–1976, volume VII, Vietnam, July 1970–January 1972, document 197, May 6, 1971

25. Foreign Relations of the United States, 1969–1976, volume VII, Vietnam, July 1970–January 1972, document 200, May 10, 1971

26. Foreign Relations of the United States, 1969–1976, volume VII, Vietnam, July 1970–January 1972, document 205, May 25, 1971

27. Memorandum of conversation, May 25, 1971, box 39, folder 1969–1977, Vietnam War, Secret Peace Talks "Mr. S," Kissinger-Scowcroft West Wing Office Files, Gerald R. Ford Presidential Library. I am grateful to Mr. Geir Gundersen, librarian at the Gerald R. Ford Presidential Library, for locating the file containing this memorandum.

28. Kissinger, *White House Years*, 277

29. "Vietnam Errors Our Own Doing, Kissinger Says," Associated Press, September 30, 2010

30. Luu Van Loi and Nguyen Anh Vu, *Le Duc Tho*, 241

31. Luke Nichter, *The Last Brahmin* (New Haven, CT: Yale University Press, 2020), 297

32. Ibid., 303

33. Document, box 1, Graham Martin, Saigon Embassy Files, Gerald R. Ford Presidential Library

34. Foreign Relations of the United States, 1969–1976, volume VII, Vietnam, July 1970–January 1972, document 185

35. "Richard Nixon and Henry A. Kissinger on 7 April 1971," conversation 001-010, Nixon Telephone Tapes

36. Saigon 0984, box 1, folder Saigon to Washington, 2, Graham Martin, Saigon Embassy Files, Gerald R. Ford Presidential Library

37. Saigon 0021, Saigon 0984, box 1, folder Saigon to Washington, 2, Graham Martin, Saigon Embassy Files, Gerald R. Ford Presidential Library

38. Lewis Sorley, *A Better War* (New York: Harcourt Brace Jovanovich, 1999), 350

39. Foreign Relations of the United States, 1969–1976, volume VII, Vietnam, July 1970–January 1972, document 206

40. Kissinger, "The Viet Nam Negotiations"

41. Memorandum of conversation, Foreign Relations of the United States, 1969–1976, volume VII, Vietnam, July 1970–January 1972, document 207

42. Luu Van Loi and Nguyen Anh Vu, *Le Duc Tho*, 172, 173, 191

43. Seymour Hersh, *The Price of Power* (New York: Summit, 1983), 429

44. Kissinger, *White House Years*, 1018

45. Ibid., 1019

46. Ibid., 1018

47. Kissinger, "The Viet Nam Negotiations"

48. Carl von Clausewitz, *On War*, trans. James John Graham (North Charleston, NC: Createspace, 2010), 15, 22, 23, 25, 92

49. Memorandum of meeting, June 3, 1971. Gerald R. Ford Library, Graham Martin, Saigon Embassy Files, Box 1, folder Saigon to Washington, 2

50. Kissinger, *White House Years*, 1314

51. Ellsworth Bunker, conversations with author

52. Military History Institute of Vietnam, *Victory in Vietnam*, 283

53. Le Duc Tho, *The Vietnam War*, 703; pre-publication copy in possession of author

54. Mao Zedong, *Quotations from Chairman Mao Tse-tun* (Peking: Foreign Languages Press, 1966), 61; Trich Loi Cua Mao Chu Tich (Beijing: Nha Zuat Ban Ngoai Van, 1967 - first edition.

55. Briefing book for Henry A. Kissinger's July 1971 trip, POLO I, box 850, National Security Council files, Richard Nixon Presidential Library

56. Foreign Relations of the United States, 1969–1976, Volume VII, Vietnam, July 1970–1972, document 231

57. Le Duc Tho, *The Vietnam War*, 703

58. Foreign Relations of the United States, 1969–1976, volume XVII, China, 1969–1972, document 140

59. Foreign Relations of the United States, 1969–1976, Volume E-13, Documents on China, 1969–1972, document 9

60. Melvin Laird, "Iraq: Learning the Lessons of Vietnam," *Foreign Affairs*, November/December 2005, https://www.foreignaffairs.com/articles/vietnam/2005-10-01/iraq-learning-lessons-vietnam

61. President Richard Nixon, conversation with author, 1985

CHAPTER 4

1. Young, *The Theory and Practice*
2. Laird, "Iraq: Learning the Lessons"
3. Foreign Relations of the United States, 1969–1970, volume VI Vietnam, document 38
4. Kissinger, *White House Years*, 262, 284, 1038
5. "Vietnam War U.S. Military Fatal Casualty Statistics," National Archives, https://www.archives.gov/research/military/vietnam-war/casualty-statistics; https://en.wikipedia.org/wiki/Vietnam_War_casualties
6. American War Library, https://www.americanwarlibrary.com/vietnam/vwatl.htm
7. Table given to author by PAVN colonel Bui Tin
8. von Clausewitz, *On War*
9. Mao Zedong, *On Guerrilla Warfare*, trans. Samuel B. Griffith II (Chicago: University of Illinois Press, 2000)
10. Pacification Attitude Analysis Survey (PAAS) results found in Ellsworth Bunker's files; author's notes; see also Ben Connable, *Embracing the Fog of War: Assessment and Metrics in Counterinsurgency* (Santa Monica, CA: RAND, 2012)
11. Military History Institute of Vietnam, "History of the Vietnamese People's Resistance War against the Americans to Save the Nation," 97
12. PAAS, June 1972
13. Howard Penniman, *Elections in South Vietnam* (Washington, DC: American Enterprise Institute for Public Policy Research, 1972)
14. Douglas Pike, ed., *The Bunker Paper* (Berkeley: Institute of East Asian Studies, University of California Berkeley, 1990)
15. "Rice Production in Vietnam," https://en.wikipedia.org/wiki/Rice_production_in_Vietnam
16. James Tyson, "Land Reform in Vietnam: A Progress Report," *Asian Affairs* 1, no. 1 (1973): 32–411
17. Pike, *The Bunker Papers*

18. Ibid.

19. Youngmin Kim, "The South Vietnamese Economy during the Vietnam War, 1954–1975," December 2007, III.I.2, *On Education*, https://www.zum.de/whkmla/sp/0708/ym/ym1.html#III12

20. Nguyen Ngoc Huy, interview with author, 1976

21. Nguyen Ngoc Huy, interview with author, 1978

CHAPTER 5

1. Bunker files; author's interview transcripts

2. Memorandum in Bunker files; author's interview transcripts

3. Bunker files; author's interview transcripts

4. Former PAVN colonel Bui Tin, interview with author

5. Kissinger, *White House Years*, 277, 278

6. Foreign Relations of the United States, volume VI, Vietnam, 1969–1970, document 103

7. Ibid., document 106

8. Ibid., document 166

9. Ibid., document 190

10. Ibid., document 191

11. Ibid., document 192

12. Luu Van Loi and Nguyen Anh Vu, *Le Duc Tho*, 123

13. Foreign Relations of the United States, volume VI, Vietnam, 1969–1970, document 200

14. Foreign Relations of the United States, volume VI, Vietnam, 1969–1970, document 198

15. Luu Van Loi and Nguyen Anh Vu, *Le Duc Tho*, 132

16. Bunker files; author's interview transcripts

17. Bunker files; author's interview transcripts

18. Foreign Relations of the United States, volume VII, Vietnam, document 223; Luu Van Loi and Nguyen Anh Vu, *Le Duc Tho*, 178; Kissinger, *White House Years*, 1022

19. Bunker files; author interview

20. Foreign Relations of the United States, 1969–1976, Volume VII, Vietnam, July 1970–January 1972, document 245; Luu van Loi and Nguyen Anh Vu, Le Duc Tho, 203, 204

21. Foreign Relations of the United States, volume VII, Vietnam, July 1970–January 1972, document 245

22. Ibid., 254

23. Memorandum of Brigadier General A. M. Haig to Henry Kissinger re: meeting with President Thieu, September 23, 1971; Bunker files, Graham Martin Files, Gerald R. Ford Presidential Library; see also Foreign Relations of the United States, volume VII, Vietnam, July 1970–January 1972, document 268

24. Luu Van Loi and Nguyen Anh Vu, *Le Duc Tho*, 181; Le Duan, *This Nation*

25. Gareth Porter, "Hanoi's Strategic Perspective and the Sino-Vietnamese Conflict," *Pacific Affairs* 57, no. 1 (spring 1984): 7–25

26. Ellsworth Bunker, interview with author

27. Nguyen Van Thieu letter, Bunker files, Graham Martin Files, Gerald R. Ford Presidential Library

28. Anthony Lewis, "At Home Abroad," *New York Times*, April 8, 1972

CHAPTER 6

1. Military History Institute of Vietnam, "History of the Vietnamese," 283; Ngo Quang Truong, *The Easter Offensive of 1972* (Washington, DC: US Army Center of Military History, 1980)

2. Luu Van Loi and Nguyen Anh Vu, *Le Duc Tho*, 239

3. Ibid., 241

4. Ibid., 303

5. Foreign Relations of the United States, volume VIII, Vietnam, 1969–1976, document 209

6. Ibid., document 216

7. Bunker files; author notes. Many originals from the Bunker files are now housed at the Gerald R. Ford Presidential Library in the Graham Martin Files, Vietnam Negotiations, boxes 1–9.

8. Foreign Relations of the United States, volume VIII, Vietnam, 1969–1976, documents 225, 251

9. Ibid., document 224

10. "Richard Nixon and Henry A. Kissinger on 3 August 1972," Conversation 760-006 (PRDE Excerpt A), Presidential Recordings Digital Edition [Fatal Politics, ed. Ken Hughes] (Charlottesville: University of Virginia Press, 2014–), http://prde.upress.virginia.edu/conversations/4006748

11. Ibid., document 243

12. Ibid., document 245

13. Nguyen Phu Duc, "The Vietnam War," 709

14. Foreign Relations of the United States, volume VIII, Vietnam, 1969–1976 245

15. Ibid.

16. Bunker files; author notes

17. Nguyen Phu Duc, "The Vietnam War," 711

18. Foreign Relations of the United States, volume VIII, Vietnam, 1969–1976, document 248

19. Ibid., document 250

20. Ibid., document 254

21. Ibid., document 258

22. Bunker files; author notes

23. Bunker files; author notes; Foreign Relations of the United States, volume VIII, Vietnam, 1969–1976, document 263

24. Ibid., document 267

25. Bunker files; author notes

26. Foreign Relations of the United States, volume VIII, Vietnam, 1969–1976, document 275

27. Ibid., document 271

28. Ibid., document 276

29. Ibid., document 277; Bunker files; author notes

30. *Meinhard v. Salmon*, 249 N.Y. 458; 164 N.E. 545

31. Foreign Relations of the United States, volume VIII, Vietnam, 1969–1976, document 270

32. Ibid.

33. Ibid., document 269

34. Nguyen Tien Hung and Jerrold L. Schecter, *The Palace File: The Remarkable Story of the Secret Letters from Nixon and Ford to the President of South Vietnam and the American Promises That Were Never Kept* (New York: Harper & Row, 1986), 91

35. Bunker files; author notes, document 283

36. Luu Van Loi and Nguyen Anh Vu, *Le Duc Tho*, 303

37. Ibid.

38. Letters from President Nixon to President Thieu are copied in Nguyen and Schecter, *The Palace File.*

39. Foreign Relations of the United States, volume VIII, Vietnam, 1969–1976, document 281

40. Ibid., document 283

41. Foreign Relations of the United States, volume IX, Vietnam, 1969–1976, document 1

42. Ibid., document 3

43. Ibid.

44. Ibid., document 5

45. Ibid., document 3

46. Ibid., document 9

47. Ibid., document 8

48. Luu Van Loi and Nguyen Anh Vu, *Le Duc Tho*, 373

49. Foreign Relations of the United States, volume IX, Vietnam, 1969–1976, document 13

50. Bunker files; Ellsworth Bunker, interview with author

51. Foreign Relations of the United States, volume IX, Vietnam, 1969–1976, document 16

52. Ibid., document 24

53. Richard Nixon, *The Memoirs of Richard Nixon, vol. 2* (New York: Warner , 1978), 188

CHAPTER 7

1. The events discussed in this chapter are also covered in Larry Berman's book *No Peace, No Honor: Nixon, Kissinger and Betrayal in Vietnam* (New York: Free Press, 2001) and Robert K. Brigham's book *Reckless: Henry Kissinger and the Tragedy of Vietnam* (New York: Public Affairs, 2018)

2. Bunker files; author notes

3. Nguyen Phu Duc, "The Vietnam War," 720

4. See, generally, Kissinger, *White House Years*; Loi and Vu, *Le Duc Tho.*

5. Author notes

6. Foreign Relations of the United States, vol. IX, Vietnam 1969–1976, document 27

7. Ibid.

8. Nixon, *The Memoirs*, 197

9. Foreign Relations of the United States, vol. IX, Vietnam 1969–1976, document 27

10. Ibid., document 32

11. Ibid.

12. Ibid., document 32; Duc, "The Vietnam War," 721–723; Bunker files; author notes

13. Foreign Relations of the United States, vol. IX, Vietnam 1969–1976, document 36

14. Bunker files; author notes

15. Nguyen Phu Duc, "The Vietnam War," 722, 723

16. Bunker files; author notes

17. Ibid.

18. Foreign Relations of the United States, vol. IX, Vietnam 1969–1976, document 34

19. Nguyen Phu Duc, "The Vietnam War," 725; Foreign Relations of the United States, vol. IX, Vietnam 1969–1976, document 42

20. Foreign Relations of the United States, vol. IX, Vietnam 1969–1976, document 42

21. Ibid., document 33

22. Ibid., document 39

23. Ibid., document 49

24. Ibid., document 41; Bunker files, author notes

25. Ibid., document 43

26. Nguyen and Schecter, *The Palace File*, 104–105

27. Bunker files; author notes; Foreign Relations of the United States, vol. IX, Vietnam 1969–1976, document 58

28. Foreign Relations of the United States, vol. IX, Vietnam 1969–1976, document 50

29. Ibid., document 57

30. Ibid., document 53

31. Ibid.,document 44

32. Ibid., document 57

33. Ibid., document 70

34. Alexander Haig, *Inner Circles* (New York: Grand Central, 1992), 302

35. Nixon, *The Memoirs*, 705

36. Foreign Relations of the United States, 1969-1976, Vietnam, Vol IX, document 77

37. Bunker files; author notes

38. Foreign Relations of the United States, 1969-1976, Vietnam, Vol IX, documents 84 and 79

39. Foreign Relations of the United States, 1969-1976, Vietnam, Vol IX, document 84

40. Ibid., document 94

41. Ibid., document 96

42. Ibid., document 99; Bunker files; author notes

43. Ibid., document 100; Bunker files, author notes

44. Ibid., document 105

45. Nguyen and Schecter, *The Palace File*, 385

46. Ibid., document 245

47. Ibid., document 120

48. Ibid, document 121

49. Bunker files; author notes

50. Foreign Relations of the United States, vol. IX, Vietnam 1969–1976, documents 118, 122

51. Ibid., document 123

52. Ibid., document 124

53. Ibid., document 125

54. Bunker files; author notes

55. H. R. Haldeman, *The Haldeman Diaries*, 543; Foreign Relations of the United States, vol. IX, Vietnam 1969–1976, document 131

56. Nguyen and Schecter, *The Palace File*, 136

57. Haldeman, *The Haldeman Diaries,* 346

58. Foreign Relations of the United States, vol. IX, Vietnam 1969–1976, document 132

59. Ibid., document 133

60. Ibid., document 135

61. Luu Van Loi and Nguyen Anh Vu, *Le Duc Tho*, 387

62. Foreign Relations of the United States, 1969-1976, Vietnam, Vol IX, Doc 144

63. Ibid., document 145

64. Ibid., document 147

65. Ibid., document 148

66. Ibid., document 165

67. Bunker files; author notes

68. Foreign Relations of the United States, vol. IX, Vietnam 1969–1976, document 163

69. Ibid., documents 159, 161

70. Ibid., document 166

71. Forcign Rclations of thc Unitcd Statcs, vol. IX, Victnam 1969–1976, document 170

72. William Butler Yeats, "The Second Coming"
73. Foreign Relations of the United States, vol. IX, Vietnam 1969–1976, document 167
74. Ibid., document 171
75. Ibid., document 175
76. Bunker files; author notes
77. Ibid.
78. Foreign Relations of the United States, vol. IX, Vietnam 1969–1976, document 175
79. Henry Kissinger, *Leadership* (New York: Penguin Press, 2022), 162
80. Foreign Relations of the United States, vol. IX, Vietnam 1969–1976, document 179
81. Ibid., document 209
82. Ibid., documents 197 and 189
83. Ibid., document 220
84. Bunker files; author notes
85. Foreign Relations of the United States, vol. IX, Vietnam 1969–1976, document 248
86. Ibid., document 252
87. Ibid., document 254
88. Ibid., document 278
89. Ibid., document 289
90. "Harold MacMillan," Wikipedia, https://en.wikiquote.org/wiki/Harold_Macmillan
91. Foreign Relations of the United States, vol. IX, Vietnam 1969–1976, document 285
92. Ibid., documents 280, 289
93. Vietnam War, Secret Peace Talks "Mr. S," 1969–1972, box 39, 1, Kissinger-Scowcroft West Wing Office Files, Gerald R. Ford Presidential Library.
94. Text of letter in Nguyen and Schecter, *The Palace File*, 393
95. Foreign Relations of the United States, vol. IX, Vietnam 1969–1976, document 292

96. Ibid., document 310

97. Ibid., document 311

98. Ibid., document 313

99. Bunker files; author notes

100. Foreign Relations of the United States, 1969-1976, Vietnam, Vol IX, Doc 320

101. Ibid.

CHAPTER 8

1. Van Tien Dung, *Our Great Spring Victory* (New York: Monthly Review Press, 1977), 7; see also George J. Veith, *Black April* (New York: Encounter, 2013); Merle L. Pribbenow, "North Vietnam's Final Offensive: Strategic Endgame Nonpareil," Parameters 29, no. 4 (1999), https://press.armywarcollege.edu/parameters/vol29/iss4/5

2. Le Duan, *This Nation*, 58; see also Le Duan, *Selected Writings* (Hanoi: Foreign Languages Publishing House, 1977)

3. Le Duan, *This Nation*, 61, 63, 64

4. Ibid., 65

5. Ibid., 55

6. Ibid., 71

7. Ibid., 91

8. Ibid., 20, 29

9. Ibid., 21, 30

10. Nguyen Thi Lien Hang, *Hanoi's War*

11. "Agreement on Ending the War and Restoring Peace in Viet-Nam. Signed at Paris on 27 January 1973," United Nations, vol. 935-1-13295, https://treaties.un.org/doc/Publication/UNTS/Volume%20935/volume-935-I-13295-English.pdf

12. William E. Le Gro, *Vietnam from Cease-Fire to Capitulation* (Washington, DC: US Army Center of Military History, 1981)

13. Ibid.

14. Ibid., 34; Nguyen Phu Duc, "The Vietnam War," 788

15. *"Quan So MB Tang Cuong cho Mien Nam,"* Ministry of Defense, Democratic Republic of Vietnam

16. Cao Van Vien, *The Final Collapse* (Washington, DC: US Army Center of Military History, 1983), 35

17. Ibid., 39

18. Van Tien Dung, *Our Great Spring*, 13, 14

19. Stephen Hosmer, Konrad Kellen, and Brian Jenkins, *The Fall of South Vietnam* (Santa Monica, CA: RAND, 1978), 63; US government analysis, February 24, 1975

20. Hosmer, Kellen, and Jenkins, *The Fall*, 63

21. Ibid; Van Tien Dung, *Our Great Spring*

22. Van Tien Dung, *Our Great Spring*

23. Henry Kissinger, *Years of Upheaval* (New York: Little, Brown, 1982), 370

24. Flora Lewis, "Tho Rejects Nobel Prize, Citing Vietnam Situation," *New York Times*, https://www.nytimes.com/1973/10/24/archives/tho-rejects-nobel-prize-citing-vietnam-situation-careful-decision.html

25. "Presentation Speech by Mrs. Aase Lionaes, Chairman of the Nobel Committee of the Norwegian Storting," https://www.nobelprize.org/prizes/peace/1973/ceremony-speech/

26. Van Tien Dung, *Our Great Spring*, 10

27. Ibid., 11

28. Ibid., 18

29. Ibid., 20

30. Frances FitzGerald, "Journey to North Vietnam", *The New Yorker*, April 28, 1975; see also Clarke, *Honorable Exit*, 15

31. Van Tien Dung, *Our Great Spring*, 20

32. Le Gro, *Vietnam from Cease-Fire*, chapter 8

33. Ibid., 88

34. Hosmer, Kellen, and Jenkins, *The Fall*, 68, 69; Le Gro, *Vietnam from Cease-Fire*, 85

35. Le Gro, *Vietnam from Cease-Fire*, 86

36. John W. Finney, "Nixon Asks $2.2-Billion in Emergency Aid for Israel," *New York Times*, October 20, 1973, https://www.nytimes.com/1973/10/20/archives/nixon-asks-2.2billion-in-emergency-aid-for-israel.html

37. Cao Van Vien, *The Final Collapse*, 67

38. Van Tien Dung, *Our Great Spring*, 21

39. Ibid., 23

40. Ibid., 24

41. Veith, *Black April*, 120

42. Le Gro, *Vietnam from Cease-Fire*, 138; "Text of U.S. Note on Vietnam Conflict," *New York Times*, January 14, 1975, https://www.nytimes.com/1975/01/14/archives/text-of-us-note-on-vietnam-conflict.html

43. Le Gro, *Vietnam from Cease-Fire*, 139

44. Ibid., 144

45. Van Tien Dung, *Our Great Spring*, 43–45

46. Ibid., 33

47. Ibid., 28

48. Ibid., 41

49. Ibid., 44

50. Ibid., 63

51. General Ngo Quang Truong, interview with author, 1988

52. Ngo Quang Truong, "Why I Abandoned I Corps," Doi (*Life*) October 1982; cited by Veith, *Black April*, 279

53. Tran Van Don, *Our Endless War* (San Rafael, CA: Presidio, 1978), 231

54. Hosmer, Kellen, and Jenkins, *The Fall*, 51

55. Tran Van Don, *Our Endless War*, 245

56. Cao Van Vien, *The Final Collapse*, 95

57. Military History Institute of Vietnam, *Victory in Vietnam*, 375

58. Edward J. Lee, *Nixon, Ford, and the Abandonment of South Vietnam* (Jefferson, NC: McFarland & Co., 2002), 91; Hosmer, Kellen, and Jenkins, *The Fall*, 89

59. Veith, *Black April*, 172, 278

60. Hosmer, Kellen, and Jenkins, *The Fall*, 25

61. Ibid., chapters 3 and 4

62. Veith, *Black April*, 310

63. Ibid., 309

64. Le Gro, *Vietnam from Cease-Fire*, 170

65. Veith, *Black April*, 311

66. Frank Snepp, *Decent Interval* (New York: Vintage, 1978), 295

67. Military History Institute of Vietnam, *Victory in Vietnam*, 397; Veith, *Black April*, 358

68. Military History Institute of Vietnam, *Victory in Vietnam*, 398

69. Le Gro, *Vietnam from Cease-Fire*, 170

70. Clarke, *Honorable Exit*, 48

71. Van Tien Dung, *Our Great Spring*, 129

72. Ibid., 158

73. Veith, *Black April*, 360

74. Le Gro, *Vietnam from Cease-Fire*, 171

75. Veith, Black April, 380

76. Military History Institute of Vietnam, *Victory in Vietnam*, 401

77. Le Gro, *Vietnam from Cease-Fire*, 173

78. Van Tien Dung, *Our Great Spring*, 182, 184

79. Ibid., 197

80. Ibid., 172

81. Ibid., 190, 191

82. Military History Institute of Vietnam, *Victory in Vietnam*, 411

83. Lam Quang Thi, *The Twenty-Five Year Century* (Denton, TX: University of North Texas Press, 2001), 382, 383; Clarke, *Honorable Exit*, 254

84. Cao Van Vien, *The Final Collapse*, 148

85. Veith, *Black April*, 480

86. Truong Nhu Tang, *A Vietcong Memoir*, 265

87. Truong Nhu Tang, "A New Look at the Old Enemy," *New York Times Magazine*, March 31, 1985; https://archive.nytimes.com/www.nytimes.com/library/world/asia/033185vietnam-enemy.html

88. "Anti-Social Personality Disorder," Mayo Clinic, https://www.mayoclinic.org/diseases-conditions/antisocial-personality-disorder/symptoms-causes/syc-20353928#:~:text=Overview,rights%20and%20feelings%20of%20others. Antisocial Personality Disorder (ASPD) is one of four cluster-B personality disorders within the *Diagnostic and Statistical Manual of Mental Disorders*, 5th Edition, which also includes narcissistic, borderline, and histrionic personality disorders.

89. Oriana Fallaci, *Interview with History* (Boston Houghton Mifflin Harcourt, 1976) 29, https://archive.org/stream/InterviewWithHistoryByOrianaFallaciInterviewArtEbook/Interview%20with%20History%20-%20by%20Oriana%20Fallaci%20(Interview%20Art%20Ebook)_djvu.t; Kissinger, *White House Years*, 1409, 1410

90. Kissinger, *Leadership*, 162

91. Laura Secor, "Henry Kissinger Is Worried About Disequilibrium," *Wall Street Journal*, August 12, 2022, https://www.wsj.com/articles/henry-kissinger-is-worried-about-disequilibrium-11660325251

AFTERWORD

1. Kissinger, *Leadership*, 162

POSTSCRIPT

1. U.S. Census Bureau American Community Survey: https://www.census.gov/programs-surveys/acs

2. Amy Budiman, "Cambodians in the U.S. Fact Sheet," Pew Research Center, https://www.pewresearch.org/social-trends/fact-sheet/asian-americans-cambodians-in-the-u-s/

DOCUMENTS

1. Edward C. Keefer, C. Geyer, and Douglas E. Selvage, eds., *Soviet-American Relations: The Détente Years*, 1969–1972 (Washington, DC: US Government Printing Office, 2007), document 110, 258

2. Foreign Relations of the United States, 1969–1976, volume XIII, Soviet Union, October 1970–October 1971, document 90, January 9, 1971

3. Memorandum of conversation, May 25, 1971, box 39, folder 1969–1977, Vietnam War, Secret Peace Talks "Mr. S," Kissinger-Scowcroft West Wing Office Files, Gerald R. Ford Presidential Library

4. Document, box 1, Graham Martin, Saigon Embassy Files, Gerald R. Ford Presidential Library

5. Briefing book for Henry A. Kissinger's July 1971 trip POLO I, box 850, National Security Council files, Richard Nixon Presidential Library

6. "Today in History: Operation Eagle Pull, 1975," Cambodia News English, https://cne.wtf/2020/04/12/today-in-history-operation-eagle-pull-1975

7. Letters in possession of author

8. *Wall Street Journal* letter to the editor about Vietnam, 1996

9. Henry A. Kissinger Papers, Part II (MS 1981), manuscripts and archives, Yale University Library, https://hdl.handle.net/10079/digcoll/558647

DOCUMENTS

THE WRITTEN EVIDENCE OF KISSINGER'S BETRAYAL

May 25, 1971, meeting between Kissinger and Anatoly Dobrynin

On January 9, 1971, Henry Kissinger met with Soviet Ambassador Anatoly Dobrynin.[1] During the meeting, Kissinger offered thoughts about how Hanoi might be left in a position to win the Vietnam War at the end of the day. Ambassador Dobrynin reported to his superiors in writing what he understood Kissinger to have said. For his part, Kissinger made a written report to his superior, President Nixon, of what he had told the Soviet diplomat. Kissinger's report to Nixon does not align with Dobrynin's report to Moscow of the same conversation.[2]

On January 9, 1971, Kissinger said to Dobrynin:

—*What if the U.S. were to commit to withdraw all of its troops by some absolutely specific deadline, of which they would inform the Vietnamese?*

—*At the same time, the Americans could refrain from demanding a reciprocal withdrawal of North Vietnamese troops from South Vietnam, since that would be clearly unacceptable to Hanoi, which has never acknowledged the presence of its troops there.*

It is important, however, that the North Vietnamese, for their part, then commit to a cease-fire for the period of the U.S. troop withdrawal plus at least some brief amount of time after the withdrawal.

Dobrynin reported:

Kissinger made a rather curious remark that ultimately it will no longer be their, the Americans', concern, but that of the Vietnamese themselves if some time after the U.S. troop withdrawal they start fighting with each other again.

Dobrynin quoted Kissinger saying:

The U.S. will deal with this matter, like the other great powers that have an interest in this region, but no longer as "a direct party to the Vietnam conflict."

On January 9, 1971, Kissinger reported to Nixon only:

We then turned to Vietnam. ... Dobrynin then said he wanted to ask me a hypothetical question. If Hanoi dropped its demands for a coalition government, would we be prepared to discuss withdrawal separately. I said as long as the matter was hypothetical, it was very hard to form a judgment, but I could imagine that the issue of withdrawals was a lot easier to deal with than the future composition of a government in South Vietnam. Indeed, if he remembered an article I had written in 1968, I had proposed exactly this procedure.

Dobrynin asked whether I still believed that this was a possible approach. I said it certainly was a possible approach and, indeed, I had been of the view that it would be the one that would speed up matters.

Dobrynin said he would report this to Moscow.

109. Memorandum of Conversation (U.S.)[1]

Washington, January 9, 1971,
10:30 a.m.–12:25 p.m.

The meeting took place at Dobrynin's invitation.[2] He had been called back to the Soviet Union unexpectedly for consultation only 24 hours after he had submitted to me the attached note on Berlin.[3] He delayed his departure for 24 hours so that he could see me.[4]

Dobrynin began the conversation by expressing his outrage over the behavior of the Jewish Defense League.[5] I told him that the President was unhappy about these actions; that we were seeking indictments where that was possible; and that we would use whatever Federal resources were available to increase the protection for Soviet installations.

Dobrynin said that what rankled most in the Soviet Union was the absence of any court action. It was inconceivable in the Soviet Union that such actions could take place without connivance by the authorities. While he was taking a slightly more tolerant view of that aspect of it, he was at one with his colleagues in his inability to understand why there had been no court action of any kind.

Dobrynin added that, in a synagogue in New York, right across the street from the Soviet Mission, a loudspeaker had been set up that was blaring obscene words at the Soviet Embassy every day. This was intolerable.

I repeated that we were taking the measures that were possible and expressed the personal regret of the President. I said there was no official connivance, but the overlapping of authority between Federal and State governments presented particular complications for us; however, we would seek court action wherever that was appropriate.

We then turned to substance. I told Dobrynin that I had an answer from the President to the Soviet note on Berlin—specifically, whether the President still stood by his conversation with Gromyko.[6] I said a lot depended, of course, on how one interpreted the President's conversation with Gromyko. In the sense that the President said that he would be well disposed towards the negotiations if they did not cut the umbilical cord between West Berlin and the Federal Republic, there was no problem. With respect to the Soviet proposal that the process be accelerated and that we review again the Soviet propositions, I said the following: I had reviewed the Soviet propositions and wanted to distinguish the formal from the substantive part. If the Soviet Union could give some content to the transit procedures and if the Soviet Union could find a way by which it could make itself responsible, together with the four allies, for access, we would, in turn, attempt to work out some approach which took cognizance of the concerns of the East German regime. I would be prepared, at the request of the President, to discuss this with him in substance, and if we could see an agreement was possible, we could then feed it into regular channels.

Dobrynin said that this was very important because Rush was clearly an obstacle to negotiations since he either didn't understand them or was too intransigent. I told him this was not an attempt to bypass Rush, but to see whether we could use our channel to speed up the procedure. I was prepared to have conversations with high German officials to find out exactly what they were prepared to settle for and then to include this in our discussions. Dobrynin said he would check this in Moscow and let me have an answer by the end of the week.

We then turned to SALT. I told Dobrynin that the President had decided the following: We were

[1] Source: National Archives, Nixon Presidential Materials, NSC Files, Box 490, President's Trip Files, Dobrynin/Kissinger, 1970, Vol. 4 [Pt. 2]. Top Secret; Sensitive. The meeting was held at the Soviet Embassy. The time of the meeting is taken from Kissinger's Record of Schedule. (Library of Congress, Manuscript Division, Kissinger Papers, Box 438, Miscellany, 1968–76)

[2] Kissinger and Dobrynin agreed on December 22, 1970, to meet at the Soviet Embassy on January 7, 1971; the meeting was subsequently postponed two days, presumably due to an extension of Kissinger's "working vacation" in California.

[3] See Document 108.

[4] Dobrynin called Kissinger in California at 12:05 p.m., PST, on January 7 both to report his recall to Moscow and to request a written reply to the Soviet note on Berlin. "I am a little reluctant to put it in writing," Kissinger replied, "because it depends on a number of explanations. But I wanted to make [a] very concrete proposal on how to proceed on the subject you made yesterday and another concrete proposal in another area." (National Archives, Nixon Presidential Materials, Henry Kissinger Telephone Conversation Transcripts, Box 27, Dobrynin File) Kissinger called Dobrynin back at 1:35 p.m. and added: "I wanted to mention one thing on a semi-personal basis. I think it would be very hard to be understood by the President if you were pulled out in light of the communication of yesterday without waiting for an answer." Dobrynin replied: "I understand and will check with Moscow." (Ibid.)

[5] On January 8, a bomb exploded near a Soviet cultural building in Washington, causing moderate damage. The Jewish Defense League, which had been linked to similar attacks on Soviet facilities in the United States, denied responsibility for the incident.

[6] October 22, 1970.

prepared to make an ABM agreement only, provided it was coupled with an undertaking to continue working on offensive limitations and provided it was coupled with an undertaking that there would be a freeze on new starts of offensive land-based missiles during the period of these negotiations. There might be some special provision that would have to be made for submarines, but we would have to leave this to detailed negotiations. I told Dobrynin that if he were prepared to proceed on this basis, I would be prepared to talk to him about it on behalf of the President. We could settle the basic issues in February. Prior to the resumption of the SALT talks there could be an exchange of letters or public statements between the President and the Chairman of the Council of Ministers. The SALT talks in Vienna could then concentrate on implementing the agreement in principle.

Dobrynin asked how I understood limitations on submarines to operate. I said I had no specific proposal to make, and I mentioned it only in case we wanted to raise it later so that he would not feel that he had been mistaken. I thought, however, that the question of equality was recognized in principle. Dobrynin said he would have an answer when he returned.

Dobrynin then raised the Middle East. He wanted to know whether the President was prepared to move that discussion into our channel also. I told him we would have to see how the Jarring negotiations went first. Secondly, we would have to then see whether the Four-Power forum might not be more appropriate. In any event, he could be sure that the President would take an interest in the negotiations and whomever he negotiated with would have Presidential backing.

Dobrynin then launched into his usual recitation of Mid-East events—how he had been misled by Sisco; how the Secretary of State had never told him the stand-still and the ceasefire were linked; how he Soviet Union could not be held responsible for a document that was handed to it after it had already been given to the Egyptians; and how, above all, the Soviet Union had never had a reply to its last note to Joe Sisco. He said if he talked to Sisco, it would be an endless series of legalistic hairsplittings that wouldn't lead anywhere. I told him that we would have to see what progress we were making on other matters before I could give him an answer.

We then turned to Vietnam. I said to Dobrynin that we had read Kosygin's interview with the Japanese newspaper with great interest.[7] We had noticed that Kosygin had listed the usual unacceptable Hanoi demands, but he had also indicated a Soviet willingness to engage itself in the process of a settlement. This was stated, it seemed to me, more emphatically than had been said in the past. Was I correct?

Dobrynin merely said that he noticed that sentence also. I asked whether the two statements were linked; in other words, whether the Soviet willingness to engage itself was linked to our prior acceptance of Hanoi's demands. Dobrynin then said he wanted to ask me a hypothetical question. If Hanoi dropped its demands for a coalition government, would we be prepared to discuss withdrawal separately. I said as long as the matter was hypothetical, it was very hard to form a judgment, but I could imagine that the issue of withdrawals was a lot easier to deal with than the future composition of a government in South Vietnam. Indeed, if he remembered an article I had written in 1968,[8] I had proposed exactly this procedure. Dobrynin asked whether I still believed that this was a possible approach. I said it certainly was a possible approach and, indeed, I had been of the view that it would be the one that would speed up matters. Dobrynin said he would report this to Moscow.

At the end of the meeting, Dobrynin gave me an art book with an inscription for my son, since he had read somewhere that my son was very interested in art.

110. Memorandum of Conversation (USSR)[1]

Washington, January 9, 1971.

Kissinger came to see me at our Embassy on January 9. He said he had flown in specially for one day from California on the instructions of President Nixon, who is there right now, to have

---

[7] *Asahi Shimbun* published its interview with Kosygin on January 2. For a condensed English text, see *Current Digest of the Soviet Press*, Vol. XXIII, No. 1 (February 2, 1971), pp. 7, 11.

[8] See footnote 5, Document 13.

[1] Source: AVP RF, f. 0129, op. 55a, p. 426, d. 1, l. 5–15. Top Secret. From Dobrynin's Journal.

May 25, 1971, meeting between
Kissinger and Jean Sainteny

The following document is the record of a luncheon meeting at the White House between Henry Kissinger and Jean Sainteny on May 25, 1971. The memorandum records that Sainteny opened his remarks by reporting on Hanoi's acceptance of Kissinger's January 9, 1971, proposal to Soviet Ambassador Dobrynin that the United States would not object to Hanoi leaving its army inside South Vietnam if Hanoi would give South Vietnam a few years of freedom and independence after the coming into force of a peace agreement.[3]

MEMORANDUM

THE WHITE HOUSE

WASHINGTON

TOP SECRET/SENSITIVE/EYES ONLY   May 25, 1971

MEMORANDUM OF CONVERSATION

PARTICIPANTS: Dr. Henry A. Kissinger
                                 M. and Mme. John Paul Sainteny
                                 Brig. General Alexander M. Haig
                                 W. Richard Smyser, NSC Staff
                                 Winston Lord, NSC Staff

PLACE: Dr. Kissinger's Office

TIME: Luncheon, May 25, 1971

Substantive portions of the luncheon conversation centered on Vietnam
and China. Following are the highlights of M. Sainteny's observations.

Vietnam

   M. Sainteny said that:

   -- Hanoi does not fully believe that the Americans will leave
      Vietnam. If they were assured of that and of a certain number
      of seats for the NLF in the Assembly, they would come to terms
      on POWs, ceasefire, and the separation of the two Vietnams for
      a number of years. (M. Sainteny actually was somewhat ambiguous
      about North Vietnamese political demands but appeared to suggest
      that Assembly representation might satisfy them for the time being
      anyway.)

   -- The NLF is really quite independent of North Vietnam and there
      could be significant differences between them. However, M. Sainteny
      thought Hanoi would be willing to deal with us without the NLF.

   -- The North Vietnamese are still determined to pursue their struggle
      although he sensed a certain degree of uncertainty. Le Duan is
      in charge, but he clearly does not have the authority of Ho Chi Minh.

TOP SECRET/SENSITIVE/EYES ONLY

400

May 25, 1971, message from Kissinger to Ambassador Ellsworth Bunker in Saigon

In this cable, written most likely after his meeting with Jean Sainteny, Kissinger indirectly and obliquely informs Ambassador Bunker that the United States will no longer demand that Hanoi withdraw its army from South Vietnam. Kissinger refers only to the requirement that "peoples of Indochina should discuss this question among themselves."[4]

TOP SECRET 250211Z MAY 71 SENSITIVE EYES ONLY VIA

BUNKER CHLS

FROM: HENRY A. KISSINGER

TO: AMBASSADOR BUNKER, SAIGON

CITE: WHS1047

REF: SAIGON 0270 DTG 171210Z APRIL 71

1. OTHER SIDE HAS AGREED TO MEET MAY 31 AFTER TAKING ALMOST THREE WEEKS TO RESPOND TO OUR MESSAGE.

2. BECAUSE WE CAN USE THE CHANNEL ONLY SPARINGLY THE PRESIDENT HAS DECIDED TO MOVE AHEAD IN THE FIRST MEETING ALONG THE LINES YOU SUGGESTED IN REFTEL FOR THE SECOND MEETING.

3. OUR PROPOSALS WILL ESSENTIALLY BE WHAT YOU SUGGESTED IN REFTEL WITH THE FOLLOWING DIFFERENCES:

-- ON YOUR PACKAGE'S I AND III WE WILL NOT OFFER SPECIFIC DATES IN OPENING STATEMENT, ALTHOUGH MAKING CLEAR OUR WILLINGNESS TO DO SO AS PART OF SETTLEMENT.

-- ON YOUR POINT VI WE WILL SAY THAT PEOPLES OF INDOCHINA SHOULD DISCUSS THIS QUESTION AMONG THEMSELVES BUT WE WILL NOT SET DATE.

4. ACCORDINGLY, I PLAN TO DO THE FOLLOWING:

Declassified
Photocopy from Gerald R. Ford Library

Kissinger's handwritten note
on wanting a "Decent Interval"

This document is a part of page 5 of the briefing book prepared for Kissinger for his July 1971 meeting with Chinese Premier Zhou Enlai. On the upper left, in the margin, Kissinger adds in his handwriting: "we want a decent interval." In the last sentence, he confirms that the United States will not object to a future Communist conquest of South Vietnam, speaking of the "Vietnamese people"—both North and South—as one nation.[5]

On behalf of President Nixon I want to assure the Prime Minister solemnly that the United States is prepared to make a settlement that will truly leave the political evolution of Vietnam to the Vietnamese alone.

We are ready to withdraw all of our forces by a fixed date and let objective realities shape the political future.

As the President has consistently declared, we believe the following principles should govern a fair political settlement in South Vietnam:

-- A political solution must reflect the will of the South Vietnamese people and allow them to determine their future without outside interference.

-- A fair political solution should reflect the existing relationship of political forces within South Vietnam.

-- We will abide by the outcome of the political process agreed upon.

But I must emphasize with equal seriousness that the United States will never agree to ~~predetermine the political future of~~ South Vietnam or make a dishonorable peace.

If the Vietnamese people themselves decide to change the present government, we shall accept ~~this~~. But we will not make that decision for them.

"I have committed this mistake of believing in you, the Americans."

In the early months of 1975 as Hanoi instructed its divisions in South Vietnam to go on the offensive, the Khmer Rouge in Cambodia similarly began a general offensive against the nationalist government in Phnom Penh. In April the United States abandoned its embassy in Phnom Penh and ended its efforts to support the Cambodian government against the Khmer Rouge. Just before Khmer Rouge forces established their control over Phnom Penh, Cambodia acting premier and later deputy prime minister Sisowath Sirik Matak wrote this letter of farewell to American ambassador John Gunther Dean.[6]

Phnom Penh April 16, 1975

Dear Excellency and Friend,

I thank you very sincerely for your letter and your offer to transport me towards freedom. I cannot, alas, leave in such a cowardly fashion. As for you, and in particular for your great country, I never believed for a moment that you would have this sentiment of abandoning a people, which has chosen liberty. You have refused us your protection, and we can do nothing about it. You leave, and my wish is that you and your country will find happiness under this sky. But, mark it well, that if I shall die here on the spot and in my country that I love, it is too bad, because we are all born and must die one day. I have committed this mistake of believing in you, the Americans."

Regards,
Sirik Matak

LETTERS FROM NIXON

The following two letters were sent to me by former President Nixon. The first refers to his 1985 book *No More Vietnams*.[7]

RICHARD NIXON

February 22, 1985

26 FEDERAL PLAZA
NEW YORK CITY

Dear Stephen:

Since April 30th will mark the tenth anniversary of the fall of Saigon, we shall probably be inundated in the weeks ahead with scores of books, columns, and television documentaries criticizing and lamenting the American role in Vietnam.

The enclosed book presents a different point of view. There can be an honest difference of opinion over whether we should have become involved in Vietnam and how the war was conducted. But after witnessing the reign of terror that has been imposed upon the people of Vietnam and Cambodia by the Communist regimes we opposed, fair-minded observers can reach only one conclusion: Whatever our mistakes, the United States tried and failed in a just cause in Vietnam.

As I put it in the last paragraph of this book, "'No more Vietnams' can mean that we should not <u>try</u> again. It <u>should</u> mean we must not <u>fail</u> again."

Sincerely,

Dean Stephen B. Young

Your advice was indispensable!

May 29, 1986

Dear Stephen,

    I never cease to marvel at your tenacity on
setting the record straight on Vietnam. No wonder
the <u>Times</u> refuses to print it. They can't bear
admitting that they might have been wrong in Vietnam
as they were with Castro and the Shah.

    With warm regards,

               Sincerely,

Dean Stephen B. Young
Hamline University School of Law
1536 Hewitt Avenue
St. Paul, Minnesota 55104

LETTERS TO THE EDITOR

A Response to Kissinger

On December 22, 1996, I read in the *Wall Street Journal* a Letter to the Editor from Henry Kissinger. In his letter, Kissinger provided a defense of his actions in seeking to end the Vietnam War. Since he had gone on record with his narrative of that history, and since I had knowledge of different facts from my working with the former ambassador to Saigon, Ellsworth Bunker, and from reading a book written by two North Vietnamese diplomats, I wrote my own Letter to the Editor (shown here) pointing out what I believed to be the truth about Kissinger's secret negotiations with the North Vietnamese Communists.[8]

Letters to the Editor

The Betrayal of South Vietnam

Henry Kissinger did not like television's recent portrayal of his efforts to negotiate an end to the Vietnam War (Letters to the Editor, Dec. 22). He was at emotional pain to portray himself as completely in step with the Vietnam policy of President Nixon. Yet the serious accusation made by the TV program about Mr. Kissinger's negotiation of the 1973 Paris Peace Accords was not his up-staging Nixon, but his betrayal of South Vietnam and the 58,000 American soldiers who had died to keep that small country free.

The peace agreement negotiated and fully accepted by Mr. Kissinger in October 1972 allowed North Vietnam to keep its army in the South. This provision, not agreed to in advance by Saigon's President Thieu, provided the U.S. with a decent interval before Hanoi's conquest of South Vietnam, but no peace with honor.

Mr. Kissinger's letter overlooked this criticism of his negotiating skills. He got off lightly in television's history of his ending of the Vietnam War. The truth is more condemning of his machinations. Once, as a colleague of the late Ellsworth Bunker, American ambassador in Saigon from 1967 to 1973, I had occasion to read all of Mr. Kissinger's secret correspondence to Bunker detailing Mr. Kissinger's negotiations with Hanoi. I had a proper security clearance and the documents were given to me by the State Department. A draft manuscript of Bunker's role in Vietnam was written, including the negotiations, and given clearance for publication by the State Department.

The still secret communications prove that Mr. Kissinger decided to let Hanoi leave its divisions inside South Vietnam in early May 1971, long before the climactic October 1972 negotiating sessions that produced the basic shape of the peace accords. Mr. Kissinger took his decision just after the May Day protests when Washington was inundated with demonstrators (many of whom were unconstitutionally arrested), the White House was surrounded by school buses as a barricade against the mob and Nixon's senior staff had lost its cool.

Previously, Mr. Kissinger's secret negotiations with Hanoi had achieved only impasse. Hanoi would not budge under his blandishments. He therefore asked Ambassador Bunker to propose a new approach to the negotiations. He wanted to try out ideas with Hanoi before discussing them with South Vietnam's President Thieu. One such proposal "modified" Bunker's requirement that North Vietnamese forces leave South Vietnam, Laos and Cambodia to prescribe only that the Indochinese countries discuss this topic among themselves. The U.S. would no longer insist on North Vietnamese withdrawal.

In his memoirs of 1979, Mr. Kissinger proudly wrote of his "modification" that: "We gave up the demand for mutual withdrawal . . . ." Misled by Mr. Kissinger's vagueness, Bunker then told President Thieu that, under Mr. Kissinger's new proposals, all foreign troops would be out of South Vietnam, Laos and Cambodia after U.S. troops had withdrawn. Bunker reported to Mr. Kissinger that he had so advised Thieu, but Bunker's misunderstanding of the proposal was not corrected by Mr. Kissinger. Not until October 1972 would Bunker learn that Mr. Kissinger would not insist on North Vietnam's withdrawal from the South as part of a final peace agreement.

In 1972 Hanoi sent its entire army to invade South Vietnam. The invasion was defeated by South Vietnamese ground forces with much help from American airpower, but then all Hanoi's units stayed on in the South as permitted by Mr. Kissinger's "modification" of Bunker's plan.

On May 31, 1971, Mr. Kissinger presented his plan to the North Vietnamese. His new proposal brought movement in the negotiations for the first time. Hanoi now agreed to accept the continued presence of the Saigon government in South Vietnam. Having secured the means to kill off its Vietnamese rival after the Americans had gone home, Hanoi was willing to give Mr. Kissinger his "decent interval" before the killing would occur.

In his memoirs Mr. Kissinger claims great credit for this May 31 proposal. He claims that it put forth the essential shape of the final peace agreement. Indeed it had. Hanoi recognized it for the sell-out of South Vietnam that it was and pocketed Mr. Kissinger's concession on troops while seeking even more concessions on the political side.

Several years ago, I asked President Nixon if he had ever discussed Bunker's two-step approach to ending the war with Mr. Kissinger and did he know of Mr. Kissinger's modification of Bunker's proposal. Nixon looked puzzled and said, "No." I asked if he remembered such a proposal from Bunker. He said, "No. What difference would it have made?" When I explained, he withdrew into himself and changed the subject of our conversation.

From May 1971 until he had finalized a peace agreement with Hanoi, Mr. Kissinger never disclosed to Thieu the implications of Bunker's proposal. Not until he read Mr. Kissinger's peace agreement in October 1972 did Thieu know that the U.S. had aborted South Vietnam's chances of long-term survival. The origin of Mr. Kissinger's disdain for Thieu and the South Vietnamese lay in his understanding of the Hanoi Communists as the more authentic and important Vietnamese leaders. Mr. Kissinger had not believed in Nixon's policy of Vietnamization, which assumed that South Vietnam was viable and valuable. Also, Mr. Kissinger, far more than Nixon, wanted to negotiate a deal with Hanoi.

Mr. Kissinger went so far as to argue that the issue of separate legal statuses for North and South Vietnam was "a theological issue," which would be a red flag for Hanoi and disrupt progress toward an agreement. This disrespect for our allies had been engendered by Mr. Kissinger's mentor on Vietnamese affairs, Jean Sainteny. Sainteny, oddly enough, had been the operative sent to Vietnam in 1945 by De Gaulle to reimpose French colonial rule on the Vietnamese after the Japanese had overthrown the French administration earlier that year. Sainteny accomplished his mission through an alliance with Ho Chi Minh, supporting him against all other Vietnamese leaders. Ho was the only Vietnamese leader who would negotiate with the French for their return to Vietnam.

Sainteny and his Free French associates, therefore, created the image of Ho Chi Minh as the quintessential Vietnamese patriot and the sole Vietnamese leader worthy of respect in order to further French colonial interests.

Mr. Kissinger, blinded by this ploy of colonial intrigue, never had faith in the non-Communist Vietnamese and consigned them to a harsh destiny, one he hammered out in Paris behind their backs in October 1972.

STEPHEN B. YOUNG

Minneapolis

Kissinger's draft response to my Wall Street Journal letter

In the following draft Letter to the Editor of the *Wall Street Journal* responding to my critique of his secret negotiations with the Vietnamese Communists, Kissinger proposes to refute the revelation of his 1971 decision to allow the Vietnamese Communists to keep their army in South Vietnam after the coming into effect of a peace agreement to end the war.[9]

The Letters to the Editor page is of course designed to let readers express their personal, and not the newspaper's, opinion. But when the Wall Street Journal publishes a two-column letter accusing a former Secretary of State of betraying an ally and 58,000 American dead under the headline "The Betrayal of South Vietnam", it cannot escape its responsibilities quite so cavalierly. One wonders why a minimum of checking was not done regarding the accuracy of the allegations or, better yet, why I was not given an opportunity to reply on the same page. Either course would have revealed the lies, half-truths and hallucinations of this late hit, twenty-five years after the events in question.

1

Failure of the Wall Street Journal to adhere to

elementary standards of fairness obliges me to recycle the

charge a second time. Mr. Young alleges that because I had

lost my nerve and was opposed to Vietnamization, and under

the influence of a Frenchman, Jean Sainteny, I agreed to the

continued presence of North Vietnamese troops in the South

in May 1971, that neither Ambassador Bunker nor President

Thieu were aware of this until October 1972, and that I

consigned South Vietnam to defeat because I considered Hanoi

a more authentic government. Almost every word is a lie in

this sick inversion of history.

The final set of American proposals was drafter in the

fall of 1971. It was submitted to President Thieu by both

Ambassador Bunker and General Haig. It was approved by

President Thieu. It was made public by President Nixon on

2

January 25, 1972, labeled as a joint South Vietnam-U.S.

peace proposal; President Nixon explicitly stated that the

proposal had President Thieu's approval, and he was not

contradicted from Saigon. Articles 5 and 6 of the proposal

deal explicitly with the withdrawal obligations in the

language substantially adopted in the final agreement. The

proposal, either when first made secretly on May 31, 1971 or

when repeated publicly in January 1972, did not bring

movement in the negotiations but was rejected by Hanoi,

which launched an offensive. The break in the negotiations

came only after the defeat of that offensive when we

_____ North Vietnamese _____ in addition to

other measures.

The reasons for the change in our position were as

follows:

3

a.   The policy of Vietnamization obliged us to draw down

our troops, which we did at the rate of 150,000 a year.

By 1971 it was obvious that a point would soon be

reached where their value as a bargaining chip had

disappeared.

b.   Congress was passing literally scores of resolutions

seeking to speed up the withdrawal and legislating a

prohibition against any terms other than the release of

prisoners.

c.   Unanimous media pressure in that direction was even

greater.

For all these reasons, Nixon approved a modification of

our previous proposal for mutual withdrawal to a prohibition

against new infiltration.   This we thought would cause the

forces remaining in the South to atrophy.   We believed that

4

the South Vietnamese could handle Hanoi's residual forces -

as indeed they had - and that we would assist them if Hanoi

broke its commitment against infiltration. A Congressional

prohibition prevented this course of action. All this is

explained in detail in "White House Years" in a passage from

which Mr. Young quotes half a sentence while suppressing the

rest.

As for Mr. Young's other charges, they are too

contemptible for an extended reply.

-- A minimum of research would show that I was a strong

supporter of Vietnamization and indeed, next to Nixon, the

principal person to hold it together.

-- Jean Sainteny was known to President Nixon and me

separately. We used him to set up the first meeting with

North Vietnamese negotiators in August 1969. He had no

5

impact on the negotiations afterwards and was never at any

point consulted with the rest of this.

-- Mr. Young tells a weird story of some unanswered

cable from Ambassador Bunker. I do not know what he is

talking about, but I do know that there is no public servant

I respected, indeed revered, more than Ambassador Bunker.

He and I worked in the closest harmony and trust at all

times. Mr. Young writes that he told this tale to Nixon who

"withdrew into himself" on learning it. I wish I could have

avoided Mr. Young this easily.

The Nixon administration had the agonizing task of

extricating half a million Americans from Vietnam while

giving the people who had relied on our predecessor's

promises an opportunity to determine their fate. It was a

tough challenge which I will believe to my dying day we had

6

managed, but for the collapse of our _____ position

due to Watergate. South Vietnam fell not to the battered

remnants of Hanoi's force which had been left behind in

1972, but because of the massive new infiltrations which we

were prohibited by Congress from resisting.